Contemporary Moral Issues

WADSWORTH CONTINUING EDUCATION SERIES
Leonard Freedman, General Editor

CONTEMPORARY MORAL ISSUES, Third Edition
edited by Harry K. Girvetz
University of California, Santa Barbara

CONTEMPORARY RELIGIOUS ISSUES
edited by Donald E. Hartsock
University of California, Los Angeles

ISSUES OF THE SEVENTIES
edited by Leonard Freedman
University of California, Los Angeles

THE NEW TECHNOLOGY AND HUMAN VALUES, Second Edition
edited by John G. Burke
University of California, Los Angeles

Contemporary Moral Issues
Third Edition

edited by

HARRY K. GIRVETZ

University of California, Santa Barbara

Wadsworth Publishing Company, Inc.
Belmont, California

1 2 3 4 5 6 7 8 9 10–78 77 76 75 74

ISBN–0–534–00349–4

L.C. Cat. Card No. 73–89982

Printed in the United States of America

ACKNOWLEDGMENTS

The American Scholar—for "In Favor of Capital Punishment" by Jacques Barzun. Copyright © 1962 by the United Chapters of Phi Beta Kappa. Reprinted by permission of the publishers. **The Atlantic Monthly Company**—for "The Dilemma of Punishment" ("The Imperative to Punish") by The Honorable David L. Bazelon. Copyright © (July 1960) by The Atlantic Monthly Company, Boston, Massachusetts. Reprinted by permission of the author. **The Honorable David L. Bazelon**—for "Eighteen Years After" from a speech to the Southern California Psychiatric Association by permission of Judge Bazelon. **Brandeis University**—for "The Dilemma of Punishment" by David L. Bazelon. From the Louis D. Brandeis Memorial Lecture, March 14, 1960. Reprinted by permission of Brandeis University. **Ramsey Clark**—for "Liberty vs Security: The False Conflict" from *Crime in America* by Ramsey Clark; published by Simon & Schuster, Inc. Reprinted by permission of the author. **Commentary**—for "Sexism in the Head" by Arlene Croce. Reprinted from *Commentary*, by permission; copyright © 1971 by the American Jewish Committee. Reprinted also by permission of the author. **The Crisis Publishing Company, Inc.**—for "Black Progress or Illiberal Rhetoric" by John A. Morsell from *The Crisis* (June/July 1973). Reprinted with permission of The Crisis Publishing Company, Inc. **Midge Decter**—for "Toward the New Chastity" by Midge Decter. Reprinted by permission of the author. The article first appeared in *The Atlantic Magazine*. **Fortune Magazine**—for "A Sentimental View of Crime" by Sidney Hook. Reprinted from the February 1971 issue of *Fortune Magazine* by special permission; © 1971 by Time, Inc. Reprinted also by permission of the author. **Harcourt Brace Jovanovich, Inc.**—for "Toward a More Human Society" by Kenneth Keniston from *The Uncommitted*, copyright, © 1960, 1962, 1965 by Kenneth Keniston. Reprinted by permission of Harcourt Brace Jovanovich, Inc. **Harold Matson Company, Inc.**—for "Black Progress and Liberal Rhetoric" from *Black Progress and Liberal Rhetoric* by Ben J. Wattenberg and Richard M. Scammon. Copyright 1973 by B. Wattenberg and R. Scammon. Reprinted by permission of Harold Matson Company, Inc. **Harper's Magazine**—for "The Obscenity Muddle" by Paul Bender. Copyright 1973 by *Harper's Magazine*. Reprinted from the February 1973 issue by special permission. **Harper & Row, Publishers, Incorporated**—for "Corporation Giving in a Free Society" from *Corporation Giving in a Free Society* by Richard Eells, copyright © 1956 by Harper & Row, Publishers, Incorporated; for "The Arts of Selling" from *Brave New World Revisited* by Aldous Huxley, copyright © 1958 by Aldous Huxley; for "Stride Toward Freedom" from *Stride Toward Freedom* by Martin Luther King, Jr., copyright © 1958 by Martin Luther King, Jr. All of these selections reprinted by permission of the publisher. **Harvard Business Review**—for "The Dangers of Social Responsibility" by Theodore Levitt. Reprinted from the September–October 1958 issue of *Harvard Business Review*. © 1958 by the President and Fellows of Harvard College; all rights reserved. **Houghton Mifflin Company**—for "The Theory of Social Balance" from *The Affluent Society* by John Kenneth Galbraith. Copyright © 1958 by Houghton Mifflin Company. Reprinted by permission of the publisher. **International Affairs Commission**

—for "What We Want" from *The New York Review of Books* (September 22, 1966). Reprinted by permission of SNCC International Affairs Commission. **The John Day Company, Inc.**—for "The Profit Motive" from *The Concept of the Corporation* by Peter F. Drucker. Copyright © 1946 by Peter F. Drucker. Reprinted by permission of the publisher. **Liveright, Publishers**—for "Marriage and Morals" from *Marriage and Morals* by Bertrand Russell. Copyright 1929 by Horace Liveright, Inc. Copyright © 1957 by Bertrand Russell. Reprinted by permission of the publisher. **The Macmillan Company**—for "Love in the Great Society" from *A Preface to Morals* by Walter Lippmann. Copyright 1929 by The Macmillan Company; renewed 1957 by Walter Lippmann. Reprinted by permission of the publisher. **The McCall Publishing Company**—for "An Interview with Gloria Steinem" from "Gloria Steinem, Writer and Social Critic, Talks about Sex, Politics and Marriage" by Liz Smith. Reprinted from *Redbook Magazine,* January 1972, copyright © 1972 The McCall Publishing Company. Reprinted by permission of the publisher. **Karl Menninger, M.D.**—for "Therapy, Not Punishment" from "Verdict Guilty—Now What?" in *Harper's Magazine* (August 1959). Reprinted by permission of the author. **The New Republic**—for "Crime in the Suites" by Ralph Nader and Mark Green. Reprinted by permission of *The New Republic,* © 1972 by Harrison–Blaine of New Jersey, Inc. **The New York Times Company**—for "Softheaded Judges" by Marvin Frankel, © 1973 by The New York Times Company; for "Needed: A Counter Counterculture" from "After the Fall—What This Country Needs Is a Good Counter Counterculture" by David French, © 1971 by The New York Times Company; for "A Program for Racial Justice" by Father Theodore M. Hesburgh, © 1972 by The New York Times Company and reprinted by permission of Father Hesburgh. All of these articles reprinted by permission of The New York Times Company. **Oxford University Press**—for "Morals and the Criminal Law" from the Maccabean Lecture in Jurisprudence read at the British Academy on March 18, 1959; printed in the *Proceedings of the British Academy,* vol. xlv, and reprinted in *The Enforcement of Morals* by Lord Devlin. Copyright © 1965 by Oxford University Press. Reprinted by permission of the publisher. **A. Philip Randolph Institute**—for "The Failure of Black Separatism" by Bayard Rustin. Reprinted by permission of the author. This article first appeared in *Harper's Magazine.* **Prentice–Hall, Inc.**—for "Crimes without Victims" from *Crimes without Victims: Deviant Behavior and Public Policy, Abortion, Homosexuality, Drug Addiction* by Edwin M. Schur. Copyright © 1965 by Prentice–Hall, Inc., Englewood Cliffs, New Jersey. Reprinted by permission of the publisher. **The Public Interest**—for "Pornography, Obscenity, and the Case for Censorship" by Irving Kristol. Reprinted by permission of *The Public Interest* and the author. **G. P. Putnam's Sons**—for "The House Divided Against Itself" from *Individualism, Old and New* by John Dewey. Copyright 1929, 1930 by John Dewey. Reprinted by permission of the publisher. **Ramparts Magazine**—for "Looking Backward" by Andrew Kopkind. Reprinted from the July 1973 issue of *Ramparts Magazine* with permission. **Marie Rodell**—for "Can an Executive Afford a Conscience"? by Albert Z. Carr. Reprinted by permission of Ann Carr. Copyright © 1970 by Albert Z. Carr. **Stanford University Press**—for "Law, Liberty and Morality" by H. L. A. Hart. Reprinted from *Law, Liberty and Morality* by H. L. A. Hart with the permission of the publishers, Stanford University Press. Copyright © 1963 by the Board of Trustees of the Leland Stanford Junior University. **Henry E. Wallich**—for "Private vs. Public" by Henry E. Wallich from *Harper's Magazine* (October 1961). Copyright © 1961 by Harper's Magazine, Inc. Reprinted by permission of the author. **The Williams & Wilkins Company**—for "A Psychiatrist Dissents from Durham" by Thomas S. Szasz from *The Journal of Nervous and Mental Disease* (July 1960). Copyright © 1960 by The Williams & Wilkins Company, Baltimore, Maryland 21202. Reprinted by permission of the publisher. **James Webb Young**—for "Wanted: Responsible Advertising Critics" by James Webb Young from *Saturday Review* (April 23, 1960). Reprinted by permission of the author.

Preface

This book deals with some of the major moral issues of our time. To call them issues is to say that they are not yet resolved, at any rate not among thoughtful and responsible men of goodwill; or, if they are resolved, the manner of resolution is not one that has decisively affected practice. Admittedly the determination of goodwill, wisdom, and responsibility involves judgments of value and might be said, therefore, to reflect the editor's personal bias. But, quite apart from the quality of the readings and the competence and distinction of their authors, I have employed a principle of selection that should commend itself to reasonable readers of every persuasion. I have chosen authors who might be presumed to encounter dissent without branding it as evidence of malice or stupidity—authors who, in short, claim no monopoly of wisdom and virtue. Presumably these are people who could engage in debate without denouncing each other as knaves or fools.

I have employed another related principle of selection, although obviously with no pretense to infallibility in its application. The authors are, it will be evident, committed people. But for the most part they have not, in my judgment, subordinated the pursuit of truth to defense of their commitments; their loyalties, however strong and even passionate, have not blinded them to alternatives.

Such, in addition to evidence of scholarship, are the requirements by which great universities recruit their faculties. The upshot of adherence to such principles is the exclusion of bigots and blind partisans. Their utterances too are of interest, for they often have an impact on history and afford interesting evidence of the extremes to which men may be led by their passions and prejudices, but our concern here is a different one—namely, better understanding of some of the still unsettled moral problems of our day. This is not a project to which fanatics can make a significant contribution. However, such a view does not imply endorsement of what has been called the "ultramiddle"; to reject blind partisanship is not to praise moral timidity or apathy.

The selections in this volume are not concerned with the problems that would occupy a theoretical treatise on ethics. Such a study, although it would do well to deal with specific moral problems and issues, would by necessity go beyond them to an analysis of the concepts of right and good and ought, of moral law and conscience, concepts that most moral controversy takes for granted— as it does the relevance and demonstrability of judgments of moral value. How judgments of value are demonstrated (if indeed they can be demonstrated at all), and the sense in which they may therefore be regarded as meaningful, is a cause of much difference of opinion among professional philosophers. I have dealt with such questions elsewhere.[1] But this is not a question that will concern us here beyond one important comment. Behind the assertions of the writers included in these pages is the assumption that there exists a difference between good and evil that is more than a simple affirmation of preference. The point to moral discourse—unless those who partake of it are in quest of emotional catharsis—is to persuade. Quite obviously, if nothing but preferences were involved, all efforts to persuade would founder on the retort that there is no disputing about tastes.

Persuasion is often and most simply accomplished by calling attention to facts concerning the antecedents and consequences of a course of action, or to its consistency or inconsistency with accepted values or standards. One may point out, for example, that the repeal of capital punishment has or has not been followed by an increase of the crimes previously punishable by death, that loyalty oaths have or have not been helpful in exposing subversives or that such oaths are or are not consistent with heretofore accepted standards concerning test oaths. One may cite evidence to indicate the discrepancy between precept and practice in sex conduct, or refer to what psychologists have told us about the causes and consequences of the state of mind that required loincloths to be painted over Michelangelo's nudes in the Sistine Chapel. In all such cases persuasion is accomplished and agreement effected within the framework of a common set of values.

---

[1] Girvetz, Harry K., *Beyond Right and Wrong: A Study in Moral Theory* (New York: Free Press, 1973).

Often, however, the facts do not prevail, and considerations of consistency become hopelessly obscured. When this happens one may conclude that the conflict lies deeper and involves values themselves. It is here, in disputes over standards of value, that our differences are crucial. Can such differences be reconciled?

The question here raised concerns moral suasion in the true sense. When the President and Vice-President of the United States in the early 1970s clashed bitterly with most American journalists and publishers over their fairness in reporting on the activities of government and the right of the press to protect its sources, they were not merely differing over matters of fact—although many facts were, of course, relevant and in need of clarification. One may assume that they had different notions concerning what *ought* to be the prevailing conduct in our society, a basic difference over values that no amount of appeal to verbally identical principles like "the common welfare" or "the public good" can conceal.

Some years ago the city of Coventry completed a cathedral to replace the great Gothic church destroyed by Germany's *Luftwaffe* on the night of November 14, 1940. However, during the years following the war the city council of Coventry refused a building permit for a new cathedral, arguing that there was a prior need for schools, houses, and clinics. The council was overruled, it so happened, by the British Minister of Works, who wrote: "Can we be sure that a cathedral would be so useless? We have never had a greater need for an act of faith." The difference, although perhaps not as acrimonious as the dispute between President Nixon and the press, surely reflects competing sets of values.

Those who are part of what we have been taught to call the "counterculture" reject middle-class values. Work, discipline, ambition are scorned, as are their fruits in money, status, and power. Often the offspring of middle-class parents, they think of their parents as chained to a treadmill and of themselves as having repudiated what William James once called the "bitch-goddess, Success." Others think of them as shiftless and slovenly free-loaders seeking escape from responsibility in drugs and antic affectations. The difference between them and their critics hardly arises from disputes about questions of fact; it is a deep divergence over ideals and standards.

If such differences are to be reconciled and moral suasion is indeed to occur, an *act of will* must take place. This is something more than the act of perception or act of thought required of those who differ because of obscured facts or inconsistent reasoning from accepted moral premises. People must be *willing* (in the double sense of that word) to suspend their prevailing standards of value in order to entertain an alternative—an alternative not envisaged when they first formulated their standards. In the ensuing reevaluation they may reaffirm or revise their heretofore accepted values, but one thing is certain: such values will have new meaning to them by virtue of having been thus tested. Moreover, in this way they may find enhancement that would otherwise have been denied them had they resisted such reappraisal.

For an in-depth discussion of the precise circumstances that occasion such reevaluations and of what happens as we reappraise our prevailing standards of value, I again refer the reader to my *Beyond Right and Wrong.* But this much is clear: bigots and fanatics will not submit their position to reexamination. Neither, for other reasons, will members of preliterate or authoritarian societies, where the individual is so submerged in the group or so submissive that he would not think of challenging the prevailing mores. Reappraisal is possible only for free men conscious of themselves as agents capable of guiding their own development—capable, that is, of an exercise of free will in what is perhaps the only meaningful sense of that term. Such a capacity is not an original endowment, but an achievement laboriously won over the long centuries during which a relatively few men have emancipated themselves from tyranny, whether of law and custom or of their own unrestrained impulses and appetites.

The issues discussed in this volume are arranged into five groupings, although other ways of relating them might be equally appropriate. With each grouping are brief introductory comments, which suggest the main problems in that area and indicate the rationale for that particular grouping. The groupings are subdivided into topics, and accompanying each topic is a brief formulation of the issue. With each selection are comments concerning the author's background. For the most part I have made an attempt to represent important differences in point of view and to emphasize the contributions of living Americans.

Constraints imposed by limitations of space have required me to omit discussion of many important issues. During this new period of *détente,* the great moral issues brought to the fore by the Cold War and our disastrous intervention in Southeast Asia—pacifism, loyalty, and civil disobedience—are not as exigent as they were during the tumultuous turn of the decade. If some readers are disappointed over the omission in this edition of a section dealing with such issues, they will at least derive consolation from the change of climate that makes this neglect defensible. A gratifying response to the first two editions of *Contemporary Moral Issues* has made this third edition possible. I am especially indebted to the many readers who have sent in comments and suggestions.

Contents

PART FIVE / ALIENATION IN THE MODERN WORLD   347

Part One

Crime and Punishment

Safety of person and property is the first concern of a well-ordered society. When other restraints fail, society sets up a system of laws, police, courts, and sanctions to secure this objective. Provision is made for a penal system to deter would-be criminals, to isolate those who have not been deterred, to reform criminals who are not incorrigible, and to deter criminals from repeating criminal acts after their release. The purposes of an enlightened penal system are thus to deter, to reform, and to protect society when deterrence fails. Another purpose, which penologists acknowledge but rarely condone, is punishment, which vents the wrath of society on those who flout its rules. The message to Congress (March 14, 1973) in which President Nixon declared that "the only way to attack crime in America is the way crime attacks our people—without pity" reflects the retributive mood in which many respond to certain (but not all) crimes.

In an area beset by many differences, there is agreement that our system of law enforcement has failed. Crime is rampant and, with it, fear. Fear battens on itself. When people can no longer walk in safety on their streets or use parks and public conveyances (not to mention elevators and hallways) without risking assault, they understandably panic. Complex issues calling for cool judgment and careful discrimination are muddled in a fog of fright and frustration. People become prey to nostrums and those who purvey them. Demagogues ride high. It is hardly necessary to cite the dismal statistics to understand the alarm felt by Americans over the vaulting rate of crime. Even so, it is startling to read that in 1970 Vienna with two million inhabitants had only 42 willful homicides and Chicago with twice the population had 810 such homicides. There is a strong and understandable feeling that we have had enough.

However, caught in this common predicament, we suddenly find ourselves polarized into those who are "hard" on crime and those who are "soft" on crime, a dichotomy that completely obscures the real issues involved. These issues concern disagreement over the means for curbing crime that might be resolved by experts. As so often happens when such disagreements over facts become irreconcilable, differences also prevail over fundamental values. Several related issues are involved here which will be distinguished in the sections that follow: the effectiveness of severer punishment in curbing crime; the role of the severest of all penalties, capital punishment, as a deterrent; the point at which individual rights should be subordinated to the need for apprehending, convicting, and incarcerating criminals; and, the extent to which criminals are the product of conditions that may be regarded as psycho- or sociopathic and, to that extent, not responsible for their misdeeds.

1

Punishment and Deterrence

Are harsher penalties, including mandatory sentences which eliminate judicial discretion, effective in reducing crime? Those who demand a crackdown on lawbreakers and a tough, no-nonsense approach to crime are in the majority. They attribute the growth in crime to weak-minded sentimentalists who coddle criminals at the expense of their victims. Opponents of this view retort that fear of punishment is only one, and often the least, of many factors that determine the incidence of crime. They insist that by relying on a prison system that demonstrably encourages recidivism, we invite more rather than less crime: 67 percent of federal prisoners have been incarcerated previously; few—no more than 15 percent—are reformed; and the proportions are similar in state prisons. All parties agree that most prisoners, when their terms are over, are released into society more hardened and brutalized and potentially more dangerous than they were before imprisonment.

It is appropriate to begin the debate with Richard Nixon's call for a hard line. He and former Attorney General John Mitchell made this a major issue in both the 1968 and the 1972 presidential campaigns, and there can be no doubt that they spoke for a large segment of Americans. It is equally appropriate to provide, as a response, the comments of a member of the attacked judiciary.

LAW ENFORCEMENT

Richard Nixon

President Nixon delivered the following address over nation-wide radio on March 10, 1972, shortly before incorporating the proposals in his sixth State of the Union message to Congress. In this message (March 14, 1973), he proposed a war "without pity" against crime and proclaimed with some pride that "the capital of the United States no longer bears the stigma of also being the Nation's crime capital."

Nothing is so precious to Americans as the freedoms provided in our Constitution. In order that these freedoms may be enjoyed to their fullest, there must be another freedom—freedom from the fear of crime.

The senseless shooting of Senator John Stennis in January gave tragic emphasis to the fact that there is still a high risk of crime on our Nation's streets. These acts of violence are the natural residue of an atmosphere in America that for years encouraged potential lawbreakers.

Americans in the last decade were often told that the criminal was not responsible for his crimes against society, but that society was responsible.

I totally disagree with this permissive philosophy. Society is guilty of crime only when we fail to bring the criminal to justice. When we fail to make the criminal pay for his crime, we encourage him to think that crime will pay.

Such an attitude will never be reflected in the laws supported by this Administration, nor in the manner in which we enforce those laws. The jurisdiction of the Federal Government over crime is limited, but where we can act, we will act to make sure that we have the laws, the enforcement agencies, the courts, the judges, the penalties, the correctional institutions and the rehabilitation programs we need to do the job.

Next week I will propose a revision of the entire Federal Criminal Code, modernizing it and strengthening it, to close the loopholes and tailor our laws to present day needs. When I say "modernize," incidentally, I do not mean to be soft on crime; I mean exactly the opposite.

Our new Code will give us tougher penalties and stronger weapons in the war against dangerous drugs and organized crime. It will rationalize the present patchwork quilt of punishments for crime. It will substantially raise current limits on monetary fines. And it will restrict the present absurd use of the insanity defense.

I am further proposing that the death penalty be restored for certain Federal crimes. At my direction, the Attorney General has drafted a statute consistent with the Supreme Court's recent decision on the death penalty. This statute will provide capital punishment for cases of murder over which the Federal Government has jurisdiction, and for treason and other war-related crimes.

Contrary to the views of some social theorists, I am convinced that the death penalty can be an effective deterrent against specific crimes. The death penalty is not a deterrent so long as there is doubt whether it can be applied. The law I will propose would remove this doubt.

The potential criminal will know that if his intended victims die, he may also die. The hijacker, the kidnaper, the man who throws a fire bomb, the convict who attacks a prison guard, the person who assaults an officer of the law—all will know that they may pay with their own lives for any lives that they take.

This statute will be a part of my proposed reform of the Federal Criminal Code. However, because there is an immediate need for this sanction, I have directed the Attorney General to submit a death penalty statute as a separate proposal so that the Congress can act rapidly on this single provision.

Drug abuse is still Public Enemy No. 1 in America. Let me tell you about some of the tragic letters I have received at the White House from victims of drugs.

One tells about a 5-year-old boy hospitalized in Missouri. Someone gave him LSD.

One is from a boy 18 years old who had spent 11 months in a mental hospital trying to get rid of his drug addiction. He started with marijuana. He is asking me for help because his 14-year-old brother has begun to use drugs.

Another is from a mother in California. Her son committed suicide. He could not end his drug habit, so he ended his life.

One of the things that comes through so forcefully in these letters is the sense of despair of people who feel they have no place to turn for help, and so they write to the White House. I intend to help them.

We have already made encouraging progress in the war against drug abuse. Now we must consolidate that progress and strike even harder.

One area in which I am convinced of the need for more immediate action is that of putting heroin pushers in prison and keeping them there. A recent study by the Bureau of Narcotics and Dangerous Drugs revealed that more than 70 percent of those accused of being narcotics violators are freed on bail for a period of 3 months to 1 year between the time of arrest and the time of trial. They are thus given the opportunity to go out and create more misery, generate more violence, commit more crimes while they are waiting to be tried for these same activities.

The same study showed that over 25 percent of the federally convicted narcotics violators were not even sentenced to jail. When permissive judges are more considerate of the pusher than they are of his victims, there is little incentive for heroin pushers to obey the law, and great incentive for them to violate it. This is an outrage. It is a danger to every law-abiding citizen, and I am confident that the vast majority of Americans will support immediate passage of the heroin trafficking legislation I will propose to the Congress next week.

This legislation will require Federal judges to consider the danger to the community before freeing on bail a suspect for heroin trafficking. That is something they cannot legally do now. It will require a minimum sentence of 5 years in prison for anyone convicted of selling heroin. It will require a minimum sentence of 10 years to life imprisonment for major traffickers in drugs. And for offenders with a prior conviction for a drug felony, those who persist in living off the suffering of others, it will require life imprisonment without parole.

This is tough legislation, but we must settle for nothing less. The time has come for soft-headed judges and probation officers to show as much concern for the rights of innocent victims of crime as they do for the rights of convicted criminals.

In recent days, there have been proposals to legalize the possession and use of marijuana. I oppose the legalization of the sale, possession or use of marijuana. The line against the use of dangerous drugs is now drawn on this side of marijuana. If we move the line to the other side and accept the use of this drug, how can we draw the line against other illegal drugs? Or will we slide into an acceptance of their use, as well?

My Administration has carefully weighed this matter. We have examined the statutes. We have taken the lead in making sanctions against the use of marijuana more uniform, more reasonable. Previously, these sanctions were often unrealistically harsh. Today, 35 States have adopted our model statute on drugs, including marijuana. I hope others will.

But there must continue to be criminal sanctions against the possession, sale or use of marijuana.

Law enforcement alone will not eliminate drug abuse. We must also have a strong program to treat and assist the addict. Two-thirds of my proposed anti-narcotics budget goes for treatment, rehabilitation, prevention and research. We are approaching the point where no addict will be able to say that he commits crimes because there is no treatment available for him.

By providing drug offenders with every possible opportunity to get out of the drug culture, we need feel no compunction about applying the most stringent sanctions against those who commit crimes in order to feed their habits.

The crimes which affect most people most often are not those under Federal jurisdiction, but those in which State and local governments have jurisdiction. But while the Federal Government does not have full jurisdiction in the field of criminal law enforcement, it does have a broad, constitutional responsibility to insure domestic tranquility. That is why I am doing everything I can to help strengthen the capacity of State and local governments to fight crime.

Since I took office, Federal assistance for State and local law enforcement authorities has grown from over $100 million to over $1 billion. We are training over 40,000 law enforcement officers in the control and prevention of drug abuse.

This year more than 1,200 State and local police officers will graduate from the new FBI Academy, and I plan to increase assistance next year to local law enforcement to over $1 billion 200 million.

Crime costs Americans twice. It costs first in lives lost, in injuries, in property loss, in increased insurance rates, in being fearful for your own safety as you go about your work.

And second, crime costs in the taxes that go to maintain police forces, courts, jails, other means of enforcement.

It is a breach of faith with those who are paying the cost of crime, human as well as financial, to be lenient with the criminal. There are those who say that law and order are just code words for repression and bigotry. That is dangerous nonsense. Law and order are code words for goodness and decency in America.

Crime is color blind. Let those who doubt this talk to the poor, the minorities, the inner-city dwellers, who are the most frequent victims of crime. There is nothing disgraceful, nothing to be ashamed of, about Americans wanting to live in a law-abiding country.

I intend to do everything in my power to see that the American people get all the law and order they are paying for. Our progress in this effort has been encouraging. The latest FBI figures show that for the first 9 months of 1972, the growth rate of serious crime in America was reduced to 1 percent. That is the lowest rate of increase since 1960.

In 83 of our major cities, serious crime has actually been reduced, and in the District of Columbia it has been cut in half since 1969. Convictions for organized crime have more than doubled in the last 4 years. The rate of new heroin addiction has dramatically decreased.

These are the positive results of refusing to compromise with the forces of crime, refusing to accept the notion that lawlessness is inevitable in America. We have the freedom to choose the kind of Nation we want, and we do not choose to live with crime.

The Federal Government can help provide resources. It can help provide leadership. It can act with its own jurisdiction. But in the end, one of the best resources we have, one of the greatest safeguards to public peace, is the active concern of the law-abiding American citizen. The war against crime is not just the job of the FBI and the State and local police; it is your job, everybody's job. It is the very essence of good citizenship to act when and where we see crime being committed.

Citizens in some high crime areas have gathered together to work with the police to protect lives and property, to prevent crime. They have recognized the simple fact that we are going to have a crime problem as long as we are willing to put up with it, and most Americans are not willing to put up with it any longer.

When I saw and heard the remarks of our returning prisoners of war, so strong and confident and proud, I realized that we were seeing men of tough moral fiber, men who reflected, despite their long absence from America, what America is all about.

Just as they are returning home to America, I believe that today we see America returning to the basic truths that have made us and kept us a strong and a free people. I am encouraged by that vision. It points the way toward a better, safer future for all Americans. It points the way toward an America in which men and women and children can truly live free from fear in the full enjoyment of their most basic rights.

To accept anything less than a Nation free from crime is to be satisfied with something less than America can be and ought to be for all our people.

SOFTHEADED JUDGES

Marvin E. Frankel

Marvin Frankel is a United States District Judge for the Southern District of New York. He is the author of a recently published book, Criminal Sentences. *His title for this article is taken from President Nixon's speech dealing with the same subject.*

President Nixon recently turned the glare of his Administration's intelligence onto the problems of crime and punishment, and showed us once again that the main thing is to identify the villains. Prominent among the night creatures thus exposed: the "softheaded judge." Judges are too soft on criminals. Soft, mind you, not in the heart, a quality that might seem at least humane, though still a failing; but soft in the head, a condition of either severe disability or calculated subversion of the public interest. "The time has come," the President said, "for softheaded judges . . . to show as much concern for the rights of innocent victims of crime as they do for the rights of convicted criminals."

The rest of the message and the promised "tough legislation" the President sent to Capitol Hill shortly afterward reveal that the Administration proposes to harden, or, perhaps, wall off, the softheaded judges by imposing stiff *mandatory minimum* terms for certain kinds of crimes and even by reviving and extending the death penalty. The theory is, of course, that measures of this kind—taken "without pity," as the President said—will reduce crime.

Federal trial judges themselves ought to know something about crime and punishment, and this is no time for the demure silence on public issues commonly affected by most judges outside their courthouses. Accordingly, I am moved to submit here that, with all deference to the top Federal officer, his theories on reducing crime are open to serious question and his strictures against softness in judges are without basis in hard fact. His proposals for severity are neither new nor useful, but only invite us to official cruelties unlikely to accomplish anything beneficial. Probably worst of all, the heroes-and-villains approach, by focusing on grim punishment as a cure, diverts attention from our real problems and the possibilities of reform that lie in other directions.

If we overlook the unloveliness of the term and accept for the sake of argument that it is wicked to be softheaded, what is the evidence for the prevalence of this quality among judges, Federal or other? (I say "for the sake of argument" because there has been a respectable tradition for some millennia that sympathy and a willingness to consider claims for leniency are not altogether incongruous traits for judges.) That there are degrees of hardness (punitiveness) and softness among the wide varieties of judges no one could doubt. But enough to be a major evil and a major cause of anything, let alone crime? That everyone should doubt—or, simply, reject. Two grounds for rejection (leaving aside that the accuser—thus far—should have the burden of proof) seem sufficient for now: (1) some concrete, if unscientific, observations of my own; (2) the statistics of American judicial punishment.

As to the first, I have, as man and judge, been judge-watching more than a quarter of a century. Judges, like folks, come in an array of sizes, shapes and qualities. Insofar as they invite generalizations, they may tend, positioned as they are, to softness in their physical condition. Allowing always for exceptions, however, the general population of the bench is scarcely notable for emotional, moral or even cerebral "softness." On the contrary, I would have to confess that we run more to the toughness and arrogance that go with a pervasive sense of righteousness and respectability. Who are we, after all? The average judge, if he was ever a youth, is no longer. If he was ever a firebrand, he is not discernibly an ember now. If he ever wanted to lick the Establishment, he has long since joined it. Does he identify more with the criminal than with the victim?

Anyone who would answer "yes" has not spent much time in criminal courtrooms. Judges actually prefer law and order to lawlessness and disorder. Our judges give out long, hard, stern sentences in quantity, as reflected in statistics I shall mention. There are exceptions, to be sure. Every knowledgeable person knows of sentences that, at least superficially, sound light for the crimes. Even such cases, of course, can be appraised only by knowing and studying the individual defendant, as the sentencing judge is supposed to have done. But granting that one can find many lenient sentences in the nation at large, they are neither frequent nor, most importantly, a plausible explanation or "cause" of crime.

Students of the subject report unanimously that courts in the United States impose on the whole—and by a wide margin—the longest prison sentences in the civilized world. And the relatively small band of Federal judges do their share. A committee of the American Bar Association reported in 1968 that the average Federal prison sentence being served in 1963 was nearly six years, and that some 5 per cent of all Federal prisoners were serving sentences in excess of 20 years. In contrast, the committee reported, sentences of over five years "are rare in most European countries." Sentences of over 20 years in England are "entirely exceptional . . . and are generally disapproved." Sweden in 1964 had eight commitments out of 11,227 to terms of over 10 years and only 38 to terms exceeding four years. Comparative figures like these (basically the same today as in the years cited) come close to the sad heart of the matter—close to pinpointing the intellectual bankruptcy of promising the American people genuine progress in reducing crime through the inspired novelty of harsher punishments. As everyone knows, along with our leadership position in locking people up, we enjoy a similar ascendancy in our crime rates. Doesn't that say something vivid? Does it not at least suggest that we should be asking some new and intelligent questions rather than repackaging worn fallacies?

If clobbering criminals (those who get caught, that is) were any real solution for a society like ours, the problem would long ago have become a memory. We have known since before Hammurabi about flaying, drawing and quartering, life and death sentences, etc. England, in the 18th century, made more than 20 felonies capital, only to see its conviction rate slip while the crime rate rose. Juries, the British discovered, can't be counted on to act mercilessly against live defendants. Jurors refused on a large scale to convict evidently guilty people when the consequence would be disproportionately harsh. English judges, sometimes bloody but rarely bleeding-hearted, strained for technicalities that would avoid the death penalty. Pickpockets picked pockets, a trade itself punishable by death, among the throngs at public hangings. There were other, typically British, compromises (like the escape through "benefit of clergy" with "clergymen" coming to mean people who could read) to soften the heady ferocity of the law books.

Consider now the innovation the President proposes of five- and ten-year mandatory minimum sentences for first offenders trafficking in heroin.[1] This is a wry touch, acquiring its supposed appeal and novelty from the citizenry's short memory. The fact is that we had this sort of Federal law (though a bit less Draconian) for many years, ending way back in October, 1970! In 1970, having found the mandatory minimum unworkable (and

---

[1] Under the bill proposed by the Administration, a first offender dealing in less than four ounces would get from at least five years to a maximum of fifteen. For more than four ounces he would get ten years to life. The Administration is also proposing mandatory minimums for crimes where weapons are used and for defendants identified as leaders of "organized crime."

not for softness or love of criminals), the Congress repealed it. In explaining the repeal, the Congressional spokesmen said such things as this:

> The severity of existing penalties, involving in many instances mandatory sentences, have [*sic*] led in many instances to reluctance on the part of prosecutors to prosecute some violations where the penalties seem to be out of line with the seriousness of the offense. In addition, severe penalties, which do not take into account individual circumstances, and which treat casual violators as severely as they treat hardened criminals, tend to make convictions somewhat more difficult to obtain. The committee feels, therefore, that making the penalty structure in the law more flexible can actually serve to have a more deterrent effect . . . , through eliminating some of the difficulties prosecutors and courts have had in the past arising out of minimum mandatory sentences.

In other words, the Congress relearned by 1970 what had been found out in England 200 years earlier. When he signed the bill into law on Oct. 27, 1970, President Nixon gave no hint of dissent.

Why the swift change (hardening) of head scarcely more than two years later? Because of softheaded judges, we are told. Explaining in his message to Congress on March 14, 1973, the President said: "In a study of 955 narcotics drug violators who were arrested by the Bureau of Narcotics and Dangerous Drugs and convicted in the [Federal] courts, a total of 27 per cent received sentences other than imprisonment. Most of these individuals were placed on probation. . . . This situation is intolerable."

The bare numbers—never mind that they are numbers of miscellaneous *people*—disclose to the President a "situation" not to be tolerated. But let me mention some of the most likely kinds of flesh-and-blood people —kinds I've placed on probation—who make up that 27 per cent. Some are college students—not quite "entrapped" legally, but perhaps persuaded a little to negotiate a sale of cocaine to a narcotics agent—students who are now traumatized, terrorized, clearly convinced that they'd better get back and stay back on the conventional trolley. Some are ghetto addicts who've "cooperated"—turned state's evidence—and for whom the prosecutors, needing such cooperation in future cases, implicitly or explicitly urge probation and treatment. One case I remember vividly was of an orchestra leader, a devoted father, whose first conviction was clearly going to be his last—a judgment shared by the prosecutor as well as the probation office and me— and whom no jury would have convicted in the first place if it knew he faced anything like five or ten years in prison. Again, we all agreed that probation was right.

For all such people—and comparable cases we could multiply—the President would compel a rigid, uncompromising five- or ten-year minimum term because anything less is "intolerable." Can he mean that? Perhaps so, when the enemy is a specter named "crime" compounded of fungible numbers without actual smiles, eyes, knees, etc. Presumably Mr. Nixon concludes that some percentage less than 27 could merit probation. (The 27 per cent sounds high for my own narcotics cases but I stand shoulder to shoulder with other softheaded judges nonetheless.) How does one then select the right figure? How do we know what the "right" and suitably "hard" percentage would be? The President did not say.

Criminal lawyers and judges, among many others, have long been asking relatively concrete questions, and evolving judgments of human value, to guide the choice between probation and the lockup. There has lately been a widening consensus (though nothing approaching unanimity) that since imprisonment is horrible, often ineffective and occasionally socially detrimental, it should perhaps be avoided unless or until it seems reasonably plain that measures less severe won't do. An influential reflection of this view is the Model Penal Code, a monumental product of years of study and debate led by Columbia Law Professor Herbert Wechsler and engaging the hardheaded efforts of scholars and members of bar and bench. The distinguished National Commission on Reform of Federal Criminal Laws, composed of leading lawyers, members of Congress and judges, followed closely the provisions on sentencing in the Model Penal Code when it proposed a revised Federal code in 1971, after several years of intensive study of its own. Embodying the view of prison as the last, not first, resort, the relevant Model Code provision says:

> The Court shall deal with a person who has been convicted of a crime without imposing sentence of imprisonment unless, having regard to the nature and circumstances of the crime and the history, character and condition of the defendant, it is of the opinion that his imprisonment is necessary for protection of the public because: (a) there is undue risk that during the period of a suspended sentence or probation the defendant will commit another crime; or (b) the defendant is in need of correctional treatment that can be provided most effectively by his commitment to an institution; or (c) a lesser sentence will depreciate the seriousness of the defendant's crime.

Following that quoted provision, there is a list of factors to "be accorded weight in favor of withholding sentence of imprisonment." These call upon the judge to *judge:* to study the particular crime, the defendant's condition and circumstances, his record, his "character and attitudes," his family situation and a number of other variables.

To dwell briefly on only one relevant characteristic of every defendant, age, judges are reminded every day that the "typical" criminal is a young male. Here statistics may mean something. Roughly eight of every ten crimes is the work of a man or boy 14 to 29 years old. This means that most of the time those of us who sentence people confront someone who probably has many years of his life to be lived—or taken away—years possibly for repair or revenge, for some constructive role or for more crime. Is it hard or soft, or merely realistic, to consider whether a measure of concern for the defendant as a person may be repaid to the community, quite apart from the promptings of ordinary humanity? Would you want to live under a system of law, or with a breed of judges, that outlawed such considerations?

I am not saying that a young defendant always gets probation—not at all. Most of the people sent to prison are young. I mention youth only because it is an inescapable fact in most cases, a human fact, one of the multitude of mixed and variable facts faced regularly by judges and omitted from the President's statistics.

It was important to me that the man I sent to prison the other day sold narcotics strictly for profit though he was not addicted, that he had lived to be 50 without learning better, that he seemed to be lying when he explained his action and that it appeared likely he would revert to his criminal ways if released soon to the streets. It was relevant that another narcotics seller was now on methadone and evidently in earnest about it, that he was finally ready to work at a legitimate job, that his loyal young wife was expecting their child, that the recent murder of his brother, apparently in underworld warfare, was appraised by an astute probation officer as a potentially chastening trauma. The defendant struck me on balance as a suitable probation risk (risk is always with us in this business), having in mind that the probationer is supervised and subject to revocation and a prison sentence if he misbehaves.

The decision to grant probation is meant as a reasoned calculation, not an emotional beneficence. The defendant on probation, if he merits the opportunity, supports himself and his family. Instead of costing us every year the price of a college education to be maintained in prison (plus welfare for his family), he costs the much smaller expense of supervision. He is —what may be the vital thing for a salvageable man—challenged by the trust we have placed in him. Of course judges make mistakes. Defendants betray that trust and go wrong. But other mistakes involve the tragic victims who would make it on probation and become useful citizens but instead live condemned as enemies behind walls, at incalculable expense all around.

Look closely, then, at this supposed division between hard (good) sentencers and soft (bad) ones. Some of our best and toughest (using "tough" in the sense of strong, not stiff) minds have discerned for a long time that lengthy prison sentences, so easy and gratifying for the grandiose sentencer, may have just the opposite effect from what was intended. They may tend in a variety of ways to promote rather than reduce crime. Some of the most dread crimes and criminals may actually be incited, rather than deterred, by the dark allure of violent penalties, including death. The weight or incidence of this phenomenon is not documented in neat statistics, but it is widely known. It is not only psychotherapists who have observed, in some human behavior, this urge to be punished; few criminal court judges sit for long without seeing it. The judge who reckons with it is not necessarily soft; he is merely doing his job of dealing with realities in all their slovenly complexities.

In the same way, responsible judges know the huge extent to which prisons breed crime rather than quell it. To be sure, the defendant in prison is not for the time being committing crimes—not against us respectables anyhow. And this purpose of incapacitation, modest though it is, does indeed rank high among the few positive reasons for imprisonment At the same time, like any decision maker aspiring to rationality, the judge ought to calculate costs along with benefits. He must weigh in the balance some familiar learning about prison life, about the steadily corrosive influences of the prison's negative values upon the inmate exposed to them for 24 daily hours. Every society has its culture, and "the society of captives," to borrow the title of a thoughtful book by Gresham M. Sykes, is not excluded. The acculturation that goes on behind walls is often deep, vicious and ineradicable. The man imprisoned for up to a few years may resist or recover. The long-termer eventually released again into the community is likely to rejoin us as one of our most assuredly dangerous (and, very possibly, cunning and undetectable) neighbors.

If we are really interested in reducing crime we cannot ignore the extent to which the behavior of community leaders determines the attitudes of the people toward law and order. We live in an era during which the candor and the integrity of our highest officials—not excluding judges, but not mainly judges—have been drawn into acute question. The people have been misled on a huge scale respecting questions of war and peace, life and death. Fortunes of money have changed hands for electoral uses and abuses, while the furtive seekers of corrupt advantage have not infrequently been glimpsed in palace corridors. Lately, unspeakably criminal assaults upon democracy's roots have appeared to be organized at levels of which the frightening heights and depths seem yet to be discovered. All this is far graver for our national morale, and surely for our crime rate, than some superficial and unconsidered probation statistics compiled for an official message.

If we are really interested in reducing crime, there is a good deal of arduous, unromantic, unheroic work to be done. We must continue to attack social ills that are at least partly responsible. We must do a large number of large and small things about particular crimes. We must light the streets better. We must understand that the British device of treatment (and an enormously lower rate of addict-related crime) is probably closer to the mark than our criminal "war" on drugs with its sordid rounds of govern ment "buys," informers, death, savagery, and the pervasive threat of provocation, entrapment and corruption all around. We must press forward with our studies of what "crimes" (like gambling, dirty books, crossing state lines for sex play, etc.) deserve continued investment of Federal resources. We must control firearms better. We must improve police effectiveness and pay policemen better, aware that only a small number of criminals is apprehended and punished at all and that the number of crimes committed is probably about five times the number reported. We must explore more fully the alternatives to standard prison confinement, expanding, and adding to, devices like work release, small community-treatment centers and halfway houses. And our scholars should be encouraged to learn whether a society so preeminent in selling deodorants may hope to persuade more people positively (rather than by threats) that criminal conduct is not splendid— or whether a nation that honors "The Godfather" so lavishly really abhors crime as much as we profess to.

My main purpose here, however, is to expose the President's strictures against judges and pity as both empty and harmful. I do agree that sentencing practices in this country are bad, but for wholly different reasons. Our sentencing laws (such as they are) give the judges more power than any official should have—power, for example, to sentence a given defendant to anything from probation to 50 years or some (any) term in between, all at the judges unfettered and commonly unappealable discretion. Prisoners know and justly resent that with laws so lax the sentence depends on the accident of which judge happens to have the case. They know that, as much or more than the judges, parole boards exercise arbitrary and unregulated power. Our sentencing practices are themselves essentially lawless, and this regime of unregulated power is a source of hatred and contempt, rather than respect, for the law.

My proposals for sentencing reform begin with a code of *law,* to guide sentencers with a measure of precision and to unify basic policies. I would make sentences reviewable on appeal, as they are not now in Federal and most state courts. I would, in short, channel the authority of judges which now leads too often to capricious, widely disparate and frequently excessive sentences.

The cure is not to banish pity. Nor is it to make an iron code of cruel, relentless sentences. It is to evolve a system of orderly, rational, detailed criteria for making fair, consistent and humane judgments in the cases of individual defendants. That would indeed diminish the power of the judge, but not by making him a robot programed to throw the same book indiscriminately at each defendant. Instead, it would compel the judge to *judge, to decide according to law* with as much sense, wisdom, and, yes, mercy as we have historically sought.

In sum, the notion that we American punishers par excellence do not punish enough—if and when we get around to catching and trying people—is both simpleminded and wrong. Whatever has happened to our credulity, our sense of security, our national nerve and other things, it is not the quality of mercy that has been strained.[2]

---

[2] Editor's Note: The National Advisory Commission on Criminal Justice Standards and Goals, appointed in 1971 by the Nixon administration and consisting mostly of hard-line police chiefs, sheriffs, mayors, judges, and other criminal justice authorities, has issued a 1973 report opposing mandatory sentences and favoring the decriminalization of so-called victimless crimes including the possession and use of marihuana.

2

Capital Punishment

The foregoing considerations come to a dramatic focus on the issue of capital punishment. Two voices separated by an astronomic social distance provide an unusual contrast in the selections appearing below. The first is that of a distinguished scholar and teacher, Jacques Barzun, who defends capital punishment as a means of ridding society of undesirable elements; the other is that of Caryl Chessman, who was executed on May 9, 1960, twelve years after he was installed in Death Row and shortly after his last reprieve. In retrospect it is difficult to believe that the fate of one individual with a long record of criminal misbehavior could have occasioned the vast uproar that preceded his execution. In the end, the governor would have commuted Chessman's sentence, but under the laws of California he was powerless to do so.[1] In a last-minute effort to alter the outcome, the governor called the state legislature into special session to consider repeal of capital punishment, at least for a trial period. In doing so he jeopardized his political career. Clearly, the execution of Chessman was no routine act of retribution. The great causes célèbres—Dreyfus, Sacco and Vanzetti, Tom Mooney—had ideological involvements that were completely lacking in the Chessman case. No issue of anti-semitism, radicalism, or the like, was involved in the spontaneous protest against Caryl Chessman's execution. His case was unique because it evoked such worldwide concern over the life of a single person and the moral right of the state to take such a life.

---

[1] Chessman was convicted of assault and kidnapping. Assault alone is not a capital crime in California. The kidnapping charge was a strictly "technical" one. The governor may not under California law commute the sentence of a twice-convicted felon without a recommendation from the state supreme court.

Much has happened since Chessman's execution. The California Supreme Court outlawed capital punishment under the "cruel and unusual punishment" clause of the state constitution, unmoved by Governor Ronald Reagan's protest that "there's cruelty when you execute a chicken to have a Sunday afternoon dinner." However, California voters by a large majority amended their constitution in 1972 to restore the stricken statutes and to declare that these statutes "shall not be deemed to be, or constitute infliction of cruel or unusual punishments within meaning of [the] California Constitution." In the same year, the U.S. Supreme Court held in *Furman v. Georgia* that a capital sentence is unconstitutional in cases where the jury or court has discretion to impose a lesser sentence.[2] Later, in a 1973 State of the Union message, President Nixon proposed to Congress a statute which he hoped would be consistent with the Supreme Court's decision. This proposed statute would provide capital punishment for cases of murder over which the federal government has jurisdiction—including war-related sabotage and espionage—and where death results from such federal offenses as skyjacking, kidnapping, and assaulting a federal official. His reasons are given in the reprint above of a March 10, 1973, nationwide address.

---

[2] In effect *Furman v. Georgia* rejected laws that give judges and juries unrestricted and essentially unreviewable power to determine who among those found guilty of capital crimes should live and who should die. The Court was not called upon to decide the constitutionality of mandatory capital punishment laws under which conviction for a capital offense results automatically in a death sentence. However, American law has long disapproved of mandatory death penalties which preclude mercy and efforts to reckon with a criminal's background or mental capacity, and juries have generally refused to enforce such sentences, preferring in some cases to acquit a guilty man rather than have him executed. *Furman* struck down the death penalty in thirty-nine states but, in point of fact, there had been no executions since 1967 and only one out of ten convicted of a capital crime had been sentenced to die. However, in the year following *Furman,* nineteen states restored the death penalty for homicide and several for rape and other felonies. Nominally mandatory, these laws have yet to be tested in the courts.

IN FAVOR OF CAPITAL PUNISHMENT

Jacques Barzun

Jacques Barzun is a well-known historian and critic and dean of faculties and provost of Columbia University. His works include Darwin, Marx, Wagner (*1941*); The House of Intellect (*1959*); Classic, Romantic, and Modern (*1961*); Science, The Glorious Entertainment (*1964*); The American University (*1968*); *and* A Catalogue of Crime *with W. H. Taylor (1971). Professor Barzun's defense of capital punishment is all the more interesting in that it comes from an unexpected quarter.*

. . . I readily concede at the outset that present ways of dealing out capital punishment are as revolting as Mr. Koestler says in his harrowing volume, *Hanged by the Neck.* Like many of our prisons, our modes of execution should change. But this objection to barbarity does not mean that capital punishment—or rather, judicial homicide—should not go on. The illicit jump we find here, on the threshold of the inquiry, is characteristic of the abolitionist and must be disallowed at every point. Let us bear in mind the possibility of devising a painless, sudden and dignified death, and see whether its administration is justifiable.

The four main arguments advanced against the death penalty are: (1) punishment for crime is a primitive idea rooted in revenge; (2) capital punishment does not deter; (3) judicial error being possible, taking life is an appalling risk; (4) a civilized state, to deserve its name, must uphold, not violate, the sanctity of human life.

I entirely agree with the first pair of propositions, which is why . . . I replace the term capital punishment with "judicial homicide." The uncontrollable brute whom I want put out of the way is not to be punished for his misdeeds, nor used as an example or a warning; he is to be killed for the protection of others, like the wolf that escaped not long ago in a Connecticut suburb. No anger, vindictiveness or moral conceit need preside over the removal of such dangers. But a man's inability to control his violent impulses or to imagine the fatal consequences of his acts should be a presumptive reason for his elimination from society. This generality covers drunken driving and teen-age racing on public highways, as well as incurable obsessive violence; it might be extended (as I shall suggest later) to other acts that destroy, precisely, the moral basis of civilization.

But why kill? I am ready to believe the statistics tending to show that the prospect of his own death does not stop the murderer. For one thing he is often a blind egotist, who cannot conceive the possibility of his own death. For another, detection would have to be infallible to deter the more imaginative who, although afraid, think they can escape discovery. Lastly, as Shaw long ago pointed out, hanging the wrong man will deter as effectively as hanging the right one. So, once again, why kill? If I agree that moral progress means an increasing respect for human life, how can I oppose abolition?

I do so because on this subject of human life, which is to me the heart of the controversy, I find the abolitionist inconsistent, narrow or blind. The propaganda for abolition speaks in hushed tones of the sanctity of human life, as if the mere statement of it as an absolute should silence all opponents who have any moral sense. But most of the abolitionists belong to nations that spend half their annual income on weapons of war and that honor research to perfect means of killing. These good people vote without a qualm for the political parties that quite sensibly arm their country to the teeth. The West today does not seem to be the time or place to invoke the absolute sanctity of human life. As for the clergymen in the movement, we may be sure from the experience of two previous world wars that they will bless our arms and pray for victory when called upon, the sixth commandment notwithstanding.

"Oh, but we mean the sanctity of life *within* the nation!" Very well: is the movement then campaigning also against the principle of self-defense? Absolute sanctity means letting the cutthroat have his sweet will of you, even if you have a poker handy to bash him with, for you might kill. And again, do we hear any protest against the police firing at criminals on the street—mere bank robbers usually—and doing this, often enough, with an excited marksmanship that misses the artist and hits the bystander? The absolute sanctity of human life is, for the abolitionist, a slogan rather than a considered proposition.

Yet it deserves examination, for upon our acceptance or rejection of it depend such other highly civilized possibilities as euthanasia and seemly suicide. The inquiring mind also wants to know, why the sanctity of *human* life alone? My tastes do not run to household pets, but I find something less than admirable in the uses to which we put animals—in zoos, laboratories and space machines—without the excuse of the ancient law, "Eat or be eaten."

It should moreover be borne in mind that this argument about sanctity applies—or would apply—to about ten persons a year in Great Britain and to between fifty and seventy-five in the United States. These are the average numbers of those executed in recent years. The count by itself should not, of course, affect our judgment of the principle: one life spared or forfeited is as important, morally, as a hundred thousand. But it should inspire a comparative judgment: there are hundreds and indeed thousands whom, in our concern with the horrors of execution, we forget: on the one hand, the victims of violence; on the other, the prisoners in our jails.

The victims are easy to forget. Social science tends steadily to mark a preference for the troubled, the abnormal, the problem case. Whether it is poverty, mental disorder, delinquency or crime, the "patient material" monopolizes the interest of increasing groups of people among the most generous and learned. Psychiatry and moral liberalism go together; the application of law as we have known it is thus coming to be regarded as an historic prelude to social work, which may replace it entirely. Modern literature makes the most of this same outlook, caring only for the disturbed spirit, scorning as bourgeois those who pay their way and do *not* stab their friends. All the while the determinism of natural science reinforces the assumption that society causes its own evils. A French jurist, for example, says that in order to understand crime we must first brush aside all ideas of Responsibility. He means the criminal's and takes for granted that of society. The murderer kills because reared in a broken home or, conversely, because at an early age he witnessed his parents making love. Out of such cases, which make pathetic reading in the literature of modern criminology, is born the abolitionist's state of mind: we dare not kill those we are beginning to understand so well.

If, moreover, we turn to the accounts of the crimes committed by these unfortunates, who are the victims? Only dull ordinary people going about their business. We are sorry, of course, but they do not interest science on its march. Balancing, for example, the sixty to seventy criminals executed annually in the United States, there were the seventy to eighty housewives whom George Cvek robbed, raped and usually killed during the months of a career devoted to proving his virility. "It is too bad." Cvek alone seems instructive, even though one of the law officers who helped track him down quietly remarks: "As to the extent that his villainies disturbed family relationships, or how many women are still haunted by the specter of an experience they have never disclosed to another living soul, these questions can only lend themselves to sterile conjecture."

The remote results are beyond our ken, but it is not idle to speculate about those whose death by violence fills the daily two inches at the back of respectable newspapers——the old man sunning himself on a park bench and beaten to death by four hoodlums, the small children abused and strangled, the middle-aged ladies on a hike assaulted and killed, the family terrorized by a released or escaped lunatic, the half-dozen working people massacred by the sudden maniac, the boatload of persons dispatched by the skipper, the mindless assaults upon schoolteachers and shopkeepers by the increasing hordes of dedicated killers in our great cities. Where does the sanctity of life begin?

It is all very well to say that many of these killers are themselves "children," that is, minors. Doubtless a nine-year-old mind is housed in that 150 pounds of unguided muscle. Grant, for argument's sake, that the misdeed is "the fault of society," trot out the broken home and the slum environment. The question then is, What shall we do, not in the Utopian city of tomorrow, but here and now? The "scientific" means of cure are more than uncertain. The apparatus of detention only increases the killer's antisocial animus. Reformatories and mental hospitals are full and have an understandable bias toward discharging their inmates. Some of these are indeed "cured"—so long as they stay under a rule. The stress of the social free-for-all throws them back on their violent modes of self-expression. At that point I agree that society has failed—twice: it has twice failed the victims, whatever may be its guilt toward the killer.

As in all great questions, the moralist must choose, and choosing has a price. I happen to think that if a person of adult body has not been endowed with adequate controls against irrationally taking the life of another, that person must be judicially, painlessly, regretfully killed before that mindless body's horrible automation repeats.

I say "irrationally" taking life, because it is often possible to feel great sympathy with a murderer. Certain *crimes passionnels* can be forgiven without being condoned. Blackmailers invite direct retribution. Long provocation can be an excuse, as in that engaging case of some years ago, in which a respectable carpenter of seventy found he could no longer stand the incessant nagging of his wife. While she excoriated him from her throne in the kitchen—a daily exercise for fifty years—the husband went to his bench and came back with a hammer in each hand to settle the score. The testimony to his character, coupled with the sincerity implied by the two hammers, was enough to have him sent into quiet and brief seclusion.

But what are we to say of the type of motive disclosed in a journal published by the inmates of one of our Federal penitentiaries? The author is a bank robber who confesses that money is not his object:

> My mania for power, socially, sexually, and otherwise can feel no degree of satisfaction until I feel sure I have struck the ultimate of submission and terror in the minds and bodies of my victims. . . . It's very difficult to explain all the queer fascinating sensations pounding and surging through me while I'm holding a gun on a victim, watching his body tremble and sweat. . . . This is the moment when all the rationalized hypocrisies of civilization are suddenly swept away and two men stand there facing each other morally and ethically naked, and right and wrong are the absolute commands of the man behind the gun.

This confused echo of modern literature and modern science defines the choice before us. Anything deserving the name of cure for such a man presupposes not only a laborious individual psychoanalysis, with the means to conduct and to sustain it, socially and economically, but also a re-education of the mind, so as to throw into correct perspective the garbled ideas of Freud and Nietzsche, Gide and Dostoevski, which this power-seeker and his fellows have derived from the culture and temper of our times. Ideas are tenacious and give continuity to emotion. Failing a second birth of heart and mind, we must ask: How soon will this sufferer sacrifice a bank clerk in the interests of making civilization less hypocritical? And we must certainly question the wisdom of affording him more than one chance. The abolitionists' advocacy of an unconditional "let live" is in truth part of the same cultural tendency that animates the killer. The Western peoples' revulsion from power in domestic and foreign policy has made of the state a sort of counterpart of the bank robber: both having power and neither knowing how to use it. Both waste lives because hypnotized by irrelevant ideas and crippled by contradictory emotions. If psychiatry were sure of its ground in diagnosing the individual case, a philosopher might consider whether such dangerous obsessions should not be guarded against by judicial homicide *before* the shooting starts.

I raise the question not indeed to recommend the prophylactic execution of potential murderers, but to introduce the last two perplexities that the abolitionists dwarf or obscure by their concentration on changing an isolated penalty. One of these is the scale by which to judge the offenses society wants to repress. I can for example imagine a truly democratic state in which it would be deemed a form of treason punishable by death to create a disturbance in any court or deliberative assembly. The aim would be to recognize the sanctity of orderly discourse in arriving at justice, assessing criticism and defining policy. Under such a law, a natural selection would operate to remove permanently from the scene persons who, let us say, neglect argument in favor of banging on the desk with their shoe. Similarly, a bullying minority in a diet, Parliament or skupshtina would be prosecuted for treason to the most sacred institutions when fists or flying inkwells replace rhetoric. That the mere suggestion of such a law sounds ludicrous shows how remote we are from civilized institutions, and hence how gradual should be our departure from the severity of judicial homicide.

I say gradual and I do not mean standing still. For there is one form of barbarity in our law that I want to see mitigated before any other. I mean imprisonment. The enemies of capital punishment—and liberals generally—seem to be satisfied with any legal outcome so long as they themselves avoid the vicarious guilt of shedding blood. They speak of the sanctity of life, but have no concern with its quality. They give no impression of ever having read what it is certain they have read, from Wilde's *De Profundis* to the latest account of prison life by a convicted homosexual. Despite the infamy of concentration camps, despite Mr. Charles Burney's remarkable work, *Solitary Confinement,* despite riots in prisons, despite the round of escape, recapture and return in chains, the abolitionists' imagination tells them nothing about the reality of being caged. They read without a qualm, indeed they read with rejoicing, the hideous irony of "Killer Gets Life"; they sigh with relief instead of horror. They do not see and suffer the cell, the drill, the clothes, the stench, the food; they do not feel the sexual racking of young and old bodies, the hateful promiscuity, the insane monotony, the mass degradation, the impotent hatred. They do not re-member from Silvio Pellico that only a strong political faith, with a hope of final victory, can steel a man to endure long detention. They forget that Joan of Arc, when offered "life," preferred burning at the stake. Quite of another mind, the abolitionists point with pride to the "model prisoners" that murderers often turn out to be. As if a model prisoner were not, first, a contradiction in terms, and second an exemplar of what a free society should not want.

I said a moment ago that the happy advocates of the life sentence appear not to have understood what we know they have read. No more do they appear to read what they themselves write. In the preface to his useful volume of cases, *Hanged in Error*, Mr. Leslie Hale, M.P., refers to the tardy recognition of a minor miscarriage of justice—one year in jail: "The prisoner emerged to find that his wife had died and that his children and his aged parents had been removed to the workhouse. By the time a small payment had been assessed as 'compensation' the victim was incurably insane." So far we are as indignant with the law as Mr. Hale. But what comes next? He cites the famous Evans case, in which it is very probable that the wrong man was hanged, and he exclaims: "While such mistakes are possible, should society impose an irrevocable sentence?" Does Mr. Hale really ask us to believe that the sentence passed on the first man, whose wife died and who went insane, was in any sense *revocable?* Would not any man rather be Evans dead than that other wretch "emerging" with his small compensation and his reasons for living gone?

Nothing is revocable here below, imprisonment least of all. The agony of a trial itself is punishment, and acquittal wipes out nothing. Read the heart-rending diary of William Wallace, accused quite implausibly of having murdered his wife and "saved" by the Court of Criminal Appeals—but saved for what? Brutish ostracism by everyone and a few years of solitary despair. The cases of Adolf Beck, of Oscar Slater, of the unhappy Brooklyn bank teller who vaguely resembled a forger and spent eight years in Sing Sing only to "emerge" a broken, friendless, useless, "compensated" man—all these, if the dignity of the individual has any meaning, had better have been dead before the prison door ever opened for them. This is what counsel always says to the jury in the course of a murder trial and counsel is right: far better hang this man than "give him life." For my part, I would choose death without hesitation. If that option is abolished, a demand will one day be heard to claim it as a privilege in the name of human dignity. I shall believe in the abolitionist's present views only after he has emerged from twelve months in a convict cell.

The detached observer may want to interrupt here and say that the argument has now passed from reasoning to emotional preference. Whereas the objector to capital punishment *feels* that death is the greatest of evils, I *feel* that imprisonment is worse than death. A moment's thought will show that feeling is the appropriate arbiter. All reasoning about what is right, civilized and moral rests upon sentiment, like mathematics. Only, in trying to persuade others, it is important to single out the fundamental feeling, the prime intuition, and from it to reason justly. In my view, to profess respect for human life and be willing to see it spent in a penitentiary is to entertain liberal feelings frivolously. To oppose the death penalty because, unlike a prison term, it is irrevocable is to argue fallaciously.

In the propaganda for abolishing the death sentence the recital of numerous miscarriages of justice commits the same error and implies the same callousness: what is at fault in our present system is not the sentence but the fallible procedure. Capital cases being one in a thousand or more, who can be cheerful at the thought of all the "revocable" errors? What the miscarriages point to is the need for reforming the jury system, the rules of evidence, the customs of prosecution, the machinery of appeal. The failure to see that this is the great task reflects the sentimentality I spoke of earlier, that which responds chiefly to the excitement of the unusual. A writer on Death and the Supreme Court is at pains to point out that when that tribunal reviews a capital case, the judges are particularly anxious and careful. What a left-handed compliment to the highest judicial conscience of the country! Fortunately, some of the champions of the misjudged see the issue more clearly. Many of those who are thought wrongly convicted now languish in jail because the jury was uncertain or because a doubting governor commuted the death sentence. Thus Dr. Samuel H. Sheppard, Jr., convicted of his wife's murder in the second degree is serving a sentence that is supposed to run for the term of his natural life. The story of his numerous trials, as told by Mr. Paul Holmes, suggests that police incompetence, newspaper demagogy, public envy of affluence and the mischances of legal procedure fashioned the result. But Dr. Sheppard's vindicator is under no illusion as to the conditions that this "lucky" evader of the electric chair will face if he is granted parole after ten years: "It will carry with it no right to resume his life as a physician. His privilege to practice medicine was blotted out with his conviction. He must all his life bear the stigma of a parolee, subject to unceremonious return to confinement for life for the slightest misstep. More than this, he must live out his life as a convicted murderer."[1]

What does the moral conscience of today think it is doing? If such a man is a dangerous repeater of violent acts, what right has the state to let him loose after ten years? What is, in fact, the meaning of a "life sentence" that peters out long before life? Paroling looks suspiciously like an expression of social remorse for the pain of incarceration, coupled with a wish to avoid "unfavorable publicity" by freeing a suspect. The man is let out

---

[1] Editor's note: Dr. Sheppard has since been freed.

when the fuss has died down; which would mean that he was not under lock and key for our protection at all. He *was* being punished, just a little—for so prison seems in the abolitionist's distorted view, and in the jury's and the prosecutor's, whose "second-degree" murder suggests killing someone "just a little."[2]

If, on the other hand, execution and life imprisonment are judged too severe and the accused is expected to be harmless hereafter—punishment being ruled out as illiberal—what has society gained by wrecking his life and damaging that of his family?

What we accept, and what the abolitionist will clamp upon us all the more firmly if he succeeds, is an incoherence which is not remedied by the belief that second-degree murder merits a kind of second-degree death; that a doubt as to the identity of a killer is resolved by commuting real death into intolerable life; and that our ignorance whether a maniac will strike again can be hedged against by measuring "good behavior" within the gates and then releasing the subject upon the public in the true spirit of experimentation.

These are some of the thoughts I find I cannot escape when I read and reflect upon this grave subject. If, as I think, they are relevant to any discussion of change and reform, resting as they do on the direct and concrete perception of what happens, then the simple meliorists who expect to breathe a purer air by abolishing the death penalty are deceiving themselves and us. The issue is for the public to judge; but I for one shall not sleep easier for knowing that in England and America and the West generally a hundred more human beings are kept alive in degrading conditions to face a hopeless future; while others—possibly less conscious, certainly less controlled—benefit from a premature freedom dangerous alike to themselves and society. In short, I derive no comfort from the illusion that in giving up one manifest protection of the law-abiding, we who might well be in any of these three roles—victim, prisoner, licensed killer—have struck a blow for the sanctity of human life.

---

[2] The British Homicide Act of 1957, Section 2, implies the same reasoning in its definition of "diminished responsibility" for certain forms of mental abnormality. The whole question of irrationality and crime is in utter confusion, on both sides of the Atlantic.

A LETTER TO THE GOVERNOR

Caryl Chessman

The voice of Caryl Chessman is stilled; he was executed at San Quentin on May 20, 1960. His words, in a letter written to the Governor after a temporary reprieve, survive as a remarkable commentary on the moral implications of capital punishment.

Name: Caryl Chessman
Box 66565, San Quentin, Calif.
Date: February 26, 1960

The Hon. Edmund G. Brown
Governor of the State of California
State Capitol
Sacramento, California

Dear Governor Brown:

As you know, at approximately 4:45 P.M. on Thursday, February 18, 1960, I was removed from the Death Row Unit located on the fifth floor of the North Block here at San Quentin and locked in the small holding cell, just a few feet from the State's lethal gas chamber, where California's condemned spend their last night on earth. The death watch began. So far as I knew, I would be put to death at ten o'clock in the morning.

I was permitted to see an early edition of a Friday newspaper. Its headlines were large and black: CHESSMAN MUST DIE, BROWN SAYS. Again, only an hour earlier, the members of the California Supreme Court had voted 4 to 3 against a recommendation to you for clemency. Thus, by a simple vote, you were foreclosed from exercising your commutation powers. The court had made its order "final forthwith." I had been notified of that action a few hours before being taken downstairs to the holding cell. In anticipation of it, had put my affairs in order and executed a new will. . . .

And death appeared inevitable. I held out no feverish, desperate hope for a life-sparing miracle. On the contrary, what sustained me, what made it possible for me to await the morning and oblivion with a detached, almost clinical calm was hope of an entirely different sort: the burning hope that my execution would lead to an objective reappraisal of the social validity or invalidity of capital punishment, and that such a reexamination would lead, in turn, to an awareness on the part of all Californians that Death Rows, and death chambers and executioners were unworthy of our society, that the former, in fact, were gross obscenities, solving nothing but rather confounding solution.

The minutes passed, the hours. The prison's Catholic Chaplain, Father Edward Dingberg, visited me. Associate Wardens Walter D. Achuff and Louis S. Nelson saw me for a few minutes. Dr. David G. Schmidt, San Quentin's chief psychiatrist, came in. Attorney George Davis conferred with me hurriedly, intending to return later. Warden Fred R. Dickson dropped by for a talk.

Contrary to published accounts that I consumed the condemned man's traditional hearty meal of "fried chicken, French fried potatoes, vegetable salad, coffee and two kinds of pie—apple and chocolate cream," I am compelled to confess these reports, seemingly attesting to my capacity as a trencherman, are somewhat exaggerated. Actually, my wants were more modest. I had a hamburger and a coke about 7:30, and during the course of the evening I drank three cups of coffee. I also puffed on a cigar, although I normally do not smoke.

I waited. Midnight came. All my visitors had left but Warden Dickson. Then the telephone rang mutedly, and one of the death watch officers said, "It's for you, Warden." I watched Mr. Dickson disappear around a bend in the hallway. I paced the floor, my steps reduced to almost soundlessness by the cloth slippers. The radio outside the cell played quietly. Over it I had listened to a succession of newscasts. The news was all negative. One commentator reported Miss Asher[1] had been unable to see you but, in vain, had talked with two members of your staff. A second commentator solemnly quoted you as having said, "Only an act of God can save Caryl Chessman now."

My eyes fell on the newspaper I had been allowed whose stark headline I quoted above. One of its front-page lead paragraphs reads: "The world was disturbed last night as the hour for Caryl Chessman's execution drew near. Protests echoed from continent to continent." This San Francisco daily also reported: "There was little question that the Governor . . . was undergoing great emotional stress as Chessman's last hours ticked away," and: "The mail—most of it running about three to one for clemency—continued to pour in. So did the telegrams and the zero-hour telephone calls. . . ."

On page two were pictures of the gas chamber and this account of how I would die in less than ten hours:

> . . . He'll get a physical examination from the prison's chief physician, Dr. Herman H. Gross, at 9 A.M. and undoubtedly will once again be found to be in perfect condition.

---

[1] Editor's note: Chessman's attorney.

At 9:45 A.M. come the last, formal visits from Warden Dickson and his aide to hear any last requests. Once again the chaplains will wait silently.

Over a carpeted floor, his stockinged feet should take the last walk at 10 A.M. on the dot.

There have been 164 people in the gas chamber before him, and experience gives the prison staff an almost split-second foretelling of the rest.

By 10:01 A.M. he should be in one of the two death chairs— chair B. in his case.

Two straps for each arm and leg, one across the chest and another for the waist. That, and the final slamming of the great iron door—less than three minutes.

At 10:03½, by schedule, Warden Dickson would nod at a guard and a lever will send the cyanide pellets into the sulphuric acid basins.

I smiled, grimly, I'm sure. I knew how it felt to be a dead man. Only the ritualized formalities of physically extinguishing my life with hydrocyanic acid gas remained.

"Has the Warden gone?" I asked one of the death watch. "No," I was told, "he's still on the phone."

I gave no thought to the significance of the call. Then, audibly, I heard Warden Dickson say, "All right, Governor." A few seconds later the Warden reappeared. I'd glanced up from the paper I was reading. As he approached the cell, the Warden's face was a thoughtful mask.

"I have some news for you, Caryl." Mr. Dickson paused. "Oh?" I responded. He nodded, smiled. "The Governor has just granted you a 60-day reprieve."

The words had been spoken softly—but they crashed and reverberated in my mind like thunder in an echo chamber. Except possibly in a mocking, sadistic nightmare, they were words I truly never had expected to hear up to the instant of their utterance. I had been prepared to die; now I must be ready to go on living, I realized, for at least another 60 days.

I drew a deep breath as my thoughts raced. My words have been reported in the press: "Thank you. This is a great surprise. I really didn't expect it. Tell the Governor I thank him. I am surprised and grateful."

The Warden said he would see me again later in the morning. We said goodnight. Swiftly I was taken back upstairs in the elevator to Death Row. Swiftly, in the office, I changed into my regular clothing. Accompanied by the officers, I was passed through the "Bird Cage"—with its double doors and multiplicity of bolts and bars and locks—into the Row proper. From most of the occupied cells, yellow light spilled out into the corridor. The condemned were awake, listening to their earphones, silent, waiting—for what? Somehow, even better than I, they had sensed their fate was tied to mine, and mine to a pressing social issue of far greater significance than what might, individually or collectively, happen to any or all of us. They had heard me say repeatedly that obviously the greatest hope for abolition of the death penalty lay with my death. They—even the tortured and troubled ones—knew this to be true. Their obvious course was to accept this fact and hope it might lead them out from the cold shadow of the gas chamber. But, as I later learned, they had sent you a telegram, urging your intercession in my behalf. They had refused to believe that death—even another's—was a solution. I don't know whether that telegram ever came to your attention in the flood of messages you were receiving. I do know it had a profound effect on me. . . .

I continued along the corridor, stopping for a moment or two to speak to the occupant of each cell. The reaction was the same. Here was a genuine and spontaneous expression of brotherhood, commingled for them with a miracle. And make no mistake, Governor, I was for my doomed fellows no arrogant, swaggering hero returned after breathing defiance into the teeth of the cosmos. On the contrary, since they had come to know the man rather than the counterfeit black criminal legend, I was a flesh and blood human being whose appointment with man-imposed death had come to symbolize the critical and yet unresolved basic struggle of social man to rise above wrath and vengeance, to trust not the executioner, but their—mankind's—own reason and humanity in building a saner world for their children and their children's children. These men had been accused and convicted of homicidal violence, and so, better than any, they knew the futility of such violence. Now, after a bitter contest, life in my case had claimed at least a temporary victory. . . .

We got the word [that] you had granted the reprieve because, since the people of California were sharply divided on the issue, you wanted "to give the people . . . an opportunity, through the Legislature, to express themselves once more on capital punishment." . . .

And then, as well as in the hectic days to come, before there were calmer reflections and clearer analysis, the paradoxical evidence mounted: While the Chessman case had made evident the urgent need for a calm, careful and objective reexamination of the question whether capital punishment should not be discarded as a barbarous anachronism, productive finally of nothing but division and uneasy doubt among us, my continued existence, if only for another few weeks, and the fearful Chessman legend, which portrayed me as a cunning, fiendish, Cataline-like mocker of justice, threatened to throttle such a reexamination and reevaluation at the outset.

I remain haunted by that paradox. Beyond the descriptive power of words, these have been troubled and difficult days for me. I do not resort to hyperbole when I say they have been hell, even more than the past 11½ years have been hell. I cannot escape the fact I owe you my life for whatever days remain to me. I cannot forget that literally millions of people from nations around the world spoke out for me. In terms of the larger social good that is your goal, my obligation is a heavy one, and I refuse to try to rationalize it away. Over and over I have asked myself the questions. What possibly can I do, if anything, to divorce the ugly, emotion-inflaming image of Caryl Chessman from the grave social issue of capital punishment? What can I say—and mean, and demonstrate?

. . . I decided I can and I do, without theatrics, offer them my life. If the hysteria and the mob wrath that surrounds the problem only can be propitiated by my death and if otherwise they agree that the death penalty should be abolished, then I earnestly urge the members of our Legislature to frame their bill in such a way as to exclude me. This can be done readily—for example, by a declaration in the law that anyone convicted of a capital offense during or subsequent to the year 1950, whose sentence of death remains in force and unexecuted, shall be treated as though serving a sentence of life imprisonment. I give my solemn word before the world that I will never challenge such a law in the courts and I will disavow any attempt by any attorney purporting to act in my behalf.

. . . If the legislators do not necessarily demand my death but do believe the final question of my fate, under the California Constitution, should be resolved by yourself and the majority opinion of the State Supreme Court, then I urge them so to indicate. This way, by the passage of the type of bill mentioned above, they can sever the two problems. . . .

Except for the days I was out to court, I have occupied a death cell continuously since Saturday morning, July 3, 1948. I have had eight dates for execution in California's lethal gas chamber fixed and then canceled, some in the very last hours. A ninth date soon will be set. Ninety-odd men have taken that last, grim walk by my cell to their deaths since I came to Death Row. If it gives them any satisfaction, Californians may be assured my prolonged half-life in the shadow of the gas chamber has been an indescribably punishing ordeal. The shock of it, I think, has brought me to maturity; it has forced upon me keen social awareness of the problem that, in exaggerated form, I am said to typify.

I am now 38 years of age. I was 26 when arrested. Behind me is a long record of arrest. I am a graduate of California reform schools and prisons. I have been called a "criminal psychopath." Certainly, as a young man, I was a violent, rebellious, monumental damn fool. I was at odds with my society; I resisted authority. I am ashamed of that past but I cannot change it. However, with my writings, I have tried to salvage something of larger social significance from it. Without shifting responsibility for my conduct, I endeavored in my first book to tell the story of my life and hence to explain how young men like myself got that way. I realized that Death Rows made sense only because people like Caryl Chessman didn't.

After being brought to the death house, the change in me and my outlook came slowly and painfully. Defiantly, I stood and fought in the courts for survival, asking no quarter and expecting none. But, ironically, to have any chance for survival, I had to turn to the law; I had to invoke the protections of the Constitution; I had to study, often as much as 18 to

20 hours a day; I had to learn to impose upon myself a harsh self-discipline; I had to think and to be ruthlessly honest with myself; in time, I forced myself to admit, "Chessman, you have been, and to some degree still are, an irrational, impossible fool. What are you going to do about it?"

At that juncture, the traditional thing, the conventional response almost certainly would have been for me to confess my past folly and to beg for mercy. But I hesitated, not out of pride or false pride. I couldn't escape the fact that such a response on my part would, in practical effect, amount to affirmation that gas chambers and a system of justice ultimately based upon retribution possessed a genuine—rather than a mistakenly conceived and defended—social validity. I knew they did not possess such a validity. Without mock heroics, I became aware then that the greatest contribution I could make was to cause people, all people, to become angrily aware of places like Death Row and the administration of criminal justice in general. This, in my own way, I did: by continued total resistance. I was told I could not write another line for publication and I wrote anyway. When concerted efforts were made to suppress my manuscripts, I found a way to smuggle them from the prison. I intensified my court fight, winning some battles, losing others. Vituperation was heaped upon me. I became known as a mocker of justice. Editorial writers and public officials roundly denounced me. The public clamored for "this cunning fiend's" execution. Often I was half-mad with doubt; often I was ready to collapse with a brutal fatigue; often I sardonically sneered at myself and my goal. But I kept on somehow. A remorseless voice within told me, "This is your penance, fool—to be reviled and hated. This, if you call yourself a man, is the price you must pay."

I had certain advantages, and almost impossible handicaps. Among others, I had been convicted of unsavory sex offenses, sordid acts that, when recounted, inflamed the mind of the listener. They had inflamed the judge, the prosecutor, the jury. A Red Light Bandit—so-called because the bandit had operated, according to trial testimony, with a car equipped with a red spotlight such as those on police cars. He had accosted couples in lonely lovers' lanes. Armed with a gun, he would sometimes rob the couples, if they had any money. On two occasions testified to at my trial, he took the woman to his car. In one of these instances, under threat of death, he compelled her, the victim, to commit an unnatural sex act before letting her out and driving off. On a second occasion, he drove off with a 17-year-old girl to another secluded area, compelled her, too, to commit a perverted sexual act and attempted to rape her. Then he let her off near her home. (This tragic young woman, who had a history of serious mental disturbance, was committed to a mental hospital some 19 months after her traumatic experience. "Today," the wire services have quoted her mother as saying, "she just sits and stares"—lost in the withdrawn unreal world of the schizophrenic.)

It is no wonder, then, that the Red Light Bandit crimes so aroused judge, jury and prosecutor and antagonized them against the man accused of their commission. They angered and outraged me to an equal or greater degree, to an extent where in a red haze of emotion, I was unable to defend myself as effectively as otherwise I might. Stupidly and stubbornly, as well, I had withheld certain vital facts about my involvement in a violent internecine struggle for control of an illegal but police protected book-making syndicate. The convict's code said I shouldn't talk, or name names. I didn't. Then, not by myself, other critical evidence got suppressed. Witnesses disappeared. And a damning net was drawn around me. The jury returned verdicts of guilty, doomed me. I was brought to Death Row, twice sentenced to death and to 15 consecutive prison terms. The question of guilt or innocence was closed unless I could convince an appellate court I had been convicted illegally. Otherwise, branded a loathsome sex predator, I would die. I would have no chance to establish California had convicted the wrong man. It would make no difference that the description furnished the police of the bandit didn't remotely fit me; that the 17-year-old girl said her attacker had been "shorter than the usual man" and had weighed nearly 50 pounds less than the evidence showed I did, while I was six feet tall; or that she said the bandit had spoken with a slight accent, had appeared to be Italian and had a linear cut scar extending back from his right ear; or that this bandit usually gave his victims a look at his face before pulling up a handkerchief mask, while I just had been released from prison on parole and knew that my photographs almost certainly would be the first shown robbery victims; or that I had absolutely no history as a sex offender; or that I had been refused the right to produce witnesses at the trial who would testify to my reputation for sexual normality as well as to produce expert psychiatric evidence that I did not possess the psychological disposition to commit sexual crimes, particularly those involving force or violence, and that I was not a sexual psychopath.

All this made no difference. In the eyes of the law, I was guilty and would remain guilty unless I could win a new trial and acquittal. This galled but it also drove and sustained me. . . .

I wait to die. I remain locked in a death cell. More than 12 years have passed since my arrest. The State has spent nearly a million dollars in trying to kill me.

Now, in a few days, the California Legislature will be called into special session to consider abolition of capital punishment. Disturbed that a vote against the death penalty will be a vote for me, the man they believe has embarrassed their State and made a mockery of their laws, many legislators have vowed publicly to see that capital punishment is retained. I do not presume to tell them what to do; I do pray they will reconsider and reevaluate. . . . I am more than willing that they separate me decisively from the greater issue. I am quite willing to die if that will bring about this desperately needed social reform. I do suggest that if our positions were reversed and they had found themselves occupying a death cell under the conditions I have they too, and honorably, would have done as I have done, even though it meant bringing the wrath of the State down upon them. Happily, they will never know what it means to be doomed, to be within hours and minutes of execution, to feel the full, terrible impact of mob wrath, to have a claim of innocence brushed impatiently aside, to be called a "monster" and vilified, to seek redemption, not through hypo-critical groveling, but by a harder, perhaps impossible road, to win friends and want desperately to justify their friendship and their faith, to want to live and to believe, humbly, that within them is a gift for words that can enrich our literature and, their own case aside, contribute significantly to the pressing social problems of our day.

I do not overstate when I say I gladly would die ten thousand gas chamber deaths if that would bring these truths into the hearts and minds of those who make our laws: A vote for either abolition or a moratorium is not an indication of approval of murder or other capital crimes, for the death penalty does not deter; it does not protect society. On the contrary, it leaves it defenseless, since as long as we have an executioner and a gas chamber, we will be content to believe that we can bury the problem with the offender. We will think that revenge is enough. It isn't. We must find why men kill and we must learn to prevent killing. We must become as intensely concerned with tomorrow's prospective victims as yesterday's actual ones. We must learn how to save lives and to salvage lives.

As long as the death penalty is on our statute books, there will be too much emotionality and circus atmosphere tainting our administration of justice. And for those who doubt this, there is a ready and rational test at hand: Let a moratorium be ordered on the supreme penalty for a period of, say, five years. I am certain during that period there will be no rise in the per capita crimes. Rather, I am convinced the crime rate will drop appreciably, and that justice will function in a far more even-handed and fair way. The sensationalism inevitably attending capital cases will vanish. The citizen will be reassured. He will know that the man who has killed has been isolated. The accused is more likely, if he is guilty, to plead guilty. Our courts thus will be able to perform their duties more efficiently. And if an innocent man is later found to have been mistakenly convicted, it will not be too late to correct the error.

Unfortunately, as investigation will confirm, too often it is the friendless and the fundless upon whom the death penalty is imposed. The man with means or who knows the angles does not come to Death Row. As well, under our outmoded tests for legal sanity or insanity, too often the man who is executed is one who, while not legally insane, suffers from some serious mental disability. It needlessly demeans our society to engage in killing the mentally ill. Still further, among this group, as psychiatrists and penologists will attest, is the type of personality who is inflamed by the thought and threat of the gas chamber. His response to it, his overt expression of defiance, is to strike out homicidally. In effect, he gets his revenge in advance, and we in turn get ours after the tragedy.

That is why so many thoughtful citizens advocate abolition or a moratorium. They feel, as I do, a sense of guilty responsibility at a lethal act that is both more than futile and less than futile when the State takes a life. They want their laws to express humanity's ideal of nobility, compassion, understanding and social awareness. They know that our laws can do so without endangering the citizens of California. The basis for their opposition to man's government killing man is thus, in the highest sense, ethical, social, practical and religious. They do not want to see their society needlessly degraded, their system of justice compromised.

I must close, and in closing I again earnestly urge you to ask the Legislature to consider the question of capital punishment apart from Caryl Chessman and the Chessman case. I urge you to request that they consider framing their bill as suggested above, to exclude me. You can do this honorably by taking my life back into your hands alone. You can let me die. Indeed, as the matter now stands, you are powerless to do otherwise because of the present 4–3 vote against me in the California Supreme Court. But, at the same time, you can give your proposal to the Legislature a chance.

It deserves that chance. It deserves your forceful leadership. You are right in the position you have taken. It is time to speak out, for too seldom does unlightened humanity in this age of fear and awesome nuclear devices have a spokesman with the courage to advocate that death and hate are not and never can be an answer to the problems that beset our civilization. Mankind and future generations ever will remain in your debt and ever will honor your name.

Yours respectfully,
/s/ Caryl Chessman

3

Human Rights and the War on Crime

Stiffer penalties are only one factor in deterrence, according to the hard-line school; deterrence is also achieved by increasing the likelihood of apprehension and punishment. If this involves infringement of individual rights presently incorporated in our basic law, so be it. Advocates of the hard line believe that in recent years we have been so zealous of the rights of accused culprits that we have forgotten their victims. Misled by the Warren Court, we have given free rein to criminals; they perpetrate acts of violence secure in the knowledge that the chance of getting caught and convicted is negligible. For example, if a defendant believes that the government has used illegal tactics in developing a case against him (as in the celebrated Ellsberg break-in), he can ask to see the raw material in order to establish his right to have it thrown out. Thus, lawyers for the Mafia have demanded and received years of tape-recorded phone conversations and have been able to get otherwise foolproof cases thrown out of court.

Opposed to the hard-line view are those who argue that the rights protecting criminals guard against tragic errors. These rights shield the innocent, including the great law-abiding majority. No-knock entry (i.e., raids without search warrants), indiscriminate wiretaps, bugs, third degree interrogations, and preventive detention may help in the capture of suspected pushers, assassins, muggers, gangsters, and violence-prone radicals; they are also the favored weapons of the police state. The Fourth Amendment protection against "unreasonable searches and seizures"[1] may give the pusher a chance to get rid of the evidence before it can be appropriated by the police; it also reflects long-standing practice evolved to protect innocent parties from tyrannical rulers and overzealous police.

Which is more important? A distinguished philosopher and a former attorney general answer this question in the following selections. The reader, if he thinks in terms of stereotypes, will be surprised to find the philosopher cast in the role of Lord High Executioner.

---

[1] Fourth Amendment: "The right of the people to be secure in their persons, houses, papers, and effects, against unreasonable searches and seizures, shall not be violated, and no Warrants shall issue, but upon probable cause, supported by Oath or affirmation, and particularly describing the place to be searched, and the persons or things to be seized."

When, two centuries ago, the British House of Lords was debating no-knock entry, William Pitt closed his argument in opposition to such government invasion of privacy with one of the most celebrated statements ever made before that august body. It was repeated by Senator Sam Ervin at the Watergate hearings when the inquiry turned to the break-in of Daniel Ellsberg's psychiatrist, an illegal act defended at that time by the President's former assistant, John Ehrlichman, in the name of national security:

"The poorest man may, in his cottage, bid defiance to all the forces of the Crown. It may be frail. Its roof may shake. The wind may blow through it. The storm may enter. The rain may enter. But the King of England cannot enter. All his force dares not cross the threshold of that ruined tenement."

LIBERTY VS. SECURITY: THE FALSE CONFLICT

Ramsey Clark

Ramsey Clark was U.S. attorney general and, as such, chief law officer in President Johnson's administration. During the 1968 presidential campaign he was warmly denounced by Nixon partisans as a "permissivist." Tom Wicker of the New York Times *describes him as "the most revolutionary public voice in America today" and as "distinguished among our public men for his ability to see that crime is not an isolated matter . . . or merely the culpable result of evil men and lax officials" (1970). The following comments are taken from his widely read book,* Crime in America.

Our system of criminal justice fails to reduce crime. It is not working well Police are not professional, courts are unable to process case loads, prisons make criminals of boys they could rehabilitate. We see the reforms that are desperately needed, yet we do not make them. But even if these public agencies were working at the most effective level possible, they could not substantially or permanently reduce crime while conditions exist that breed crime. Mere words of prohibition, with force and the threat of force their only sanction, cannot shape human conduct in mass society.

As turbulence, doubt and anxiety cause fear to increase, fear in turn seeks repressiveness as a source of safety. But experience tells us that the result of repressiveness is more turbulence and more crime. In frustration over the failure of law enforcement to control crime, new, quick and cheap methods by which police and courts and prisons might be made more effective are sought amid desperate hope and rising hatred. A public that believes the police alone are responsible for crime control, and therefore no other effort is needed, will vest any power in the police that seems to prom ise safety when fear of crime is great. But there is no such power.

Excessive reliance on the system of criminal justice is terribly dangerous. It separates the people from their government. . . . The dialogue over the proper limits of police action and barely relevant court rulings consumes most of the emotion and much of the energy that could be constructively used to strengthen the system of criminal justice. Instead of efforts to raise police standards, expand training, increase salaries, and improve judicial machinery, we debate in ignorance and anger whether police should be authorized to stop and frisk whenever they choose and whether the *Miranda* decision[1] should be reversed. The resulting diversion of attention, emotionalization of concern and polarization of attitude damage the system of criminal justice. Those who stimulate prejudices in public opinion, who appeal to base instincts of fear, who protest their willingness—even desire—to sacrifice freedom on the altar of order add immeasurably to the burdens of achieving excellence in the performance of criminal justice agencies and commitment to eradication of the underlying causes of crime. . . .

There are degrees of repression. Each demeans the dignity of the individual in its different way. Intimidation of speech or conduct by force or threat of force in essence says the state is supreme, the individual has no rights, he must do as he is told. We see this when police tell people to move along, when they stop and frisk without cause, arrest on suspicion, enter premises without a warrant or without knocking, deny permits to speak and

---

[1] Editor's note: *Miranda v. Arizona* outlaws all police interrogations not held in the presence of the suspect's lawyer, unless the suspect has been clearly informed of and has waived his right to free or paid counsel and his right to remain silent. The decision was intended to end "squeal rooms" where police obtain confessions by duress or more refined "psychological" methods.

assemble, break up meetings and raid places where unpopular people live or work, without legal justification.

Stealth and trickery as methods of repression mean that the state has no respect for the individual. It will deceive, lie, invade privacy, steal documents, do whatever it thinks necessary to catch people in crime. By wiretapping, the government says to its citizens: Do not trust us, for we do not trust you. We will hide, overhear, wait secretly for months for you to do wrong. If you do anything to displease us, we may choose to watch your every move.

Denial of bail and preventive detention are essentially premised on the belief that the individual must yield his liberty to the state if he is poor, ignorant, despised—and apparently dangerous. He can be tried later. Society will not presume him innocent. No respecters of human dignity, these measures imply that judges can tell who the bad people—the dangerous ones—are and can say that they should be denied freedom and punished as guilty until proven innocent.

The desire to compel confessions and to repeal the Fifth Amendment admits the impotence of the system of criminal justice to find truth and do justice. Instead, it seeks to crush the individual, to make him bend his knee to its sovereignty, to coerce from his own mouth words that will convict him, to question him—if he is poor, ignorant or afraid—until he cracks. Frustrated and frightened in its impulse, it ignores the unreliability of the emotional or psychotic response, seeking only conviction. . . .

In bygone days the risks arising from eavesdropping were not great. Only by hiding could a person overhear. With the telephone the danger increased. . . . Developments in electronics beyond the telephone make it possible to totally destroy privacy. Privacy will exist tomorrow only if society insists on it. By placing a radio receiver-transmitter in a room, by directing a laser beam through a wall and focusing it on a resonant surface, by directing a parabolic scope toward two men in the middle of a field, every sound can be heard from afar. The speaker has no way of knowing who hears.

This invasion is only the beginning. Technology will soon bring the capability for audio-visual intrusion into every place. We can create a society where no one will know whether his every act is watched, his every word heard—or everyone will know they are. A generation later no one will see any wrong in it. The individual will be a different creature then.

Privacy has always been a precious commodity, but never so rare as in our times. . . . Invasions of privacy demean the individual. Can a society be better than the people composing it? When a government degrades its citizens, or permits them to degrade each other, however beneficent the specific purpose, it limits opportunities for individual fulfillment and national accomplishment. If America permits fear and its failure to make basic social reforms to excuse police use of secret electronic surveillance, the price will be dear indeed. The practice is incompatible with a free society.

Why do we think that the wiretap and the bug offer security? What is the evidence that they are either effective or efficient? Surely those who favor their use have the burden of proving their value to law enforcement and that other means equally effective are not available before sacrificing privacy. This has not been done.

Manifestly, for most crime electronic surveillance has little utility. In murder, assault, mugging, shoplifting, robbery, burglary, larceny, no one seriously contends that tapping and bugging are useful, with rarest exceptions. . . .

The one area of criminal activity where proponents most fervently believe wiretapping to be essential is against organized crime. This is in part because law enforcement officials have played a losing game with organized crime for too long. Organized crime can be eliminated. Why should we merely dabble with it? There have been whole cultures free of its scourge, and today there are entire nations without it. There are states and major cities in America with no significant organized crime.

In several cities where organized crime is most severe, police and prosecution have in the past used wiretap without inhibition. It has not been effective. Organized crime still flourishes in these communities. In other cities where there has never been organized crime, police have never used wiretap. The massive programs required to end organized crime have no place for wiretap. It is too slow, too costly, too ineffective.

Organized crime cannot exist where criminal justice agencies are not at least neutralized and probably corrupted to some degree. The syndicates deal in goods and services people want. Gambling, dope, unsecured loans at high rates of interest and prostitution account for probably 90 per cent of the illegal income of organized crime. Their customers include hundreds of people in any city where they operate and thousands in some cities. Anyone able to flash a roll of bills who wants to gamble can find a game within a few hours if there is gambling in the city. The difficulty of finding a dope peddler or prostitute is little if any more difficult. The police know—they cannot escape knowing—of much of this illegal activity. The slightest investigation will reveal it.

Urban slums are the natural environment of organized crime. Here are tens of thousands of powerless people who can be victimized with impunity. Much of the activity of organized crime is visible and viewed from passing squad cars on ghetto streets. The numbers runners, addicts buying and selling, and prostitutes looking for a pickup are known throughout the communities in which they live. . . .

How will wiretaps help law enforcement control organized crime against this background? Police know where numbers are sold, they know who's running the dice game, they know the prostitutes and bookies—they do not need a bug to tell them. They know the big shots, too. Most have criminal records. Their activities are knowable and known without wiretapping. If we really want to eliminate organized crime, we will not be distracted from the major effort necessary by cheap and degrading proposals to wiretap. . . .

The FBI used electronic surveillance in the organized crime area from at least the late 1950's until July 1965. Hundreds of man-years of agent time were wasted. . . . In 1967 and 1968, without the use of any electronic surveillance, FBI convictions of organized crime and racketeering figures were several times higher than during any year before 1965. The bugs weren't necessary. Other techniques such as the strike force proved far more effective. . . . The great bulk of the conversations intercepted by tap or bug involve private conversations unrelated to crime. Most people overheard on nearly any surveillance are not criminals. Nearly everyone has family, friends, associates and acquaintances who are not partners in crime. They talk together and to others.

No technique of law enforcement casts a wider net than electronic surveillance. Blind, it catches everything in the sea of sound but cannot discriminate between fish and fowl. It is ineffective and inefficient because this world is too big to detect crime by gathering all the noise and silence of whole areas to sift for evidence. . . .

Since authorization of wiretaps and electronic surveillance in 1968, we have been repeatedly told by the FBI, by prosecutors and by the Attorney General [John Mitchell] himself that various indictments and arrests resulted from wiretaps. Nearly all have referred to gambling and narcotics activities. Some announcements have referred to hundreds, even thousands, of incriminating conversations. Obviously, had someone cared to, these activities could have been broken up and important seizures made without wiretaps. Police knew of the activity before the taps were placed. Some prosecutors seem more interested in justifying wiretaps than in controlling crime. . . . Surreptitiousness is contagious. If you invade privacy with a bug, why not break and enter? Why not remove and photostat documents? . . .

Many believe that if court orders are required before police may tap or bug, the risks will be eliminated. This is doubtful. The history of court approval in New York City reveals widespread rubber stamp approval without real judicial consideration. This has been a common experience with bail and search warrants. The opportunity of the judge to decide intelligently is limited. Only the police present the application. The judge knows little, if anything, of the individuals involved except what the police allege. Some judges in most major jurisdictions will probably give automatic approval.

If the Supreme Court establishes a standard of probable cause, comparable to that required by the Constitution for search warrants, the lawful use of electronic surveillance will be drastically limited. Under this standard a phone could be tapped only when the police can demonstrate by evidence that there is reason to believe a specific crime has been or is about to be committed. There will rarely be such evidence and when it exists, a tap will rarely be needed. Such a test is the minimum protection the public should have. . . .

There is a profound and tragic moral in the fact that Congressional forces that favor wiretapping generally oppose professionalization of police, prisoner rehabilitation and research. They want to ignore any relationship between crime and slums, racism, poverty or mental health. . . . Somehow, the hard-liners believe that all that is needed to stop crime is to catch crooks. . . .

There is no conflict between liberty and safety. We will have both, or neither. You cannot purchase security at the price of freedom, because freedom is essential to human dignity and crime flows from acts that demean the individual. We can enlarge both liberty and safety if we turn from repressiveness, recognize the causes of crime and move constructively.

The major contribution the law can make is moral leadership. Only then can it hope to permanently influence the conduct of its citizens. The law cannot therefore impose immoral rules or act immorally. The government of a people who would be free of crime must always act fairly, with integrity and justice.

A SENTIMENTAL VIEW OF CRIME

Sidney Hook

Sidney Hook is one of America's most distinguished philosophers. Until his recent retirement he was professor of philosophy at New York University. Among his voluminous writings are From Hegel to Marx (*1936*), John Dewey: An Intellectual Portrait (*1950*), The Hero in History (*1943*), *and* The Paradoxes of Freedom (*1962*). *He is a spirited polemicist, not given to espousing causes popular with his academic brethren.*

Ramsey Clark ranges over the entire field of crime including the methods of detection and the procedures of arrest, parole, and corrections. At every point he displays a heart-warming and commendable interest in the human rights of criminals—but alas, little concern for the human rights of their victims. The fundamental weakness of his analysis is his failure to realize that there are conflicts of human rights, and that the requirements of wise decision making impose an order of priority. In the long run, were crime totally abolished in Clark's utopia, the human rights of all would be safeguarded; but in the succession of short runs that constitute the continuing present, we must often choose between the rights of the potential criminal and the rights of his potential victims. In a period when the number of violent crimes is rising rapidly, when in almost every large city citizens fear to leave their homes at night, it is psychologically unrealistic as well as morally unjustifiable to expect the potential victims of criminal behavior to give priority to the human rights of criminals if these conflict with their own rights.

Clark's failure to face up to the necessity for hard choices in the prevention and control of crime results in a shocking absence of common sense. "There is no conflict between liberty and safety," he declares. "We will have both, or neither." This is sheer balderdash. In many situations, liberty and safety are inversely related. If plane passengers were free to carry anything they please in their baggage and enjoy freedom from search, the safety of passengers in this age of hijacking would be correspondingly reduced. The safety of a traffic system depends upon restriction of motorists' freedom to drive in any lane or at any speed they please. Clark himself, with characteristic inconsistency, urges that, in the interest of safety and crime prevention, we severely abridge the freedom to acquire handguns and other lethal weapons.

The uncritical use of large abstractions leads Clark to positions that are little short of bizarre. He reiterates again and again that the end of law is justice. But surely this is not the only end of law, or always the most important. Most philosophers of law consider other ends to be at least as important: security (or reliability) and the ordered regulation of human affairs, so that human beings, knowing what to expect, can arrange their lives and business accordingly.

If justice were the sole end of law, then many of the procedural safeguards that shield the criminal from prosecution—and in defense of which Clark is rightly vehement—would have to be abandoned. For example, if conclusive evidence of a defendant's guilt has been acquired without a proper search warrant, justice in the case would certainly require that the evidence be admitted. And the privilege against self-incrimination, it has often been pointed out, has nothing to do with the ends of justice, for it is more often a shelter for the guilty than a shield for the innocent. One may of course say, as Blackstone did, "It is better that ten guilty persons escape than one innocent suffer." But no one can say this in the name of *justice*.

Clark's prejudices and one-sidedness are also manifest in his case against creation of a national police force in this country. (The F.B.I. is primarily an investigative agency.) The idea deserves fairer treatment than he gives it. He contends that concentration of police power would pose a threat to liberty. He believes in the dominance of local law enforcement, although in some areas of our country it is local law enforcement that has violated the basic rights of citizens, especially minorities. Nor is citizen participation in local law enforcement the unmixed blessing Clark apparently thinks it is. The lynch mobs and vigilante parties of yesteryear were made up of local citizens insisting on participation in law enforcement. And it certainly cannot be argued that in recent years local law enforcement has adequately protected the citizenry against criminal outrage.

It seems at least possible that a federal police force could be co-ordinated with local police in such a way as to avoid the danger of concentration of power and at the same time afford all citizens greater protection of the laws. But Clark disregards the possibility. He does not even ask, much less examine, the central question of whether, granting all the difficulties, dangers, and potential corruption in both local and federal police authorities, it would be easier to cope with them if we had a central police agency.

Clark makes some sound points, to be sure. He is certainly right in contending that we should put more effort and resources into rehabilitation of imprisoned criminals. And he is certainly right that speedier trials would be more effective than harsher punishments in reducing the incidence of crime. The book's merits, however, are outbalanced by faulty thinking and ritualistic rhetoric. Clark speaks eloquently of justice, of human dignity, and of reverence for life, but his words have a hollow ring because they are combined with judgments, exhortations, and sometimes insinuations that are incompatible with elementary fairness. It is possible, for example, to criticize the arguments for preventive detention of repeated offenders or for limitations upon abuse of the Fifth Amendment, without smearing those who hold such views as demagogues. (In a contrasting spirit, Clark refers to the Black Panthers and the Weathermen as "poor and unpopular groups and individuals" who might suffer from preventive-detention laws.)

On the whole, *Crime in America* holds the police up to obloquy. One gets the impression, indeed, that the country has more to fear from its police (who, of course, are not undeserving of criticism) than from its criminals. "A major portion of the American public, for a variety of reasons," Clark tells us, "feels a little shudder when a squad car goes by."

On the basis of my own experience—as one born and raised in a big-city slum, a lifelong city dweller, and a visitor to many of the nation's large metropolitan centers—I doubt that Ramsey Clark knows what a "major portion of the American public" feels. There have been times in the past, to be sure, when activist radicals were harried by municipal ordinances. But today the police squad car is usually welcomed as a sign of safety. The most common complaint about the police I have recently heard from people who live in cities (as opposed to people who write books about city problems) is that there are not enough policemen around.

Typical of Clark's book as a whole is the final sentence (final, that is, if we disregard a hectic, italicized Epilogue). "Our greatest need," it runs, "is reverence for life—mere life, all life—life as an end in itself." Like many other dubious assertions in *Crime in America,* this seems vaguely appealing on a first, hurried reading. But on scrutiny, it is a dangerously muddled sentiment. Devotion to life as an end in itself is incompatible with, among many other things, the passionate devotion to justice that Clark also urges upon us. Whoever glorifies "mere life, all life" is evading the necessity for making the distinctions that are required for a life worthy of man.

4

Crime and Responsibility

There must be some leniency and flexibility in the law to provide for mitigating circumstances ranging from consideration of the mental condition of the accused to his social background. Central to such consideration is the most difficult problem of ethics—when is an individual responsible for his conduct and when is he the victim (or beneficiary) of circumstances over which he has no control? This problem ultimately involves the basic issue of freedom and determinism.

Clearly there are many conditions under which an individual cannot be held accountable. We have a long legal tradition that reckons with such circumstances as extreme youth, the presence of duress, entrapment, etc. Long ago England dealt in a formal way with the crucial question of sanity as a mitigating condition in the M'Naghten rule by which most American jurisdictions are now bound: the perpetrator of an illegal act may not be found guilty if he was unable at the time of the crime to distinguish between right and wrong; if, in other words, he "was laboring under such a defect of reason, from disease of the mind, as not to know" what he was doing or that it was wrong. Supplemented by the "irresistible impulse" test, the M'Naghten rule represents the limits to which adherents of the retributive justice school are willing to go in reckoning with mental defect or disease.

In recent years the M'Naghten rule has been subject to much criticism. Psychiatrists and penologists see it as unjust and symptomatic of a limited approach to criminal conduct that accounts for the glaring failures in our penal system. The now celebrated Durham rule laid down by Judge David Bazelon in *Durham v. United States* (1954) sought to reformulate the responsibility test and bring it to the fore. The principle of *Durham* was "to impose responsibility only if an act was the product of a free choice on the part of the defendant, and not of a mental disease or defect." The key word is "product." The court hoped, as Judge Bazelon later explained in *United States v. Brawner,* that the requirement of productivity would permit a jury to decide that "the illness was too slight or the causal connection too remote to have causal significance."

Psychiatrists and advanced criminologists hailed the Bazelon opinion as a breakthrough in the treatment of criminals and as marking a new *rapprochement* between psychiatry and criminology. Dr. Karl Menninger, whose comments appear below, described it as "more revolutionary in its total effect than the Supreme Court decision regarding segregation." Objections to the Durham rule were largely limited to frustrated police and prosecuting attorneys, to incensed citizens who achieve a sense of civic responsibility and moral righteousness by denouncing crime and demanding severer penalties, and to moralists genuinely concerned about whether the Durham rule hopelessly confounds the meaning of responsibility as a moral category. An exception among psychiatrists was Dr. Thomas S. Szasz, whose trenchant criticism is reprinted below.

However, the Durham rule has failed to satisfy the high hopes its author reposed in it; eighteen years later in a unanimous decision Judge Bazelon's court abandoned Durham and adopted the American Law Institute test that "a person is not responsible for criminal conduct if at the time of such conduct as a result of mental disease or defect he lacks substantial capacity either to appreciate the criminality [wrongfulness] of his conduct or to conform his conduct to the requirements of law" [Model Penal Code, #4.01 (1)]. Judge Bazelon's reasons are given below; they afford an important insight into the problems faced by our courts as they try to steer a line between those who would treat all criminals as patients to be cured and those who would treat them as sinners to be punished.

THE DILEMMA OF PUNISHMENT

David L. Bazelon

Judge David L. Bazelon, member of the U.S. Court of Appeals, Washington, D.C., has written more than twenty-five opinions on the insanity defense in criminal cases, of which the Durham opinion is the most famous. The American Psychiatric Association has recognized his work by awarding him a certificate of commendation, declaring that "he has removed massive barriers between the psychiatric and legal professions and opened pathways wherein together they may search for better ways of reconciling human values with social safety." The following are selections from his Brandeis Lecture delivered at Brandeis University in 1960.

. . . In the criminal law, where one might expect the assistance of the behavioral sciences and especially psychiatry to be most eagerly solicited—because most obviously relevant—the fact of the matter is that they are not. . . . I will not burden your patience by recounting again the century-old struggle against the exclusionary M'Naghten Rules. These Rules have dominated the administration of the insanity defense in England and most American jurisdictions. It should suffice to remind you of their continued vitality. The M'Naghten formula emphasizes the rational capacity of the mind, and excuses from criminal responsibility only the individual who at the time of the crime "was laboring under such a defect of reason, from disease of the mind, as not to know" what he was doing or that it was wrong. However this test *might* have been interpreted—volumes have been written on the possible meanings of the words—it has in fact worked to exclude medical evidence. I am almost tempted to say that under M'Naghten practice the psychiatrist appears in the proceeding at all only to testify to the irrelevance of psychiatry—that is, to confirm the irrelevance that "the law" has already decided upon. It assigns to the psychiatric expert in court a sacrificial role in a ritual of condemnation. The expert is asked a question which—most leaders of the profession inform us—cannot be answered within the terms of their discipline. And unless the Rules are breached—as they frequently are on the trial level— the psychiatrist is not encouraged or permitted to address himself to the clinical questions which are the only ones he is truly expert in answering.

That is the scientific expert testifying at the trial level. But on appeal, you may ask, have there been no "Brandeis briefs" setting forth the relevant facts and insights of modern scientific psychiatry? Yes, for example many psychiatric works were referred to in the appellant's brief in the *Durham* case, which, as many of you know, resulted in the adoption in the District of Columbia of a broadened insanity test—a rule designed to relax the rigors of M'Naghten and to welcome genuine psychiatric testimony presented in its own terms. *The Durham test simply asks whether the accused was suffering from a mental disease or defect, and inquires as to the relation between any such condition and the criminal act. . . .*[1]

In the administration of the criminal law today, we desperately need all the help we can get from modern behavioral scientists—before trial, during trial, and after trial. The law by itself, without these workers, is cast in the hopeless role of a socially isolated, traditional bulwark against the welter of personal, social and economic forces which create today's problem of crime and the so-called criminal population. And in this losing struggle, the law—by which I mean police, judges, lawyers, and prison guards—would have at its disposal a limited set of concepts honored largely by time alone. In brief, the law would have the *lex talionis*—the idea of retributive punishment based on absolute moral principles of purportedly universal application. *By itself,* the law would dispose of both the problem of crime and the criminal himself with the one idea of punishment. The "program" would be: Repress crime and all antisocial behavior by punishment alone; rehabilitate the offender by punishment alone; achieve social understanding of wrongdoing and the wrongdoer by the sole mechanical response—"Punish them—they deserve it!"

If the foregoing remarks seem intemperate, that is of course because they do *not* describe our actual system of criminal law administration. For one thing, stern retributive justice has always been tempered by mercy and forgiveness—by the ubiquitous impulse to afford the transgressor a "second chance." This happens in practice even when it is not allowed by theory. We simply find it too difficult, too non-human to punish, punish, punish—even though we may hold most seriously the moral imperative to punish, and even though our feeling is that we are wrong when we do not. And for another thing, the behavioral scientists—along with their facts, ideas, and methodology—have as a matter of fact intervened increasingly at many stages of the administrative process. Social workers, clinicians, welfare agencies, even the police, as well as many others, attempt to deal constructively with the juvenile delinquent before he is sent to a reformatory to begin his professional training as the criminal of the future. The psychiatrist comes to court and sometimes his presence

---

[1] My emphasis. Editor.

there *does* have something other than a ritualistic effect on the outcome of the proceeding. . . .

So clearly our criminal system is a very mixed affair—some would say a very *mixed-up* affair. But things are happening, there is agitation and movement, much heat and a certain amount of light. To put it simply, it is a system in transition. We are, painfully and slowly, coming to a clearer understanding of alternatives and necessities. . . .

If our system is in transition, then the question properly arises— Transition from what to what? From M'Naghten to Durham? Hardly. Certainly *from* M'Naghten—but not *just* from that ritualistic phrase, except perhaps symbolically. And Durham—even viewed as a concept, as an approach, which is the way I prefer to view it, rather than nineteen words of a jury instruction—is merely one way of welcoming the psychiatrist into the courtroom. It is a beginning, not an ending—and it relates to the insanity defense, which is only [the] visible one-ninth of the iceberg.

I believe that the deeper part of the iceberg consists of the retributive urge to punish irrespective of effect, and the accompanying intellectual justification of this primitive urge, the so-called theory of deterrence. A deep emotion and a complicated rationalization. . . .

Wherever one turns in an effort at reform in the treatment of offenders, one comes up against this need to punish and its defense by the theory of deterrence. Of course there are many other arguments put forward at various times in justification of the present system, with its great emphasis on punishment for its own sake or punishment as the answer to all problems. For example, both Judge Learned Hand in this country and Lord Justice Denning in England—the first sadly and the latter more firmly—have referred to the *public's* demand that the sinner shall suffer. Judge Hand stated that he did "not share that feeling, which is a vestige . . . of very ancient primitive and irrational beliefs and emotions." Lord Justice Denning spoke more strongly by saying:

> It is a mistake to consider the objects of punishment as being deterrent or reformative or preventive, and nothing else. . . . The truth is that some crimes are so outrageous that society insists on adequate punishment, because the wrongdoer deserves it, irrespective of whether it is a deterrent or not.

I can assure you that similar views are frequently expressed from the bench in courts throughout our land—and often enough when the crime is no more "outrageous" than juvenile car-theft. Sometimes the court in relieving itself of these sentiments will refer to society's demand for retribution— communicated to the court by some unknown intermediary, or perhaps so obvious as not to require communication. On other occasions a court will abandon that rhetorical flourish and speak directly, saying—"You are going to be punished good and proper because you deserve it, and because too many of you hoodlums have been getting away with it."

. . . The excessive emphasis on punishment, with the consequent neglect of genuine rehabilitation, is accompanied by a disastrously high level of recidivism. In the relatively progressive Federal Prison System, for example, the rate increased between 1949 and 1958 from 61 percent to 67 percent. In this same period, the number of serious offenders who have had two or more previous commitments has grown from 39 percent to 46 percent. Please realize what these figures mean: In two-thirds of the cases, punishment neither reforms nor deters the individual who has served one sentence. And with those who have served a second sentence, it fails again in nearly half of the cases. . . .

. . . Most of us who have been good for many years—or at least haven't been caught—have not maintained our high estate because of witnessing frequent public hangings and whippings or stopping to observe a malefactor being drawn-and-quartered on the corner of a busy intersection. Quite the opposite. . . .

Perhaps one should be encouraged by the fact that the modern urge to punish is no longer so immediately personal. I suppose we should all be pleased by the recent report from Saudi Arabia announcing an important reform in criminal law administration—that hereafter a thief's hand will be cut off by an "expert surgeon" using anesthetics rather than by an amateur with a hatchet. An accompanying reform is that adulteresses will no longer be stoned to death, as in biblical times. As Saudi Arabia enters the modern world, they will now be shot.

So there is something like progress in these matters. I would remind you that not half a century before the M'Naghten Rules were enunciated, more than 200 crimes were punishable by death in England. It is interesting to speculate as to whether England could possibly have become the civilized place it is today if the number of capital crimes had not been reduced. But Lord Justice Denning still believes in punishment for its own sake—or still believes that society believes in it. . . .

. . . what has to be explained—and finally understood—is the really frightening scope of the irrationality of our notions and practices regarding punishment. It seems that we just do not know how to be practical about the matter. For example, most of us, I imagine, have achieved major control over our own aggressive and vindictive impulses. We would be revolted to watch a hanging or a beating, and even more to participate in one. When we are personally called upon to administer punishment or any form of serious deprivation, we take the task as a heavy duty and think very hard to make certain that we do no more and no less than we feel to be necessary and effective in the circumstances. This would be so in the disciplining of our own children or any subordinates. But when it comes to the administration of crime, we hand the whole matter over to a distant bureaucratic machine, and we want to hear no more about it. Our attitude is—"Let the State take care of them."

Isn't it strange that the criminal law tradition which not so long ago was based on the supposedly deterrent spectacle of public punishment has come full circle and now can be said to be based in effect on the distance and even the secrecy of actual punishment? I wonder how many . . . have ever seen the inside of a prison? What you would see there can be justified only on the assumption that the prisoners are less than human, and that therefore the obviously de-humanizing process they are undergoing is appropriate for them. Because they have stolen property or committed acts of violence, they are outside the pale of human society, and that is the end of the matter. But of course after having further brutalized them, after having failed to deal with the causes of their behavior, and having failed to effect any serious rehabilitation, we then release them into society where they can experience their second or third or fourth opportunity to fail. As Karl Menninger has said, these people are failures first and "criminals" later. To be a criminal is not strictly speaking merely to have committed a crime—it is a social branding plus penitentiary training, all of which serves only to confirm the initial personal failure which led to the first antisocial act. (As I speak of crime and the criminal tonight, I should emphasize that I am thinking of the delinquent car-thief, the mugger, the amateur burglar and the armed robber, the sex offender, and the man who commits assault and other crimes of violence—my attention is not directed toward the special problems represented by the criminal elite consisting of competent professionals, the organization men of the syndicates, or the whole separate area of white-collar crime.)

It is as if society cooperates with certain human beings who are social failures to create this object called the criminal. Our present system of punishment is an essential part of *this* process, not of any process that can be called reforming or rehabilitative. Why does society go to all the trouble and expense of creating this special class of human beings? I think chiefly because we really do not comprehend what we are doing, because we do not want to deal with the facts of social failure to begin with, and because we are not prepared to follow out the logic of our attitude and "dispose" of these failures outright. There results a sort of half-way house, neither disposal nor rehabilitation, but a new class of human beings to mirror society's confusion on the profound issue of failure in the educative process—and reliance on punishment to cure or cover over all such failure.

Another point to be understood about punishment is that it is not a universal solvent. Different people react differently to it. This is perfectly obvious with regard to children, and needs no elaboration. Our response to punishment is like anything else we learn; some learn better than others, and some learn the same lesson differently than others. In this broad sense, the criminal is the person who has been miseducated with respect to punishment and the threat of punishment. His re-education must consist of something in addition to just more of the same, more punishment. To conceive otherwise would be like giving harder and harder lessons in algebra to a student who has already evidenced his inability to absorb the basic lessons. Only an incompetent teacher, a man of ill-will or one with very limited resources, would go about destroying a student in such a fashion. But that is just what we do with so many people who, if they had had the proper capacity to respond to punishment, would not have gotten into trouble in the first place. We do just the wrong thing by confirming all of their wrong feelings about punishment. And so we create a class of hopelessly recidivistic criminals. . . .

I would not want to leave you with the impression that I am opposed to all measures of punishment, or deprivation. It seems superfluous to state that I recognize their necessity, but perhaps I had better do so because thinking in this field tends to be characterized by an either-or, all-or-nothing attitude. It is just this attitude which I object to and from which I wish to dissociate myself. Let me illustrate its unfortunate effects. When the *Durham* case was decided in the District of Columbia, a great hue and cry was raised that great numbers of vicious criminals would soon be roaming the streets of the city. Nothing could have been more off the mark, as subsequent events have shown. But at the time many people felt that *either* offenders are punished by execution or a penitentiary term, *or* they in effect get off scotfree—that *all* of them must be punished and just punished, or *nothing* would be done to protect society against them. . . . The Court now requires a positive instruction to the effect that the defendant acquitted by reason of insanity will be put in a mental institution until cured and judicially determined to be no longer a danger to himself or others. Such commitments, incidentally, may continue for a longer term than would have been served in a penitentiary for the offense charged. They are clearly a deprivation, a negative sanction—and in this sense a "punishment"—but with the very important difference that it is not retributive, it is no more than may be necessary, and it is punishment subordinate to the purpose of rehabilitation.

. . . Some people seem to feel that whenever trained workers including psychiatric therapists supplement the work of police and prison guards, or play any independent role at all, the offender will be mollycoddled and consequently society's bulwark against crime will crumble. This is nonsense, but the attitude persists. Dr. Melitta Schmideberg of the Association for the Psychiatric Treatment of Offenders . . . feels that— "Fear of punishment and guilt keep normal people in check, but an overdose of anxiety can react in the opposite direction on criminals." She states the problem as follows: "If the therapist condemns the offender out and out, he cannot treat him; if he condones his offense, he cannot change him."

This is certainly not a mollycoddling approach. On the other hand, she objects eloquently to the psychological effect on offenders of a period in the usual penitentiary. She feels one of the most imperative uses of therapy is to help the ex-convict overcome the effects of prison! Now does it strike anyone here as sensible to deny early treatment of first offenders, send them to a penitentiary where their dangerous problems will be dangerously augmented, and then end up with an infinitely more difficult problem-personality to deal with later on?

Why do we treat offenders this way? . . . When we transcend our emotional urge to punish, and begin to think seriously about crime and the criminal without such undue reliance on the one idea of punishment, we very shortly come right up against an intellectually much more formidable barrier. And that is the ubiquitous theory of deterrence. On the intellectual level, it turns out to be the greatest barrier to progress in the criminal law.

This theory proposes that actual malefactors be punished in order to deter potential malefactors. In its pure form, it is willing to assume arguendo that punishment may not reform and may even damage the particular individual being punished. But this unfortunate person must be sacrificed to the common good—he must be punished as an example to all, to keep all the rest of us from committing his crime. Of course the theory is not always stated in this pure form. Indeed, there is a common confusion which you may notice in arguments based on the premise of deterrence—a confusion between deterrence of the person being punished and deterrence of all others. Now clearly the convicted prisoner was not deterred by the prior punishment of others from committing the crime which placed him in prison. And to speak of deterring him from committing another offense later takes us back to the previous discussion of the effectiveness of punishment, and concerns rehabilitation not deterrence. So the theory, properly considered, involves only the justification of punishment because of its show-effect, its supposed effect on others. . . . The individual so used is a scapegoat, a sacrificial victim. . . .

Logically, of course, the more we witness the pains of punishment, the more apt they would be actually to deter us from crime. (That is, if active fear deters.) Originally, this logic was a part of the deterrence theory. But in our day it is not. To illustrate this I would like to quote from the 1953 Report of the Royal Commission on Capital Punishment:

> In the first half of the nineteenth century executions still took place in public. This indeed was thought to be an essential part of the deterrent value of the death penalty. But public executions, "though the publicity was deterrent in intention . . . became in practice a degrading form of popular entertainment, which could serve only to deprave the minds of the spectators."

Parliament ended the practice in 1868. . . . A common argument offered in support of deterrence is this: The ordinary citizen would not obey traffic signals if sanctions were not imposed on all drivers for breach of the rules. This argument . . . depends for its persuasiveness on a supposed identity between a traffic violation, on the one hand, and murder, assault, and grand theft, on the other—all these being "breach of the rules." Although I suppose they all do come under this category, the empirical differences are more impressive to me than the abstract similarity. But more important, because of the preconditioning of licensing, the persons to whom traffic rules are addressed are a select group to begin with: Those who are incompetent to conform to the rules, for whatever reasons, are weeded out before the sanction system is applied. And that is an important point. Although traffic rules have very little moral force behind them, the system works tolerably well just because reliance is not placed solely on sanctions, but also on the judgment of competence.

I think we all understand that the maintenance of public order must be backed up by a system of sanctions . . . deprivations . . . *punishments,* if you please. Neither law nor morality can sustain itself, from generation to generation, without the threat of some form of punishment. But the difficult point to be comprehended here is that the system requires the *threat* of punishment, not punishment itself. An internal control system generated by our mores and received beliefs keeps most of us from stealing. For those who require external controls, it is the threat of going to jail, not actual time spent there, that keeps them from stealing. Actual sanctions are needed—as far as the system is concerned—only to give substance to the threat, to keep it from being reduced to impotence. The problem really posed by the question of deterrence is, how much actual punishment—and what kind of actual punishment—is required in order to sustain the threat of punishment at an effective level? . . .

I do not propose to solve this problem [now], even stated in such fashion. . . . But I do want to conclude with a few observations about this critical and perplexing question. First of all, I believe that in the absence of decisive empirical data, we should take a developmental approach. That is, we should view the issue historically and not assume that any particular status quo is ultimate and unalterable. I will confess that I am subjectively distrustful of many ponderous proponents of deterrence who answer the question, how much punishment is necessary, with the quick reply, exactly as much as we now have. And those who use the necessity of deterrence to justify the scandal of our prison system, also earn my suspicion.

Some people have argued in favor of the M'Naghten ritual on the grounds of a deterrent effect—that the mentally ill offender should not be recognized as such and treated as such because to do so would encourage crime and perhaps even mental illness. This argument I consider beneath contempt. The M'Naghten Rules were adopted twenty-five years before the English saw fit to do away with public hangings. . . . Why I wonder, are these Rules considered still necessary to deter crime, when public hangings and capital punishment for petty offenses are not? And if M'Naghten is so necessary for this purpose, why do the same people justify it by reminding us that trial courts frequently ignore it?

To sum up briefly: Punishment has a role to play in the education and re-education of the individual. The threat of some form of deprivation is of course essential in the functioning of any moral or legal system—and the threat must have substance. But these basic requirements of the criminal law have been used—I will say misused—to justify the present system which contains a preposterous predominance of senseless punitive elements. The theory of deterence, as too frequently applied, results in degrading the individual for a purported social purpose—contrary to the democratic ethos and with no convincing evidence that the purpose is promoted. In doing so, in casting the individual offender in the role of a scapegoat, it begs the entire question of justice. . . .

If we were not so set on punishing the offender for the sake of punishment, if we did not justify this practice by reference to its deterrent effect, we could understand that rehabilitation lies at the spiritual heart of any vital moral system. The alternative can only be destructiveness. Even the violent corporal punishments of the past were designed to rehabilitate the wrongdoer's soul, which was held to be of much greater concern than his body. In our secular age, we have lost sight of this spiritual truth. But we still punish—without hope of reformation, without belief in saving the soul by damning the earthly body. And our entire moral system necessarily suffers thereby.

Would it really be the end of the world if all jails were turned into hospitals, or "Rehabilitation Centers"? The offender would then—just as the committed mental patient is today—be deprived of his dearest possession, his personal liberty. "Punishment" enough, I should think—to satisfy our punitive urge and to induce a deterrent fear. The offender's purpose in such a Rehabilitation Center would be to change his personality, his very style of responding to life. I would like to suggest, quite seriously, that the effort toward such a personal alteration is the greatest sanction of them all. To make this is indeed the true command of all religion and all morality. And it is the normal law-abiding person's most profound and continuous "punishment." The difference between the offender or the mental patient and the rest of us happily normal citizens, is that "they" have a special problem and need special help in living up to society's expectations. A few of us have had "special problems" in the course of our lives but were lucky enough to get the help we needed, or strong enough to get by on our own.

We are entitled to congratulate ourselves on the superiority of our endowment or good fortune—but not, I think, to celebrate our triumphs by degrading our less fortunate neighbors. Is it in any way necessary for our own benefit to perpetuate the shame of our penitentiaries—where a youthful offender, having been processed through the homosexual auction block, will be taught the ways of crime and perversity by a hardened expert? . . .

Among the many serious issues I have not discussed, . . . prominent mention should be made of the current and future limits of that omnibus grouping called the behavioral sciences. How much of their promise is valid hope, how much wishful thinking? We can only find out by trying—by experimenting. Take the question of psychiatric "treatment," for example. It seems clear that new, more sophisticated techniques will have to be developed with more pointed relevance to the problems of offenders. But where are the experimental clinics, where are the budgets to attract competent staff, where is the administrative approach that would welcome and facilitate this urgent work? Blocked, I have suggested, by the belief in punishment. . . .

Crime and criminals belong very much to their particular time and place. They grow out of very specific social settings. Moreoever, any system of sanctions and any system of rehabilitation applies to and within a society, it does not substitute for one. And these systems cannot be much better than the society in which they exist. On the other hand, they should not be worse.

THERAPY, NOT PUNISHMENT

Karl Menninger, M.D.

Dr. Karl Menninger is one of America's most distinguished psychiatrists, with headquarters at the famous Menninger Clinic in Topeka, Kansas. His is the psychiatrist's verdict on the principles enunciated by Judge Bazelon in the Durham case. Dr. Menninger has written The Human Mind *(1930)*, Man against Himself *(1938)*, Love against Hate *(1942)*, Theory of Psychoanalytic Technique *(1958), and* The Vital Balance *(1963)*.

. . . Most lawyers have no really clear idea of the way in which a psychiatrist functions or of the basic concepts to which he adheres. They cannot understand, for example, why there is no such thing (for psychiatrists) as "insanity." Most lawyers have no conception of the meaning or methods of psychiatric case study and diagnosis. They seem to think that psychiatrists can take a quiet look at a suspect, listen to a few anecdotes about him, and thereupon be able to say, definitely, that the awful "it"—the dreadful miasma of madness, the loathsome affliction of "insanity"—is present or absent. Because we all like to please, some timid psychiatrists fall in with this fallacy of the lawyers and go through these preposterous antics.

It is true that almost any offender—like anyone else—when questioned for a short time, even by the most skillful psychiatrist, can make responses and display behavior patterns which will indicate that he is enough like the rest of us to be called "sane." But a barrage of questions is not a psychiatric examination. Modern scientific personality study depends upon various specialists—physical, clinical, and sociological as well as psychological. It takes into consideration not only static and presently observable factors, but dynamic and historical factors, and factors of environmental interaction and change. It also looks into the future for correction, re-education, and prevention.

Hence, the same individuals who appear so normal to superficial observation are frequently discovered in the course of prolonged, intensive scientific study to have tendencies regarded as "deviant," "peculiar," "unhealthy," "sick," "crazy," "senseless," "irrational," "insane."

But now you may ask, "Is it not possible to find such tendencies in any individual if one looks hard enough? And if this is so, if we are all a little crazy or potentially so, what is the essence of your psychiatric distinctions? Who is it that you want excused?"

And here is the crux of it all. We psychiatrists don't want *anyone* excused. In fact, psychiatrists are much more concerned about the protection of the public than are the lawyers. I repeat; psychiatrists don't want anyone excused, certainly not anyone who shows antisocial tendencies. We consider them all responsible, which lawyers do not. And we want the prisoner to take on that responsibility, or else deliver it to someone who will be concerned about the protection of society and about the prisoner, too. We don't want anyone excused, but neither do we want anyone stupidly disposed of, futilely detained, or prematurely released. We don't want them tortured, either sensationally with hot irons or quietly by long-continued and forced idleness. In the psychiatrist's mind nothing should be done in the name of punishment, though he is well aware that the offender may regard either the diagnostic procedure or the treatment or the detention incident to the treatment as punitive. But this is in. *his* mind, not in the psychiatrist's mind. And in our opinion it should not be in the public's mind, because it is an illusion.

It is true that we psychiatrists consider that all people have potentialities for antisocial behavior. The law assumes this, too. Most of the time most people control their criminal impulses. But for various reasons and under all kinds of circumstances some individuals become increasingly disorganized or demoralized, and then they begin to be socially offensive. The man who does criminal things is less convincingly disorganized than the patient who "looks" sick, because the former more nearly resembles the rest of us, and seems to be indulging in acts that we have struggled with and controlled. So we get hot under the collar about the one and we call him "criminal" whereas we pityingly forgive the other and call him "lunatic." But a surgeon uses the same principles of surgery whether he is dealing with a "clean" case, say some cosmetic surgery on a face, or a "dirty" case which is foul-smelling and offensive. What we are after is results and the emotions of the operator must be under control. Words like "criminal" and "insane" have no place in the scientific vocabulary any more than pejorative adjectives like "vicious," "psychopathic," "bloodthirsty," etc. The need is to find all the *descriptive* adjectives that apply to the case, and this is a scientific job—not a popular exercise in name-calling. Nobody's insides are very beautiful; and in the cases that require social control there has been a great wound and some of the insides are showing.

Intelligent judges all over the country are increasingly surrendering the onerous responsibility of deciding in advance what a man's conduct will be in a prison and how rapidly his wicked impulses will evaporate there. With more use of the indeterminate sentence and the establishment of scientific diagnostic centers, we shall be in a position to make progress in the science of *treating* antisocial trends. Furthermore, we shall get away from the present legal smog that hangs over the prisons, which lets us detain with heartbreaking futility some prisoners fully rehabilitated while others, whom the prison officials know full well to be dangerous and unemployable, must be released, *against our judgment,* because a judge far away (who has by this time forgotten all about it) said that five years was enough. In my frequent visits to prisons I am always astonished at how rarely the judges who have prescribed the "treatment" come to see whether or not it is effective. What if doctors who sent their seriously ill patients to hospitals never called to see them!

As more states adopt diagnostic centers directed toward getting the prisoners *out* of jail and back to work, under modern, well-structured parole systems, the taboo on jail and prison, like that on state hospitals, will begin to diminish. Once it was a lifelong disgrace to have been in either. Lunatics, as they were cruelly called, were feared and avoided. Today only the ignorant retain this phobia. Cancer was then considered a *shameful* thing to have, and victims of it were afraid to mention it, or have it correctly treated, because they did not want to be disgraced. The time will come when offenders, much as we disapprove of their offenses, will no longer be unemployable untouchables.

To a physician discussing the wiser treatment of our fellow men it seems hardly necessary to add that under no circumstances should we kill them. It was never considered right for doctors to kill their patients, no matter how hopeless their condition. True, some patients in state institutions have undoubtedly been executed without benefit of sentence. They were a nuisance, expensive to keep and dangerous to release. Various people took it upon themselves to put an end to the matter, and I have even heard them boast of it. The Hitler regime had the same philosophy.

But in most civilized countries today we have a higher opinion of the rights of the individual and the limits to the state's power. We know, too, that for the most part the death penalty is inflicted upon obscure, impoverished, defective, and friendless individuals. We know that it intimidates juries in their efforts to determine guilt without prejudice. . . . We know that in practice it has almost disappeared—for over seven thousand capital crimes last year there were less than one hundred executions. But vast sums of money are still being spent—let us say wasted—in legal contests to determine whether or not an individual, even one known to have been mentally ill, is now healthy enough for the state to hang him. (I am informed that such a case has recently cost the State of California $400,000!)

Most of all, we know that no state employees—except perhaps some that ought to be patients themselves—want a job on the killing squad, and few wardens can stomach this piece of medievalism in their own prisons. For example, two officials I know recently quarreled because each wished to have the hanging of a prisoner carried out on the other's premises.

Capital punishment is, in my opinion, morally wrong. It has a bad effect on everyone, especially those involved in it. It gives a false sense of security to the public. It is vastly expensive. Worst of all it beclouds the entire issue of motivation in crime, which is so importantly relevant to the question of what to do for and with the criminal that will be most constructive to society as a whole. Punishing—and even killing—criminals may yield a kind of grim gratification; let us all admit that there are times when we are so shocked at the depredations of an offender that we persuade ourselves that this is a man the Creator didn't intend to create, and that we had better help correct the mistake. But playing God in this way has no conceivable moral or scientific justification. . . .

We, the agents of society, must move to end the game of tit-for-tat and blow-for-blow in which the offender has foolishly and futilely engaged himself and us. We are not driven, as he is, to wild and impulsive actions. With knowledge comes power, and with power there is no need for the frightened vengeance of the old penology. In its place should go a quiet, dignified, therapeutic program for the rehabilitation of the disorganized one, if possible, the protection of society during his treatment period, and his guided return to useful citizenship, as soon as this can be effected.

A PSYCHIATRIST DISSENTS FROM DURHAM

Thomas S. Szasz, M.D.

Dr. Szasz was a staff member of the Institute for Psychoanalysis, Chicago, and when the following article was written, a member of the Department of Psychiatry, State University of New York. His Ethics of Psychoanalysis *and* Psychiatric Justice *both appeared in 1965. His most recent book is* Second Sin *(1973).*

The following brief comments are intended to call attention to what I believe are inroads of serious import which organized psychiatry is making into the area of civil liberties. The significance of this encroachment transcends the specialized interests of psychiatry and jurisprudence, for it involves the most basic value of Anglo-American democracy, namely, the worth of the individual's autonomy and dignity. Cast in the context of current political and social events, it would seem that what the Western democracies can put against the claims of opposing ideologies is not a high standard of living; nor is it the abstract notions of free enterprise, capitalism, or even the Christian ethic. What democracies, and *only* democracies, possess, and what can not be imitated by other ideologies—without themselves becoming democracies—is respect for the dignity and autonomy of the individual. Stripped of proud adjectives, this simply means that people must be taken seriously for what they do; and this implies holding them accountable for their actions.

Having argued elsewhere that psychiatric testimony concerning mental illness (as presently conceived) is distracting to judicial proceedings, and that acquittal from a criminal charge by reason of insanity followed by commitment to a mental hospital constitutes a serious infringement of a person's civil liberties, I shall turn, without further comment, to a recent case to illustrate and add to the points made previously.

The case is that of Miss Edith L. Hough. The following are the salient facts, as abstracted from the records of her appeal to the U.S. Court of Appeals for the District of Columbia Circuit. On May 30, 1957, Miss Hough shot and killed a male friend who came to call on her to express his sympathy over the recent death of her father. The next day she was ordered to St. Elizabeths Hospital for determination of her competency to stand trial. She was subsequently found incompetent to stand trial and was committed to the hospital until restoration of her competency. In May, 1958, she was declared competent. She was tried for her offense—first degree murder—on July 10, 1958, and was acquitted by reason of insanity. She was then committed to St. Elizabeths Hospital.

On October 20, 1958, the Superintendent of St. Elizabeths Hospital filed in the District Court a certificate stating in part:

> Miss Hough has now recovered sufficiently to be granted her conditional release from Saint Elizabeths Hospital pursuant to section 927 (e) of Public Law 313.

The District Court denied conditional release, whereupon the "patient" appealed to a higher court seeking reversal of this decision. The U.S. Court of Appeals for the District of Columbia Circuit heard the case and, on September 14, 1959, affirmed the decision of the lower court. In hearing the appeal, psychiatric testimony was obtained from Doctors Benjamin Karpman and Winfred Overholser, and judicial opinions were rendered by Judges David Bazelon and Wilbur K. Miller. In the context of decision-making in an actual, real-life situation, the opinions and actions of the various participants become clearer than any statement, concerning psychiatry and law, that could be made in the abstract. My comments will be based on testimony and opinion recorded in the transcript of the decision rendered by the Appellate Court.

The first point on which I shall comment is the problem of acquitting a person of a crime and then committing him. Once he is acquitted, he must be considered (legally) innocent. If he is not so considered, the word "acquittal" and the deed it designates will lose their customary meanings.

Commitment of the insane—a complex, and in my opinion, highly questionable procedure as presently practiced—must now be scrutinized. Courts are legally empowered to commit people to mental hospitals, provided that certain conditions obtain. Illustrative is the case of a person who manifests such behavior as is considered patently deranged in our culture. A young man, for example, may become increasingly withdrawn and uncommunicative; he may stop eating and start masturbating in the presence of others. Sooner or later in the course of these events, the patient's family would very likely seek the aid of a physician (who may or may not be a psychiatrist). The latter would then make out the necessary papers *certifying* that the patient is in need of involuntary hospitalization. Finally, the judge under whose jurisdiction this matter falls would, in the ordinary course of events, order the patient *committed*.

Another type of situation in which people might be committed as mentally ill has traditionally been associated with the general area of criminal behavior. Without entering into the complexities of this matter, I wish to note only that according to the Durham Rule and its implementations, persons charged with offenses but acquitted by reason of insanity are committed to St. Elizabeths Hospital. If this practice were to be carried out *seriously* such persons would have to be treated as if they were *bona fide innocent.* This is required by the fact that they have been tried and have been pronounced *"not guilty* (by reason of insanity)." While the court has the right to order commitment, once a patient has been committed he comes under the jurisdiction of the hospital authorities. Hospital psychiatrists should be able to release the patient should they wish to do so. In cases of ordinary civil commitment, the court has no jurisdiction over the actions of the hospital staff vis-à-vis patients. To be more exact, the courts do have a say concerning hospital-patient relationships even in such cases, but this is essentially limited to giving the patient freedom. In other words, if the patient wishes to be released from the hospital over the opposition of the psychiatrists, he can, by availing himself of the appropriate legal safeguards, *e.g., habeas corpus,* enlist the aid of the court to gain his freedom. The reverse of this does not obtain! Should the hospital wish to release the patient, the court cannot interfere and keep the patient confined. It can not do this simply because commitment is legally justified— and this shows how poor this justification really is—by the psychiatric testimony of the physicians involved. Hence, if they (*i.e.,* the state hospital physicians) testify that the patient is sane, how can the court commit?

In the present case, it is to be noted that the court had the power not only to commit but also to regulate the patient's movements in and out of the hospital. This was in accord with a statute of the District of Columbia (D.C. Code #24.301 (e) Supp. VII, 1959). This meant, in effect, that the hospital functioned as an arm of the court. It had no real autonomy, but was merely a subordinate body to the superordinate power of the courts. If a hospital superintendent and his staff can not discharge a patient from their "hospital" when they wish, then, I submit, they are but the functionaries of those who do have the power to make this decision.

All this points to the fact that hospitals functioning in such a fashion are, in fact, jails. But we can go further than this, for jails have a high degree of regulatory autonomy over their inmates. Parole boards, for example, can decide—within certain legally set limits—when prisoners may be released. The courts, once having passed sentence, can not interfere in this process. The regulations governing the release of mental patients from St. Elizabeths Hospital thus give the staff of this institution *less* jurisdiction over (some of) its "patients" than have jails over their prisoners.

We must infer from this that the courts, after having relinquished their responsibility to the psychiatrists for judging and sentencing criminals, have turned around and have arrogated to themselves the responsibilities of physicians and psychiatrists. This conclusion must be drawn from the fact that the courts take it upon themselves to decide when a person—

officially designated a "patient," and one who has been acquitted of a criminal charge in a duly conducted trial, and is therefore "innocent"—may or may not be released from a place called "hospital." As matters now stand, psychiatric testimony in criminal trials—to the effect that the accused is mentally ill—makes it virtually unnecessary to have juries and judges, for acquittal follows almost automatically. Similarly, judicial authority of the type considered makes it virtually unnecessary, for patients of *this type* at least, to have psychiatrists and psychotherapists in mental hospitals—for it is the court, in the last analysis, that will decide when the "patient" is well enough to be released. The tragi-comedy that has been called "psychiatric testimony" has traversed a full circle: The psychiatrists who displaced the legal authorities (the latter having abdicated their responsibilities for decision-making of this type) have, in their turn, been displaced by the legal authorities, who now function in the guise of psychiatrists and social therapists.

All this leads finally and inevitably to the psychiatrist's surrender of his professional responsibility. For, if a psychiatrist in charge of a patient—who is *not* a convicted criminal!—regards him, in his own best judgment, as ready to leave a hospital and assume the duties of a job, how can he, in his professional conscience, let a court tell him that this he can not do? What is the psychiatrist "treating" the patient for, anyway? To make him a good "prisoner"? The farcical, were it not tragic, character of the notion of mental illness is well illustrated by these impossible dilemmas into which psychiatrists and lawyers place themselves, each other, their patients, and their clients.

The peculiar legal condition of a person such as Miss Hough has not escaped the participants in this difficult affair. Judge Bazelon expressly affirmed that such a person is a "patient," not a "prisoner." The facts of the matter, however, vitiate the practical meaning of these terms. Judge Bazelon's words illustrate the crux of the problem:

> Nothing in the history of the statute—and nothing in its language—indicates that an individual committed to a mental hospital after acquittal of a crime by reason of insanity is other than a patient. The individual is confined in the hospital for the purpose of treatment, not punishment; and the length of confinement is governed solely by considerations of his condition *and* the public safety. Any preoccupation by the District Court with the need of punishment for crime is out of place in dealing with an individual who has been acquitted of the crime charged.
>
> It does not follow, however, that the hospital authorities are free to allow such a patient to leave the hospital without supervision. We readily grant that periodic freedom may be valuable therapy. So, we suppose, may outright release sometimes be. But the statute makes one in appellant's situation a member of "an

exceptional class of people." It provides generally, that the District Court have a voice in any termination of her confinement, whether unconditional or conditional.

There is an attempt here to circumvent the problem by creating the somewhat mystical entity of "an exceptional class of people." What is meant by this? Are these people who are "legally innocent but really guilty"? Or are these people who, by virtue of their actions, shall henceforth and forever after be considered second-class citizens? Does this mean that we shall have two sets of laws, one for ordinary citizens and ordinary criminals, and another for the "mentally ill"? If these questions are answered in the affirmative—as they seem to be in this case—then surely we ought to ask: Is this in accord with the spirit and the letter of our Constitution, our Bill of Rights, and with the ethics of democracy?

Before bringing this discussion to an end, I wish to comment briefly on two other items found in this record. One is an opinion by Judge Wilbur K. Miller, stating:

It is, of course, much easier to believe that a sane person will not in the reasonable future be dangerous to himself or others than to believe that an insane person will not be.

Here is an ancient view, equating violence and insanity, dressed in slightly more modern garb. What is being asserted here, if anything? Both "insanity" and "dangerousness" are such vague terms that it is impossible to know what is being asserted by such a statement. But not only is this statement vague, worse, it is tautologous, for we habitually infer a condition of "insanity" from acts of violence. This was precisely the case in the present instance, for Miss Hough was considered legally sane until after she committed a murder. But if we infer insanity from violence, naturally we shall always expect violence when we speak of insanity, even though, in everyday life, the latter term is often used quite independently of whether or not a person is considered "dangerous."

In this connection, we must also note that the common-sense formulation of "insanity" propounded by Judge Miller seems to serve the function of enabling the observer—and this means all of us, and especially juries and judges—to wrestle with the problem of a person's so-called possible future dangerousness. At the very least, by codifying acts of violence as expressions of "mental illness" and some sort of irrationality (which, according to *certain* criteria, they might well be), we neatly rid ourselves of the task of dealing with criminal offenses as rational, goal-directed acts in principle no different from other forms of conduct.

Finally, I wish to call attention to a portion of Doctor Overholser's testimony. Being challenged by the attorney for the appellee to show reason why the patient should be released from the hospital, he was asked this question:

> Now, if this woman, who has this major mental disease, were released conditionally into the community and met a great number of frustrations in adjusting herself in getting along, isn't there a probability or possibility that she might explode, so to speak, and even do harm to herself or to others?

His answer was:

> Well, there is that possibility with a great many people, some of whom have never been in mental hospitals. I can't make any guarantee about permanence, or even about the conduct.

Here, it seems to me, Doctor Overholser spoke as a psychiatric scientist. As such, he could not predict with certainty, and surely could not guarantee, that this woman would not kill again. But if this is true, how can psychiatrists justify hospitalizing and "psychiatrically treating" someone whose "illness" appears to be mainly that she killed someone. Is being a murderer an illness? And if psychiatric treatment still leaves open the possibility of future crime, as obviously it must, then why use it as a *substitute* for legally codified imprisonment?

Does all this not mean that a logically simpler, and legally and psychiatrically clearer approach to a problem such as this might lie in treating persons in Miss Hough's predicament with the same dignity and firmness as we treat others confronted by serious problems? Why could she not be found guilty of a crime she obviously committed? Why could she not be imprisoned for a given term and, if necessary, given psychiatric help in jail? Is it not a truism that in a democracy, imprisonment (or loss of liberty) is justified only by conviction for a crime? But Miss Hough, and others in similar positions, were never convicted of a crime, but are, nevertheless, deprived of their liberty. This is clearly done as a *preventive measure!* Herein lies, I think, the worst and most dangerous feature of this procedure: it establishes legal precedent, and hence a measure of sanction, for prophylactic imprisonment! Let us not forget that this social act has, and with good reason, been regarded as the hallmark of the totalitarian state. The legal restraint of a person justified by *what he might do* (in the future) is there used with the explicit aim of social reform. Although not explicitly formulated, and perhaps only as an unwitting and undesired side-effect, this tactic of preventive restraint seems to be implicit in the operations of the Durham Rule and its subsequent modifications and applications.

The merits and risks of preventive imprisonment—even if some choose to call it "hospitalization"—are well worth the attention of every informed and intelligent person. This was my reason for stating at the outset that many problems of psychiatry and law transcend the boundaries of these disciplines and rightly concern all the people of the land. Let us at least entertain the possibility that by engaging in certain modifications of social living—for this is what we are doing—we run the risk of squandering the greatest asset of our Nation and its distinctive form of government, namely, the autonomy, integrity, responsibility, and freedom of the individual.

A recent decision rendered by the United States Court of Appeals for the District of Columbia Circuit was examined for the light it threw on some problems concerning crimes, psychiatry, and civil liberties. It was shown that acquittal by reason of insanity, followed by automatic commitment, seems to lead by easy steps to preventive jailing (hospitalization) of persons because of their alleged future dangerousness.

Increased psychiatric participation in the disposition of criminals seems to invite its corollary, namely, increased legal participation in psychiatric operations. We might raise the question: Do the questionable benefits of the Durham Rule (and its implementation) justify the risks of this "social therapy"? Could it be, perchance, that the cure, in this case, is worse than the disease? In other words, are the political and ethical risks of preventive jailing (preventive mental hospitalization) worth running, even if the psychiatric value of this measure were firmly established? (The psychiatric-scientific rationale of this procedure is hardly clear-cut or well established.) Personally, I hold that the value of formal psychiatric therapy for "criminals"—under present medico-legal conditions—is, at best, highly questionable. But beyond this, I believe that even if this psychiatric-legal procedure could be shown to be highly efficacious in restoring offenders of a certain type to useful social existence (which is the most that even its proponents claim for it), I would doubt that, *in a hierarchy of values,* such therapy of a small group could be justified *if* its results could be achieved *only* at the cost of a significant reduction in the autonomy and dignity of the majority of the people. In any case, the problem of crime and "mental illness" should be cast in a much broader context, and should be scrutinized by many more people, than it is at present.

EIGHTEEN YEARS AFTER

David L. Bazelon

The following comments are adapted from a speech delivered by Judge Bazelon at a 1973 meeting of the Southern California Psychiatric Society. They reflect an important change from the position taken eighteen years earlier in the celebrated Durham case. That change culminated in the unanimous decision of the same court in United States v. Brawner *rejecting the Durham rule.*

Psychiatry has been called upon to help answer a number of questions concerning the balance of power between the state and the individual: Who can morally be convicted of a crime? Who can be ordered into a hospital for compulsory treatment? What kinds of treatment can be imposed involuntarily, and for how long?

At the beginning of my judicial career I had hoped that the decisionmakers in psychiatry would willingly open up the reservoirs of their knowledge in the courtroom, and that this knowledge would have a significant impact on the law. What I saw instead was that psychiatrists in court quickly adopted a protective stance; they refused to submit their opinions to the scrutiny which the adversary process demands.

Challenging an expert, and questioning his expertise, is the lifeblood of our legal system, whether it is a psychiatrist discussing mental disturbance, a physicist testifying on the environmental impact of a nuclear power plant, or a General Motors executive insisting on the impossibility of meeting federal auto pollution standards by 1975. It is the only way a judge or a jury can decide whom to trust.

In the early 1950s psychiatry and the law were at a standstill on the issue of criminal responsibility, the so-called insanity defense. The traditional legal test permitted psychiatric testimony to focus only on a single narrow issue—whether the defendant knew what he was doing, and knew whether it was right or wrong. Strictly construed, this might mean whether he knew that a knife in his hand was not a toothbrush.

The psychiatric profession was critical of this test. It seemed to ignore the modern theories of man as an integrated personality; it concentrated on one aspect of that personality, cognitive reason, as being the sole determinant of conduct. Psychiatrists publicly claimed that, if the law would let them, they could give a more adequate account of psychic realities and present a vast array of scientific knowledge.

The law recognizes that the question of guilt or innocence is essentially a moral one. I believe that morality cannot be determined solely by abstract philosophical principles, without the facts which generate human behavior in the real world.

To help obtain these facts, I formulated a new test of criminal responsibility in 1954 in the Durham case, which held that an accused is not criminally responsible if his unlawful act was the "product" of a mental disease or defect. The announced purpose was to unfreeze psychiatric knowledge, to irrigate a field parched by a lack of information, and to restore to the jury its traditional function of applying "our inherited ideas of moral responsibility" to those accused of crimes.

Initial psychiatric reaction was enthusiastic. Dr. Karl Menninger, for one, described the decision as "more revolutionary in its total effect than the Supreme Court decision (of the same year) regarding segregation."

But there were problems from the start. Psychiatrists continued to use conclusory labels without explaining the origin, development or manifestations of a disease in terms meaningful to the jury. A war of words began to be waged in the courtroom. Psychiatrists argued about whether a defendant had a "personality defect," a "personality problem," a "personality disorder," a "disease," an "illness" or simply a "type of personality." How could a jury make any sense out of this?

Before long, the psychiatric profession turned against the Durham rule, and many of its leaders were delighted when my court abandoned it last year.[1]

---

[1] In *United States* v. *Brawner* (U.S. Court of Appeals, District of Columbia Circuit, June 23, 1972). "Ever since this court announced its new test of responsibility in 1954, we have been struggling with the problem of distinguishing between the uniquely psychiatric elements of the determination of responsibility, and the legal and moral elements of that determination. We have repeatedly urged psychiatrists to avoid using the conclusory labels of either psychiatry or law. Testimony in terms of the legal conclusion that an act was or was not the product of mental disease invites the jury to abdicate its function and acquiesce in the conclusion of experts. Testimony in terms of psychiatric labels obscures the fact that a defendant's responsibility does not turn on whether or not the experts have given his condition a name and the status of a disease . . . psychiatric labels which often served to hide the fact that the experts were providing virtually no information about the defendant's underlying condition" [pp. 95–97].

Judge Bazelon continues: "In *Washington* v. *United States* we reluctantly took the step of prohibiting all psychiatric testimony in terms of the issue of productivity on the ground that such testimony was particularly likely to usurp the jury's function of resolving the ultimate question of guilt. We said that the existence of disease was a medical question which psychiatrists could properly answer, but the question of productivity was the ultimate question for the jury, involving a mixture of medical information and moral judgment. . . . In practice, however, under *Durham* . . . psychiatrists have continued to make moral and legal judgments beyond the scope of their professional expertise" [pp. 99–100].

At one point, I discussed the problems with the late Dr. Winfred Overholser, superintendent of St. Elizabeth's Hospital in Washington, D.C., and one of the foremost forensic psychiatrists of his day. He told me that the kind of information sought by Durham would take from 50 to 100 manhours of interviewing and investigation, and that the hospital simply could not provide those resources.

I told him that psychiatrists should then frankly explain on the witness stand how their opinions were affected by the limitations of time and facilities. This would cast no aspersions on their expertise. It was a far greater disservice to the legal process and the administration of justice for them to create the distorted impression that they had learned substantially all that could be known about someone on the basis of admittedly insufficient exploration and study.

Later, when courts began to evaluate the treatment in mental hospitals and to establish standards, the APA again panicked. It adopted a position statement which began: "The definition of treatment and the appraisal of its adequacy are matters for medical determination."

Such assumptions and declarations are inevitably questioned whenever psychiatric decisions are exposed in the public sector—whether in the courtroom or in the community. When people are confined by psychiatrists on behalf of the state, this necessarily introduces the potential for misuse of that power, and it is a court's duty, on behalf of society, to scrutinize all governmental intrusions on freedom and liberty.

Part Two

Sex and Society

Many of our moral problems concern sex: institutional restraints have been pitted against persistent drives, there are radical discrepancies between what we preach and what we practice,[1] and values are in a state of tension and flux.

Most of us know where we stand on pornography, prostitution, and promiscuity. Differences arise, however, over the obscenity of a particular book or motion picture. Prudery can be as objectionable as prurience; in our time, prudery—which is not to be confused with modesty—is regarded with as much misgiving as promiscuity. Other differences arise concerning the kind of measures to take: shall pornography and prostitution be outlawed, or shall we avoid legal curbs and rely on the power of education and public opinion? Even among those who acknowledge the evil of both pornography and prostitution, there is the recurrent problem of not courting a greater evil as we endeavor to combat a lesser one.

Moral problems concerning such issues as feminism, premarital and extramarital sexual experience, divorce, and birth control are more acute. Here standards have undergone drastic change as reflected in the women's liberation movement, new attitudes toward the use of contraceptives, greater ease in obtaining divorce and an enormous increase in the divorce rate, and surveys indicating a significantly large proportion of women reporting extramarital sexual experience. Everywhere one encounters perplexity and a need for moral guidance. But authorities are themselves in doubt and disagreement, and the counsel we get is conflicting.

---

[1] It is reliably estimated, for example, that in the United States where until 1972 abortion was illegal unless the life of the mother was at stake, five thousand women died each year at the hands of illegal, unqualified abortionists, and from one to three million abortions were performed each year. Since it was illegal to abort a woman who contracted an illness (e.g., German measles) that might result in the birth of a blind or mentally retarded child, or even to abort a victim of rape, flouting of the law was almost certain. The issue is by no means dead.

Conflicts are best dramatized by particular events, as are changes in the attitudes we bring to bear on them. It was not many years ago that Bertrand Russell, by common consent one of the greatest philosophers and one of the greatest men of our age, was dismissed by the City College of New York where he was visiting lecturer because, in a book written many years before, he had advocated experimental marriage. That one of the most cosmopolitan and reputedly tolerant cities of the world suffered an agony of shame over this episode suggests the dimensions of the conflict, as does the invitation to teach at Harvard which was promptly extended to him. Today authorship of such a book by a prominent philosopher would hardly create a ripple.

Topics dealing with sexual conduct fall logically into three parts. One part embraces deviant or aberrational sexuality, specifically perversion, obscenity, prudery, and prostitution. Here concern is with the psychopathic or sociopathic and with how to deal with it. The second part embraces "normal" sexuality, that is, questions concerning guidance of the sexual development of adolescents, the role of love, extramarital relationships, marriage and divorce, and birth control. Here sex deviancy is irrelevant, and psycho- or sociopathic behavior is only indirectly if at all involved. A third part, recently come into new prominence, concerns the status of women.

Considerations of space limit the number of selected topics to four: extramarital sex, the women's liberation movement, pornography and how to control it, and homosexuality.

5

Extramarital Sexual Experience[1]

Until recently the mores were flexible with reference to male chastity and comparatively rigid as regards female chastity. Such a double standard in a society that frowned upon prostitution and did not, like ancient Corinth, accept hetairas (or what the French call "women of the demimonde") was, of course, contradictory. The great disparity between what was preached about chastity and what was practiced should come as no surprise. In the samples studied prior to the mid-1950s by three authoritative surveys of premarital sexual behavior (Terman, Burgess and Wallen, and Kinsey), approximately 50 percent of the women born after 1900 had entered marriage "nonvirginal."

In 1971, with the sexual revolution in full swing, Johns Hopkins demographers Melvin Zelnik and John Kentner, surveying a representative sample of white women, found 40 percent reporting intercourse before the age of 20. By contrast, Kinsey's 1953 survey had indicated 23 percent before the age of 21. Clearly, the proportion of young women reporting premarital intercourse has been increasing rapidly. A 1973 Gallup poll indicated that, although four years earlier two out of every three Americans held that premarital sex relations are wrong, only 48 percent had come to believe sex before marriage wrong as compared with 43 percent holding the opposite opinion. The change was most pronounced among Catholics who now hold more permissive views on this issue

---

[1] "Extramarital" is used here to designate all relationships outside of marriage and hence to include premarital sexual experience.

than Protestants. As one might expect, the same poll disclosed generation differences: only 29 percent of young persons (eighteen to twenty-nine) believed that premarital sex is wrong. Interestingly, a larger proportion of American youth say premarital sex is wrong than do their counterparts in Yugoslavia, the United Kingdom, Switzerland, France, West Germany and Sweden.

The sexual revolution has broken down unhealthy restraints and generated a refreshing atmosphere of honesty and candour about sex. We are well rid of the penumbra of guilt, embarrassment, and evasion with which sex was once surrounded. But the sexual revolution has also brought with it, as revolutions generally do, a train of unexpected and unwanted consequences. Reference here is not to such disturbing results as the mounting rate of pregnancy among unmarried women—illegitimate births have increased per thousand from 8.3 in 1940 to 19.8 in 1972, and the rate of abortion has spiralled—and the spread of venereal disease to epidemic proportions, but to profounder if less immediately visible consequences. Where is the line to be drawn between a healthy reassertion of the role of sex and sexual neuroticism? Are individuals able to shoulder the burden of choice and decision which the abandonment of guidelines thrusts upon them? What will be the impact of the new sex ethic on the family? What are the psychological hazards and what is the final loss in happiness of sex without love? If marriage and, with it, loyalty to family and one's wife in her later years is the unwritten and unarticulated (and appropriately romanticized) *quid pro quo* exacted by peer females for making themselves constantly available and functioning as more preferable sex partners than demimonde and prostitutes, what will happen as peer women (especially young ones) become available without such a *quid pro quo?*[2] Questions such as these are explored in the selections reprinted below.

Two of these selections first appeared in the late twenties and there are several reasons for including them. They were written by two supremely enlightened and civilized men during the decade when the modern sexual revolution began. Beyond this, they may serve to remind readers that emancipated thinking about sex is not an invention of this generation, but began with their parents, if not their grandparents. There is nothing old hat about these selections; they are astonishingly contemporary, especially when one considers what has happened in the half-century since they were written. They put current questions about sex in historical perspective and

---

[2] No crass calculation of interests is implied; only a functional interpretation of the mores and the suggestion that they may embody a wisdom notoriously neglected by revolutionaries.

help to remind us that the central issue is still the same, only more acute now that abortion and contraceptives are easily available. That issue involves the question of intimacy without commitment, of how one avoids prudery without courting promiscuity. For those who are able, it is the problem of achieving the kind of sexual union that transforms and enhances far beyond the brief gratification—and perhaps ultimate frustration—of transient sexual encounters.

MARRIAGE AND MORALS

Bertrand Russell

Many who read the following selection from Bertrand Russell's Marriage and Morals *will wish that this ruthlessly frank philosopher had limited himself to such harmless pursuits as logic, epistemology, and metaphysics. Russell was no sexologist, of course, and not an authority on marriage and the family. The volume from which the following selection is taken may well be regarded as among the less important of his works. The selection is simply offered as a sample of what one of the most profound thinkers of our time had to say about a delicate and still much neglected subject.* Marriage and Morals *was published in 1929, but there is no reason to believe that Russell, who died in 1970, would change it materially if he were writing now. Those who would savor the details of this great man's personal life are advised to read his autobiography, completed shortly before his death. It begins with these memorable words: "Three passions, simple but overwhelmingly strong, have governed my life: the longing for love, the search for knowledge, and unbearable pity for the suffering of mankind . . . Love and knowledge, as far as they were possible, led upward toward the heavens. But always pity brought me back to earth."*

In a rational ethic, marriage would not count as such in the absence of children. A sterile marriage should be easily dissoluble, for it is through children alone that sexual relations become of importance to society, and worthy to be taken cognisance of by a legal institution. This, of course, is not the view of the Church, which, under the influence of St. Paul, still views marriage rather as the alternative to fornication than as the means to the procreation of children. In recent years, however, even clergymen have become aware that neither men nor women invariably wait for marriage before experiencing sexual intercourse. In the case of men, provided their lapses were with prostitutes and decently concealed, they were comparatively easy to condone, but in the case of women other than professional prostitutes, the conventional moralists find what they call immorality much harder to put up with. Nevertheless, in America, in England, in Germany, in Scandinavia, a great change has taken place since [World War I] . . . many girls of respectable families have ceased to think it worth while to preserve their "virtue," and young men, instead of finding an outlet with prostitutes, have had affairs with girls of the kind whom, if they were richer, they would wish to marry. It seems that this process has gone farther in the United States than it has in England, owing, I think, to Prohibition and automobiles. Owing to Prohibition, it has become *de rigueur* at any cheerful party for everybody to get more or less drunk. Owing to the fact that a very large percentage of girls possess cars of their own, it has become easy for them to escape with a lover from the eyes of parents and neighbours. The resulting state of affairs is described in Judge Lindsey's books.[1] The old accuse him of exaggeration, but the young do not. As far as a casual traveller can, I took pains to test his assertions by questioning young men. I did not find them inclined to deny anything that he said as to the facts. It seems to be the case through America that a very large percentage of girls who subsequently marry and become of the highest respectability have sex experience, often with several lovers. And even when complete relations do not occur, there is so much "petting" and "necking" that the absence of complete intercourse can only be viewed as a perversion.

I cannot say myself that I view the present state of affairs as satisfactory. It has certain undesirable features imposed upon it by conventional moralists, and until conventional morality is changed, I do not see how these undesirable features are to disappear. Bootlegged sex is in fact as inferior to what it might be as bootlegged alcohol. I do not think anybody can deny that there is enormously more drunkenness among young men, and still more among young women, in well-to-do America than there was before the introduction of Prohibition. In circumventing the law there is, of course, a certain spice and a certain pride of cleverness, and while the law about drink is being circumvented it is natural to circumvent the conventions about sex. Here, also, the sense of daring acts as an aphrodisiac. The consequence is that sex relations between young people tend to take the silliest possible form, being entered into not from affection but from bravado, and at times of intoxication. Sex, like liquor, has to be taken in forms which are concentrated and rather unpalatable, since these forms alone can escape the vigilance of the authorities. Sex relations as a dignified, rational, wholehearted activity in which the complete personality

---

[1] *The Revolt of Modern Youth*, 1925. *Companionate Marriage*, 1927.

co-operates, do not often, I think, occur in America outside marriage. To this extent the moralists have been successful. They have not prevented fornication; on the contrary, if anything, their opposition, by making it spicy, has made it more common. But they have succeeded in making it almost as undesirable as they say it is; just as they have succeeded in making much of the alcohol consumed as poisonous as they assert all alcohol to be. They have compelled young people to take sex neat, divorced from daily companionship, from a common work, and from all psychological intimacy. The more timid of the young do not go so far as complete sexual relations, but content themselves with producing prolonged states of sexual excitement without satisfaction, which are nervously debilitating, and calculated to make the full enjoyment of sex at a later date difficult or impossible. Another drawback to the type of sexual excitement which prevails among the young in America is that it involves either failure to work or loss of sleep, since it is necessarily connected with parties which continue into the small hours.

A graver matter, while official morality remains what it is, is the risk of occasional disaster. By ill luck it may happen that some one young person's doings come to the ears of some guardian of morality, who will proceed with a good conscience to a sadistic orgy of scandal. And since it is almost impossible for young people in America to acquire a sound knowledge of birth-control methods, unintended pregnancies are not infrequent. These are generally dealt with by procuring abortion, which is dangerous, painful, illegal, and by no means easy to keep secret. The complete gulf between the morals of the young and the morals of the old, which exists very commonly in present-day America, has another unfortunate result, namely that often there can be no real intimacy or friendship between parents and children, and that the parents are incapable of helping their children with advice or sympathy. When young people get into a difficulty, they cannot speak of it to their parents without producing an explosion—possibly scandal, certainly a hysterical upheaval. The relation of parent and child has thus ceased to be one performing any useful function after the child has reached adolescence. How much more civilized are the Trobriand Islanders, where a father will say to his daughter's lover: "You sleep with my child: very well, marry her."[2]

In spite of the drawbacks we have been considering, there are great advantages in the emancipation, however partial, of young people in America, as compared with their elders. They are freer from priggery, less inhibited, less enslaved to authority devoid of rational foundation. I think also that they are likely to prove less cruel, less brutal, and less violent than their seniors. For it has been characteristic of American life to take out in

---

[2] Malinowski, *The Sexual Life of Savages*, p. 73.

violence the anarchic impulses which could not find an outlet in sex. It may also be hoped that when the generation now young reaches middle age, it will not wholly forget its behaviour in youth, and will be tolerant of sexual experiments which at present are scarcely possible because of the need of secrecy.

The state of affairs in England is more or less similar to that in America, though not so developed owing to the absence of Prohibition and the paucity of motor-cars. There is also, I think, in England and certainly on the Continent, very much less of the practice of sexual excitement without ultimate satisfaction. And respectable people in England, with some honourable exceptions, are on the whole less filled with persecuting zeal than corresponding people in America. Nevertheless, the difference between the two countries is only one of degree.

Judge Ben B. Lindsey, who was for many years in charge of the juvenile court at Denver, and in that position had unrivalled opportunities for ascertaining the facts, proposed a new institution which he calls "companionate marriage." Unfortunately he has lost his official position, for when it became known that he used it rather to promote the happiness of the young than to give them a consciousness of sin, the Ku Klux Klan and the Catholics combined to oust him. Companionate marriage is the proposal of a wise conservative. It is an attempt to introduce some stability into the sexual relations of the young, in place of the present promiscuity. He points out the obvious fact that what prevents the young from marrying is lack of money, and that money is required in marriage partly on account of children, but partly also because it is not the thing for the wife to earn her own living. His view is that young people should be able to enter upon a new kind of marriage, distinguished from ordinary marriage by three characteristics. First, that there should be for the time being no intention of having children, and that accordingly the best available birth-control information should be given to the young couple. Second, that so long as there are no children and the wife is not pregnant, divorce should be possible by mutual consent. And third, that in the event of divorce, the wife should not be entitled to alimony. He holds, and I think rightly, that if such an institution were established by law, a very great many young people, for example students at universities, would enter upon comparatively permanent partnerships, involving a common life, and free from the Dionysiac characteristics of their present sex relations. He brings evidence to bear that young students who are married do better work than such as are unmarried. It is indeed obvious that work and sex are more easily combined in a quasi-permanent relation than in the scramble and excitement of parties and alcoholic stimulation. There is no reason under the sun why it should be more expensive for two young people to live together than to live separately, and therefore the economic reasons which at present lead to postponement of marriage would no longer operate. I have not the faintest doubt that Judge Lindsey's plan, if embodied in the law, would have a very beneficent influence, and that this influence would be such as all might agree to be a gain from a moral point of view.

Nevertheless, Judge Lindsey's proposals were received with a howl of horror by all middle-aged persons and all newspapers throughout the length and breadth of America. It was said that he was attacking the sanctity of the home; it was said that in tolerating marriages not intended to lead at once to children he was opening the floodgates to legalized lust; it was said that he enormously exaggerated the prevalence of extramarital sexual relations, that he was slandering pure American womanhood, and that most businessmen remained cheerfully continent up to the age of thirty or thirty-five. All these things were said, and I try to think that among those who said them were some who believed them. I listened to many invectives against Judge Lindsey, but I came away with the impression that the arguments which were regarded as decisive were two. First, that Judge Lindsey's proposals would not have been approved by Christ; and second, that they were not approved by even the more liberal of American divines. The second of these arguments appeared to be considered the more weighty, and indeed rightly, since the other is purely hypothetical, and incapable of being substantiated. I never heard any person advance any argument even pretending to show that Judge Lindsey's proposal would diminish human happiness. This consideration, indeed, I was forced to conclude, is thought wholly unimportant by those who uphold traditional morality.

For my part, while I am quite convinced that companionate marriage would be a step in the right direction, and would do a great deal of good, I do not think that it goes far enough. I think that all sex relations which do not involve children should be regarded as a purely private affair, and that if a man and a woman choose to live together without having children, that should be no one's business but their own. I should not hold it desirable that either a man or a woman should enter upon the serious business of a marriage intended to lead to children without having had previous sexual experience. There is a great mass of evidence to show that the first experience of sex should be with a person who has previous knowledge. The sexual act in human beings is not instinctive, and apparently never has been since it ceased to be performed *a tergo*. And apart from this argument, it seems absurd to ask people to enter upon a relation intended to be lifelong, without any previous knowledge as to their sexual compatibility. It is just as absurd as it would be if a man intending to buy a house were not allowed to view it until he had completed the purchase. The proper course, if the biological function of marriage were adequately recognized, would be to say that no marriage should be legally binding until the wife's first pregnancy. At present a marriage is null if sexual intercourse is impossible, but children, rather than sexual intercourse, are the true purpose of marriage, which should therefore be not regarded as consummated until such time as there is a prospect of children. This view depends, at least in part, upon that separation between procreation and mere sex which has been brought about by contraceptives. Contraceptives have altered the whole aspect of sex and marriage, and have made distinctions necessary which could formerly have been ignored. People may come together for sex alone, as occurs in prostitution, or for companionship involving a sexual element, as in Judge Lindsey's companionate marriage, or, finally, for the purpose of rearing a family. These are all different, and no morality can be adequate to modern circumstances which confounds them in one indiscriminate total.

LOVE IN THE GREAT SOCIETY

Walter Lippmann

Over a long period Walter Lippmann has been a brilliant political analyst and commentator. Through his syndicated column and numerous books and articles he has influenced public policy in America at least as much as any living writer. He is now retired. The Good Society (*1937*), The Public Philosophy (*1955*), The Communist World and Ours (*1959*), The Coming Test with Russia (*1961*), *and* Western Unity and the Common Market (*1962*) *are among his many works. Because in his later years he limited himself to questions of public policy—if, indeed, such an interest can be viewed as restricted—it is not always remembered that in an older work,* A Preface to Morals, *he wrote about the foundations of belief and conduct. Unlike behavior, which is the province of the psychologist, conduct is the concern of the humanist and moralist; and it is as such that Lippmann writes about sexual conduct. Although these comments were published in the same year as Russell's (*1929*), it is doubtful that Lippmann any more than Russell would find a need to change the text (except perhaps the frequency of his reference to Havelock Ellis) if he were writing it today.*

. . . In the popular mind it is immediately assumed that when morals are discussed it is sexual morals that are meant. The morals of the politician and the voter, of the shareholder and executive and employee, are only moderately interesting to the general public: thus they almost never supply the main theme of popular fiction. But the relations between boy and girl, man and woman, husband and wife, mistress and lover, parents and children, are themes which no amount of repetition makes stale. The explanation is obvious. The modern audience is composed of persons among whom only a comparatively negligible few are serenely happy in their personal lives. Popular fiction responds to their longings: to the unappeased it offers some measure of vicarious satisfaction, to the prurient an indulgence, to the worried, if not a way out, then at least the comfort of knowing that their secret despair is a common, and not a unique, experience.

Yet in spite of this immense preoccupation with sex it is extraordinarily difficult to arrive at any reliable knowledge of what actual change in human behavior it reflects. This is not surprising. In fact this is the very essence of the matter. The reason it is difficult to know the actual facts about sexual behavior in modern society is that sexual behavior eludes observation and control. We know that the old conventions have lost most of their authority because we cannot know about, and therefore can no longer regulate, the sexual behavior of others. It may be that there is, as some optimists believe, a fine but candid restraint practiced among modern men and women. It may be that incredible licentiousness exists all about us, as the gloomier prophets insist. It may be that there is just about as much unconventional conduct and no more than there has always been. Nobody, I think, really knows. Nobody knows whether the conversation about sex reflects more promiscuity or less hypocrisy. But what everybody must know is that sexual conduct, whatever it may be, is regulated personally and not publicly in modern society. If there is restraint it is, in the last analysis, voluntary; if there is promiscuity, it can be quite secret.

The circumstances which have wrought this change are inherent in modern ways of living. Until quite recently the main conventions of sex were enforced first by the parents and then by the husband through their control over the life of the woman. The main conventions were: first, that she must not encourage or display any amorous inclinations except where there was practical certainty that the young man's intentions were serious; second, that when she was married to the young man she submitted to his embraces only because the Lord somehow failed to contrive a less vile method of perpetuating the species. All the minor conventions were subsidiary to these; the whole system was organized on the premise that procreation was the woman's only sanction for sexual intercourse. Such control as was exercised over the conduct of men was subordinate to this control over the conduct of women. The chastity of women before marriage was guarded; that meant that seduction was a crime, but that relations with "lost" or unchaste women was tolerated. The virtuous man, by popular standards, was one who before his marriage did not have sexual relations with a virtuous woman. There is ample testimony in the outcries of moralists that even in the olden days these conventions were not perfectly administered. But they were sufficiently well administered to remain the accepted conventions, honored even in the breach. It was possible, because of the way people lived, to administer them.

The woman lived a sheltered life. That is another way of saying that she lived under the constant inspection of her family. She lived at home. She worked at home. She met young men under the zealous chaperonage of practically the whole community. No doubt, couples slipped away occasionally and more went on than was known or acknowledged. But even then there was a very powerful deterrent against an illicit relationship. This deterrent was the fear of pregnancy. That in the end made it almost certain that if a secret affair were consummated it could not be kept secret and that terrible penalties would be exacted. In the modern world effective chaperonage has become impracticable and the fear of pregnancy has been virtually eliminated by the very general knowledge of contraceptive methods. The whole revolution in the field of sexual morals turns upon the fact that external control of the chastity of women is becoming impossible.

. . . . liberal reformers have . . . been urging for the removal of prohibitory laws [on birth control] and they have built their case on two main theses. They have argued, first, that the limitation of births was sound public policy for economic and eugenic reasons; and second, that it was necessary to the happiness of families, the health of mothers, and the welfare of children. All these reasons may be unimpeachable. I think they are. But it was idle to pretend that the dissemination of this knowledge, even if legally confined to the instruction of married women by licensed physicians, could be kept from the rest of the adult population. Obviously that which all married couples are permitted to know every one is bound to know. Human curiosity will make that certain. Now this is what the Christian churches, especially the Roman Catholic, which oppose contraception on principle, instantly recognized. They were quite right. They were quite right, too, in recognizing that whether or not birth control is eugenic, hygienic, and economic, it is the most revolutionary practice in the history of sexual morals.

For when conception could be prevented, there was an end to the theory that woman submits to the embrace of the male only for the purpose of procreation. She had to be persuaded to cooperate, and no possible reason could be advanced except that the pleasure was reciprocal. She had to understand and inwardly assent to the principle that it is proper to have sexual intercourse with her husband and to prevent conception. She had, therefore, to give up the whole traditional theory which she may have only half-believed anyway, that sexual intercourse was an impure means to a noble end. She could no longer believe that procreation alone mitigated the vileness of cohabiting with a man, and so she had to change her valuation and accept it as inherently delightful. Thus by an inevitable process the practice of contraception led husbands and wives to the conviction that they need not be in the least ashamed of their desires for each other.

But this transvaluation of values within the sanctity of the marital chamber could hardly be kept a secret. What had happened was that married couples were indulging in the pleasures of sex because they had learned how to isolate them from the responsibilities of parenthood. When we talk about the unconventional theories of the younger generation we might in all honesty take this fact into account. They have had it demonstrated to them by their own parents, by those in whom the administering of the conventions is vested, that under certain circumstances it is legitimate and proper to gratify sexual desire apart from any obligation to the family or to the race. They have been taught that it is possible to do this, and that it may be proper. Therefore, the older generation could no longer argue that sexual intercourse as such was evil. It could no longer argue that it was obviously dangerous. It could only maintain that the psychological consequences are serious if sexual gratification is not made incidental to the enduring partnership of marriage and a home. That may be, in fact, I think it can be shown to be, the real wisdom of the matter. Yet if it is the wisdom of the matter, it is a kind of wisdom which men and women can acquire by experience alone. They do not have it instinctively. They cannot be compelled to adopt it. They can only learn to believe it.

That is a very different thing from submitting to a convention upheld by all human and divine authority.

With contraception established as a more or less legitimate idea in modern society, a vast discussion has ensued as to how the practice of it can be rationalized. In this discussion the pace is set by those who accept the apparent logic of contraception and are prepared boldly to revise the sexual conventions accordingly. They take as their major premise the obvious fact that by contraception it is possible to dissociate procreation from gratification, and therefore to pursue independently what Mr. Havelock Ellis calls the primary and secondary objects of the sexual impulse. They propose, therefore, to sanction two distinct sets of conventions: one designed to protect the interests of the offspring by promoting intelligent, secure, and cheerful parenthood; the other designed to permit the freest and fullest expression of the erotic personality. They propose, in other words, to distinguish between parenthood as a vocation involving public responsibility, and love as an art, pursued privately for the sake of happiness.

As a preparation for the vocation of parenthood it is proposed to educate both men and women in the care, both physical and psychological, of children. It is proposed further that mating for parenthood shall become an altogether deliberate and voluntary choice: the argument here is that the duties of parenthood cannot be successfully fulfilled except where both parents cheerfully and knowingly assume them. Therefore, it is proposed, in order to avert the dangers of love at first sight and of mating under the blind compulsion of instinct, that a period of free experimentation be allowed to precede the solemn engagement to produce and rear children. This engagement is regarded as so much a public responsibility that it is even proposed, and to some extent has been embodied in the law of certain jurisdictions, that marriage for parenthood must be sanctioned by medical authority. In order, too, that no compulsive considerations may determine what ought to be a free and intelligent choice, it is argued that women should be economically independent before and during marriage. As this may not be possible for women without property of their own during the years when they are bearing and rearing children, it is proposed in some form or other to endow motherhood. This endowment may take the form of a legal claim upon the earnings of the father, or it may mean a subsidy from the state through mothers' pensions, free medical attention, day nurseries, and kindergartens. The principle that successful parenthood must be voluntary is maintained as consistently as possible. Therefore, among those who follow the logic of their idea, it is proposed that even marriages deliberately entered into for procreation shall be dissoluble at the will of either party, the state intervening only to insure the economic security of the offspring. It is proposed, furthermore, that where women find the vocation of motherhood impracticable for one reason or another, they may be relieved of the duty of rearing their children.

Not all of the advanced reformers adopt the whole of this program, but the whole of this program is logically inherent in the conception of parenthood as a vocation deliberately undertaken, publicly pursued, and motivated solely by the parental instincts.

The separate set of conventions which it is proposed to adopt for the development of love as an art have a logic of their own. Their function is not to protect the welfare of the child but the happiness of lovers. It is very easy to misunderstand this conception. . . .

There are two arts of love and it makes a considerable difference which one is meant. There is the art of love as Casanova, for example, practiced it. It is the art of seduction, courtship, and sexual gratification: it is an art which culminates in the sexual act. It can be repeated with the same lover and with other lovers, but it exhausts itself in the moment of ecstasy. When that moment is reached, the work of art is done, and the lover as artist "after an interval, perhaps of stupor and vital recuperation" must start all over again, until at last the rhythm is so stale it is a weariness to start at all; or the lover must find new lovers and new resistances to conquer. The aftermath of romantic love—that is, of love that is consummated in sexual ecstasy—is either tedium in middle age or the compulsive adventurousness of the libertine.

 . . . When a man and woman are successfully in love, . . . sexual intimacy is not the dead end of desire as it is in romantic or promiscuous love, but periodic affirmation of the inward delight of desire pervading an active life. Love of this sort can grow; it is not, like youth itself, a moment that comes and is gone and remains only a memory of something which cannot be recovered. It can grow because it has something to grow upon and to grow with; it is not contracted and stale because it has for its object, not the mere relief of physical tension, but all the objects with which the two lovers are concerned. They desire their worlds in each other, and therefore their love is as interesting as their worlds and their worlds are as interesting as their love.

It is to promote unions of this sort that the older liberals are proposing a new set of sexual conventions. . . .

They ask public opinion to sanction what contraception has made feasible. They point out that "a large number of the men and women of today form sexual relationships outside marriage—whether or not they ultimately lead to marriage—which they conceal or seek to conceal from the world." These relationships . . . differ from the extramarital manifestations of the sexual life of the past in that they do not derive from prostitution or seduction. Both of these ancient practices, he adds, are diminishing, for prostitution is becoming less attractive and, with the education of women, seduction is becoming less possible. The novelty of these new relations, the prevalence of which is conceded though it cannot be measured, lies in the fact that they are entered into voluntarily, have no obvious social consequences, and are altogether beyond the power of law or opinion to control. The argument, therefore, is that they should be approved, the chief point made being that by removing all stigma from such unions, they will become candid, wholesome, and delightful. The objection of the reformers to the existing conventions is that the sense of sin poisons the spontaneous goodness of such relationships.

The actual proposals go by a great variety of fancy names such as free love, trial marriage, companionate marriage. When these proposals are examined it is evident they all take birth control as their major premise, and then deduce from it some part or all of the logical consequences. Companionate marriage, for example, is from the point of view of the law, whatever it may be subjectively, nothing but a somewhat roundabout way of saying that childless couples may be divorced by mutual consent. It is a proposal, if not to control, then at least to register publicly, all sexual unions, the theory being that this public registration will abolish shame and furtiveness and give them a certain permanence. Companionate marriage is frankly an attempt at a compromise between marriages that are difficult to dissolve and clandestine relationships which have no sanction whatever.

The uncompromising logic of birth control has been stated more clearly, I think, by Mr. Bertrand Russell than by anyone else. Writing to Judge Lindsey during the uproar about companionate marriage, Mr. Russell said:

> I go further than you do: the things which your enemies say about you would be largely true of me. My own view is that the state and the law should take no notice of sexual relations apart from children, and that no marriage ceremony should be valid unless accompanied by a medical certificate of the woman's pregnancy. But when once there are children, I think that divorce should be avoided except for very grave cause. I should not regard physical infidelity as a very grave cause and should teach people that it is to be expected and tolerated, but should not involve the begetting of 'll/gitimate children—not because illegitimacy is bad in itself, but because a home with two parents is best for children. I do not feel that the main thing in marriage is the feeling of the parents for each other; the main thing is cooperation in bearing children.

In this admirably clear statement there is set forth a plan for that complete separation between the primary and secondary function of sexual intercourse which contraception makes possible.

It is one thing, however, to recognize the full logic of birth control and quite another thing to say that convention ought to be determined by that logic. One might as well argue that because automobiles can be driven at a hundred miles an hour the laws should sanction driving at the rate of a hundred miles an nour. Birth control is a device like the automobile, and its inherent possibilities do not fix the best uses to be made of it.

What an understanding of the logic of birth control does is to set before us the limits of coercive control of sexual relations. The law can, for example, make divorce very difficult where there are children. It could, as Mr. Bertrand Russell suggests, refuse divorce on the ground of infidelity. On the other hand the law cannot effectively prohibit infidelity, and as a matter of fact does not do so to-day. It cannot effectively prohibit fornication though there are statutes against it. Therefore, what Mr. Russell has done is to describe accurately enough the actual limits of effective legal control.

But sexual conventions are not statutes, and it is important to define quite clearly just what they are. In the older world they were rules of conduct enforceable by the family and the community through habit, coercion, and authority. In this sense of the word, convention tends to lose force and effect in modern civilization. Yet a convention is essentially a theory of conduct and all human conduct implies some theory of conduct. Therefore, although it may be that no convention is any longer coercive, conventions remain, are adopted, revised, and debated. They embody the considered results of experience: perhaps the experience of a lonely pioneer or perhaps the collective experience of the dominant members of a community. In any event they are as necessary to a society which recognizes no authority as to one which does. For the inexperienced must be offered some kind of hypothesis when they are confronted with the necessity of making choices: they cannot be so utterly open-minded that they stand inert until something collides with them. In the modern world, therefore, the function of conventions is to declare the meaning of experience. A good convention is one which will most probably show the inexperienced the way to happy experience.

Just because the rule of sexual conduct by authority is dissolving, the need of conventions which will guide conduct is increasing. That, in fact, is the reason for the immense and urgent discussion of sex throughout the modern world. It is an attempt to attain an understanding of the bewilderingly new experiences to which few men or women know how to adjust themselves. The true business of the moralist in the midst of all this is not to denounce this and to advocate that, but to see as clearly as he can into the meaning of it, so that out of the chaos of pain and happiness and worry he may help to deliver a usable insight.

It is, I think, to the separation of parenthood as a vocation from love as an end in itself that the moralist must address himself. For this is the heart of the problem: to determine whether this separation, which birth control has made feasible and which law can no longer prevent, is in harmony with the conditions of human happiness.

Among those who hold that the separation of the primary and secondary functions of the sexual impulse is good and should constitute the major premise of modern sexual conventions, there are, as I have already pointed out, two schools of thought. There are the transcendentalists who believe with Mr. Havelock Ellis that "sexual pleasure, wisely used and not abused, may prove the stimulus and liberator of our finest and most exalted activities," and there are the unpretentious hedonists who believe that sexual pleasure is pleasure and not the stimulus or liberator of anything important. Both are, as we say, emancipated: neither recognizes the legitimacy of objective control unless a child is born, and both reject as an evil the traditional subjective control exercised by the sense of sin. Where they differ is in their valuation of love.

Hedonism as an attitude toward life is, of course, not a new thing in the world, but it has never before been tested out under such favorable conditions. . . . There is now a generation in the world which is approaching middle age. They have exercised the privileges which were won by the iconoclasts who attacked what was usually called the Puritan or Victorian tradition. They have exercised the privileges without external restraint and without inhibition. Their conclusions are reported in the latest works of fiction. Do they report that they have found happiness in their freedom? Well, hardly. Instead of the gladness which they were promised, they seem . . . to have found the wasteland. . . .

If you start with the belief that love is the pleasure of a moment, is it really surprising that it yields only a momentary pleasure? . . . This much the transcendentalists understand well enough. They do not wish to isolate the satisfaction of desire from our "finest and most exalted activities." They would make it "the stimulus and the liberator" of these activities. They would use it to arouse to "wholesome activity all the complex and interrelated systems of the organism." But what are these finest and most exalted activities which are to be stimulated and liberated? The discovery of truth, the making of works of art, meditation and insight? Mr. Ellis does not specify. If these are the activities that are meant, then the discussion applies to a very few of the men and women on earth. For the activities of most of them are necessarily concerned with earning a living and managing a household and rearing children and finding recreation. If the art of love is to stimulate and liberate activities, it is these prosaic activities which it must stimulate and liberate. But if you idealize the logic of birth control, make parenthood a separate vocation, isolate love from work and the hard realities of living, and say that it must be spontaneous and carefree, what have you done? You have separated it from all the important activities which it might stimulate and liberate. You have made love spontaneous but empty, and you have made home-building and parenthood efficient, responsible, and dull.

What has happened, I believe, is what so often happens in the first enthusiasm for a revolutionary invention. Its possibilities are so dazzling that men forget that inventions belong to man and not man to his inventions. In the discussion which has ensued since birth control became generally feasible, the central confusion has been that the reformers have tried to fix their sexual ideals in accordance with the logic of birth control instead of the logic of human nature. Birth control does make feasible this dissociation of interests which were once organically united. There are undoubtedly the best of reasons for dissociating them up to a point. But how completely it is wise to dissociate them is a matter to be determined not by saying how completely it is possible to dissociate them, but how much it is desirable to dissociate them.

All the varieties of the modern doctrine that man is a collection of separate impulses, each of which can attain its private satisfaction, are in fundamental contradiction not only with the traditional body of human wisdom but with the modern conception of the human character. Thus in one breath it is said in advanced circles that love is a series of casual episodes, and in the next it transpires that the speaker is in process of having himself elaborately psychoanalyzed in order to disengage his soul from the effects of apparently trivial episodes in his childhood. On the one hand it is asserted that sex pervades everything and on the other that sexual behavior is inconsequential. It is taught that experience is cumulative, that we are what our past has made us and shall be what we are making of ourselves now, and then with bland indifference to the significance of this we are told that all experiences are free, equal, and independent.

It is not hard to see why those who are concerned in revising sexual conventions should have taken the logic of birth control rather than knowledge of human nature as their major premise. Birth control is an immensely beneficent invention which can and does relieve men and women of some of the most tragic sorrows which afflict them: the tragedies of the unwanted child, the tragedies of insupportable economic burdens, the tragedies of excessive child-bearing and the destruction of youth and the necessity of living in an unrelenting series of pregnancies. It offers them freedom from intolerable mismating, from sterile virtue, from withering denials of happiness. These are the facts which the reformers saw, and in birth control they saw the instrument by which such freedom could be obtained.

The sexual conventions which they have proposed are really designed to cure notorious evils. They do not define the good life in sex; they point out ways of escape from the bad life. Thus companionate marriage is proposed . . . not as a type of union which is inherently desirable, but as an avenue of escape from corrupt marriages on the one hand and furtive promiscuity on the other. The movement for free divorce comes down to this: it is necessary because so many marriages are a failure. The whole theory that love is separate from parenthood and home-building is supported by the evidence in those cases where married couples are not lovers. It is the pathology of sexual relations which inspires the reformers of sexual conventions.

There is no need to quarrel with them because they insist upon remedies for manifest evils. Deep confusion results when they forget that these remedies are only remedies, and go on to institute them as ideals. It is better, without any doubt, that incompatible couples should be divorced and that each should then be free to find a mate who is compatible. But the frequency with which men and women have to resort to divorce because they are incompatible will be greatly influenced by the notions they have before and during marriage of what compatibility is, and what it involves. The remedies for failure are important. But what is central is the conception of sexual relations by which they expect to live successfully.

They cannot—I am, of course, speaking broadly—expect to live successfully by the conception that the primary and secondary functions of sex are in separate compartments of the soul. I have indicated why this conception is self-defeating and why, since human nature is organic and experience cumulative, our activities must, so to speak, engage and imply each other. Mates who are not lovers will not really cooperate, as Mr. Bertrand Russell thinks they should, in bearing children; they will be distracted, insufficient, and worst of all they will be merely dutiful. Lovers who have nothing to do but love each other are not really to be envied; love and nothing else very soon is nothing else. The emotion of love, in spite of the romantics, is not self-sustaining; it endures only when the lovers love many things together, and not merely each other. It is this understanding that love cannot successfully be isolated from the business of living which is the enduring wisdom of the institution of marriage. Let the law be what it may be as to what constitutes a marriage contract and how and when it may be dissolved. Let public opinion be as tolerant as it can be toward any and every kind of irregular and experimental relationship. When all the criticisms have been made, when all supernatural sanctions have been discarded, all subjective inhibitions erased, all compulsions abolished, the convention of marriage still remains to be considered as an interpretation of human experience. It is by the test of how genuinely it interprets human experience that the convention of marriage will ultimately be judged.

The wisdom of marriage rests upon an extremely unsentimental view of lovers and their passions. Its assumptions, when they are frankly exposed, are horrifying to those who have been brought up in the popular romantic tradition of the Nineteenth Century. These assumptions are that, given an initial attraction, a common social background, common responsibilities, and the conviction that the relationship is permanent, compatibility in marriage can normally be achieved. It is precisely this that the prevailing sentimentality about love denies. It assumes that marriages are made in heaven, that compatibility is instinctive, a mere coincidence, that happy unions are, in the last analysis, lucky accidents in which two people who happen to suit each other happen to have met. The convention of marriage rests on an interpretation of human nature which does not confuse the subjective feeling of the lovers that their passion is unique, with the brutal but objective fact that, had they never met, each of them would in all probability have found a lover who was just as unique. . . .

This is the reason why the popular conception of romantic love as the meeting of two affinities produces so much unhappiness. The mysterious glow of passion is accepted as a sign that the great coincidence has occurred; there is a wedding and soon, as the glow of passion cools, it is discovered that no instinctive and preordained affinity is present. At this point the wisdom of popular romantic marriage is exhausted. For it proceeds on the assumption that love is a mysterious visitation. There is nothing left, then, but to grin and bear a miserably dull and nagging fate, or to break off and try again. The deep fallacy of the conception is in the failure to realize that compatibility is a process and not an accident, that it depends upon the maturing of instinctive desire by adaptation to the whole nature of the other person and to the common concerns of the pair of lovers.

The romantic theory of affinities rests upon an immature theory of desire. It springs from an infantile belief that the success of love is in the satisfactions which the other person provides. What this really means is that in child-like fashion the lover expects his mistress to supply him with happiness. But in the adult world that expectation is false. Because nine-tenths of the cause, as Mr. Santayana says, are in the lover for one-tenth that may be in the object, it is what the lover does about that nine-tenths which is decisive for his happiness. It is the claim, therefore, of those who uphold the ideal of marriage as a full partnership, and reject the ideal which would separate love as an art from parenthood as a vocation, that in the home made by a couple who propose to see it through, there are provided the essential conditions under which the passions of men and women are most likely to become mature, and therefore harmonious and disinterested.

They need not deny, indeed it would be foolish as well as cruel for them to underestimate, the enormous difficulty of achieving successful marriages under modern conditions. For with the dissolution of authority and compulsion, a successful marriage depends wholly upon the capacity of the man and the woman to make it successful. They have to accomplish wholly by understanding and sympathy and disinterestedness of purpose what was once in a very large measure achieved by habit, necessity, and the absence of any practicable alternative. It takes two persons to make a successful marriage in the modern world, and that fact more than doubles its difficulty. For these reasons alone the modern state ought to do what it would none the less be compelled to do: it ought to provide decent ways of retreat in case of failure.

But if it is the truth that the convention of marriage correctly interprets human experience, whereas the separatist conventions are self-defeating, then the convention of marriage will prove to be the conclusion which emerges out of all this immense experimenting. It will survive not as a rule of law imposed by force, for that is now, I think, become impossible. It will not survive as a moral commandment with which the elderly can threaten the young. They will not listen. It will survive as the dominant insight into the reality of love and happiness, or it will not survive at all. That does not mean that all persons will live under the convention of marriage. As a matter of fact in civilized ages all persons never have. It means that the convention of marriage, when it is clarified by insight into reality, is likely to be the hypothesis upon which men and women will ordinarily proceed. There will be no compulsion behind it except the compulsion in each man and woman to reach a true adjustment of his life. . . . It is in the hidden issues between lovers, more than anywhere else, that modern men and women are compelled, by personal anguish rather than by laws and preachments or even by the persuasions of abstract philosophy, to transcend naive desire and to reach out towards a mature and disinterested partnership with their world.

SEX: THE QUIET REVOLUTION

David Boroff

David Boroff wrote frequently about university life and is the author of Campus, U.S.A. *(1961). He was until his recent death an associate professor of English at New York University.*

What has happened to sex during the last fifteen years? Among those over thirty-five, there is a feeling, half-envious and half-appalled, that the younger generation is calmly but insatiably erotic. What was tense sexual melodrama twenty years ago seems to be little more than reflex action today. If the sophisticated young are no longer agitated about sex, it is because sex is no longer a problem for them. We appear to be living through a sexual revolution. It is a quiet revolution—not a rebellion—without ideological fireworks or flamboyance or protest.

The nature of the change-over was expressed by a man in his thirties who recently spent a year at Harvard. "During the day," he recalled, "you never saw a couple on campus holding hands. Yet you knew damn well that these same kids were quietly having affairs." And there is the editor in his early forties who remarked about one of his charges, a talented novelist of twenty-six: "When . . . and I discuss ideas, I feel I have to pin up his diapers; but when we talk about sex, I feel he has to pin up mine."

If a new sex ethic is beginning to crystallize, it is the culmination of the efforts of a long line of sex libertarians—from Wilhelm Reich through Henry Miller to Norman Mailer and the Beats. Norman Brown, author of *Life Against Death,* is only the last of the champions of a freer sexuality. Dr. Brown, whose revaluation of Freud has been widely discussed in intellectual circles, sees in present society the dominion of death-in-life. He calls for the "resurrection of the body," for "erotic exuberance," and for an end to repression. Significantly, many of the official custodians of our culture are beginning to be influenced by such ideas. Lionel Trilling describes Brown's book as "one of the most interesting and valuable books of our time." And Norman Podhoretz, the editor of *Commentary* who just a few years ago derogated the Beats, [became] a fervid proponent of Mailer's talent and hipster ideas.

The New Freedom even gains qualified support from liberal church people. Dr. Roger Shinn, who teaches a course in "The Christian Meaning of Sex" in the Union Theological Seminary, summed up the position of liberal Protestantism: "A good deal of the old repressiveness is gone—what we generally associate with the word puritanism. Arising out of Biblical scholarship of the last twenty years is the recognition that the Bible's attitude toward sex is affirmative and that the repressive attitude is actually a heresy. Sex is God-given, and man realizes himself through it. Simultaneously, we have been influenced by the psychological studies that many clergymen now engage in. There is no longer the feeling that the true meaning of sin is sexual. However, the real meaning of the sexual encounter is still the commitment expressed through marriage vows."

During the last dozen years, there have been some striking changes in American culture with implications for sexual behavior. There has been a loosening in restraints about language. The vindication of the right to distribute *Lady Chatterley's Lover* through the post office was merely a legal consolidation of a development which has been obvious to many people. World War II opened the floodgates of language. In *The Naked and the Dead* Mailer used the familiar four-letter words, but prissily modified. Then James Jones, in *From Here to Eternity,* employed the idiom of the barracks without disguise and won a National Book Award. When James Gould Cozzens, hardly a literary insurgent, used plain Anglo-Saxon diction in *By Love Possessed,* the forces of conservatism were in full retreat. At the Post Office Department hearings for *Lady Chatterley's Lover,* critic Malcolm Cowley sounded the obsequies for the old restrictions: "There are a certain number of short Anglo-Saxon words for bodily functions that were regarded as a secret language of men. These words were used in the smoking room, in the barroom, in the barbershop, but no woman was supposed to know them unless she was an utterly degraded woman. . . . There is no more secret language of males. That has been abolished."

It is perhaps more accurate to say that women have been admitted to the club. Language that a respectable woman would not permit herself to hear years ago, much less use, is now the lingua franca of the sexes. One can hear the newly liberated idiom at cocktail parties, in plays, and even, occasionally, in that most circumspect of media, television. (*The Iceman Cometh* was *not* bowdlerized for TV presentation.) And plain Anglo-Saxon language has even gained a tenuous handhold in academia. A number of professors all around the country who have invited poets to give readings have listened in stunned silence to naked utterance, while wondering nervously what the Dean would say about all this.

Our culture today is highly sexualized. We see it in changing culture heroes. The late Clark Gable, the archetypal hero of the Thirties and Forties, was unquestionably virile, but an ingenuous boy scout in comparison with the stridently phallic movie heroes of today. Even James Dean, who set the new vogue, for all his dark and moody sensitivity, had a kind of sullen but demanding eroticism. And if Marlon Brando is inarticulate it is because his arrogant sexuality clearly announces his intentions. We have been inundated in movies, each one bolder than the next, so that titillation no longer titillates. And in the publishing world, sleazy paperbacks compete with each other in a gaudy Olympiad of sex and sadism. But, contrary to vulgar opinion, it takes more than sex to make a best seller. This merely proves that the sexual beachheads have been achieved, the campaigns won, and the old battle cries no longer rouse. It is only in an atmosphere of repression that lasciviousness can provide kicks. And there are even those who deplore the passing of the delicious pleasures of the Forbidden.

For many, sex is the last arena of adventure in the quasi-welfare state in which we now live. The old dramas have subsided into silence. Sex, according to David Riesman, is the last frontier of our culture. In an era of affluence and muffled sensibilities, "sex provides a kind of defense against the threat of total apathy. . . . [The other-directed person] looks to it for reassurance that he is alive."

In a very real sense, sex [was] the politics of the Sixties. There was a vivid demonstration of that . . . when Norman Mailer gave a reading at the Poetry Center in New York City. He started out tamely enough reading an excerpt from a magazine piece; then, in an atmosphere of mounting excitement, he began to read short verse selections, some of which could be regarded as obscene. Showing a mock solicitude for the squares in the audience, he said he would "semaphore" if a selection he was about to read would jar their sensibilities. He was wagging his arms before reading his seventh or eighth selection when the curtain came down; the management of the Poetry Center decided they had done enough for one evening to advance the cause of freedom. For a while, it looked as if there might be trouble. Many of the young people in the audience, for whom Mailer oozes *charisma,* were hurling imprecations at the weak-kneed guardians of public morality. It was only after Mailer came out, in duffel coat and mischievous smile, and asked them to leave to show their "discipline" that the crowd grumblingly dispersed. . . .

The ascendancy of psychology in our time has given the new sex ethic a solid intellectual underpinning. According to Philip Rieff, author of *Freud: The Mind of the Moralist,* the New Man is psychological man who substitutes health values for moral values. "Freud," says Rieff, "can conceive of a person's feeling guilty not because he has been bad, but because, as a result of his repressions, he is too moral. This is one source of his influence: his diagnosis that we are sick from our ideals and that the one practical remedy lies in an infusion from below." It is clear that sex and sex pleasure are obligatory today. Dr. Albert Ellis, a psychologist who has written extensively about sex, recently remarked: "Instead of coming with problems of guilt about sex, my patients express concern if they don't enjoy it, or if they're fearful or shy."

How much change in sex behavior has there been? Nobody really knows. But one thing is certain: attitudes towards sex among those who grew up after World War II—those under thirty in other words—are strikingly different from those of earlier generations. It can be summed up in this way: Sex is one of life's principal goods. The degree of pleasure one derives from it is a measure of one's self-realization. And since the old moral sanctions have lost much of their authority, there is far less reluctance about premarital sex. In fact, Dr. Ellis reveals that when he lectures on sex before college students, there is almost invariably a wild cheer when he endorses premarital sex. Before World War II, to be a virgin was good; today, after a certain age, it is bad. The loss of chastity is no longer the fall from innocence; it is the fall upwards, so to speak, to maturity and self-fulfillment. . . .

But this does not mean that carnal anarchy prevails. Young people acknowledge the claims of society. Early marriages constitute one imposing piece of evidence for this. The ethos of the under-thirty generation is that sex is fine—nay, indispensable—but it has to be validated either by love or by a steady relationship. This was borne out by the Kinsey Report which revealed that although about half the women interviewed had premarital coitus, forty-six per cent of this group had relations only with their fiancés And in a recent study of college youth only two per cent of the girls had intercourse with acquaintances, six per cent with friends (men they knew well, but did not love), and seventeen per cent with lovers.

What we have, in other words, is a shift from the old-fashioned double standard—sex is fine for men, but not for women—to a modified single standard. The old sexual serfdom is dead or dying. Sex is being democratized. Confronting the new sexual freedom for women, a college boy I talked with said: "I'm in favor of it—with reservations. You figure that, one time or another, a girl was in love and had an affair. But I wouldn't want to marry a girl who had too many affairs." Another young man, determinedly egalitarian, said: "I can't condemn a girl for having sex. She has the same feelings I have." He pondered the implications of this for a moment: "You know, I say all this, but I'm not sure I really believe it."

Among girls, there is a range of attitudes from the girl who chanted with horror, "If a girl has sex before she is married, she is ruined!" to the twenty-four-year-old worldling who said haughtily, "In my milieu I don't know any virgins." A mainstream response was that of the girl who said: "I used to think it was terrible if people had intercourse before marriage. Now I think each person should find his own values. And if they won't suffer and feel guilty, why not?" But among sophisticated young women there is a cheerful appropriation of sex which is remarkably masculine in tone. "You feel that you can't really communicate with a virgin," a graduate of a good woman's college remarked. "You want to talk about your current affair—it's not true that girls don't share confidences with each other—and you can't with an inexperienced girl." . . .

Despite their sexual divagations, sophisticated girls are as fierce about marriage as their less-venturesome sisters. It's just that their time-table is arranged differently. Marriage for them comes later, after a few discreet, developmental affairs. "The same girls who may be terribly sophisticated and have one affair after another," a psychoanalyst re-marked, "still want to marry and have families." And Professor William Barrett of New York University, author of *Irrational Man,* remarked: "There may be a new freedom, but women are different from men. After a while, the sexual bravado of even the most sophisticated woman disap-pears. Men are interested in sex, but women are interested in curtains and babies."

But . . . amid evidence of greater permissiveness, there are un-answered questions. What about the quality of sex experience? And where are we headed?

There are the beginnings of a second stage in the new sex ethos. If sex is good, then perhaps it's always good—and the more the better. This may account for the sex predators that some girls complain of—the males who make perfunctory overtures as a kind of reflexive gesture of malehood, Dr. Margaret Mead had some harsh things to say about youthful behavior: "We have jumped from puritanism to lust. The breakdown of the double standard means that all girls—not just bad girls—are fair game today. The average college boy is an unprincipled wolf. The reason they stick so close to their dates at college parties is that they won't trust their girls with their friends, since they don't really trust themselves."

Then, here is another corollary. If sex is good—the basic premise of our culture—then perhaps *all* kinds of sex are good. We encounter this in some of the evangelists of a richer, freer sexuality. For example, Paul Goodman, the brilliant author of *Growing Up Absurd,* was recently asked his view of premarital sex by a college student. "In sex, anything you get pleasure from is good," he said peremptorily. "And that's all there is to it." . . .

But serious students of sex are generally agreed about one thing: the sexual freedom we now have is spurious. Dr. Sandor Lorand, an eminent psychiatrist, said soberly: "The reason youth is on a rampage is that we now have a sexual freedom which does not free." And Dr. Alexander Lowen, a Reichian analyst, said: "Superficially, sexual sophistication is increasing, but on an unconscious level there is almost the same measure of guilt and anxiety as in the past. Sociologist Ernest van den Haag talks of the gap between our verbal culture and our actual sex sophistication. Some New York college girls use a blunt acrostic, Nato, which stands for "No action—talk only!"

Dr. Roger Shinn, the Protestant clergyman cited earlier, also took a measured view of the new freedom. "The so-called emancipation," he observed, "has led some people to adopt a hurrah-for-sex attitude. I'm prepared to say hurrah-for-sex too, but it doesn't solve very much. Sex can be an expression of love, or it can be a form of exploitation. We must start with a post-Victorian appreciation of sex, but we must also be aware of its corruptions."

And even among the sophisticates, there is the feeling that surely there must be more to it than this. Pleasure is not enough. Sexual health is not enough. Instead of relieving anxiety, today's sex culture compounds it. For in addition to residual Puritan guilt and anxiety, there is the new pressure that both men and women feel to be sexually omnicompetent. With the new erotic hedonism, people are constantly appraising their sexual performance.

"Among women," Dr. Douglas Spencer said, "there is a tremendous concern about orgasm. They ask themselves, 'Am I missing something?' And this tension actually blocks orgasm. There used to be a time when women hardly knew about these matters. Now it's become a goal, like a Diners' Club credit card. They lose sight of the real joy—even the humor of sex."

For the man, the sexual virtuosity demanded of him may have something to do with the asserted increase in homosexuality. In other words, some precariously poised males may be scared out of heterosexuality by the very demands made upon them. And today sexual pressure is increased by the fact that men can define their masculinity through their sexual role alone as the occupational, social, and even sartorial space between the sexes narrows.

Turn-of-the-century sports, for example, defined their masculinity through jobs, masculine dress, and all-male recreations. In the brothels which they frequented nobody measured their potency. And their wives had to pretend an indifference to sex—and an ignorance of it—in the same fashion that women today have to simulate ardor and appreciation.

What is the impact of the New Freedom on marriage? Very little thus far. We seem to be moving toward increasing premarital sex freedom, but with the same tight restraints after marriage. This is startlingly similar to the pattern of most primitive cultures. According to Charles Rolo, the author of a forthcoming book about the impact of psychoanalysis on our culture, the psychological revolution is responsible for this.

"Premarital sexual freedom no doubt derives from the influence of psychoanalysis. The psychological revolution placed a premium on sex as hygiene. However, as applied to marriage, psychoanalysis is a conservative influence. In marriage, you don't use adultery as hygiene. We disapprove, on psychological grounds, of the Don Juan and the nymphomaniac. We perceive their pathology all too clearly."

In short, the institution of marriage is well-armored. A Westport, Connecticut, resident pointed out that a single man who turns up for a week end in the company of a girl with whom he is having an affair provokes no comment, "but there would be hell to pay if he went off into the bushes with someone's wife." The only marked development, according to most observers, is that when infidelity occurs it is less likely today to break up a marriage. The couple is more likely to sit down and explore psychologically what is wrong with their relationship.

Sex is still a vast, mysterious country. Freud and Kinsey are perhaps the Livingstone and Stanley of this dark continent. Only one thing is certain: at a time of the swiftest technological change in the history of mankind, it would be naïve to expect sexual mores to stand comfortably still. That our institutions have shown so much survival power is astonishing. But only a reckless prophet would predict the shape of things to come.

TOWARD THE NEW CHASTITY

Midge Decter

Midge Decter is a frequent contributor to leading periodicals and has served in an editorial capacity at Midstream *and* Commentary, *and most recently as executive editor of* Harper's. *In recent years she has concentrated on the women's liberation movement, an interest reflected not only in numerous articles, but in two books,* The Liberated Woman and Other Americans *(1971) and* The New Chastity and Other Arguments Against Women's Liberation *(1972). In this context it is perhaps not irrelevant to add that she is married and the mother of four children. The following selection is included because in it a liberated woman suggests that the sexual revolution may not be all that liberating.*

By the Sixties, there were numerous different notions in currency about the sex life of the American female, and while these notions did not altogether comfortably cohere, they did all stem from one basic assumption: namely, that sexual activity was less of a problem to her than to any other group of women since at least the onset of Christianity. We were, after all—so it was said over and over from every corner of the culture—passing through a sexual revolution, a revolution, moreover, of which she was proving to be the main beneficiary.

Thus the declaration by Women's Liberation that women were nowadays more than ever mere sexual "objects" and that the sexual revolution was more than ever a sexual enslavement must have been experienced by many people, especially many men—but even by many young women—as a rude awakening. . . .

Women's Liberation calls it enslavement, but the real truth about the sexual revolution is that it has made of sex an almost chaotically limitless and therefore unmanageable realm in the life of women. A young girl begins in the awareness that she has a strange, abstract power over young men. The playmates of her childhood have ceased to be playmates, for they are in the grip of lust. The adolescent boy begins to react to, and to make judgments upon, the females around him in an entirely new way. He may like or dislike them, yearn for their company or flee from it in terror, but they are now necessary to him. For the young girl, the situation is exactly the obverse. She has no such lust—her yearnings toward the males around her are of another sort—and so, briefly, she is in a position of superior power. She has the control over herself that enables her to control the conditions between them. Her power on the other hand is not *personal* power; it resides in her femaleness. Her own erotic fantasies are entirely personal, her own need—precisely to the extent that she has now become an undifferentiated member of a species—is to establish herself as a differentiated individual. So she, too, but from the other side, places herself in a position of dependence on the other sex. Men have placed her in the crowd; thus they have unique authority to single her out from it. If she does not find the reflection of her individual value in their eyes, she will continue, perhaps all her life, to be uncertain about whether she has any. She must use the power of her abstract desirability to wrest the acknowledgment of her concrete irreplaceableness. She does this in anxiety, with all the means available. She tries to enhance her beauty so as to be more desirable than others. Or she may flirt so as to promise more than others. Or dress so as to make those around her mindful of the delights it would be hers, if she chose, to bestow. In any case, her one trump card—for the time being—is that though her dependence may in the larger picture of life be of more lasting consequence, she is far less vulnerable to the sexual needs and pressures of the moment.

This imbalance and incomparability of needs constitutes the beginning of that which is sometimes referred to as the war between the sexes. As the armies for this war first mobilize, each has its own tactics, its own fortifications, its own natural weaponry of attack and defense. Moreover, the battle conducted by these armies was once a relatively orderly affair, culminating in a mutually recognized resolution—marriage. From generation to generation this warfare produced many casualties—young men whose lust had sickened and withered or scattered irretrievably—and young women whose sense of individual worth had been permanently shattered—but it continued at least to leave the possibility of an orderly procession of workable settlements.

At some relatively recent point, however, American society, through the combined offices of Freudian thought and liberal hubris, decreed that no further field of battle in life should yield up any casualties, and certainly not sexual ones. For every potential human wound there was now to be a preemptive remedy. Wherever possible, battle should cease altogether. With respect to sex, this meant that everyone, male and female, was to seek the experience of individuality in the same way. The young girl was no longer to withhold her sexual favors as a bargaining point for the right to impose herself, and the young boy was no longer to succumb to the blind dictates of lust without her private, individual assent.

She was to become the equal, the partner, and no longer the antagonist, of her male. Sex was to be taken for granted, like youth and energy themselves. It was to be deemed "good" for her or "bad" for her not on moral grounds, nor on grounds of its increasing or impairing her worth in the eyes of future candidates for marriage, but simply as it served or did not serve the imperatives of her being. These last were things that no one, not even her best friend, could tell her about. Sex became an issue of her private welfare, like her eating habits or her choice of friends. "It all depends on the individual," she was likely to be told if she were ever so innocent as to seek out advice in the matter. "For some it will be good immediately, for others, not yet."

Since there were no standards of conduct either to obey or to violate, since she herself was to be the arbiter and the standard, she was pressed into a species of self-knowledge it had once been one of the purposes of sexual games and encounters to help her attain to. Far from being a sexual object, as Women's Liberation claimed, she was a sexual subject *par excellence.* She had been deprived of a large measure of her accustomed power over men, the power in clear conscience to withhold from them a sexual victory or save them from a sexual defeat; and she had in exchange been granted an unprecedented amount of power over herself, the power in equally clear conscience to accede to her own wishes. If, that is, she could know what these were.

For the problem of her having been left to the operations of her own lust is that young girls do not lust in any way that gives proper drive or guidance to action. Constructed to be the receptor, the reactor—and even all but the most homosexually frenzied of the advocates of the clitoris in Women's Liberation concede that the erotic force of that organ resides in its capacity to respond rather than to initiate—a young girl's sexual tendency is to deal with the alternatives set before her by others. Her "lust," insofar as it is proper at all to use that term, is for an image of herself as erotically aroused. Her erotic fantasies are not of the penis but of the man, complete with identity and personality, who is able to create in her and minister to an ever-growing feeling of arousal. This character of her eroticism need offer no difficulty in the actual event of sexual play or intercourse; she and her lover can then be in pursuit of a common quest and moved by a common erotic stimulant: namely, herself as an aroused female. (It is sometimes noted, and exactly as frequently misunderstood, that women are not moved by the sight of the male body as men are moved by the sight of the female body. This fact does not point to a different amount or strength of erotic fantasy between men and women, but to a different *kind,* the one precise and specific, the other diffuse and narcissistic. For this reason, on the other hand, women and heterosexual men are excited by the same pornography— heterosexual pornography focusing as it does mainly on images of a wildly stimulated and responsive woman.)

But the nature of her sexuality creates a great deal of difficulty within the new social dispensation that seeks to make her a free and autonomous being. She has been forced—at a time of life when she feels the greatest need for the protection of a fixed set of manners—to make up her own code of conduct. Should she sleep with this boy or that—or with none? By what criterion? Should she claim a pure and undiscriminating lust—which she does not feel—or a genuine emotional commitment whose nature or requirements she does not yet understand or, in her orgies of self-consciousness, wish to be adequate to?

The imposition upon sex of her need to find her individual self, sex being, after all, among the least individuating of human activities, will only be the beginning of her difficulties. For however successfully or unsuccessfully she goes about fulfilling this need, sex itself, the mere fact of her involvement in it, is at first an adventure and a realm of new discovery. It engages her more intimately than ever before with the otherness of males, and it places her, at least in her own eyes, among the grown-ups—even if only to share in their miseries. But once sex has become a fixed element in her life—the adventure of the simple possibility of it departed—she is left to face yet another disjunction between her experience and that of men. And this disjunction will be a permanent, and a permanently experienced, one.

She will find, against the teachings of many a historical legend and certainly against the most prominent sexual teachings of her own time, that sex is something which requires no effort on her part. As she has become indispensable to men by nothing more than the accident of having been born female, so she is to give and, when such should occur, to take pleasure by nothing more than an offer of her assent. Wars had been fought, murders and suicides had been committed, great poems had been written, on the question of the momentary possession of that tiny bit of territory that for her could at best be only among the mundane accoutrements of her physical being. Even in the act of coition, when that hallowed tract might become the sole focus of her entire capacity for sensual response, its evident significance as a symbol of male striving and conquest would really, deep down, elude her. Women have been accused of an earthbound incapacity for the higher romance, of a sluggardly obtuseness in the presence of a male inclination to flights of the spirit. And this in turn has been chalked up to such grand womanly operations as keeping the species alive and the home fires burning. Whereas the truth is probably something far more intimate: namely, that a woman is a person who nightly, so to speak, witnesses a man in the grip of some kind or some degree of will to valor in an activity that for her is the very definition of ordinary natural function.

In her case, the real issues of the spirit are those of whether, and how—in what atmosphere, under the sway of which of the many possible fantasies—she will lend herself to lovemaking. Once these issues are settled and her body yielded up to the joint proceedings, the rest is simple. It may produce ecstasy in her, or well-being, or a number of lesser conditions all the way down on a sliding scale to nothing; in any of these cases it will have been something easy for her to do and thus of little impinging consequence to the other areas of her life. Unlike a man, she enters each sexual encounter with no pressure further than that of her willingness or unwillingness to do so. If she likes sex, does not mind it, or positively hates it, that which is basically required of her in its proper fulfillment will be the same and will present her—whatever complaints and claims of need she has lately been encouraged to give utterance to—with no difficulty. Unlike a man, and the difference is absolutely crucial, she need never produce living, visible, upright evidence of her sexual potency. Regardless of the level of her potency, if such a term can even be applied to her, her performance will be just as successfully realized. Prominent among pornographic archetypes is that of the young virgin who, on being deflowered, immediately becomes a sexual glutton, heedless and insatiable. Only a slight adaptation would bring this fantasy into the realm of truth: for a woman the crucial sexual drama resides in her overcoming the initial, and largely social, resistance to having intercourse at all; once that drama has been resolved, she may become quite heedless (though certainly never insatiable) in the sense that she has no further obligation but just to be there and to open herself to the exertions of others. The very reason that women are able to dissemble and pretend to a sexual response they have not felt—the necessity that the Women's Liberationists find to be so deplorably widespread—is that nothing will involuntarily betray the truth. But what is to stop them then, it might be asked, from spending their whole lives lying about like the beasts in the field or the ladies in the pornographic stories, perpetually ready to receive the sexual advances made upon them? The answer is—nothing. Nothing, that is, but such entirely extra-erotic considerations as that there are other things they wish or need to do or that they fear pregnancy—and also of course the workings of such entirely extra-erotic forces of the ego as vanity, pride, ambition, or jealousy. For a man, sex is an attainment like the other attainments of his life; it is indeed often felt by him to be paradigmatic of them: each incidence of potency in bed providing some intestinal reassurance of his adequacy to deal with the world outside it. For a woman, coitus is a happenstance, roused and dispensed with on the same occasion, being only itself and touching nothing else. Since she has not been tested by it, it speaks very little one way or the other to the rest of her life. The heterosexual woman who struggles with a man frequently discovers that these struggles they undergo together, which can sometimes be heated nearly to the point of mutual destruction, concern two very different experiences, his and on the other hand hers, but not theirs. She does not understand how much of him is at stake; he does not understand how very little of her.

This natural disjunction between them has been exacerbated a thousandfold by the recent preoccupation with her pleasure—that is, the world-famous quest for the female orgasm. For implicit in this quest is the idea that a man and a woman locked in sexual intercourse are meant to be directly "equal." This equality is to be tokened in their capacity to share very nearly the same rhythm of arousal, action, and release (a certain biologically determined difference in rhythm between them to be overcome by a number of disciplines enabling him to defer and her to accelerate). Thus under the right conditions—for every act of sex its full mutual orgasmic consummation—sex would take on the same significance for women as it has for men.

The truth is, of course, that the pursuit of orgasm for a woman is an entirely irrelevant undertaking. Not that she has no "need" of sex; nor is she indifferent to the "quality" of her sexual encounters. But what that need really is, and what the qualities really are which for her become the true determinants of pleasure, cannot be understood by an analogy with these terms in the experience of men. She may, for instance, have an orgasm in an unpleasurable way, or fail to have one in an entirely pleasurable way. Her need for sex is diffuse, not focused on its consummation but on a hundred different small reminders of the nature that is by daily circumstance mostly hidden from her. She needs, that is, to be reminded of the game for which so much of her existence is after all the candle. And her pleasure in sex is not found in, or determined by, explosive release—for that which is diffuse can never be decisively settled, even for a moment—but rather in the general erotic atmosphere: in the engagement of her fantasies, in the enhancement of her experience and sense of self, in the power to elicit affirmations of her worth and desirability, in the excitements of *giving* pleasure. The relative weights of such elements in the erotic atmosphere will vary from woman to woman or, within the same woman, from time to time. Sometimes, for instance, she will delight in the sensation that sex is a pestilential swamp in which she is helplessly enmired; sometimes, that it is the simplest of all simple human contacts. Always she will be playing out an inner drama whose pleasures will be available to her in exact proportion as she is enabled to feel and to taste the various subtleties of her role. Orgasm may or may not result; an *occupation* with it will be a distraction.

It may be that this very possibility for distraction is precisely one of the things that has set her on the quest at all—that the problem of having "good" sex has been introduced to substitute for the former limits, now removed, on her freedom of choice in sexual encounter. No longer expecting or expected to be chaste, and yet without the active force of lust to guide her, she finds herself without natural boundaries to set the term to her complicity. Where it was once required of her that she be married, it came then, by the earliest fiat of the sexual revolution, to be required of her that she be in love before putting herself in the way of sexual experience. Love itself, however, was now something circularly defined as an emotion to be given full credence only after attaining to a state called "sexual compatibility." Thus it, too, could provide no prior guidance. Accordingly, love has given way to a whole range of even vaguer conditions—such as sexual attraction, personal "need," or even the momentary whim to seek experience—as limiting criteria for sex. She is left, in short, without any orderly or persuasive terms, save those she devises for herself, by which to arrive at any decisions about her conduct as a sexual being.

It is very likely that she will often not know whether she "wishes" to sleep with some man or not—or why, if she should decide in the affirmative in one case, she is entitled to decide in the negative in another. For her it is all so easy: she may in the end decide simply on the basis of which course of action presents the lesser social difficulty. There are occasions on which explaining oneself promises to engender far more of what Simone de Beauvoir would call an unwanted "struggle" than does offering oneself. And conversely, there are other occasions on which refusal, even should her desire be not to refuse, will seem to make matters a good deal simpler for her. The point is, that each encounter with a man which contains in it the possibility of sex will be one in which she has full responsibility for herself.

Flirtation, for instance, has become, in an era which offers no sanction to chastity, an activity fraught with consequence. Which is to say, of course, that there is no longer by definition such a thing as real flirtation— whose purpose is to denote a relation between a man and a woman in which each offers full tribute to the presumed erotic attractions of the other, playfully, securely, if need be quite insincerely, freed by the assumption that nothing but conversational pleasure could or was intended to follow from it. The woman who flirts now labors under the consciousness that her behavior might easily be seen as an invitation, that it might, for all she knows, or ought to *be* an invitation, that it thus carries both for herself and her interlocutor either the possibility of sleeping together or of humiliating one another. She will, in other words, run the risk of being either a prig or a tease. Apart from the serious impoverishment of the everyday relations between men and women wrought by this new load of consciousness—for innocent flirtation has always been one of the mainstays of the peaceable and mutually helpful coexistence of the sexes—women have been prodded by it even further into an altogether inauthentic relation to the nature of their own sexual desires.

Nor, while considerably lessened, does the burden of decision disappear when she marries. Without chastity, marital fidelity, too, becomes a matter of individual responsibility and choice. Such fidelity, in order to be maintained, requires a rationale, a purpose, a justification that each individual marriage must now separately provide. She cannot tell herself that her husband is the only man in the world to whose caresses she can surrender, for her life has already shown this not to be so. In order to know why she must be a faithful wife, a woman must either define marriage in such a way as to set it off uniquely from all the rest of her experience or she must define herself as a person with her own special reasons, her own private, arbitrary moral feelings or ethical principles vis-à-vis her husband, for conducting herself in a new way. In either case, her exclusive sexual commitment as a wife will be *experienced* as something she has chosen by virtue of her own intention to make a certain kind of marriage or to be, from now on, a certain kind of woman.

Single or married, therefore, the lives of women have suffered certain inner distortion in the sexual revolution. For in seeking to free themselves from an unnaturally constricted relation to their bodies—constricted in the way they were permitted to dress them, to think of them, to feel about them, to experience them, or to bestow them upon the experience of others —women were, perhaps inevitably, led to give their sexuality a false importance. It is no paradox, though it may at first seem to be one, that in an age in which sex had been proclaimed to be as right, as taken for granted, as rain, sexual fulfillment should have taken on the aura of a holy grail. Giving up the harsh impositions of chastity, women took upon themselves an entirely new kind of accountability for their behavior—an accountability, moreover, whose main elements did not flow naturally from their own sexual nature and so had to be extracted from will and consciousness. They undertook the obligations of an impersonal lust they did not feel but only believed in; they set out in quest of a pleasure whose dimensions did not match their own and whose attainment was a willed accomplishment; they rendered up to the realm of active choice that about which they felt little genuine inner pressure to choose. Far from being mere objects—which Women's Liberation claimed the sexual revolution had reinforced their being—women had relinquished a good deal of their former right to trade on their sexual desirability as something apart from themselves. Far from having become merely the more available to men, women's availability or lack of it had now been given over entirely to their discretion. Sex may indeed have become a newly beneficent force in the life of women. It is, however, a force which is anything but taken for granted.

Has the sexual revolution brought women nothing, then—nothing but the anxieties and puzzlements of a life lived out of touch with one's authentic demands and feelings? Has women's experience of sex been given no richer coloration, opened to no greater release, softened none of their former crippling fastidiousness? Have all those couples working through all those long nights to attune themselves, both, to the special rhythms of her pleasure—all those dutiful workers in the vineyards of orgasm—been simply duped and deluded, the objects of a vast and not very amusing prank? Who would think confidently and serenely to answer these questions in the affirmative must be very arrogant: as arrogant, indeed, as were the sexual revolutionists who once spoke so confidently in their new scientific wisdom of the universal frigidity and sexual loathing of all the generations of women before them; as arrogant as Women's Liberationists today, who dismiss such things as the relative comfort and good health in the life of modern Western woman as phony. It nevertheless cannot be denied, the much-hailed presence in our midst of busy sexual engineers like Masters and Johnson, the existence of Women's Liberation itself would confirm—that the promised dissolution of all erotic tension and hostility between men and women, the promised resulting happiness and completeness of women particularly, have failed to materialize.

What the new sexual freedom of women has indisputably brought them, however, is . . . new sexual freedom: the freedom of each and every individual woman to have a large hand in the determination of her own sexual conduct and destiny, the freedom to decide very largely for herself what to do, and that other freedom, which is its inevitable concomitant, to entertain the possibility of paying very dearly for her decision.

6

Equality of the Sexes

Following a recent 8 to 1 decision that female members of the armed services are entitled to the same dependency benefits for their husbands that servicemen have always received for their wives, a four-justice plurality of the United States Supreme Court issued a noteworthy judgment that all laws which treat men and women differently are "inherently suspect."[1] Associate Justice William Brennan, Jr., in writing the ruling, declared that there must be "compelling justification" for any law that discriminates between the sexes. An astronomic distance separates this judgment from an 1872 decision in which the Court, as it sustained the exclusion of women from practicing law, declared that "the natural and proper timidity and delicacy which belongs to the female sex unfits it for many of the occupations of civil life."

An even greater distance separates the present position of Catholic theologians from the view of Thomas Aquinas that woman is "defective and accidental . . . a male gone awry" and probably "the result of some weakness in the [father's] generative powers," although stubborn feminists are bound to doubt that God is yet in her heaven so long as there are no female cardinals (not to mention a paucity of Protestant and Jewish clergywomen).

Well into this century, Sigmund Freud, the putative source of much of our enlightenment about sex, found a predominance of envy in the mental life of the female. He attributed this envy to her sense of lack in not possessing male genitalia, thereby accounting

---

[1] It was a judgment instead of a decision because it lacked a five-person majority.

for the "fact" that she has so "little sense of justice."[2] Such flagrant prejudice would not be displayed by a man of comparable stature today. It is likely, now that American women are addressing themselves vigorously to such projects, that we shall soon see a decisive breach in the double standard governing chastity and fidelity, a decline in discrimination against female candidates for the most desirable occupations, and the attainment of parity in compensation. Even so, there are deep differences concerning the best strategies for achieving such goals and sometimes concerning the goals themselves, as the two articles included here suggest.

[2] Sigmund Freud, *New Introductory Lectures,* **Vol.** 16, *Complete Works* (New York: Macmillan), chap. 33.

AN INTERVIEW WITH GLORIA STEINEM

Liz Smith

Liz Smith's newspaper work has been widely syndicated, and she has contributed articles to numerous major magazines. She has also worked as a radio and television producer. A convert to Women's Lib, she reports that her interview with Gloria Steinem "raised my consciousness almost to an unbearable point of self-recognition and self-castigation for what I came to feel were my blindnesses in an area I had been carefully avoiding considering too seriously."

In the mid '60s, at the pinnacle of her success as a magazine writer, Gloria Steinem had become an almost legendary figure on the New York "pop" scene. She knew everyone who was anyone, the men in her life all were big-name "eligibles" and she was much in demand socially and professionally.

After she became a regular writer-observer on more serious matters for *New York* magazine in 1968, Gloria's own life underwent alteration. Long an activist in liberal politics and the peace movement, a champion of oppressed minorities, a defender of all equal and human rights, she had come to believe that the movement for women's liberation was the one in which she should be most deeply involved. In fact, she believes all these causes to be one cause and that all "out" groups must unite against the white male power structure.

I did not come an early or an easy believer to Women's Liberation. My attitude toward Gloria often put me in mind of Plato's words from *The Apology:* "Socrates, can you not go away from us and live quietly without talking?" I thought when I began this dialogue that Gloria might concede at some point that she and the Movement might go away and live quietly without talking. But the more we discussed it, the more I knew she must talk— and women listen.

LIZ: Gloria, I think a good way to start is for me to ask if you don't feel perhaps you've become a bit of a fanatic about Women's Liberation? I mean, are you in the class of that character Marlon Brando played in *The Wild One?* When he was asked, "What are you rebelling against?" Brando as the cyclist said, "What have you got?"

GLORIA: Yes, maybe I am a fanatic, but it's difficult not to be, once you accept the idea that all people are equal human beings. Then you can see very clearly what is wrong with the system that calls women inferior; see what's wrong with marriage, the patriarchal family, the economic structure and how women are exploited. Until you see these things the cause of Women's Liberation may seem illogical. But once understood, it is very logical—and more than vital enough to be fanatical about.

LIZ: You don't feel your life has been somewhat distorted by this cause?

GLORIA: No, my life has been clarified and strengthened. My life really became my own only since I realized that women are adults and should control their own lives.

LIZ: Well, who is Women's Lib for? Whom can it benefit?

GLORIA: It's for housewives, who should get a legally determined percentage of their husbands' salaries and work only the regular nine-to-five day. After all, if their husbands were widowers, how much would they have to pay a housekeeper?

It's for working women who make about half what men make for doing the same jobs.

It's for older women who are made to feel as if they no longer have human value because they've outgrown their identity as sex objects and breeders.

It's for little girls trapped by family and school into taking secondary positions, who play at nurse rather than doctor, who find themselves kept out of athletic training, who see the money for education in the family going to their brothers.

It's for women students who get inferior teachers and who suffer from quotaism in colleges and graduate schools and in medicine and in law. No, it's not even quotaism—it's tokenism.

It's for every woman who ever faked an orgasm because science has denied or misunderstood the nature of woman's sexuality and husbands and lovers tend to know even less about it than the scientists.

It's for Black women. They are really at the bottom of the economic structure, kept there by both racism *and* sexism. A white woman with a college education makes less money working full time than a Black man with a high-school education. Black women make even less than that —and get the most menial jobs.

It's for Hispanic women, who have the worst kind of *machismo* to deal with, that overweening male pride that I guess is best defined as "sexual fascism."

It's for women who have been subjected to a certain part of the psychiatric community, because to send a woman to a Freudian analyst, with his theories about penis envy, the nonexistent vaginal orgasm and his generally demeaning estimate of women, is like sending a Jew to a Nazi.

It's for every woman who has been made to conform to the double standard and for every woman outside the sexual norm, whether she's too heterosexual or not heterosexual enough.

It's for all the women who are dying from butchered, illegal abortions. Even in states where legal abortions are permitted, they may still be too expensive for most poor women to afford.

It's for children too, who respond to cultural and parental brainwashing about what little boys should be like and what little girls should be like. Children feel they won't be loved unless they play the roles our society casts them in. And there's another way that Women's Liberation will be children's liberation—because the notorious overdominating, possessive mother is merely a person whose normal human ambitions are confined to a house, so that she becomes hell to live with. Given a wider world in which to function, she won't be so frustrated; she'll get off her children's backs.

It's for parents. We should always talk of parenthood, not just motherhood. The whole system today is so inhuman. We think the American nuclear family is very normal, but really it's such a new idea. In the agricultural cultures, families were around the farm or patch of land together, performing similar chores and co-operating with one another. They worked together during the day and were together in the evenings. But the Industrial Revolution forced a husband to go off early and come back late, ghettoizing the wives and children at home. With suburbanization, work got farther away and the ghetto was more separate.

Liz: Gloria, you believe that, and thousands of women as involved as you are believe it, but there are even more women who dislike or disapprove of Women's Liberation. Can they be turned toward your way of thinking?

Gloria: First of all, we have to figure out whether those women are reacting to the Movement or to the way it is depicted in the press. The reason many women in Gallup polls and the like say they are not for Women's Liberation is that the idea is generally subjected to ridicule and distortion—especially by the men in the press. Ridicule has always been a weapon men used to keep women in their place.

So many women will approve of all the individual ideas and yet reject the form simply because they've been made to believe we're all crazy bra-burners. They will say, "Yes, I believe women are equal human beings who deserve equal pay, equal job opportunities," and, "Yes, I agree that we need child-care centers and that women should make their own social and political decisions." But they still say, "I'm not for Women's Liberation." That's the fault of the male-dominated media.

In fact, no bra that I know of ever got burned. Women protesting the Miss America contest in 1968 threatened to burn a bra, just as, earlier, suffragettes burned corsets. Both bra and corsets are symbols of the crazy notion that women's identities rest on their outsides more than their insides. But the women didn't actually burn the bra because they couldn't get a fire permit—we've always been too docile and law-abiding. And yet even now, four years later, male reporters write about that supposed bra burning every day.

LIZ: But truly, according to the Gallup poll, there is some grass-roots objection to the Movement.

GLORIA: Of course there is. If all women were fighting against their roles, the revolution would have been won by now. I believe the women who really oppose the Movement—both in form and in content—I think they are the ones who believe women really *are* inferior and therefore *should be* dependent, subservient. That's our biggest problem—women's low estimate of themselves.

The worst punishment society inflicts on all second-class groups is to make a group believe it is second-class. So a person is afraid to leave the security of a dependent status. Even if some women do get a little success in the world, we still think women as a *group* are inferior, and we don't want to be associated with the group. From that kind of thinking comes the terrible desire to be the only woman in the office, the only Black family on the block or the only Jew in the club.

Once we start to see that our low estimate of ourselves, as individuals and as a group, is only societal, not biological or "natural," we begin to change. But that takes time. It's much easier—and safer—not to buck the system.

LIZ: Is there any hope for change?

GLORIA: Yes, I think there is. I have been talking to groups all over the country, from Billings, Montana, to Dayton, Ohio, and I have yet to be in a town that didn't have a Women's Liberation group in it or a town where they didn't have students, Blacks, housewives, businesswomen, at least discussing the Movement. It's a very deep revolution, and women are hungry for it.

You see, it isn't so strange—women already have been politicized by either taking part in or watching other movements, so they are really ready for this one. They have worked in humanist movements, demonstrated, gone to jail. They have worked to get politicians elected and to get traffic lights at bad street crossings. They have demonstrated for peace. They've been doing all kinds of right things, but even in those meetings they find they are supposed to make coffee instead of policy. So they are ready for Women's Liberation.

As for the grass-roots women who have doubts, the key is in seeing our personal experiences honestly, seeing that our experiences are shared by most women as a class and so understanding that woman's position is political. Also, women often don't tell the truth in front of men. To assess women's real feelings about the Movement takes time.

Unlike political philosophies imposed from above, Women's Liberation is a political philosophy that grows out of individual truth, out of women's understanding of their own most intimate problems. It's very personal. It's a thing that says that women are not objects or "playthings" or sources of cheap labor—but that women are full human beings.

LIZ: Do you really believe women are exploited?

GLORIA: Yes. The American housewife works ninety-nine and six-tenths hours a week, on the average, and gets no pay for it. She has to chisel her money off the household or food budget. That's exploitation. A housewife should get a salary that she doesn't have to account for, a legally determined percentage of her husband's salary. And she should work decent hours. Which means her husband should share in the care of the children and the housework. If she is working outside the home, then the man should do half the housework and child care. As it is, working women often have to play a double role.

LIZ: But what does the Movement have to say to those women who insist —as so many do—that they like being wives and mothers and are perfectly happy in these roles?

GLORIA: The Movement says the point is *choice!* If women really like these positions, then that's fine. But women also should be able to be engineers and jockeys and truck drivers and nuclear physicists. The whole point of the Movement is individual choice—for both men and women. The point is to become individuals.

LIZ: Is it in the real interest of women to be for the Movement or is there some chance—and I believe this is a fear among some women—that they will lose their femininity or lose their men or lose their sexual satisfactions?

GLORIA: Well, there's no such thing as femininity—that's a cultural value. In some cultures it has been "feminine" to till the soil or "feminine" to take care of all the money. No woman can lose her *femaleness,* but "femininity" is just the enshrinement of cheap labor. It's being passive, doing what you're told.

LIZ: Are you the best spokeswoman for the Movement, since you're not married and have no children?

GLORIA: There is no single spokeswoman for the Movement. Anyone can speak for it—single women, grandmothers, divorced women, wives, workers, whatever. As long as you have breasts and a vagina you are discriminated against as a woman in this society. We mustn't be divided because of minor differences such as age, or whether one is married or not, or is of a special economic status, or has physical beauty or not. All women can be spokespeople.

LIZ: What about the woman who hasn't even arrived at being a spokeswoman, who has accepted her role so automatically and so long that she is numbed? What is the first thing she should do in the way of "consciousness raising"—I mean sharpening her consciousness concerning the issues?

GLORIA: She must look at her own problems. What is she now? What talents is she not using? How is her life different from what she once hoped and dreamed? The next step has to do with confidence and self-esteem. It helps us all to realize that women are full human beings and have the same rights men have to develop themselves and to be what they want to be. In this country, she will soon realize it if she's been held down, and I'm sure she'll find there are other women in her community with similar problems. For them to get together and talk would be a big help in raising consciousness.

LIZ: You seem to take a dim view of women who play passive roles. You know, the "indulgent female" roles. Isn't it narrow-minded of you to see it as wrong for women to be weaker and men more dominant if, as the saying goes, it's "whatever turns you on"?

GLORIA: No. The point is choice—freedom of choice. Men should feel free to admit weakness too. But I don't understand or welcome people who are "turned on" by putting themselves down or putting others down. And women should realize that socially we're encouraged to be passive if we're women and encouraged to be aggressive if we're men, so much so that it almost amounts to a problem of sadomasochism.

It's all a matter of conditioning. Women cling to those old ways as they play "helpless little sex object" parts. They think they have to be "feminine," and that means to be clinging, helpless, fluttering. You say they may like it that way. Well, that's fine, but what happens to this sort of woman when she gets older? In our culture, as soon as you get a few wrinkles you stop having social value. That's why so many women have much more obvious problems at menopause than men do. The cause is cultural more than physical.

At the very moment when women must go through a hormonal change, when they are no longer "sex objects" and can't have any more children, suddenly also their lives are more or less over in a social sense. It's as if they are no longer of any use to society. Men at that age are usually at the height of their careers, so any hormonal changes taking place in them don't affect them so radically.

LIZ: But you can't classify all the passive active sex roles women and men play out as real extensions of actual sadomasochism. Isn't it possible they are attitudes of genuine enjoyment?

GLORIA: But women have been trained to be masochists. What pleasure is there, really, in being a victim? Or for men in victimizing others? Women have accepted the cultural brainwashing that says they find pleasure in being passive in sex, but it is equally possible for a man to find pleasure in being passive in sex.

LIZ: Nevertheless, many women refuse to believe they can find happiness outside a certain passivity, and not only in sex. Furthermore they refuse to believe they are oppressed in any way. Many women won't even believe your simple statistics about lack of job opportunities, unequal pay for women, and so forth.

GLORIA: Well, we've been fed with the myth that women are better off in this country than in any other, which of course isn't true. We have *quid pro quos*—things we've traded for our so-called special privileges—and what we get amounts to no more than that we can dominate in the home while playing the "dear little woman" to our husbands, and wear expensive perfume. But we can't be real human beings.

If women as an oppressed group didn't agree to the oppression, they wouldn't be oppressed. What keeps oppression going is for an oppressed group to *believe* it is weaker and *believe* it is second-class. Women have been brainwashed to really believe they are inferior, so they accept the inferior role. It's the consciousness of oppression that has to come first. Once that comes, even a small percentage of women can make the revolution.

LIZ: Well, I grew up not wanting to be like my mother. She had to cook three meals a day and she hated it. But I knew my father had it made. He was always jumping in the car, never answering for his actions, doing exciting things. Incidentally, is Women's Liberation for men too?

GLORIA: Yes, but not primarily. It will be men's liberation too because feminism is an unavoidable step on the way to humanism. But men have to start their own movement. Women's Liberation is for men the way the Black movement is for whites. As labor leader Cesar Chavez says, "We have to free the victim from being the victim *and* the executioner from being the executioner." Too many men are restricted and dehumanized by foolish ideas of masculinity—masculinity seeming to mean making a lot of money; subjugating other people, whether physically or economically; beating each other up in bars; shooting small animals; suppressing emotions; being the whole support of a family.

LIZ: Ti-Grace Atkinson is certainly one of the most radical spokeswomen for Women's Lib—what do you think of her insistence that she will not willingly associate with any man unless he has actually done something for the Movement?

GLORIA: I think she has always been uncomfortably ahead of her time, so she has been treated as if she were some kind of nut. But she is very fore-sighted and not at all a nut. What she is saying today, other women will be saying two to four years from now. When she says she won't associate with any man unless he has done something for the Movement, she means she won't associate with any man unless he is a humanist and as a humanist has done something about his beliefs. That makes sense to me.

Ti-Grace also was the first to understand that lesbianism is a very important issue because it's a bludgeon with which we always are beaten into conformity. If people call a woman a "lesbian," she's supposed to shrink and say, "Oh, no! Not me!"

You know, there's this whole propaganda about lesbians. Men in-sist that all they need is a good lay and then they'll be straight. The average man can't bear to think that a woman might prefer another woman to him, and he's threatened by a woman who obviously chooses to live without a man.

LIZ: Ti-Grace Atkinson has said that she trusts only women. Do you think that's radical?

GLORIA: Well, she is different. I don't trust men as a group either, though there are individual men I love and trust.

LIZ: Do you really trust women as a group more than men?

GLORIA: Yes. Women have nothing to gain, you see, by keeping the current, oppressive system going. But men have the real power. They have the money and they run the world. They have plenty to gain by keeping us down. It's not that women are more moral or have natural rhythm or are closer to the earth or any of that, but culturally women are less violent. They are less likely to feel they have to defeat people in order to prove themselves.

LIZ: You said something in one of your speeches about how women haven't had enough power yet to be spoiled by it, that for a little while, until both sex roles got equalized and humanized, women in power would be very healthy for the country.

GLORIA: Yes, I think all human beings have the same potential for hostility, aggression and violence. But for the next fifty or a hundred years women are going to be very valuable in positions of power, because we haven't been brainwashed into thinking our identities depend on violence and controlling others. I'd much prefer to have Margaret Mead in the White House than Nixon or Johnson. At least she wouldn't be having to prove her masculinity in Indochina.

LIZ: It seems to me that real change for women is very slow in coming. Will you comment on the Census Bureau report that says women of the '70s are rapidly moving to full equality? Do you believe that's true?

GLORIA: As you say, no. Not *rapidly*. We are just approaching the point of tokenism. Women may go to college, but most of them still end up as typ-ists. What the Census Bureau statistics show us is the large number of women who are working today. So the housewife, that vivid creature of the advertising agencies' imagination, is in the minority for the first time. More women who are married work outside the home today than before.

LIZ: I've noticed that some of the women in the Movement seem very angry. Vocal too. But are women in general angry?

GLORIA: I think so. But I think women inside the Movement are somewhat less angry than the women outside because the women outside are still suppressing their anger. Women in the Movement are free to talk about how they feel, and already that makes them happier. I mean, the more you suppress anger, the angrier you become. It's much better that a woman understand why she resents doing dishes, resents living on a level where she is reduced to baby talk, resents having to stay home while her husband is off doing something interesting. It's much better, that understanding, than painful submission for twenty years and then stabbing her husband with a butcher knife, or having a nervous breakdown because all the anger has been turned inward.

And that resentment exists on all social levels, not just for the middle-class, suburban housewife. A woman who has been working all her life and making about half what a man does for the same job is angry. Whether she is scrubbing floors in an office building or is made a token vice-president —if she is in an unequal situation, she is angry. And a woman is angry if she is condemned to be a secretary forever, has no chance for promotion, even if she is qualified. Or if a teacher sees herself passed over while men become chairmen of departments or get paid more for teaching the same classes.

Unless we admit that we are angry, it can be turned inward; it can cause depression, even suicide. If it is turned outward, at least the anger can be used constructively.

LIZ: Yes, you see that anger often in our divorce-alimony arrangements, don't you.

GLORIA: In this country alimony is like war reparations. They handle these things better in Sweden. Here in the United States if there's a divorce and there are children, a woman can try to skin her husband as far as alimony and child-support payments are concerned. In Sweden there is now the beginning of a very good system. When a couple is happily married and the woman is a housewife, she gets a legally determined percentage of her husband's salary. In case of divorce, both parties treat their breakup like the end of a business relationship. The woman receives a pension based on the percentage of her husband's salary she has been earning all along. She also gets a job-training allowance from the government so that the man doesn't have to go on paying her a pension forever. If there are children, both are responsible for their welfare.

LIZ: But in this country what if a family is barely able to get along on the husband's salary? What if it just scrapes by and there is no extra money to go to the wife as "salary"?

GLORIA: If a man does not or cannot make enough to pay for all the service he needs, then there should either be a strike against his employer or a supplemental income under a welfare plan. The other way, you see, means that both the man and his wife are being exploited by the man's employer. The employer is really getting the services of two for the price of one. We have to do away with all that. And we have to stop penalizing women, using them as a cheap labor force.

LIZ: What about the American word "togetherness" and the idea of people belonging to each other? You hear a lot about that in American romances.

GLORIA: You can't *own* another human being.

LIZ: So it's a different thing from, say, two people's being committed to each other?

GLORIA: Yes. You can need each other; you can support each other; you can complement each other. But you don't belong to each other. You belong to yourself. Women are not property—and neither are men.

LIZ: You've had love affairs with some extraordinary men, a few of whom I know. Several of your former lovers seem to have understood you very well. Are they just malleable types?

GLORIA: "Lovers" is a crazy, limited word. Let's say "friends."

LIZ: Okay, I withdraw that word. But where does this man who is more understanding fit in?

GLORIA: First of all, I'm not attracted to male chauvinists because I'm not a masochist, so I would never pick a man who would destroy me as a person. I am genuinely attracted to kind, sensitive, understanding men. I couldn't be attracted to a man who doesn't respect my work as much as I respect his, a man who wouldn't be willing to rearrange his life-style for my benefit as I would be willing to rearrange mine for him. I couldn't be attracted to a man who wasn't willing to become a human being, to give up the privileges that go with a white skin or that go with being a male. For instance, if he were to be promoted over a better-qualified woman or a nonwhite man, I would expect him to refuse the promotion—just as I would have to refuse a promotion over a better-qualified Black man on racial grounds.

LIZ: Are you romantic?

GLORIA: I'm sentimental. I don't know if I'm romantic.

LIZ: But will you concede that it's all right for a woman to be carried away by a bit of romantic emotion? For her to feel a weak-in-the-knees emotion about a man that might be the very antithesis of all your Women's Liberation ideas?

GLORIA: Yes, of course. Love exists. Men and women might both feel weak in the knees at times, as you say—and I believe two people can live together as loving and compassionate partners. Anything is possible between equals. But as soon as one person is more dependent than his or her partner, then all kinds of bad things happen—pretense and fear, for instance. Love really cannot exist between unequals.

LIZ: You make it sound so serious! Don't you think there's room in the world for play-acting and kidding around between men and women?

GLORIA: Only after there's equality, only when there are father-in-law jokes to go with mother-in-law jokes and jokes about dumb blond men who can't balance their checkbooks. Now the humor is often just an acceptable way of expressing prejudice.

LIZ: But do you think sex ever can be entirely equal? I mean, aren't there elements of adoration and worship, domination, mastery and submission, in lots of good sex?

GLORIA: I suppose an ideal world would be one where for every masochist there was a sadist. Well, if people want that kind of sex, it's all right with me. I just draw the line at taking pleasure in another's suffering, humiliation and subjugation or inequality. I suppose any kind of sex is good to the degree that it is natural to the person engaging in it and bad to the degree that it is imposed by society, convention or someone else's brainwashing.

LIZ: Still, isn't it possible, for instance, that the passive-active roles are attitudes of genuine enjoyment for some individuals?

GLORIA: They could be individual attitudes. But given the fact that they go so much with what our culture dictates, I'd say usually they are not.

LIZ: What about the leering *Playboy* approach to sex, breasts and so forth? If that turns certains girls on and certain guys on, what do you think about it?

GLORIA: Well, the *Playboy* kinds of men are still treating human beings like toys or objects; that's the problem. It's just as offensive the other way around. When a woman is interested only in going to bed, when she behaves in imitation of that kind of male, when she goes to bed with just anyone . . .

LIZ: I'm not talking about promiscuity or about anybody's hitting you with a whip. But what if a woman wants the man in her life to be dominant?

GLORIA: If it's a personal choice, fine. But when all your personal choices turn out to be the same as society's choices, I think you should examine yourself and your choices—all of them. For instance, when you see yourself choosing the so-called "female" course of study in school, like home economics; choosing a big engagement ring, an early marriage, two and a half children, a house in the suburbs, membership in the country club and a trip to Florida every year—you might stop to think that you could have been brainwashed into wanting just these things.

LIZ: I read a great interview with a young Jesuit who said he simply could not allow a commercial, merchandising society to force him to forsake celibacy because sex happens to be an "in" thing now. He wanted the choice to remain celibate—that's a form of sexual choice too.

GLORIA: Yes, it is. To remain single, not to have children, not to marry, to live communally or never to live with anyone or for a woman to live with another woman or a man to live with a man—all these should be honorable personal choices. We change as we live and grow, but because of what society is or says, we often end up thinking there is something wrong with us.

If you're not like the majority, there's nothing wrong with you. You're just changing and growing in some other way. That's a freedom we all should have. And believe me, the freer you are in general, the better you make love. Most men are so accustomed to submission that they don't know what co-operation might be like.

LIZ: I'm not sure that's true, Gloria. Freedom can mean bewilderment to some people.

GLORIA: Yes, like the freedom to be and enjoy your total self. Don't forget, for instance, that the idea of a woman's having an orgasm is new. It used to be the male's prerogative. To this day textbooks are still telling women about a kind of orgasm they are supposed to have that doesn't even exist. Advertising has misled men and women about sex too, but in other ways. The ads play into the "sex kitten" and "sex object" idea. They sell women and men a phony bill of goods about women. That's why you see on ads those stickers that read: "This ad insults women." People like ourselves have put them there.

LIZ: But if women's bodies are things of beauty, why does the Movement object to the use of nude women in ads?

GLORIA: Because you almost never see a nude male body in an ad. Only the woman is an "object" in this society. Man is the consumer.

LIZ: What do you think of the ads for Virginia Slims cigarettes? Or of a magazine like *Cosmopolitan?* Is the Movement just spinning its wheels when it attacks them? After all, ninety per cent of the *Cosmopolitan* staff are women, the magazine claims it's for Women's Lib and directs its attitudes, even if misguided, toward and for women.

GLORIA: Everybody is always saying politics is "out there" some place. Well, politics begins right here with the Virginia Slims ads and with magazines that sell us a bill of goods and with who's doing the typing and who's doing the cooking. That's politics. And we have to change our lives by changing whatever else needs changing—the ads or the women's magazines, most of which, in spite of their good intentions, still see women as phony vamps, sex objects or nothing more than housewives. They play into society's sick ideas of what relations between the sexes should be. *Cosmopolitan* is much less insulting to women than *Playboy,* but it still teaches women to trick and trap men—to be male-defined instead of self-defined.

LIZ: But isn't it more important to educate people than just attack some of these trivial things that aren't doing anything really except extending advertising myths?

GLORIA: *Except!* Liz! All the myths in popular culture are terribly important. They have brainwashed us. And children are especially subject to this influence. I think they are hurt by seeing women on television and in ads behaving like mental defectives. Also, when ads show only beautiful young women, children get the idea that all women are, or should be, young and beautiful, so that an older woman, an ugly woman, has no worth.

But the ads, phony as they are, are no phonier than our so-called labor laws to protect women. In most cases those laws are really restrictive and were never designed to protect. One law says a woman can't lift more than ten pounds. Ridiculous! Any woman with a child can lift more than ten pounds. There should be a weight-lifting test for both sexes to determine whether an individual is physically capable of doing a job. The category should not be based on sex but on ability.

LIZ: And about marriage? I gather you don't think much of marriage as an institution. Why? Can you elaborate?

GLORIA: Obviously I believe it is possible for two people to live together in a loving, equal partnership, but the legal institution of marriage works against that. It's still based on the old English legal principle that a married couple are one person and that person is the man.

When a woman marries she loses many of her civil rights. In some states she can't use her own name any more without her husband's permission; she can't establish a legal residence or sign a credit agreement or incorporate a business. It varies, but in every state she loses a large part of her civil rights, becomes a kind of legal child again. Men become legally responsible for another adult human being and they shouldn't have to be. So the law works against an equal, loving relationship because it makes you into unequals the minute you sign the license.

The whole principle is all-pervasive; it's all-*corrosive.* So "I now pronounce you man and wife" means "I now pronounce you person and role," like "man and dog." It should be "man and woman" or "husband and wife"—but not "man and wife." A lot of young people today are rewriting the marriage ceremony. But even when you do that and make promises to be equal partners, you are still stuck with the state laws.

LIZ: Don't you think thousands of women get married because they really want to be cared for, because they don't want to work in the sense of going to a job, because they feel inadequate for anything but marriage?

GLORIA: Yes, but that's a cultural problem. If women had a choice, if they were allowed to do in the world what men can do, I doubt that women would feel inadequate. The serious problem is condescension toward women and the assumptions that are made about women. And of course, as we've just said, that's what's wrong with most women's magazines. They are assuming that women don't know about the Movement or don't like it or that they all simply want to bury themselves in marriage.

LIZ: What about the way the magazines tout make-up and self-embellishment in general? Is there validity to the indignant remark made by Helen Gurley Brown, the editor of *Cosmopolitan?* She said it's all very well for *you* to say no woman should spend more than fifteen minutes on herself because you're beautiful and don't have to do all the things other girls have to do to look nice.

GLORIA: I don't think I'm beautiful. Anyway, what's *presentable* is the question! I think we all should spend a fair amount of time going totally without make-up to try to find out who we are. After that, time is the important factor. If women had all the time—and money—they've been brainwashed into spending on their appearance, we could have taken over the world by now.

LIZ: I suppose that also applies to your sensitivity about women's commenting on one another's clothes. You think that's a bad idea.

GLORIA: I think it's all right to have an authentic human reaction to something a friend might be wearing. If it's beautiful or a nice color or whatever, there's no reason not to comment. But we've been so brainwashed, we've been cast into roles where clothes and appearance are too important. So women who "ooh" and "ah" about clothes and make a great fuss about them are playing into the image so many men like to have of us—of "fluffy little things." To play into that role is actually to help in the dehumanizing of women, and we should stop it. Clothes and appearance should be of only relative importance, not the silly be-all and end-all that brainwashed women make them. Women journalists should stop writing about what's on women's backs and write about what's on their minds.

LIZ: Is Women's Liberation the last of the revolutions?

GLORIA: It's the first *and* the last—the most fundamental. It's moving now into a more activist stage. A National Women's Political Caucus was recently formed, for instance. It's an organization devoted to getting women into political office—not just "Uncle Tom" women, but women who will work on women's issues or, where that is not possible right now, will see to it that male candidates rise or fall on women's issues. It's a national organization, and local caucuses are now being formed in the states and counties. We have outlined the issues one by one: the reforming of tax laws and of marriage and abortion laws, getting child-care legislation passed. We are dedicated to supporting candidates who are against sexism, racism, poverty and violence. . . .

Candidates are afraid at the gut level that women will withdraw their support, because women have traditionally done all the work at the grassroots level. We have to warn these candidates that if they don't support our issues, we will work actively against them. And we have to get real commitments from candidates, because they'll say or promise anything to get elected. We want to see women at high levels in their own campaigns and parties.

SEXISM IN THE HEAD

Arlene Croce

Arlene Croce no doubt shares most of the aspirations of the women's liberation movement. Her target is the radical version of the liberationist credo. Ms. Croce is the editor of Ballet Review *and author of a book about American film musicals. Her spirited polemic suggests that women are far from united concerning their liberation.*

There is a point in life when every woman is a feminist. Generally it's in the college years when ideas have more glamor and excitement than they ever will have again, or in the first years out on a job, which teach the truth of feminist books and pamphlets. The men during those years are still there to be argued with; they haven't been drained off by marriage. And since feminism is the only idea a woman can really grasp in her nature, can *feel* without having to know very much about the history or literature of the movement, discussing the position of women with men is a good preliminary to (or substitute for) sleeping with them, a disguised way of discussing oneself. It makes life personal again at a time when the personality feels the first thrust of the world's indifference.

And it does so again later, after a divorce or two or a number of years without satisfaction in marriage or advancement in a career, but the men are now in short supply, and a woman who feels a sense of connection with feminist philosophy in her late twenties or early thirties is apt to feel isolated by it. The position has lost its sexiness; its capacity to illuminate life in personal terms has become a negative one. To a healthy woman it becomes a burden—she can move faster and farther without it; but to the less fortunate—those who can't expel the poisons of self-pity or sexual jealousy or utopian greed—feminism is a solipsistic haven, a place in the psyche where all the bad and bitter feelings unite, where unbearably personal failures are rationalized by a belief in organic failures in society. Feminism, because it is fundamentally self-expression with nothing outside the self to express, can be outgrown even when there remain feminist issues to be cleared up. At twenty it's useful and fulfilling to be a feminist; at thirty (and over) it's indulgent and wasteful and, at the present moment in history, not a little crazy.

The short but active history of the present feminist revival is pretty well documented in the library of books by and about women now pouring from the presses. The reason there are so many books is not that women never know when enough's enough; it's that their (mostly male) publishers don't. And the (mostly male) reviewers, who might have told them, have been astonishingly receptive. These men are perhaps feeling a little guilty and a little flattered at the same time by all the imprecations against "patriarchal society." Nobody has called them patriarchs in some time—they didn't know their own strength. But what the women who write the books know is that Women's Liberation, so-called, is the only movement that has to struggle full time to persuade its constituents of their need to be liberated. The books are written not only by and about but *to* women. No intelligent man can be expected to keep his head in these gaseous effluvia compounded of reason and unreason, solid premise and hysterical deduction, legitimate gripe and invincible myth. The outstanding failure of Women's Liberation is that it has enlisted no outstanding men. It has no Havelock Ellises or John Stuart Mills. That may be because it is not a liberation movement at all but an attempt to mobilize vengeance, and the more explicitly anti-male it becomes, the more corrupt becomes its core protest. On one level it's a losing fight. Measures which might have had efficacy when applied to proximate irritations, like job discrimination, lose all their force. But on another level it's no contest at all. This blundering chauvinism encounters no resistance— nothing *formidable*. It crushes the living animus out of every decent relationship that men and women have been able to contrive. If a woman can't say "I hate men" (and I don't know an honest woman who hasn't said it sometimes) without feeling like part of a slaves' rebellion, then she *is* a slave, in thrall to a worse orthodoxy than the one her "sisters" want to liberate her from.

Men in a position to do something about sexual discrimination are paradoxically relieved of their obligations by a campaign so absurdly far-flung. If nothing less than a "revolution in consciousness," sweeping away that most repressive of male inventions, the family, will suffice to end the miseries of women, then what's one employer, one Congressman, one welfare supervisor, union official, civil-liberties lawyer to do in the meantime? He may presumably raise his consciousness by reading Women's Lib books and articles, in which every knock is a caress. If man really invented the family, then every rabbitty commuter scurrying for the 8:05 that will take him to a detestable job can relax a little in Steig-like dreams of glory. "Man is the oppressor!" What ego-satisfactions in the clank of that rusty old cowbell. Or, alternatively: "Man is not the oppressor! Woman's liberation is also the liberation of man" (provided man is homosexual, an extra-marital cheat, a begetter of illegitimate children, a patron of prostitutes, or involved in other sexually nefarious ways with women he doesn't respect).

The radicals of Women's Lib have all but preempted the field of argument with their titillating visions of patriarchal dominance, brutality, and male conspiracy. And because they don't believe in individual responsibility—they are, almost to a woman, suprasocialists with a fixed view of sex as the basis of class struggle (Kate Millet, in *Sexual Politics*,[1] adapting Engels: "Thus all the mechanisms of human inequality arose out of the foundations of male supremacy and the subjection of women, sexual politics serving historically as the foundation of all other social, political, and economic structures")—they don't believe in individual solutions either, only communal ones. Even Betty Friedan, who in the present state of things might be thought of as a moderate, rejects the idea that women can assert themselves as individual human beings *now* without waiting for ideological aid and counsel from Betty Friedan. In *Voices of the New Feminism*[2] she speaks of such women as "token spokeswomen" and "Aunt Toms," and writes, "We are beginning to know that no woman can achieve a real breakthrough alone, as long as sex discrimination exists in employment, under the law, in education, in mores, and in denigration of the image of women." As long (in short) as society remains imperfect. Yet in spite of all these horrors a great many women, in middle-class white America especially, have gone along for years achieving all kinds of "real" breakthroughs (you can only make a false breakthrough in something that doesn't resist). Mrs. Friedan is thought by some people to have made one herself.

Because they don't recognize a biological base for the distinctions commonly made between men's and women's social roles, many advocates of Women's Lib look on the classic institutions of our society as a series of tricks played on women by men. They see Western civilization, which sponsored and thrived on the patriarchal nuclear family, as an artificial construct enabling men to gain and keep power at the expense of women, and they really think they can turn the whole thing around by abolishing the family with its invidious power equation (Patriarchy equals Paternity plus Property), setting up communes, relegating child care to "professionals" (whether men or women), and reprogramming the attitudes of male and female children toward sex. They think all this is not only desirable but possible and who knows, they may be right. We live in strange times. Only eighteen months ago these notions were the hallucinations of a lunatic fringe. Now they are the common trash of daily conversation, part of the polluted air we breathe. In New York, where educated people profess boredom with feminist revolt, it is easier to get an abortion than equal pay for equal work.

The radicalization of mass consciousness now under way is introducing—I am trying to put it into words the sisterhood will understand—a mass opiate, and here is a slogan for it: Revolution is reaction to reform. One of the difficulties of dealing with revolutionary feminism is that it is

---

[1] Doubleday.

[2] Edited by Mary Lou Thompson, Beacon Press.

intellectually inane—little more than a feeling of persecution dressed up as a *Weltanschauung*. These massive revolutionary formulas that are supposed to stun the opposition and only give it a high instead—of what do they consist? The stereotypes of 1930's Marxism plus a little Wilhelm Reich plus a lot—rather too much—of Masters and Johnson, who are the unofficial mentors of Women's Lib as Marcuse was of the student Left and Fanon of the black liberation movements. The capitalist-militarist-imperialist-racist society has now become male chauvinist as well. As a set of ideas Women's Lib is about as creative and inspiring as a set of Tinker Toys, and women who like to busy themselves with mechanical playthings may properly be said, I think, to be regressing. In their books they even sound mechanical—toneless, like children repeating their lessons about the great revolution to come. In Simone de Beauvoir's *The Second Sex,* which raised the consciousness of the 50's, all feminist roads led to socialism, but de Beauvoir's position was an expression of her total personality as a writer. Some of these neo-feminist tracts seem to have been written by computers. In *The Dialectic of Sex,*[3] a self-declared disciple of de Beauvoir, Shulamith Firestone, concocts a futuristic vision of "cybernetic socialism" from which I excerpt one facet, that dealing with love and sexual freedom as they affect the child (we must assume the family to have withered away):

> . . . If a child does not know his own mother, or at least does not attach a special value to her over others, it is unlikely that he would choose her as his first love object, only to have to develop inhibitions on this love. It is possible that the child might form his first close physical relationship with people his own size out of sheer physical convenience, just as men and women, all else being equal, might prefer each other over those of the same sex for sheer physical fit. But even if he should happen to pick his own genetic mother, there would be no *a priori* reasons for her to reject his sexual advances, because the incest taboo would have lost its function. The "household," a transient social form, would not be subject to the dangers of inbreeding.

Talk about regression! This is not socialism, "cybernetic" or otherwise. This is the forest primeval. These primitive paradises where no inhibitions whatever are practiced resemble no primitive society that ever existed (for long). They also have a way of resembling those infantile utopias of escapist fiction where sex is never mentioned and nobody misses it. In the Tinker Toy paradise everything is missing *except* sex. (Note how the sexes come together—not for passion but for "sheer physical fit.") Everything that limits the release of the libido is purged. Thus the family. Thus the incest taboo. Miss Firestone is telling us that mothers should have genital

---

[3] Morrow.

sex with their sons lest they grow up repressed or homosexual (though why that should matter, when polymorphously perverse sexuality is the norm for all, isn't clear). Furthermore, she is telling us that they should have genital *intercourse* (although how coitus between an adult woman and a male child comes to be mutually desirable or even thinkable isn't clear either). To revoke the incest taboo, which applies legally only in cases where penetration has taken place, is to revoke the family, is to revoke the whole concept of motherhood except in the genetic sense. Even here, too, there are some severe qualifications, for in Miss Firestone's paradise young Oedipus is more than likely to be a test-tube baby.

Here is where Women's Lib goes off the cliff. The incest taboo (and Miss Firestone surely knows it) is based not on biological fears of inbreeding but on an almost universal compulsion to extend the family's relations with society. It is enforced in many primitive societies where nothing is known of heredity and almost nothing of the connection between the father and fertility. Since the principal evil of patriarchy, for the feminists, is male tyranny based on male succession, can patriarchy be said to exist when paternity is in doubt? (Even the normally headlong Miss Millett stops short here.) If not, and if the incest taboo is neither biological nor sexual-political, might there not be some reason for retaining it in a society not dominated by men? No again. *All* families, even matriarchies, must go. Then the feminist complaint is perhaps biological after all? Yes, says Miss Firestone, and I quote her italics: *"Pregnancy is barbaric."* Breakthrough.

Whoever said women were not logical? They are fiercely logical. It is their most depressing trait as thinkers. As Nietzsche said, nothing is a truth that doesn't contain at least one laugh, but these women seem to think that whatever follows logically, even unto the annihilation of all reason, must be truth. The New Feminists don't seem to know when they're being funny, or when they're really thinking independently and not just reacting to men. Radical Women's Liberation was born from the rib of civil-rights activism, much as the 19th-century women's rights movement had sprung from abolitionism. The militant British suffragists who chained themselves to lamp-posts have their modern counterparts in the young women who sit-in and disrupt traffic. Where the old girls threw off their corsets and wore bloomers, *we* are bra-less and wear pants suits. But here the resemblance to historical feminism ends. And so it should, say the New Feminists. The old-time feminists may have been anti-marriage, some of them; some may even have been anti-family. But they made the mistake (yes, mistake—see footnote) of narrowing their objectives to civil rights, of campaigning for the same privileges men enjoyed instead of trying to erase the functional distinctions upon which those privileges rested. And so, when they got the vote, all further protest was pinched off.

Let us not pause to wonder how the militant women of the 1960's and 1970's could ever have expected those of the 1880's and 1890's to anticipate them.[4] The women who can say "Freud was a sexist" are the same women who can say, as so many militant men do, "Abraham Lincoln was a racist." Anti-historicism is a contemporary cultural disease and a feature of the insane logic of the young. But the parallels between "racism" and "sexism," both of them manifestations of the New Left paranoia that has arisen within the last five years (and symbiotically linked in Yoko Ono's remark, "Woman is the nigger of the world"), should interest us. America is "a racist nation"; even more it is "a sexist nation." Women were the first slaves and they are the last (WL thinks wives should be paid for doing housework and taking care of children). When the New Left embraced violence, the girls in the movement found that they were up front where police could club them on television and in the back room the rest of the time, functioning as secretaries and sex partners. These are the girls who radicalized Women's Lib, turning it into a (jealous?) parody of the Black Power movement and reacting in monkey-see, monkey-do fashion to men as separatist blacks were reacting to whites.

The title of the bible of lumpen rad-lib, *Sisterhood Is Powerful,* is a play on "black is beautiful" (though you'll never hear a white sister say, "I, a woman, am beautiful." Unlike black women, who have a stake in the reconstitution of the black family, she rejects the hypocritical homage of the master sex). Along with Kate Millett, many of the contributors to this volume feel they can assail prejudice based on sexual distinctions in the same way that they assail prejudice based on racial ones—as if admitting that women (or Negroes) are different from men (or whites) would be giving prejudice a blank check. In this I think they are doubly wrong, and of course it is now fashionable—at the express wish of Black Power groups—to grant that racial differences do indeed exist and to recognize them in a form of cultural apartheid. This inconsistency doesn't seem to bother the feminist ideologues. They had discovered no egalitarianism on the Left, not even

---

[4] For some of the New Feminists, the women's movement began to go wrong as early as 1848, when Elizabeth Cady Stanton and Lucretia Mott called the convention at Seneca Falls, N.Y. that issued the Seneca Falls Declaration of Rights and Sentiments. "Although it [the Declaration] conveys a vivid sense of the depth, pervasiveness, and subtlety of women's oppression, as well as of its legal manifestations, it conspicuously avoids an analysis of the family, and of the connection between woman's primary responsibilities there, and her exclusion from public life. To question the sacred rightness of the family, and women's place in it, would have brought upon these women a storm of outrage far beyond what they actually suffered. Feminist imagination, which envisaged radically new forms of dress, rebelled at the traditional marriage ceremony and the surrender of the maiden name, attacked established religion and male dominance of education and the professions—the fearless feminist imagination balked at an attack on the family. Although the early feminists cannot be accused of the mistake of the later ones in concentrating solely on the ballot as the key to equality, they dared only to insist on sharing public life with men—not to insist on men's sharing the burdens of home and family."—Connie Brown and Jane Seitz, "You've Come a Long Way, Baby" in *Sisterhood Is Powerful* (edited by Robin Morgan, Random House.

on the black Left. Stokely Carmichael had said, "The only position for women in SNCC is prone." The racist plague faded rather quickly into the sexist terror without changing its basic character as a system of *political* oppression dedicated to perpetuating mythological differences between people. The girls seem to feel they are more like Women the less like "women" they behave: taking karate in men's classes, using foul language (in the *Sisterhood* collection of pieces, those by high-school girls are more belligerent than those by lesbians; if this is the way they talk to their boyfriends, then there's no sexiness in feminism at any age), adopting the adversary style of Black Power, which at the time of the split with the male Left was the most powerful adversary style around. While the feminist movement has yet to produce a flaming heroine on a par with Bernadette Devlin, the current media favorite—and successor to James Baldwin, LeRoi Jones, Eldridge Cleaver, and Bobby Seale—is Angela Davis. Girls have the real *machismo* spirit.

Another thing that was around at the time was *Human Sexual Response*. It is darkly suspected in Women's Lib circles that people who bought the book were so shocked by the findings on the clitoral orgasm that they clammed up about it for fear of toppling the male power structure. Certainly men can't be accused of suppressing the book; it was a best-seller, front-page news, and there were paperback trots to explain the technical language. Yet life goes on as before, a male-dominated hell. Women's Lib's answer to this has been to make the clitoral orgasm its winged victory, its revolutionary torch of truth. You cannot pick up a piece of Lib propaganda without coming across it, nor can you escape the polemical logic within which its value to the movement is as tightly sealed as a desert flower in a cube of Lucite.

Dr. Alice S. Rossi writes (in *Voices of the New Feminism*): "Implicit in both psychological theory of sex differences and the Freudian vaginal-orgasm theory was a basic assumption that women should be exclusively dependent on men for their sexual pleasure, hiding from view the realization that masturbation may be different from, but not necessarily less gratifying sexually than, sexual intercourse." (This is putting it mildly. What was "hidden from view," until Masters and Johnson, was that a female with the aid of an electric vibrator could achieve twenty to fifty orgasms in a single hour.) Susan Lydon (in *Sisterhood Is Powerful*): "The definition of normal feminine sexuality as vaginal . . . was a part of keeping women down, of making them sexually, as well as economically, socially and politically subservient." Kate Millett: ". . . the conditions of patriarchal society have had such profound effects upon female sexuality that its function has been drastically affected, its true character long distorted and long unknown. This is remarkable evidence of culture's ability to affect physiology." But is it? Where is the evidence that female sexuality has been "distorted" and "unknown"? Distorted by what standards, unknown to whom? Apart from the fact that social conditioning actively discourages masturbation in the male as well as in the female, what is there to show that women—half the human race—ever accepted the definition of their sexuality as vaginal or ever supposed they were operating in intercourse without a clitoris? Not all of them read Freud and go to analysis. Not all of them know men who do, either. That sex education doesn't stress the existence of the clitoris (another scrap of feminist "evidence") is less a reflection of Freudian error than of the fact that sex education is concerned with human reproduction, in which the clitoris plays no part. It wouldn't even if we got rid of the family. Even if we found a way for women to have their babies in bottles—like those artificial wombs scientists have already grown sheep in—the sperm would still have to travel up the river from New Orleans. I see no mark of patriarchal oppression in satisfying the curiosity of children on this point. Sex education in the schools is anyway a very recent development. What about those of us, those many millions of us, who never were formally sexually-educated— who "got it in the streets"? This is supposed to be horrible, yet is it likely that we would have learned from our little boyfriends and girlfriends that one sex was meant to be subservient to the other? The sexuality of young children is still very much underrated. I suspect "street" experiences are much more common, occur earlier, and leave a more lasting impression of the physiology of sex than the formal acquaintance with biological facts which is what most people mean when they talk about sex education. . . . It is one thing to say that male misconceptions of female sexuality have caused confusion and upset, and even—it would be fair to say—that they have caused neurotic confusion and upset. But it is nonsense to insist that they constitute a system of oppression from which we can find no escape in society as we know it. The total genital orientation of so much feminist thinking on sex is really remarkable, and it's totally non-erotic, tasteless, vegetable sex, too. This insensitive, "strong" stuff isn't the transparent bravado of girls trying to act tough; they *are* tough, and the first thought that occurs to you is how in the world anyone would manage to oppress them— just let him try. The second thought is, what contempt for women. The picture we get of women is a misogynist's delight: creatures so stupidly submissive to male authority in all things we wonder why we are supposed to think them worth rescuing.

The humiliated woman, the woman as weakling, as victim, keeps turning up in Kate Millett's book—not in her account of Victorian thought and literature, which produces some samples of a rebellious and sane feminism, but in the chapters on contemporary society. She doesn't look very hard at the world we live in. Her "literary reflection" consists of the works of Henry Miller, Norman Mailer, and D. H. Lawrence. (Poor Lawrence! First de Beauvoir and now Millett. The only woman to show him mercy has been Katherine Anne Porter, who called him a "panting, agonized man.") In Jean Genet, of whom she approves, she finds a ringing affirmation of the male principle in all its vicious splendor. Here, she says, in the parody world of the homosexual, a world of sadistic pimps and masochistic queens, is the truth about "masculine" and "feminine" roles in the straight world. . . . Nothing from Cheever, O'Hara, Styron, Salinger, or Updike—just to mention some Americans besides Miller and Mailer; no Europeans besides Lawrence; nothing from Proust, the greatest homosexual artist of the century. And—incredibly—nothing from a woman writer. If the aim is to present the literary reflection of society's attitudes toward women, surely we might look at the writings of women.

Miss Millett's literary preferences are very odd, not merely because they keep presenting the same disconcerting sexual image over and over, but because they reveal an apparent need to believe somehow that the lowest and most violent forms of sexual expression represent the truth about heterosexual relations. Miss Millett takes pornographic description literally and this leads her astray. No matter how wild or ludicrous the event—and in the Miller section you laugh even while reading her scornful denunciations—she believes she is handing us an instance of caste and conquest. Nothing that happens between the sexes is exempt from such categorization. If you were to say to Miss Millett, "Jack fell down and broke his crown and Jill came tumbling *after*," she would say, "A clear case of sexual politics," and carefully note the double significance of the word "crown." We have lately learned that she is a homosexual and the knowledge is worth a great deal to the opposition—such knowledge always is—but not if it thinks it puts her, and those of her sisters who may yet come out as lesbians, safely back in their places.

For what are their places? Do they now retire from the stage? The stars of the show?

There is no doubt that *Sexual Politics* has had an impact. Elegantly furnished with scholarly trophies—it is in fact a doctoral thesis—and written with furious energy, it was an apologia the critics could take seriously at just the time when the movement needed something to take the public's mind off the ugly women screaming on talk shows. But it is no different in substance from the main bulk of Women's Lib propaganda. As I said at the beginning of this article, feminism is just a way of talking about oneself; ideologically, it can be anything you want to make it. There is no reason why the ideological content of the present feminist revival could not be lesbianism or, as it might with more circumspection call itself, bisexuality. Much as we might cringe from such a prospect, could it be worse than what we are going through right now? And there might be some abatement in tension if the next batch of books by aggrieved women (for they *will* go on writing these testaments—it's a tenet of feminism that every woman is a philosopher) could be informally grouped around some such forthright theme as "My Life with Mary Ann" instead of "Feeling Insulted as a Woman."

It would be good if all those fed-up wives, indignant earth mothers, abused secretaries, and hounded sex objects declared themselves. If those others would all go visit them once in a while—those newly fixated on the subject of orgasm, those bemused by the new life-styles, those whimperers to whom any behavior is feminine except delivering a baby, and, above all, those who say, "I can't imagine what lesbians *do* . . ."—it would be almost as great a blessing as the perfect Pill.

And such perfect logic, too.

7

Pornography and Its Control

What is pornography? We have traveled a long distance since Walter Hines Page, then with Doubleday, Page and Co., refused to publish a book which contained the word "chaste" because it was too "suggestive." The Massachusetts Supreme Court would not now sustain the conviction of a publisher for selling Theodore Dreiser's *An American Tragedy* as it did in 1930. Even so, it was only yesterday that *Lady Chatterley's Lover* became available to American readers (pirated editions were sold, of course, from the beginning); and it was only a day before yesterday that producers of the motion picture version of *A Street-car Named Desire* were persuaded to delete the last three words from a line in the Tennessee Williams play that reads, "I would like to kiss you softly and sweetly on the mouth."

In a book he wrote in 1927 about Anthony Comstock, Heywood Broun reminded his readers that sex is not an invention of the novelists, not even the modern ones. "Both the fundamentalists and the evolutionists agree," Broun wrote, "that the scheme has at least the merit of antiquity. Anthony Comstock may have been entirely correct in his assumption that the division of living creatures into male and female was a vulgar mistake, but a conspiracy of silence about the matter will hardly alter the facts."[1]

---

[1] *Anthony Comstock* (New York: A. & C. Boni, Inc., 1927), p. 274. Written with Margaret Leech. This, with *The Censor Marches On* by Morris L. Ernst and Alexander Lindey, is a good account of early difficulties with the censors. Comstock, a professional anti-vice crusader who devoted himself chiefly to the suppression of what he regarded as salacious literature, was primarily responsible for the notorious Comstock Laws of 1873.

Today, nearly all responsible people will applaud Broun's verdict, and, with motion pictures dealing in such taboo themes as Lesbianism, incest, and even child molestation, and mass-circulation periodicals using words heretofore banned in all except the most vulgar company, the day of permissiveness has dawned. Even so, the nature of obscenity and its control remains controversial.

If the canon ecclesiastical lawyers did not spell out the meaning of the word "obscene," says Father Gardiner, this was because they did not conceive that the word was complicated or obscure. They took it for granted, as it were, that the word was rather self-evident." But Father Gardiner concedes that "in a pluralistic society such as ours" the problem *has* arisen, and he therefore defines obscenity in a book or painting as "the intrinsic tendency or bent of the work to arouse sexual passion, or, to put it more concretely, the motions of the genital apparatus which are preparatory to the complete action of sexual union." Father Gardiner adds that "a particular work . . . may not always and in all circumstances so arouse this or that individual. It is not so much a matter of the individual's own reaction here and now as the nature of the work under consideration . . . it must, of its nature, be such as actually to arouse in the viewer or reader such venereal pleasure."[2]

Psychologists Eberhard Kronhausen and Phyllis Kronhausen disagree. They distinguish between erotic realism and pornography: "In pornography . . . the main purpose is to stimulate erotic response in the reader. And that is all. In erotic realism, truthful description of the basic realities of life is of the essence. . . ." And, ". . . if while writing realistically on the subject of sex the author succeeds in moving his reader, this too is erotic realism, *and it is axiomatic that the reader should respond erotically to such writing,* just as the sensitive reader will respond, perhaps by actually crying, to a sad scene . . ."[3]

Pondering such differing views of obscenity and recalling that reproductions of Goya's famous Nude (or Naked) Maja decorate an official postage stamp in Catholic Spain whereas in "pluralistic" America reproductions were banned in the mails, we may turn for enlightenment to the U.S. Supreme Court or the report of the federal Commission on Obscenity and Pornography. The commission, provided by Congress with a two-million-dollar budget, concluded that government "should not seek to interfere with the

---

[2] Harold C. Gardiner, S.J., *Catholic Viewpoint on Censorship,* Image Books Edition (Garden City, N.Y.: Doubleday & Company, Inc., 1961), pp. 64–65.

[3] *Pornography and the Law* (New York: Ballantine Books, Inc., 1959), p 18. With an introduction by Dr. Theodore Reik.

right of adults who wish to do so to read, obtain, or view explicit sexual materials." The Supreme Court, on June 21, 1973, reversed a decade-long trend toward permissiveness and, in its controversial decisions of that date, declared that the determination of obscenity and its legality shall be left in effect to local option, and that juries and courts no longer need find that material is "utterly" without redeeming social value before they declare it obscene and subject to proscription. Excerpts from majority and dissenting opinions are included below.

Whatever the verdict of courts and commissions, to say that pornography and obscenity should be free from legal prohibition—at least so far as consenting adults are concerned—does not preclude moral judgment even in the absence of evidence indicating a "clear and present danger." It may well be that no solid evidence links obscenity with violent crime. If we conclude that legal curbs on the access of consenting adults to the obscene and pornographic are unjustified, are we not perhaps underestimating the importance of sex by ignoring consequences of its debasement that may be even more adverse than occasional acts of violence? In any event, issues more important than the pornography-obscenity question are involved here: the extent to which government action against freedom of expression in this area sets a precedent for restraint on expression in other areas; the extent to which government should act in the area of so-called victimless crimes (e.g., drug use [see below, pp. 371-90], prostitution, etc.); the related although broader and more fundamental question of the extent to which the community should use legal sanctions to control the conduct of its members or rely on other methods of social control.[4]

---

[4] Before 1957, the U.S. Supreme Court guided itself by the so-called Hicklin test of obscenity, which was first affirmed in 1868 in England by Lord Chief Justice John Campbell: "Whether the tendency of the matter charged . . . is to deprave and corrupt those whose minds are open to such immoral influences, and into whose hands . . . [it] may fall." Typical of works suppressed by this test were Hemingway's *For Whom the Bell Tolls*, Lillian Smith's *Strange Fruit* and Tolstoy's *Kreutzer Sonata*. In its famous *Roth-Alberts* decision (June 24, 1957) the Court, while affirming the constitutionality of obscenity laws, rejected the Hicklin test declaring that the test of obscenity is "Whether to the average person, applying contemporary community standards, the dominant theme of the material taken as a whole appeals to prurient interest." Hailed by the censors, the Court had in fact liberalized the test of obscenity as became clear in a series of decisions in which movies like *The Moon Is Blue* and books like Miller's *Tropics* and Lawrence's *Lady Chatterley* were given constitutional protection. However, on March 21, 1966, in three historic decisions, the Court upheld obscenity convictions in the cases of Ralph Ginzburg, publisher of *Eros,* and Edward Mushkin, a Times Square bookseller, while reversing a lower-court ruling that *Fanny Hill,* the eighteenth-century minor classic, is obscene. The significance of the Ginzburg-Mushkin decisions is the Court's finding that the context of a work's production and sales promotion is relevant. That is to say, the manner in which a purveyor promotes a work may bring it under a ban as when

the redoubtable Mr. Ginzburg sought out the town of Intercourse (Pa.) for a frank-
ing permit and, denied one there, settled for Middlesex (N.J.).

THE OBSCENITY MUDDLE

Paul Bender

*Although written several months before the June 1973 deci-
sions of the U.S. Supreme Court, the following article affords
an interesting insight into the efforts of that court to cope with
the problem of obscenity. Paul Bender is professor of law at
the University of Pennsylvania Law School. He was general
counsel to the federal Commission on Obscenity and Pornography.*

Seven years ago the Supreme Court adopted a narrow standard for
obscenity under which the pornographic classic, *Fanny Hill,* could not be
constitutionally banned. Moved to prophecy by his victory, *Fanny Hill*'s
lawyer, Charles Rembar, wrote a book, *The End of Obscenity,* that pre-
dicted a new era in American law when virtually no literature would be forbidden as "obscene." With the lifting of legal restraints, he argued, all sorts
of explicit sexual material would enter the open marketplace, and "the kind
of response in the reader—shocked or aroused or guilty—that marks what
we are accustomed to call obscene will begin to disappear."

It hasn't happened quite that way. To be sure, the *Fanny Hill* decision was followed by an outpouring of commercial erotica. And in 1970
the federal Commission on Obscenity and Pornography urged a limit to
legal obscenity by recommending that government "should not seek to interfere with the right of adults who wish to do so to read, obtain, or view
explicit sexual materials." Yet obscenity laws that do just that remain
on the books almost everywhere. Prosecutors still seek convictions—and
jail sentences—for the crime of marketing the "obscene" to those who wish
to obtain it.

Even more important, our elected leaders seem unwilling to let the
obscenity concept disappear from the popular mind. The Senate, in an election year, overwhelmingly rejected the obscenity commission's recommendation so quickly that few, if any, Senators could have read the extensive

research and findings on which it was based. President Nixon "categorically" denounced the commission's "morally bankrupt" conclusion: "So long as I am in the White House, there will be no relaxation of the national effort to control and eliminate smut from our national life." And last term the Supreme Court, although reversing a conviction, seemed to use a more inclusive test for what is "obscene" than the one applied in *Fanny Hill*. The Court even went out of its way to note that "the earmarks of an attempt at serious art," while relevant in deciding what is permissible, are "not inevitably a guarantee against a finding of obscenity." Only two Justices—William Douglas and Potter Stewart—declined to join in this opinion.

It appears that a new crisis in the law of obscenity is upon us. The Court now has before it several cases that raise a broad range of constitutional issues. On the one hand, the Court is being asked formally to reject the *Fanny Hill* test in favor of a standard that would permit much of the recent sexual explosion to be considered "obscene." On the other, it is being asked to give constitutional status to the obscenity commission's recommendation—to hold, in sum, that the Constitution prohibits government from preventing adults from privately seeing whatever sexual materials they wish, whether or not such materials are "obscene." Also before the Court are some interesting subsidiary issues, such as the procedures that police must follow in seizing allegedly obscene material. The Court's decisions in these cases may actually begin the end of obscenity—or they may give renewed life, for who knows how long, to that slippery concept.

Almost no one has a good word to say for the present state of obscenity law. To anti-pornography groups, a constitutional standard under which *Fanny Hill* can be openly sold to adults represents legal and moral anarchy. To libertarians, it is equally obnoxious that the state can still ban a book or film without demonstrating any danger to anyone, simply because of its explicit sexual contents. Tempers and feelings often run high. The outrage of both sides is compounded by law-enforcement efforts that are viewed as either too lax or too zealous, depending upon one's point of view.

The point on which everyone agrees is that the Supreme Court's tests for what is "obscene" are exquisitely obscure and incoherent. The *Fanny Hill* test requires, for example, that three elements must "coalesce" for "obscenity" to be present: the dominant theme of a book or film must appeal to a "prurient" (defined as a "shameful" or "morbid") interest in sex; the work must be "patently offensive" in the light of "contemporary community standards"; and it must be "utterly" without "redeeming social value." Who can say what sexual materials others will find shameful, offensive, or valueless, and why, in any case, should those who want to buy a book be prevented from doing so by the fact that others find it obnoxious? In actual practice the application of the Court's three criteria turns on the aesthetic, moral, and psychological judgments of the particular policemen, prosecutors, judges, and jurors who enforce the law against specific materials. Such personalized judgments about so volatile a subject hardly provide a satisfactory basis upon which to ban books and send people to jail.[1]

How did the law become so muddled? The answer goes back to 1957, when the Supreme Court first got around to weighing the constitutionality of obscenity laws in the famous case of *Roth* v. *U.S.* In that case, the Court committed a serious tactical and judgmental error, I think, and thus far it has not been able to extricate itself from the consequences.

When the Justices considered *Roth*, laws forbidding "obscene" sexual materials were about a hundred years old. The basic constitutional argument against them was quite straightforward: material deemed "obscene" nonetheless consists of books, films, and other forms of expression that ordinarily are entitled to the protection of the First Amendment—unless they are shown to create a "clear and present danger" of substantial harm to society. But, the argument continued, obscenity statutes fail to require proof of harm by the prosecution, and no one has ever shown that any class of sexual materials, no matter how defined, creates a clear and present danger to anyone.[2]

The Court didn't answer this argument—it avoided it. It held that the clear and present danger test did not apply to "obscenity" because history showed that the First Amendment had never been intended to include

---

[1] Curiously enough, the two groups (aside from the professional anti-pornographers) who may profit most from the law's current uncertainty are some purveyors of sexual materials and some candidates for public office—the purveyors because obscenity prosecutions, which are dismissed or reversed in court, can sometimes be very good for sales; the candidates because the supposed failings of incumbents or judges, in applying present law, can make a very good campaign issue.

[2] Hold on, you anti-smut crusaders. I know you have lots of "evidence" that persons arrested for sex crimes have had sexual materials in their possession. But the relevant statistic is not how many offenders read dirty books (no one really knows how many do), but whether people who read such books are more likely to commit crimes than people who do not. Before the obscenity commission was established, neither you nor anyone else had ever done extensive research on the subject. The commission tried, and one study done for it showed that adult sex offenders and "deviates" actually had *less* exposure to sexual materials during adolescence than a carefully matched control group. (Does that mean that we should require that obscenity be read?) But even if sex offenders *did* see more obscenity than the rest of us, that would only show a correlation, not a cause-and-effect relationship. It would be quite plausible that people who are perpetually inclined to sex crimes are, for the same reason, also excessively inclined to sexual materials. (Some people think that sexual materials often provide a harmless release for such persons.) Of course, sexual material may, now and then, trigger an act of violence (although no one, to my knowledge, has ever found such a case). But so may detective stories, *The Godfather*, the Bible, and who knows what else. We don't ban these things because a clear and present danger means a high degree of probability of harm, not a one-in-a-million possibility. If a freak possibility of harm from a book were enough, none of us would be able to read anything. (The obscenity commission, incidentally, concluded that "extensive empirical investigation . . . provides no evidence that exposure to or use of explicit sexual materials play a significant role in the causation of social or individual harms. . . ."

"obscene" materials within its protection. It buttressed this conclusion by noting a "universal" legal judgment "that obscenity should be restrained." As a result, the Court said that the distribution of "obscene" things may, *ipso facto,* be prohibited by any legislature that so wishes—no danger, no harm whatever need be shown.

The Court's sense of history was faulty. In fact, the offense of publishing explicit sexual materials did not fully evolve in either England or the United States until about 1850. None of the Colonies except Massachusetts had statutes regulating sexual "obscenity." The first American obscenity prosecution of any kind occurred thirty years after the First Amendment (the first federal statute wasn't passed until 1842), and the English common law of 1800 seemed to prohibit only anti-religious sexual materials.

The Court's constitutional theory was worse than its history. We simply do not believe that the meaning of the First Amendment was fixed by the understanding of the Framers in 1791 as to what could and could not be published or said. They probably thought that profanity, blasphemy, and libel of political figures were broadly prohibitable, but the First Amendment generally protects those things today. And the Court should not have needed to be reminded about the fallibility of "universal" legal judgments.

Finally, even if the First Amendment's relatively absolute protection was, indeed, inapplicable to "obscenity" on historical or other grounds, the Court should not have relieved those who wished to ban books from showing at least some legitimate reason for doing so and from coming up with an understandable definition of what exactly they wished to prohibit. Rationality and clarity are requisites of any law that substantially invades men's liberty—especially the liberty to read.

So the Court in 1957 created a monster: a thing—the "obscene"— that could be prohibited for no other reason than the "facts" that it always had been and everyone thought it should be. But how was this thing to be defined in the absence of proof that it caused any harm? Only by individualized judgments about propriety, morality, and "value." Is it any wonder that the definitional problem has been so impenetrable ever since?

This is not to say that the Court in 1957 should have forbidden any regulation of sexual materials under any circumstances. That would have been just as abstract a decision as the Court actually made—and just as wrong. What the Court should have perceived is that there is no single thing called "obscenity" but many different things deserving different governmental responses.

Pushing explicit sex in the faces of those who would rather not see it—and who may be deeply disturbed by seeing it—is quite a different thing from selling such materials to those who want them. Selling to twelve-year-olds whose parents object is miles apart from selling to married, middle-aged couples. Sex mixed with violence may be worse than depictions of sex alone. Those who wished to regulate such phenomena in various ways—it is almost inconceivable that any government today would want to treat them all alike—should have been told to give their reasons in each instance, and to draft coherent and understandable definitions reflecting those reasons. It is likely that the abstract obscenity monster would have disappeared in the face of such an approach, and we all could have turned our attention to more important things.

One hesitates to offer excuses for the Court when it has bungled so badly. I'll try anyway. The Court, it seems to me, was victimized by developments it cannot entirely be blamed for failing to foresee. Definitional and conceptual problems did not loom so large in 1957 as they do today, because there were two quite distinct classes of sexual materials at that time. With few exceptions, highly explicit descriptions and depictions were found only in "hard-core pornography," designed to be sold "under the counter" and treated by all concerned as contraband. The "obscene" thus tended to define itself in the marketplace ("psst, feelthy pictures"), and most of the Justices probably felt a little silly thinking about whether to give constitutional protection to what everyone so clearly regarded as dirty. Thus, Justice Potter Stewart could say, in his famous opinion involving the film *The Lovers,* that while he would not attempt a definition of obscenity, "I know it when I see it." (*The Lovers* was not it.) There were known to be a few hard cases where great explicitness and apparent respectability were combined—some of Henry Miller, *Lady Chatterley's Lover*—but the Court undoubtedly felt confident that it could deal successfully with those works individually when it had to. And it must have anticipated that it would eventually confer First Amendment protection on such books. Thus, the Court's incomprehensible definition of "obscene" was not originally designed to tell the good from the bad. It was meant to refer to the "smut" that everyone recognized as such.

What the Court did not perhaps anticipate was that once an unlimited degree of sexual explicitness was found constitutionally protected in a few "respectable" books, (1) it would prove enormously financially successful, and (2) other authors, publishers, and media would seek to cash in by coming out, en masse, from under the counter and similarly asserting respectability. When this happened, there was simply no way left to draw rational lines. If Justice Stewart knows it when he sees it today, he either sees it everywhere or he doesn't see it at all.

And now the Court has a chance to retrieve itself. Like most people, Justices are reluctant to admit their own mistakes. Optimism about reversing the broad dictum that "obscenity," whatever it means, is not protected by the First Amendment would seem misplaced. It also seems very likely that, where obscenity laws continue to be constitutionally applicable, the Nixon Court will now give the law relatively broad scope. It will likely permit the use of local—rather than national—community standards of offensiveness. It may relieve prosecutors of the burden of affirmatively *proving* that a work is prurient, offensive, or valueless (and permit the jury to make that decision on the basis of the work alone). And it could easily hold that some redeeming value does not automatically insulate a work from the law, but that value must merely be weighed in determining pruriency and offensiveness.

The critical question is whether the Court will examine—as it has never directly done before—the constitutionality of applying obscenity laws to consensual and noninstructive distributions of sexual materials to adults who wish to obtain those materials. At issue here, for example, is the constitutionality of censoring the contents of adult book stores and theaters that keep out children and don't display their wares in advertisements or on the public street, and the constitutionality of regulating what adults can privately order through the mails. In granting review in two cases last spring, the Court specifically asked the parties to argue this issue.

If the Court is really willing to weigh the right of adults to obtain sexual materials, without forcing them upon others, it is hard to see how there can be more than one answer. Some of us may not like the attitude toward sexual relations that some of these materials display, but bad attitudes (if that is what they are) are a subject for discussion—not governmental prohibition. Like it or not, some adults find such attitudes a very important part of their lives. Why shouldn't they be entitled to feed their fantasies, compare their experiences, get information or amusement, become aroused if they like, by whatever sexual materials they wish.

To call explicit sexual materials "filthy" unless they are serious "art" or embody a noble social message is to call an interest in sex for its own sake filthy. Everyone is entitled to hold that view if he wants, but not to enforce it or its consequences on others. The Court has recently seemed to recognize, in cases involving the distribution of contraceptive devices and information, that adults, whether married or unmarried, are constitutionally entitled to engage in private sexual relationships that do not harm others, with or without the purpose of procreation. Will the Court hold that you are constitutionally entitled to do it, but not to read about it?

The Court may thus be prepared to move in two directions at once: to broaden the permissible meaning of "obscene," while narrowing the permissible situations where that categorization is legally relevant. That would not be at all a bad result. It would permit those who are concerned about sexual materials to vindicate that concern quite effectively where it has an arguably legitimate basis—where materials are given or sold to children without parental consent or participation, and where sexual depictions are forced upon those who do not want to see them. And it would simultaneously recognize that books and films cannot be forbidden to adults who want them simply because others do not want them to want them.

From the Court's perspective, such a resolution would lighten its overcrowded docket and relieve it of the almost constant embarrassment of trying to explain and justify present obscenity doctrine. If the Court, on the other hand, broadens the scope of the "obscene" without clarifying the definition or recognizing adult prerogatives, it will have created a worse mess than ever before.

Ending obscenity for adults would not be without its significant future legal consequences, and this, more than anything else, may make the Court hesitate. Obscenity legislation for "consenting" persons is just the tip of an iceberg of adult "morals" prohibitions that pervade our criminal codes. The Court has thus far largely avoided direct constitutional confrontation with these statutes. If it holds that adults have a right to sample or wallow in pornography (so long as it does no one else any discernible harm), what about their right to gamble, to patronize prostitutes, to use drugs whose harm is only speculative, or even to use harmful drugs, when the harms are solely self-inflicted?

Our laws and practices relating to such "victimless" crimes are at present a welter of contradiction, hypocrisy, and frequent disservice to the control of serious criminal activity with real victims. They need close scrutiny and, once the Court has faced the obscenity muddle, it may find it difficult to avoid moving on from there to require rationality in other "moral" restrictions on individual liberty. The obscenity controversy will have served us well if it ultimately helps to bring some reason and restraint into these other vast areas of criminal law.

MILLER V. CALIFORNIA
PARIS ADULT THEATER CASE

United States Supreme Court

Recent appointments have led to significant changes in the view of the U.S. Supreme Court on the control of obscenity and pornography. These changes are reflected in the controversial decisions announced by the court on June 21, 1973, in Miller v. California[1] *and the Paris Adult Theater Case.*[2] *Excerpts from Chief Justice Warren E. Burger's opinion for the majority and the dissents of Associate Justices William O. Douglas and William J. Brennan appear below.*

This is one of a group of "obscenity-pornography" cases being reviewed by the Court in a re-examination of standards enunciated in earlier cases involving what Mr. Justice Harlan called "the intractable obscenity problem."

This case involves the application of a state's criminal obscenity statute to a situation in which sexually explicit materials have been thrust by aggressive sales action upon unwilling recipients who had in no way indicated any desire to receive such materials.

This Court has recognized that the states have a legitimate interest in prohibiting dissemination or exhibition of obscene material when the mode of dissemination carries with it a significant danger of offending the sensibilities of unwilling recipients or of exposure to juveniles.

It is in this context that we are called on to define the standards which must be used to identify obscene material that a state may regulate without infringing the First Amendment as applicable to the states through the Fourteenth Amendment.

Since the Court now undertakes to formulate standards more concrete than those in the past, it is useful for us to focus on two of the landmark cases in the somewhat tortured history of the Court's obscenity decisions.

In *Roth v. United States* (1957) the Court sustained a conviction under a federal statute punishing the mailing of "obscene, lewd, lascivious or filthy" materials. The key to that holding was the Court's rejection of the

---

[1] No. 70–73, *U.S. Law Week* (Bureau of National Affairs, Inc., Washington, D.C.) Vol. 41, pp. 4925–4935.

[2] No. 71–1051, *U.S. Law Week,* Vol. 41, pp. 4935–4955.

claim that obscene materials were protected by the First Amendment. Five Justices joined in the opinion stating:

"All ideas having even the slightest redeeming social importance—unorthodox ideas, controversial ideas, even ideas hateful to the prevailing climate of opinion—have full protection of the [First Amendment] guarantees, unless excludable because they encroach upon the limited area of more important interests. But implicit in the history of the First Amendment is the rejection of obscenity as utterly without redeeming social importance. . . .

> There are certain well-defined and narrowly limited classes of speech, the prevention and punishment of which have never been thought to raise any Constitutional problem. These include the lewd and obscene. . . .
> It has been well observed that such utterances are no essential part of any exposition of ideas, and are of such slight social value as a step to truth that any benefit that may be derived from them is clearly outweighed by the social interest in order and morality.
> We hold that obscenity is not within the area of constitutionally protected speech or press.

Nine years later in *Memoirs v. Massachusetts* (1966), the Court veered sharply away from the *Roth* concept and with only three Justices in the plurality opinion, articulated a new test of obscenity. The plurality held that under the *Roth* definition:

> . . . as elaborated in subsequent cases, three elements must co-alesce: it must be established that (a) the dominant theme of the material taken as a whole appeals to a prurient interest in sex; (b) the material is patently offensive because it affronts contemporary community standards relating to the description or representation of sexual matters; and (c) the material is utterly without redeeming social value.

While *Roth* presumed "obscenity" to be "utterly without redeeming social value," *Memoirs* required that to prove obscenity it must be affirmatively established that the material is *"utterly* without redeeming social value."

Apart from the initial formulation in the *Roth* case, no majority of the Court has at any given time been able to agree on a standard to determine what constitutes obscene, pornographic material subject to regulation under the States' police power.

We have seen "a variety of views among the members of the Court unmatched in any other course of constitutional adjudication." This is not remarkable for in the area of freedom of speech and press the courts must always remain sensitive to any infringement on genuinely serious literary, artistic, political or scientific expression. This is an area in which there are few eternal verities. . . .

This much has been categorically settled by the Court: that obscene material is unprotected by the First Amendment.

We acknowledge, however, the inherent dangers of undertaking to regulate any form of expression. State statutes designed to regulate obscene materials must be carefully limited. As a result, we now confine the permissible scope of such regulations to works which depict or describe sexual conduct.

That conduct must be specifically defined by the applicable state law, as written or authoritatively construed. A state offense must also be limited to works which, taken as a whole, appeal to the prurient interest in sex, which portray sexual conduct in a patently offensive way, and which, taken as a whole, do not have serious literary, artistic, political or scientific value.

The basic guidelines for the trier of fact must be: (a) whether "the average person, applying contemporary community standards" would find that the work, taken as a whole, appeals to the prurient interest; (b) whether the work depicts or describes, in a patently offensive way, sexual conduct specifically defined by the applicable state law, and (c) whether the work, taken as a whole, lacks serious literary, artistic, political, or scientific value.

We do not adopt as a constitutional standard the *"utterly* without redeeming social value" test; that concept has never commanded the adherence of more than three Justices at one time. If a state law that regulates obscene material is thus limited, as written or construed, the First Amendment values applicable to the States through the Fourteenth Amendment are adequately protected by the ultimate power of appellate courts to conduct an independent review of constitutional claims when necessary.

We emphasize that it is not our function to propose regulatory schemes for the States. It is possible, however, to give a few plain examples of what a state statute could define for regulation under the second part (b) of the standard announced in this opinion:

(a) Patently offensive representations or descriptions of ultimate sexual acts, normal or perverted, actual or simulated.

(b) Patently offensive representations or descriptions of masturbation, excretory functions and lewd exhibition of the genitals.

Sex and nudity may not be exploited without limit by films or pictures exhibited or sold in places of public accommodation any more than live sex and nudity can be exhibited or sold without limit in such public places. At a minimum, prurient, patently offensive depiction or description of sexual conduct must have serious literary, artistic, political, or scientific value to merit First Amendment protection. . . .

Under the holdings announced today, no one will be subject to prosecution for the sale or exposure of obscene materials unless these materials depict or describe patently offensive "hard-core" sexual conduct specifically defined by the regulating state law, as written or construed. . . .

Mr. Justice Brennan . . . notes, and we agree, that "uncertainty of the standards creates a continuing source of tension between state and federal courts . . . The problem is . . . that one cannot say with certainty that material is obscene until at least five members of this Court applying inevitably obscure standards, have pronounced it so." . . .

But today, for the first time since *Roth* was decided in 1957, a majority of this Court has agreed on concrete guidelines to isolate "hard-core" pornography from expression protected by the First Amendment. . . .

This may not be an easy road, free from difficulty. But no amount of "fatigue" should lead us to adopt a convenient institutional rationale—an absolutist, anything goes" view of the First Amendment—because it will lighten our burdens.

Under a national Constitution, fundamental First Amendment limitations on the powers of the States do not vary from community to community, but this does not mean that there are, or should or can be, fixed, uniform national standards of precisely what appeals to the "prurient interest" or is "patently offensive." . . .

It is neither realistic nor constitutionally sound to read the First Amendment as requiring that the people of Maine or Mississippi accept public depiction of conduct found tolerable in Las Vegas, or New York City.

As the Court made clear in *Miskin v. New York,* the primary concern with requiring a jury to apply the standard of "the average person, applying contemporary community standards" is to be certain that so far as material is not aimed at a deviant group, it will be judged by its impact on an average person, rather than a particularly susceptible or sensitive person—or indeed a totally insensitive one. . . .

The dissenting Justices sound the alarm of repression. But, in our view, to equate the free and robust exchange of ideas and political debate with commercial exploitation of obscene material demeans the grand conception of the First Amendment and its high purposes in the historic struggle for freedom. . . .

Mr. Justice Brennan finds "it is hard to see how state-ordered regimentation of our minds can ever be forestalled." These doleful anticipations assume that courts cannot distinguish commerce in ideas, protected by the First Amendment, from commercial exploitation of obscene material.

Moreover, state regulation of hard-core pornography so as to make it unavailable to nonadults, a regulation which Mr. Justice Brennan finds constitutionally permissible, has all the elements of "censorship" for adults; indeed even more rigid enforcement techniques may be called for with such dichotomy of regulation.

One can concede that the "sexual revolution" of recent years may have had useful by-products in striking layers of prudery from a subject long irrationally kept from needed ventilation. But it does not follow that no regulation of patently offensive "hard-core" material is needed or permissible; civilized people do not allow unregulated access to heroin because it is a derivative of medicinal morphine.

Dissent by Associate Justice Douglas

Today we leave open the way for California to send a man to prison for distributing brochures that advertise books and a movie under freshly written standards defining obscenity which until today's decision were never the part of any law.

The Court has worked hard to define obscenity and concededly has failed. . . .

But even those members of this Court who created the new and changing standards of "obscenity" could not agree on their application. . . .

Today the Court retreats from the earlier formulations of the constitutional test and undertakes to make new definitions. This effort, like the earlier ones, is earnest and well-intentioned.

The difficulty is that we do not deal with constitutional terms, since "obscenity" is not mentioned in the Constitution or Bill of Rights. . . .

So there are no constitutional guidelines for deciding what is and what is not "obscene." . . . We deal here with problems of censorship which, if adopted, should be done by constitutional amendment after full debate by the people.

Obscenity cases usually generate tremendous emotional outbursts. They have no business being in the courts. . . .

While the right to know is the corollary of the right to speak or publish, no one can be forced by government to listen to disclosure that he finds offensive. . . . There is no "captive audience" problem in these obscenity cases. No one is being compelled to look or to listen. . . .

The idea that the First Amendment permits government to ban publications that are "offensive" to some people puts an ominous gloss on freedom of the press. That test would make it possible to ban any paper or any journal or magazine in some benighted place. . . .

Paris Adult Theater Case, Opinion by Chief Justice Burger

It should be clear from the outset that we do not undertake to tell the States what they must do, but rather to define the area in which they may chart their own course in dealing with obscene material. . . .

We categorically disapprove the theory, apparently adopted by the trial judge, that obscene, pornographic films acquire constitutional immunity from state regulation simply because they are exhibited for consenting adults only. . . . Although we have often pointedly recognized the high importance of the state interest in regulating the exposure of obscene materials to juveniles and unconsenting adults, this Court has never declared these to be the only legitimate state interests permitting regulation of obscene material.

The States have a long-recognized legitimate interest in regulating the use of obscene material in local commerce and in all places of public accommodation, as long as these regulations do not run afoul of specific constitutional prohibitions.

In particular, we hold that there are legitimate state interests at stake in stemming the tide of commercialized obscenity, even assuming it is feasible to enforce effective safeguards against exposure to juveniles and to the passerby. Rights and interests "other than those of the advocates are involved." These include the interest of the public in the quality of life and the total community environment, the tone of commerce in the great city centers, and, possibly, the public safety itself. . . .

As Chief Justice Warren stated, there is a "right of the nation and of the states to maintain a decent society." . . .

But, it is argued, there is no scientific data which conclusively demonstrates that exposure to obscene materials adversely affects men and women or their society. It is urged on behalf of the petitioner that, absent such a demonstration, any kind of state regulation is "impermissible."

We reject this argument. . . . Although there is no conclusive proof of a connection between antisocial behavior and obscene material, the legislature . . . could quite reasonably determine that such a connection does or might exist. . . .

From the beginning of civilized societies, legislators and judges have acted on various unprovable assumptions. Such assumptions underlie much lawful state regulation of commercial and business affairs. . . .

If we accept the unprovable assumption that a complete education requires certain books, and the well nigh universal belief that good books, plays, and art lift the spirit, improve the mind, enrich the human personality and develop character, can we then say that a state legislature may not act on the corollary assumption that commerce in obscene books, or public exhibitions focused on obscene conduct, have a tendency to exert a corrupting and debasing impact leading to antisocial behavior? . . .

It is argued that individual "free will" must govern, even in activities beyond the protection of the First Amendment and other constitutional guarantees of privacy, and that Government cannot legitimately impede an individual's desire to see or acquire obscene plays, movies, and books.

We do indeed base our society on certain assumptions that people have the capacity for free choice. Most exercises of individual free choice—those in politics, religion, and expression of ideas—are explicitly protected by the Constitution. Totally unlimited play for free will, however, is not allowed in ours or any other society. . . .

The idea of a "privacy" right and a place of public accommodation are, in this context, mutually exclusive. Conduct or depictions of conduct that the state police power can prohibit on a public street does not become automatically protected by the Constitution merely because the conduct is moved to a bar or a "live" theatre stage, any more than a "live" performance of a man and woman locked in a sexual embrace at high noon in Times Square is protected by the Constitution because they simultaneously engage in a valid political dialogue.

Dissent by Associate Justice Brennan

If, as the Court today assumes, "a state legislature may . . . act on the . . . assumption that . . . commerce in obscene books, or public exhibitions focused on obscene conduct, have a tendency to exert a corrupting and debasing impact leading to antisocial behavior," then it is hard to see how state-ordered regimentation of our minds can ever be forestalled.

For if a State may, in an effort to maintain or create a particular moral tone, prescribe what its citizens cannot read or cannot see, then it would seem to follow that in pursuit of that same objective a state could decree that its citizens must read certain books or must view certain films.

However laudable its goal—and that is obviously a question on which reasonable minds may differ—the State cannot proceed by means that violate the Constitution.

Even a legitimate, sharply focused state concern for the morality of the community cannot, in other words, justify an assault on the protections of the First Amendment. Where the state interest in regulation of morality is vague and ill-defined, interference with the guarantees of the First Amendment is even more difficult to justify.

In short, while I cannot say that the interests of the state—apart from the question of juveniles and unconsenting adults—are trivial or nonexistent, I am compelled to conclude that these interests cannot justify the substantial damage to constitutional rights and to this nation's judicial machinery that inevitably results from state efforts to bar the distribution even of unprotected material to consenting adults.

I would hold, therefore, that at least in the absence of distribution to juveniles or obtrusive exposure to unconsenting adults, the First and Fourteenth Amendments prohibit the state and federal governments from attempting wholly to suppress sexually oriented materials on the basis of their allegedly "obscene" contents.

PORNOGRAPHY, OBSCENITY AND THE CASE FOR CENSORSHIP

Irving Kristol

The excesses to which permissiveness has led no doubt trouble many libertarians who find prurience as objectionable as prudery. Even so, it is still difficult to find an intellectually respectable support in academic and literary circles for censorship. Accordingly, the following article by Irving Kristol has special significance.

Irving Kristol was a founder of Encounter *and is senior editor and vice-president of Basic Books. He is professor of urban values at New York University and coeditor of a comparatively new quarterly,* The Public Interest. *His most recent book is* On the Democratic Idea in America (*1972*).

Being frustrated is disagreeable, but the real disasters in life begin when you get what you want. For almost a century now, a great many intelligent, well-meaning and articulate people—of a kind generally called liberal or intellectual, or both—have argued eloquently against any kind of censorship of art and/or entertainment. And within the past 10 years, the courts and the legislatures of most Western nations have found these arguments persuasive—so persuasive that hardly a man is now alive who clearly remembers what the answers to these arguments were. Today, in the United States and other democracies, censorship has to all intents and purposes ceased to exist.

Is there a sense of triumphant exhilaration in the land? Hardly. There is, on the contrary, a rapidly growing unease and disquiet. Somehow, things have not worked out as they were supposed to, and many notable civil libertarians have gone on record as saying this was not what they meant at all. They wanted a world in which "Desire Under the Elms" could be produced, or "Ulysses" published, without interference by philistine busybodies holding public office. They have got that, of course; but they have also got a world in which homosexual rape takes place on the stage, in which the public flocks during lunch hours to witness varieties of professional fornication, in which Times Square has become little more than a hideous market for the sale and distribution of printed filth that panders to all known (and some fanciful) sexual perversions.

But disagreeable as this may be, does it really matter? Might not our unease and disquiet be merely a cultural hangover—a "hangup," as they say? What reason is there to think that anyone was ever corrupted by a book?

This last question, oddly enough, is asked by the very same people who seem convinced that advertisements in magazines or displays of violence on television do indeed have the power to corrupt. It is also asked, incredibly enough and in all sincerity, by people—e.g., university professors and school teachers—whose very lives provide all the answers one could want. After all, if you believe that no one was ever corrupted by a book, you have also to believe that no one was ever improved by a book (or a play or a movie). You have to believe, in other words, that all art is morally trivial and that, consequently, all education is morally irrelevant. No one, not even a university professor, really believes that.

To be sure, it is extremely difficult, as social scientists tell us, to trace the effects of any single book (or play or movie) on an individual reader or any class of readers. But we all know, and social scientists know it too, that the ways in which we use our minds and imaginations do shape our characters and help define us as persons. That those who certainly know this are nevertheless moved to deny it merely indicates how a dogmatic resistance to the idea of censorship can—like most dogmatism—result in a mindless insistence on the absurd.

I have used these harsh terms—"dogmatism" and "mindless"—advisedly. I might also have added "hypocritical." For the plain fact is that none of us is a complete civil libertarian. We all believe that there is some point at which the public authorities ought to step in to limit the "self expression" of an individual or a group, even where this might be seriously intended as a form of artistic expression, and even where the artistic transaction is between consenting adults. A playwright or theatrical director might, in this crazy world of ours, find someone willing to commit suicide on the stage, as called for by the script. We would not allow that—any more than we would permit scenes of real physical torture on the stage, even if the victim were a willing masochist. And I know of no one, no matter how free in spirit, who argues that we ought to permit gladiatorial contests in Yankee Stadium, similar to those once performed in the Colosseum at Rome—even if only consenting adults were involved.

The basic point that emerges is . . . that . . . no society can be utterly indifferent to the ways its citizens publicly entertain themselves. Bearbaiting and cockfighting are prohibited only in part out of compassion for the suffering animals; the main reason they were abolished was because it was felt that they debased and brutalized the citizenry who flocked to witness such spectacles. And the question we face with regard to pornography and obscenity is whether, now that they have such strong legal protection from the Supreme Court, they can or will brutalize and debase our citizenry. We are, after all, not dealing with one passing incident—one book, or one play, or one movie. We are dealing with a general tendency that is suffusing our entire culture.

I say pornography *and* obscenity because, though they have different dictionary definitions and are frequently distinguishable as "artistic" genres, they are nevertheless in the end identical in effect. Pornography is not objectionable simply because it arouses sexual desire or lust or prurience in the mind of the reader or spectator; this is a silly Victorian notion. A great many non-pornographic works—including some parts of the Bible —excite sexual desire very successfully. What is distinctive about pornography is that, in the words of D. H. Lawrence, it attempts "to do dirt on [sex] . . . [It is an] insult to a vital human relationship."

In other words, pornography differs from erotic art in that its whole purpose is to treat human beings obscenely, to deprive human beings of their specifically human dimension. That is what obscenity is all about. It is light years removed from any kind of carefree sensuality—there is no continuum between Fielding's "Tom Jones" and the Marquis de Sade's "Justine." These works have quite opposite intentions. To quote Susan Sontag: "What pornographic literature does is precisely to drive a wedge between one's existence as a full human being and one's existence as a sexual being —while in ordinary life a healthy person is one who prevents such a gap from opening up." This definition occurs in an essay *defending* pornography —Miss Sontag is a candid as well as gifted critic—so the definition, which I accept, is neither tendentious nor censorious.

Along these same lines, one can point out—as C. S. Lewis pointed out some years back—that it is no accident that in the history of all literatures obscene words—the so-called "four-letter words"—have always been the vocabulary of farce or vituperation. The reason is clear; they reduce men and women to some of their mere bodily functions—they reduce man to his animal component, and such a reduction is an essential purpose of farce or vituperation.

Similarly, Lewis also suggested that it is not an accident that we have no offhand, colloquial, neutral terms—not in any Western European language at any rate—for our most private parts. The words we do use are either (a) nursery terms, (b) archaisms, (c) scientific terms or (d) a term from the gutter (i.e., a demeaning term). Here I think the genius of language is telling us something important about man. It is telling us that man is an animal with a difference: he has a unique sense of privacy, and a unique capacity for shame when this privacy is violated. Our "private parts" are indeed private, and not merely because convention prescribes it. This particular convention is indigenous to the human race. In practically all primitive tribes, men and women cover their private parts; and in practically all primitive tribes, men and women do not copulate in public.

It may well be that Western society, in the latter half of the 20th century, is experiencing a drastic change in sexual mores and sexual relationships. We have had many such "sexual revolutions" in the past—and the bourgeois family and bourgeois ideas of sexual propriety were themselves established in the course of a revolution against 18th century "licentiousness"—and we shall doubtless have others in the future. It is, however, highly improbable (to put it mildly) that what we are witnessing is the Final Revolution which will make sexual relations utterly unproblematic, permit us to dispense with any kind of ordered relationships between the sexes, and allow us freely to redefine the human condition. And so long as humanity has not reached that utopia, obscenity will remain a problem.

One of the reasons it will remain a problem is that obscenity is not merely about sex, any more than science fiction is about science. Science fiction, as every student of the genre knows, is a peculiar vision of power: what it is really about is politics. And obscenity is a peculiar vision of humanity: what it is really about is ethics and metaphysics.

Imagine a man—a well-known man, much in the public eye—in a hospital ward, dying an agonizing death. He is not in control of his bodily functions, so that his bladder and his bowels empty themselves of their own accord. His consciousness is overwhelmed and extinguished by pain, so that he cannot communicate with us, nor we with him. Now, it would be, technically, the easiest thing in the world to put a television camera in his hospital room and let the whole world witness this spectacle. We don't do it—at least we don't do it as yet—because we regard this as an *obscene* invasion of privacy. And what would make the spectacle obscene is that we would be witnessing the extinguishing of humanity in a human animal.

Incidentally, in the past our humanitarian crusaders against capital punishment understood this point very well. The abolitionist literature goes into great physical detail about what happens to a man when he is hanged or electrocuted or gassed. And their argument was—and is—that what happens is shockingly obscene, and that no civilized society should be responsible for perpetrating such obscenities, particularly since in the nature of the case there must be spectators to ascertain that this horror was indeed being perpetrated in fulfillment of the law.

Sex—like death—is an activity that is both animal and human. There are human sentiments and human ideals involved in this animal activity. But when sex is public, the viewer does not see—cannot see—the sentiments and the ideals. He can only see the animal coupling. And that is why, when men and women make love, as we say, they prefer to be alone—because it is only when you are alone that you can make love, as distinct from merely copulating in an animal and casual way. And that, too, is why those who are voyeurs, if they are not irredeemably sick, also feel ashamed at what they are witnessing. When sex is a public spectacle, a human relationship has been debased into a mere animal connection.

It is also worth noting that this making of sex into an obscenity is not a mutual and equal transaction, but is rather an act of exploitation by one of the partners—the male partner. I do not wish to get into the complicated question as to what, if any, are the essential differences—as distinct from conventional and cultural differences—between male and female. I do not claim to know the answer to that. But I do know—and I take it as a sign which has meaning—that pornography is, and always has been, a man's work; that women rarely write pornography; and that women tend to be indifferent consumers of pornography.[1] My own guess, by way of explanation, is that a woman's sexual experience is ordinarily more suffused with human emotion than is man's, that men are more easily satisfied with autoerotic activities, and that men can therefore more easily take a more "technocratic" view of sex and its pleasures. Perhaps this is not correct. But whatever the explanation, there can be no question that pornography is a form of "sexism," as the Women's Liberation Movement calls it, and that the instinct of Women's Lib has been unerring in perceiving that, when pornography is perpetrated, it is perpetrated against them, as part of a conspiracy to deprive them of their full humanity.

But even if all this is granted, it might be said—and doubtless will be said—that I really ought not to be unduly concerned. Free competition in the cultural marketplace—it is argued by people who have never otherwise had a kind word to say for laissez-faire—will automatically dispose of the problem. The present fad for pornography and obscenity, it will be asserted, is just that, a fad. It will spend itself in the course of time; people will get bored with it, will be able to take it or leave it alone in a casual way, in a "mature way," and, in sum, I am being unnecessarily distressed about the whole business. The New York Times, in an editorial, concludes hopefully in this vein.

"In the end . . . the insensate pursuit of the urge to shock, carried from one excess to a more abysmal one, is bound to achieve its own antidote in total boredom. When there is no lower depth to descend to, ennui will erase the problem."

I would like to be able to go along with this line of reasoning, but I cannot. I think it is false, and for two reasons, the first psychological, the second political.

The basic psychological fact about pornography and obscenity is that it appeals to and provokes a kind of sexual regression. The sexual pleasure one gets from pornography and obscenity is autoerotic and infantile; put bluntly, it is a masturbatory exercise of the imagination, when it is not masturbation pure and simple. Now, people who masturbate do not get

---

[1] There are, of course, a few exceptions—but of a kind that prove the rule. "L'Histoire d'O," for instance, written by a woman, is unquestionably the most *melancholy* work of pornography ever written. And its theme is precisely the dehumanization accomplished by obscenity.

bored with masturbation, just as sadists don't get bored with sadism, and voyeurs don't get bored with voyeurism.

In other words, infantile sexuality is not only a permanent temptation for the adolescent or even the adult—it can quite easily become a permanent, self-reinforcing neurosis. It is because of an awareness of this possibility of regression toward the infantile condition, a regression which is always open to us, that all the codes of sexual conduct ever devised by the human race take such a dim view of autoerotic activities and try to discourage autoerotic fantasies. Masturbation is indeed a perfectly natural autoerotic activity, as so many sexologists blandly assure us today. And it is precisely because it is so perfectly natural that it can be so dangerous to the mature or maturing person, if it is not controlled or sublimated in some way. That is the true meaning of Portnoy's complaint. Portnoy, you will recall, grows up to be a man who is incapable of having an adult sexual relationship with a woman; his sexuality remains fixed in an infantile mode, the prison of his autoerotic fantasies. Inevitably, Portnoy comes to think, in a perfectly *infantile* way, that it was all his mother's fault. . . .

What is at stake is civilization and humanity, nothing less. The idea that "everything is permitted," as Nietzsche put it, rests on the premise of nihilism and has nihilistic implications. I will not pretend that the case against nihilism and for civilization is an easy one to make. We are here confronting the most fundamental of philosophical questions, on the deepest levels. But that is precisely my point—that the matter of pornography and obscenity is not a trivial one, and that only superficial minds can take a bland and untroubled view of it.

In this connection, I might also point out those who are primarily against censorship on liberal grounds tell us not to take pornography or obscenity seriously, while those who are for pornography and obscenity, on radical grounds, take it very seriously indeed. I believe the radicals—writers like Susan Sontag, Herbert Marcuse, Norman O. Brown, and even Jerry Rubin—are right, and the liberals are wrong. I also believe that those young radicals at Berkeley, some . . . years ago, who provoked a major confrontation over the public use of obscene words, showed a brilliant political instinct. Once the faculty and administration had capitulated on this issue— saying: "Oh, for God's sake, let's be adult: what difference does it make anyway?"—once they said that, they were bound to lose on every other issue. And once Mark Rudd could publicly ascribe to the president of Columbia a notoriously obscene relationship to his mother, without provoking any kind of reaction, the S.D.S. had already won the day. The occupation of Columbia's buildings merely ratified their victory. Men who show themselves unwilling to defend civilization against nihilism are not going to be either resolute or effective in defending the university against anything.

I am already touching upon a political aspect of pornography when I suggest that it is inherently and purposefully subversive of civilization and its institutions. But there is another and more specifically political aspect, which has to do with the relationship of pornography and/or obscenity to democracy, and especially to the quality of public life on which democratic government ultimately rests.

Though the phrase, "the quality of life," trips easily from so many lips these days, it tends to be one of those clichés with many trivial meanings and no large, serious one. Sometimes it merely refers to such externals as the enjoyment of cleaner air, cleaner water, cleaner streets. At other times it refers to the merely private enjoyment of music, painting or literature. Rarely does it have anything to do with the way the citizen in a democracy views himself—his obligations—his intentions, his ultimate self-definition.

Instead, what I would call the "managerial" conception of democracy is the predominant opinion among political scientists, sociologists and economists, and has, through the untiring efforts of these scholars, become the conventional journalistic opinion as well. The root idea behind this "managerial" conception is that democracy is a "political system" (as they say) which can be adequately defined in terms of—can be fully reduced to —its mechanical arrangements. Democracy is then seen as a set of rules and procedures, and *nothing but* a set of rules and procedures, whereby majority rule and minority rights are reconciled into a state of equilibrium. If everyone follows these rules and procedures, then a democracy is in working order. I think this is a fair description of the democratic idea that currently prevails in academia. One can also fairly say that it is now the liberal idea of democracy par excellence.

I cannot help but feel that there is something ridiculous about being this kind of a democrat, and I must further confess to having a sneaking sympathy for those of our young radicals who also find it ridiculous. The absurdity is the absurdity of idolatry—of taking the symbolic for the real, the means for the end. The purpose of democracy cannot possibly be the endless functioning of its own political machinery. The purpose of any political regime is to achieve some version of the good life and the good society. It is not at all difficult to imagine a perfectly functioning democracy which answers all questions except one—namely, why should anyone of intelligence and spirit care a fig for it?

There is, however, an older idea of democracy—one which was fairly common until about the beginning of this century—for which the conception of the quality of public life is absolutely crucial. This idea starts from the proposition that democracy is a form of self-government, and that if you want it to be a meritorious polity, you have to care about what kind of people govern it. Indeed, it puts the matter more strongly and declares that, if you want self-government, you are only entitled to it if that "self" is worthy of governing. There is no inherent right to self-government if it means that such government is vicious, mean, squalid and debased. Only a dogmatist and a fanatic, an idolater of democratic machinery, could approve of self-government under such conditions.

And because the desirability of self-government depends on the character of the people who govern, the older idea of democracy was very solicitous of the condition of this character. It was solicitous of the individual self, and felt an obligation to educate it into what used to be called "republican virtue." And it was solicitous of that collective self which we call public opinion and which, in a democracy, governs us collectively. Perhaps in some respects it was nervously oversolicitous—that would not be surprising. But the main thing is that it cared, cared not merely about the machinery of democracy but about the quality of life that this machinery might generate.

And because it cared, this older idea of democracy had no problem in principle with pornography and/or obscenity. It censored them—and it did so with a perfect clarity of mind and a perfectly clear conscience. It was not about to permit people capriciously to corrupt themselves. Or, to put it more precisely: in this version of democracy, the people took some care not to let themselves be governed by the more infantile and irrational parts of themselves.

I have, it may be noticed, uttered that dreadful word, "censorship." And I am not about to back away from it. If you think pornography and/or obscenity is a serious problem, you have to be for censorship. I'll go even further and say that if you want to prevent pornography and/or obscenity from becoming a problem, you have to be for censorship. And lest there be any misunderstanding as to what I am saying, I'll put it as bluntly as possible: if you care for the quality of life in our American democracy, then you have to be for censorship.

But can a liberal be for censorship? Unless one assumes that being a liberal *must* mean being indifferent to the quality of American life, then the answer has to be: yes, a liberal can be for censorship—but he ought to favor a liberal form of censorship.

Is that a contradiction in terms? I don't think so. We have no problem in contrasting *repressive* laws governing alcohol and drugs and tobacco with laws *regulating* (i.e., discouraging the sale of) alcohol and drugs and tobacco. Laws encouraging temperance are not the same thing as laws that have as their goal prohibition or abolition. We have not made the smoking of cigarettes a criminal offense. We have, however, and with good liberal conscience, prohibited cigarette advertising on television, and may yet, again with good liberal conscience, prohibit it in newspapers and magazines. The idea of restricting individual freedom, in a liberal way, is not at all unfamiliar to us.

I therefore see no reason why we should not be able to distinguish repressive censorship from liberal censorship of the written and spoken word. In Britain, until a few years ago, you could perform almost any play you wished—but certain plays, judged to be obscene, had to be performed in private theatrical clubs which were deemed to have a "serious" interest in theater. In the U.S., all of us who grew up using public libraries are familiar with the circumstances under which certain books could be circulated only to adults, while still other books had to be read in the library reading room, under the librarian's skeptical eye. In both cases, a small minority that was willing to make a serious effort to see an obscene play or read an obscene book could do so. But the impact of obscenity was circumscribed and the quality of public life was only marginally affected.[2]

I am not saying it is easy in practice to sustain a distinction between liberal and repressive censorship, especially in the public realm of a democracy, where popular opinion is so vulnerable to demagoguery. Moreover, an acceptable system of liberal censorship is likely to be exceedingly difficult to devise in the United States today, because our educated classes, upon whose judgment a liberal censorship must rest, are so convinced that there is no such thing as a problem of obscenity, or even that there is no such thing as obscenity at all. But, to counterbalance this, there is the further, fortunate truth that the tolerable margin for error is quite large, and single mistakes or single injustices are not all that important.

This possibility, of course, occasions much distress among artists and academics. It is a fact, one that cannot and should not be denied, that any system of censorship is bound, upon occasion, to treat unjustly a particular work of art—to find pornography where there is only gentle eroticism, to find obscenity where none really exists, or to find both where its existence ought to be tolerated because it serves a larger moral purpose. Though most works of art are not obscene, and though most obscenity has nothing to do with art, there are some few works of art that are, at least in part, pornographic and/or obscene. There are also some few works of art that are in the special category of the comic-ironic "bawdy" (Boccaccio, Rabelais). It is such works of art that are likely to suffer at the hands of the censor. That is the price one has to be prepared to pay for censorship—even liberal censorship.

But just how high is this price? If you believe, as so many artists seem to believe today, that art is the only sacrosanct activity in our profane and vulgar world—that any man who designates himself an artist thereby acquires a sacred office—then obviously censorship is an intolerable form

---

[2] It is fairly predictable that some one is going to object that this point of view is "elitist"—that, under a system of liberal censorship, the rich will have privileged access to pornography and obscenity. Yes, of course they will—just as, at present, the rich have privileged access to heroin if they want it. But one would have to be an egalitarian maniac to object to this state of affairs on the grounds of equality.

of sacrilege. But for those of us who do not subscribe to this religion of art, the costs of censorship do not seem so high at all.

If you look at the history of American or English literature, there is precious little damage you can point to as a consequence of the censorship that prevailed throughout most of that history. Very few works of literature —of real literary merit, I mean—ever were suppressed; and those that were, were not suppressed for long. Nor have I noticed, now that censorship of the written word has to all intents and purposes ceased in this country, that hitherto suppressed or repressed masterpieces are flooding the market. Yes, we can now read "Fanny Hill" and the Marquis de Sade. Or, to be more exact, we can now openly purchase them, since many people were able to read them even though they were publicly banned, which is as it should be under a liberal censorship. So how much have literature and the arts gained from the fact that we can all now buy them over the counter, that, indeed, we are all now encouraged to buy them over the counter? They have not gained much that I can see.

And one might also ask a question that is almost never raised: how much has literature lost from the fact that everything is now permitted? It has lost quite a bit, I should say. In a free market, Gresham's Law can work for books or theater as efficiently as it does for coinage—driving out the good, establishing the debased. The cultural market in the United States today is being pre-empted by dirty books, dirty movies, dirty theater. A pornographic novel has a far better chance of being published today than a non-pornographic one, and quite a few pretty good novels are not being published at all simply because they are not pornographic, and are therefore less likely to sell. Our cultural condition has not improved as a result of the new freedom. American cultural life wasn't much to brag about 20 years ago; today one feels ashamed for it.

Just one last point which I dare not leave untouched. If we start censoring pornography or obscenity, shall we not inevitably end up censoring political opinion? A lot of people seem to think this would be the case— which only shows the power of doctrinaire thinking over reality. We had censorship of pornography and obscenity for 150 years, until almost yesterday, and I am not aware that freedom of opinion in this country was in any way diminished as a consequence of this fact. Fortunately for those of us who are liberal, freedom is not indivisible. If it were, the case for liberalism would be indistinguishable from the case for anarchy; and they are two very different things.

But I must repeat and emphasize: what kind of laws we pass governing pornography and obscenity, what kind of censorship—or, since we are still a Federal nation—what kinds of censorship we institute in our various localities may indeed be difficult matters to cope with; nevertheless the real issue is one of principle. I myself subscribe to a liberal view of the enforcement problem: I think that pornography should be illegal *and* available to anyone who wants it so badly as to make a pretty strenuous effort to get it. We have lived with under-the-counter pornography for centuries now, in a fairly comfortable way. But the issue of principle, of whether it should be over or under the counter, has to be settled before we can reflect on the advantages and disadvantages of alternative modes of censorship. I think the settlement we are living under now, in which obscenity and democracy are regarded as equals, is wrong; I believe it is inherently unstable; I think it will, in the long run, be incompatible with any authentic concern for the quality of life in our democracy.

8

Homosexuality

Britain's relaxation of its laws against homosexuality, recent disclosures (some of them at least partly misleading) of an unexpectedly high incidence of homosexuality, and the trend toward permissiveness and frankness in the discussion of once forbidden topics have all combined to increase interest in homosexuality and the problems it poses. For the student of ethics (and legal philosophy) an exploration of the general issues raised by these problems will prove more rewarding than an examination of the phenomenon itself.

The specific problems and the general questions they suggest are exasperatingly perplexing. To what extent is the homosexual a product of nature and therefore incorrigible, or a product of nurture and therefore possibly amenable to correction or "cure"? If homosexuals are such by choice, even though only in the sense that they persist in practices (and a way of life) that could be changed through counsel or treatment, how are they to be judged morally? When we remind ourselves that homosexuals were not subject to ridicule, censure, or legal sanctions in ancient Greece,[1] we may ask to what extent the adverse moral judgment that still generally prevails in our society is culturally conditioned.

---

[1] Aristophanes' *The Frogs* suggests the opposite, as far as ridicule is concerned. The homosexuality popular among Athens' upper classes and reflected in Plato's dialogues (*vide,* the *Charmides* and *Symposium*) was not shared by the poorer classes and was borrowed from Sparta where homosexuality was encouraged as a military virtue.

Our society is not exceptional, it may be noted; nearly all societies have condemned homosexuality.

Homosexuals are referred to as sex deviants in our society. Does this imply a pathological condition, whether physical or psychological, and hence an illness or disease, as Freud suggested in a widely quoted "Letter to an American Mother," or simply a behavioral departure or personality variation from the normal? But what is the "normal"? It is not the opposite of the pathological, since in a society of chain-smokers where nearly everyone was afflicted with lung cancer that would be normal—at least in one sense. Is it simply action in conformity with rules (whether or not embodied in laws) which are supported by a strong consensus and largely obeyed in practice, so that departure from them is deviance? Or is there some standard of health, which, like healthy lungs and unlike rules, is independent of any fiat, from which homosexuality is a deviation?

Finally, to what extent ought society to ban and invoke legal sanctions against practices which, whether moral or immoral, involve only consenting adults and result in no harm to others (except in the tenuous sense that one who "takes offense" is thereby "harmed")?

Many of these issues came to the fore when the British parliament, in December 1966, adopted a controversial recommendation of its now famous Wolfenden Committee and removed the legal ban against homosexual relations in private between consenting adults. Overwhelmingly defeated ten years earlier, the bill encountered only token opposition on its final passage. In the United States only Illinois has legalized private acts. With the exception of West Germany, all major European countries have eased the restrictions on deviates. Recently, there has been a marked tendency to view homosexuality with the compassion and understanding one accords the victim of an illness, rather than with loathing and contempt. Homosexuals, to be sure, as they become bolder and more visible, reject such condescension, preferring to be regarded as different rather than defective—an attitude recently reinforced by prominent Christian theologians such as Norman Pittinger who refuses to regard any "permanent union in love" as sinful.

An ancillary problem, of special interest to the student of literary criticism, is suggested by the prominence of homosexuals among authors, especially playwrights. To what extent does their deviancy influence what they have to say? If, as might be argued, the intent is to get revenge on the "straight" world from which homosexuals are excluded by denigrating and deriding heterosexual love, should the work be judged by reference to its source and its concealed, possibly subconscious, motive, or strictly on its "merits"?

Of the three readings, the first, by an able scientific observer, is primarily descriptive, although by no means morally aloof. The other two represent brilliantly argued opposing sides of the great debate precipitated by the Wolfenden Report over the role of law in regulating morals, an issue in jurisprudence which far transcends in importance the narrower question of passing judgment on homosexuality as such.

CRIMES WITHOUT VICTIMS

Edwin M. Schur

Edwin M. Schur is a sociologist and teaches at Tufts University. He is a graduate of the London School of Economics, where he received his Ph.D. and also has a law degree from the Yale Law School. Dr. Schur is Associate Editor of the journal Social Problems *and, in addition to the volume from which the following selections have been taken, has written* Narcotic Addiction in Britain and America: The Impact of Public Policy (*1962*), *and* Radical Nonintervention: Rethinking the Delinquency Problem (*1973*).*

Psychiatrist Robert Lindner has succinctly criticized some widely accepted yet inadequate definitions of homosexuality. As Lindner states, a very popular definition is based on overt appearance and mannerisms—that is, the homosexual is conceived of as a person who looks and acts like a member of the opposite sex. Actually, this is an erroneous notion. Although some homosexuals do adopt some mannerisms typical of the opposite sex, there is no simple correlation between effeminacy and homosexuality or between masculinism and lesbianism. Both scientific studies and informal accounts by participants in homosexual life confirm that the most obvious types comprise but a tiny percentage of all sexual deviants. In fact, blatant displays of effeminacy are viewed with scorn by many male homosexuals; similarly, in some cases it may be an exaggerated display of masculinity that makes one man an object of sexual desire for another.

Reporting on some observations of homosexuality in New York City, a journalist recently expressed his strong surprise that so few of the men he saw dancing with one another in "gay" (i.e., homosexual) bars "looked" homosexual.

A second misleading definition of homosexuality Lindner describes as "pseudoscientific and statistical." According to this approach, one could examine the sort of data presented in the Kinsey report (for example, cumulative incidence figures for various types of sexual activities) and classify as homosexual those individuals reporting a certain frequency of homosexual activities. Lindner asserts that such statistics confuse "outlet with inclination, activity with psychic tendency." They do not, for example, take into account whether other sexual outlets were available, or whether the activities engaged in were really satisfying to the participants. Lindner concludes that the term *homosexual* should be applied only to "those individuals who more or less chronically feel an urgent sexual desire toward, and a sexual responsiveness to, members of their own sex, and who seek gratification of this desire predominantly with members of their own sex." As he goes on to comment, this definition recognizes inversion as "an attitude basic to the personality wherein it resides, as a compulsion with all the urgency and driving energy that account for its persistence despite the obvious disadvantages of homosexuality as a way of life." The Church of England Moral Welfare Council, in its statement to the Wolfenden Committee, similarly sought to distinguish between isolated homosexual acts and homosexuality as a basic sexual condition or inclination:

> Although most males and females exhibit that decided propensity toward members of the complementary sex which is rightly regarded as normal and natural in human beings, it is incontestable that a minority display an equally marked orientation toward members of the same sex.

Homosexuality, then, can—and often does—take the form of a basic personality orientation rather than a particular type of sexual activity. An alternative definition, suggested by Erving Goffman, would limit the term *homosexual* to "individuals who participate in a special community of understanding wherein members of one's own sex are defined as the most desirable sexual objects, and sociability is energetically organized around the pursuit and entertainment of these objects." This definition has the merit of focusing on a collective or socially structured aspect of the problem which . . . is extremely important. However, given the possibility that legal policy may significantly reinforce or even indirectly generate the development of such restricted social organization and collective orientations, it would be a mistake to consider such aspects as being necessary elements in all homosexuality.

Just as there are different definitions of homosexuality, there are also highly conflicting explanations of its causes. There have long been attempts to explain homosexuality in terms of "innate" characteristics, but the results of research along these lines have been very unimpressive. According to one recent and careful report, "there is so much evidence on the side of the nurture hypothesis, and so little on the side of the nature hypothesis, that the reliance upon genetic or constitutional determinants to account for the homosexual adaptation is ill founded." It may be worth noting that such "internal" explanations have often been voiced by homosexuals themselves. This may occasionally represent an effort to find some plausible meaning for an otherwise inexplicable compulsion. On the other hand, the value for the deviant in using such statements as a defense against moral blame is obvious.

Today the view is widely accepted that homosexuality constitutes, or at least reflects, some kind of psychological disturbance. The rather vague phrase *some kind of* is used intentionally—for there is wide variation in the particular factors emphasized by different experts. Oral fixation, castration anxiety, and numerous other psychoanalytic and psychological rubrics abound in the professional literature on homosexuality. Psychoanalytic theories tend to emphasize that adult homosexuality is rooted in childhood situations. In reporting on a recent comparison of over 100 homosexual patients with a matched group of nonhomosexual patients, a team of psychotherapists stated: "Our findings point to the homosexual adaptation as an outcome of exposure to highly pathologic parent-child relationships and early life situations." Analysts also stress that homosexuality may represent a fear of the opposite sex as much as a desire for persons of the same sex. Another key element in some explanations of male homosexuality has been the concept of a flight from masculinity, an actual or feared inability to live up to male-role expectations. This concept is expanded, by some of the more sociologically oriented interpreters, to relate male homosexuality generally to changing sex roles in modern Western society—that is, to formulate a structural explanation of the condition, rather than merely to uncover predisposing factors in individual cases. . . .

There is definitely no sure and simple cure for homosexuality, and the dominant view is that in most cases therapy at best can only make the patient a better-adjusted homosexual. Not surprisingly, many homosexuals insist that they are in no sense sick, and several disinterested students of the problem also have questioned the alleged invariable pathology of the homosexual. Thus Lindner has viewed homosexuality as a form of rebellion generated by the conflict between an urgent sexual drive and the repressive measures of conventional sex morality. . . .

Although there may well be more homosexuality than the average heterosexual imagines, estimates by individual homosexuals are not likely to be very accurate. Apart from their lack of systematic data, many homosexuals have a psychological stake in exaggerating their number—in order to impress nonhomosexuals that a sizable minority is being mistreated, and in order to bolster their own morale. It is also very difficult to evaluate police figures or other official statistics on homosexuality, fluctuations in which may reflect differentials in law enforcement effort or success every bit as much as they do actual variations in behavior rates.

One point on which all observers are agreed is that official statistics reflect but a fraction of the homosexual behavior that is, in fact, occurring. Most specialists also appear convinced that there has been some increase in homosexuality in recent years—though it is extremely difficult to be sure that such apparent increase is not primarily a reflection of greater research on the problem and more open consideration and discussion of the subject. . . .

Perhaps the conclusion of the Wolfenden Committee would apply equally well to the American situation—that although the amount of homosexuality might well be "large enough to present a serious problem," such behavior is "practiced by a small minority of the population, and should be seen in proper perspective, neither ignored nor given a disproportionate amount of public attention."

In line with the prevailing misconceptions regarding the appearance and overt behavior of the homosexual (and the corresponding mistaken assumption that homosexuals are easily and quickly identified), there is a widespread belief that most homosexuals are members of a particular social stratum and are engaged in a narrow range of occupations. Research has shown—and homosexuals themselves are quick to confirm—that homosexuality cuts across all boundaries of class and occupation, race and religion.

Although the discussion thus far has related largely to male homosexuality, many of the general points would apply equally well to homosexuality among females. . . .

Although it is not a crime merely to be a homosexual, all American jurisdictions (with the recent exception of Illinois) proscribe homosexual acts—among adults as well as between adults and minors, and in private as well as in public. The homosexual, in other words, has no legal outlet for the kind of sex life to which he is drawn; his only alternative to law-breaking is abstinence. Although some statutes provide separate definitions of and penalties for particular homosexual offenses, others set forth a vaguely phrased, catch-all offense. Thus the law books are full of such phrases as *unnatural crimes, the infamous crime against nature, any unnatural copulation, the abominable and detestable crime against nature with mankind or beast, unnatural intercourse,* and *any unnatural and lascivious act.* These terms obviously reflect an attitude of moral condemnation; they do not display the degree of specificity usually required in the statutory definition of crimes. . . .

The typical over-all law enforcement policy on homosexuality . . . appears to be a fairly pragmatic one. Police realize that they must, to a certain extent, adopt a live-and-let-live outlook. They act as vigorously as possible in cases involving force or minors; furthermore, public outrage over any type of sex crime may be an occasion for stepped-up activity against known homosexuals and their gathering places. Although some law enforcement personnel certainly harbor sadistic attitudes toward homosexuals, today such attitudes may not be widespread. A handbook for plainclothesmen notes:

> In recent years the terms *fag, fairy,* and *queer* have fallen into the discard [*sic*] in law enforcement circles. The general term *degenerate* has had the same fate. The homosexual is now called a *sex deviate,* and *degenerate* is now used as a term to describe the more bestial molester of women or children.

Admittedly, the labels in themselves provide no reliable indication of attitude, yet this change seems to reflect more than a trend toward euphemisms. Even if the police do not engage in continual and all-out persecution of homosexuals, however, it may be questioned (given the relatively meager results) whether the use of policemen as decoys and for other surveillance of homosexuals is justified—particularly when there are more urgent social problems to which such efforts might be directed. . . .

Although legal stigmatization and harassment make the homosexual's life difficult, they rarely push him into a life of sexual abstinence. Often, however, such pressures do significantly color his sexual and social relationships. An important aspect of the problem of homosexuality in our society is the development of a special homosexual subculture—not merely the gathering together of homosexuals, but a more general culture-within-a-culture, with its distinctive values and behavior norms, modes of speech and dress, as well as its special patterns of interaction and social differentiation. To the extent that a homosexual immerses himself in this subculture, he must undergo a particular socialization process. Homosexual inclination, at least where it is exclusive, may reflect a basic personality orientation. But living as a homosexual, in the sense of the Goffman definition cited earlier, involves the learning of a special social role. This element is suggested by the phrase *coming out,* which is used among homosexuals to refer to "one's recognition of oneself as a homosexual or one's entrance into the ongoing stream of homosexual life, specifically into the bar system and the privately organized social affairs." . . .

Whether one says that many homosexuals experience shame or guilt or both, at least it seems valid to assert that many suffer from some form of low self-esteem. Such poor self-acceptance relates partly to the very central matter of sexual identity, as such, and partly to the social condemnation and humiliation which invariably confronts homosexuals. It is also reinforced by the very patterns of sexual behavior to which homosexuals are driven by the need for concealment. One-night stands and commercial sex transactions have been said both to reflect and to increase the considerable ambivalence of the homosexual about his condition and his behavior. . . .

It is interesting that homosexual life is called "gay," but it would seem a mistake to infer from this that the invert society is a predominantly happy one. Homosexuals may feel genuine relief and some considerable pleasure in being able to drop the mask and meet with fellow inverts. Yet many observers have noted a forced gaiety in such activities, and in any case it is questionable whether the pleasurable aspects of the invert's life can often outweigh the frequent loneliness and insecurity. An informal survey among 100 male homosexuals found that while 75 per cent considered themselves generally well-adjusted, 57 per cent did admit to some adjustment difficulties, and 90 per cent reported some concern about exposure. In another study of 300 male inverts, all but a handful stated they did not want to change their own sexual orientation, but the same respondents overwhelmingly stated that they would not want their sons to be homosexuals. . . .

Conceivably one could argue that no special public policy toward homosexuality is needed at all; an individual's sexual inclinations and behavior are strictly his own business, and inversion is just one of the possible alternatives from which people can choose. This view, according to which any attempt at controlling homosexuality is uncalled for, will be acceptable to few people in our society. There is a strong and sound belief that heterosexuality is the preferable adaptation (both for society and for the individual) and that homosexuality should at least be discouraged—to the extent that discouragement is possible. Furthermore, notwithstanding differences of opinion about the degree of psychopathology involved, there is good reason to think that full inversion is not simply an alternative that some people have freely chosen.

It is not at all clear, however, just what can be done to discourage or to prevent homosexuality. Although the causes are somewhat obscure, it seems likely that major alterations of social structure and culture would be necessary in order to reduce homosexuality to any significant degree. And if it is true that inversion is on the increase, then probably the stemming or even the reversal of broad social trends would also be required. A sharpening of sex-role differentiation, and an accompanying relaxation of the multiple burdens of the male role, might be seen as helping to curb any

flight from masculinity. Yet, even assuming that this would be effective and
that it could somehow be encouraged by policy, the strong current of social
change in the opposite direction (i.e., toward "equalizing" the roles of men
and women) would be a major obstacle. Prevention in individual cases
may be a more realistic goal. The sympathetic counselling of young persons
who seem to be heading in the direction of homosexuality may sometimes
inhibit that adaptation. If such persons are reached early enough, the likelihood of success would be increased. . . . Most psychotherapists remain
pessimistic about the likelihood of effecting complete reversals of sex
orientation.

MORALS AND THE CRIMINAL LAW

Patrick Devlin

*Lord Devlin, a Fellow of the British Academy, is one of
Great Britain's most distinguished jurists. He served as Justice
of the High Court, Queen's Bench, Lord Justice of Appeal,
and, until his retirement in 1964, as Lord of Appeal in ordinary. He has written* Trial by Jury *(1956),* The Criminal
Prosecution in England *(1957),* Samples of Lawmaking
*(1962). The following selection is from a collection of lec-
tures entitled* The Enforcement of Morals *(1965), in which
Lord Devlin reverses an earlier position supporting reform of
the criminal law dealing with homosexuality.*

What is the connexion between crime and sin and to what extent,
if at all, should the criminal law of England concern itself with the enforcement of morals and punish sin or immorality as such? The statements
of principle in the Wolfenden Report provide an admirable and modern
starting-point for such an inquiry. . . .
Early in the Report the Commiteee put forward:

> Our own formulation of the function of the criminal law so far
> as it concerns the subjects of this enquiry. In this field, its function,
> as we see it, is to preserve public order and decency, to protect the
> citizen from what is offensive or injurious, and to provide sufficient
> safeguards against exploitation and corruption of others, particu-

larly those who are specially vulnerable because they are young, weak in body or mind, inexperienced, or in a state of special physical, official or economic dependence.

It is not, in our view, the function of the law to intervene in the private lives of citizens, or to seek to enforce any particular pattern of behaviour, further than is necessary to carry out the purposes we have outlined.

The Committee preface their most important recommendation

that homosexual behaviour between consenting adults in private should no longer be a criminal offence, [by stating the argument] which we believe to be decisive, namely, the importance which society and the law ought to give to individual freedom of choice and action in matters of private morality. Unless a deliberate attempt is to be made by society, acting through the agency of the law, to equate the sphere of crime with that of sin, there must remain a realm of private morality and immorality which is, in brief and crude terms, not the law's business. To say this is not to condone or encourage private immorality.

Similar statements of principle are set out in the chapters of the Report which deal with prostitution. No case can be sustained, the Report says, for attempting to make prostitution itself illegal. The Committee refer to the general reasons already given and add: 'We are agreed that private immorality should not be the concern of the criminal law except in the special circumstances therein mentioned.' They quote with approval the report of the Street Offences Committee, which says: 'As a general proposition it will be universally accepted that the law is not concerned with private morals or with ethical sanctions.' It will be observed that the emphasis is on *private* immorality. By this is meant immorality which is not offensive or injurious to the public in the ways defined or described in the first passage which I quoted. In other words, no act of immorality should be made a criminal offence unless it is accompanied by some other feature such as indecency, corruption, or exploitation. This is clearly brought out in relation to prostitution: 'It is not the duty of the law to concern itself with immorality as such . . . it should confine itself to those activities which offend against public order and decency or expose the ordinary citizen to what is offensive or injurious'.

I must disclose at the outset that I have as a judge an interest in the result of the inquiry which I am seeking to make as a jurisprudent. As a judge who administers the criminal law and who has often to pass sentence in a criminal court, I should feel handicapped in my task if I thought that I was addressing an audience which had no sense of sin or which thought of crime as something quite different. . . . I must admit that I begin with a feeling that a complete separation of crime from sin (I use the term throughout this lecture in the wider meaning) would not be good for the moral law and might be disastrous for the criminal. But can this sort of feeling be justified as a matter of jurisprudence? And if it be a right feeling, how should the relationship between the criminal and the moral law be stated? Is there a good theoretical basis for it, or is it just a practical working alliance, or is it a bit of both? . . . In jurisprudence . . . everything is thrown open to discussion and, in the belief that they cover the whole field, I have framed three interrogatories addressed to myself to answer:

1. Has society the right to pass judgement at all on matters of morals? Ought there, in other words, to be a public morality, or are morals always a matter for private judgement?
2. If society has the right to pass judgement, has it also the right to use the weapon of the law to enforce it?
3. If so, ought it to use that weapon in all cases or only in some; and if only in some, on what principles should it distinguish?

I shall begin with the first interrogatory and consider what is meant by the right of society to pass a moral judgement, that is, a judgement about what is good and what is evil. The fact that a majority of people may disapprove of a practice does not of itself make it a matter for society as a whole. Nine men out of ten may disapprove of what the tenth man is doing and still say that it is not their business. There is a case for a collective judgement (as distinct from a large number of individual opinions which sensible people may even refrain from pronouncing at all if it is upon somebody else's private affairs) only if society is affected. Without a collective judgement there can be no case at all for intervention. Let me take as an illustration the Englishman's attitude to religion as it is now and as it has been in the past. His attitude now is that a man's religion is his private affair; he may think of another man's religion that it is right or wrong, true or untrue, but not that it is good or bad. In earlier times that was not so; a man was denied the right to practise what was thought of as heresy, and heresy was thought of as destructive of society.

The language used in the passages I have quoted from the Wolfenden Report suggests the view that there ought not to be a collective judgement about immorality *per se*. Is this what is meant by 'private morality' and 'individual freedom of choice and action'? Some people sincerely believe that homosexuality is neither immoral nor unnatural. Is the 'freedom of choice and action' that is offered to the individual, freedom to decide for himself what is moral or immoral, society remaining neutral; or is it freedom to be immoral if he wants to be? The language of the Report may be open to question, but the conclusions at which the Committee arrive answer this question unambiguously. If society is not prepared to say that homosexuality is morally wrong, there would be no basis for a law protecting youth from 'corruption' or punishing a man for living on the 'immoral' earnings of a homosexual prostitute, as the Report recommends. This attitude the Committee make even clearer when they come to deal with prostitution. In truth, the Report takes it for granted that there is in existence a public morality which condemns homosexuality and prostitution. What the Report seems to mean by private morality might perhaps be better described as private behaviour in matters of morals.

This view—that there is such a thing as public morality—can also be justified by *a priori* argument. What makes a society of any sort is community of ideas, not only political ideas but also ideas about the way its members should behave and govern their lives; these latter ideas are its morals. Every society has a moral structure as well as a political one: or rather, since that might suggest two independent systems, I should say that the structure of every society is made up both of politics and morals. Take, for example, the institution of marriage. Whether a man should be allowed to take more than one wife is something about which every society has to make up its mind one way or the other. In England we believe in the Christian idea of marriage and therefore adopt monogamy as a moral principle. Consequently the Christian institution of marriage has become the basis of family life and so part of the structure of our society. It is there not because it is Christian. It has got there because it is Christian, but it remains there because it is built into the house in which we live and could not be removed without bringing it down. The great majority of those who live in this country accept it because it is the Christian idea of marriage and for them the only true one. But a non-Christian is bound by it, not because it is part of Christianity but because, rightly or wrongly, it has been adopted by the society in which he lives. It would be useless for him to stage a debate designed to prove that polygamy was theologically more correct and socially preferable; if he wants to live in the house, he must accept it as built in the way in which it is.

We see this more clearly if we think of ideas or institutions that are purely political. Society cannot tolerate rebellion; it will not allow argument about the rightness of the cause. Historians a century later may say that the rebels were right and the Government was wrong and a percipient and conscientious subject of the State may think so at the time. But it is not a matter which can be left to individual judgement.

The institution of marriage is a good example for my purpose because it bridges the division, if there is one, between politics and morals. Marriage is part of the structure of our society and it is also the basis of a moral code which condemns fornication and adultery. The institution of marriage would be gravely threatened if individual judgements were permitted about the morality of adultery; on these points there must be a public morality. But public morality is not to be confined to those moral principles which support institutions such as marriage. People do not think of monogamy as something which has to be supported because our society has chosen to organize itself upon it; they think of it as something that is good in itself and offering a good way of life and that it is for that reason that our society has adopted it. I return to the statement that I have already made, that society means a community of ideas; without shared ideas on politics, morals, and ethics no society can exist. Each one of us has ideas about what is good and what is evil; they cannot be kept private from the society in which we live. If men and women try to create a society in which there is no fundamental agreement about good and evil they will fail; if, having based it on common agreement, the agreement goes, the society will disintegrate. For society is not something that is kept together physically; it is held by the invisible bonds of common thought. If the bonds were too far relaxed the members would drift apart. A common morality is part of the bondage. The bondage is part of the price of society; and mankind, which needs society, must pay its price. . . .

You may think that I have taken far too long in contending that there is such a thing as public morality, a proposition which most people would readily accept, and may have left myself too little time to discuss the next question which to many minds may cause greater difficulty: to what extent should society use the law to enforce its moral judgements? But I believe that the answer to the first question determines the way in which the second should be approached and may indeed very nearly dictate the answer to the second question. If society has no right to make judgements on morals, the law must find some special justification for entering the field of morality: if homosexuality and prostitution are not in themselves wrong, then the onus is very clearly on the lawgiver who wants to frame a law against certain aspects of them to justify the exceptional treatment. But if society has the right to make a judgement and has it on the basis that a recognized morality is as necessary to society as, say, a recognized government, then society may use the law to preserve morality in the same way as it uses it to safeguard anything else that is essential to its existence. If therefore the first proposition is securely established with all its implications, society has a prima facie right to legislate against immorality as such.

The Wolfenden Report, notwithstanding that it seems to admit the right of society to condemn homosexuality and prostitution as immoral, requires special circumstances to be shown to justify the intervention of the law. I think that this is wrong in principle and that any attempt to approach my second interrogatory on these lines is bound to break down. I think that the attempt by the Committee does break down and that this is shown by the fact that it has to define or describe its special circumstances so widely that they can be supported only if it is accepted that the law *is* concerned with immorality as such.

The widest of the special circumstances are described as the provision of 'sufficient safeguards against exploitation and corruption of others, particularly those who are specially vulnerable because they are young, weak in body or mind, inexperienced, or in a state of special physical, official or economic dependence'. The corruption of youth is a well-recognized ground for intervention by the State and for the purpose of any legislation the young can easily be defined. But if similar protection were to be extended to every other citizen, there would be no limit to the reach of the law. The 'corruption and exploitation of others' is so wide that it could be used to cover any sort of immorality which involves, as most do, the co-operation of another person. Even if the phrase is taken as limited to the categories that are particularized as 'specially vulnerable', it is so elastic as to be practically no restriction. This is not merely a matter of words. For if the words used are stretched almost beyond breaking-point, they still are not wide enough to cover the recommendations which the Committee make about prostitution.

Prostitution is not in itself illegal and the Committee do not think that it ought to be made so. If prostitution is private immorality and not the law's business, what concern has the law with the ponce or the brothel-keeper or the householder who permits habitual prostitution? The Report recommends that the laws which make these activities criminal offences should be maintained or strengthened and brings them (so far as it goes into principle; with regard to brothels it says simply that the law rightly frowns on them) under the head of exploitation. There may be cases of exploitation in this trade, as there are or used to be in many others, but in general a ponce exploits a prostitute no more than an impresario exploits an actress. The Report finds that 'the great majority of prostitutes are women whose psychological makeup is such that they choose this life because they find in it a style of living which is to them easier, freer and more profitable than would be provided by any other occupation. . . . In the main the association between prostitute and ponce is voluntary and operates to mutual advantage.' The Committee would agree that this could not be called exploitation in the ordinary sense. They say: 'It is in our view an over-simplification to think that those who live on the earnings of prosti-tution are exploiting the prostitute as such. What they are really exploiting is the whole complex of the relationship between prostitute and customer; they are, in effect, exploiting the human weaknesses which cause the customer to seek the prostitute and the prostitute to meet the demand.'

All sexual immorality involves the exploitation of human weak-nesses. The prostitute exploits the lust of her customers and the customer the moral weakness of the prostitute. If the exploitation of human weak-nesses is considered to create a special circumstance, there is virtually no field of morality which can be defined in such a way as to exclude the law.

I think, therefore, that it is not possible to set theoretical limits to the power of the State to legislate against immorality. It is not possible to settle in advance exceptions to the general rule or to define inflexibly areas of morality into which the law is in no circumstances to be allowed to enter. Society is entitled by means of its laws to protect itself from dangers, whether from within or without. Here again I think that the political parallel is legitimate. The law of treason is directed against aiding the king's enemies and against sedition from within. The justification for this is that established government is necessary for the existence of society and therefore its safety against violent overthrow must be secured. But an established morality is as necessary as good government to the welfare of society. Societies disintegrate from within more frequently than they are broken up by external pressures. There is disintegration when no common morality is observed and history shows that the loosening of moral bonds is often the first stage of disintegration, so that society is justified in taking the same steps to preserve its moral code as it does to preserve its government and other essential institutions. The suppression of vice is as much the law's business as the suppression of subversive activities; it is no more possible to define a sphere of private morality than it is to define one of private subversive activity. It is wrong to talk of private morality or of the law not being concerned with immorality as such or to try to set rigid bounds to the part which the law may play in the suppression of vice. There are no theoretical limits to the power of the State to legislate against treason and sedition, and likewise I think there can be no theoretical limits to legislation against immorality. You may argue that if a man's sins affect only himself it cannot be the concern of society. If he chooses to get drunk every night in the privacy of his own home, is any one except himself the worse for it? But suppose a quarter or a half of the population got drunk every night, what sort of society would it be? You cannot set a theoretical limit to the number of people who can get drunk before society is entitled to legislate against drunkenness. . . .

In what circumstances the State should exercise its power is the third of the interrogatories I have framed. But before I get to it I must raise a point which might have been brought up in any one of the three. How are the moral judgements of society to be ascertained? By leaving it until now, I can ask it in the more limited form that is now sufficient for my purpose. How is the law-maker to ascertain the moral judgements of society? It is surely not enough that they should be reached by the opinion of the majority; it would be too much to require the individual assent of every citizen. English law has evolved and regularly uses a standard which does not depend on the counting of heads. It is that of the reasonable man. He is not to be confused with the rational man. He is not expected to reason about anything and his judgement may be largely a matter of feeling. It is the viewpoint of the man in the street—or to use an archaism familiar to all lawyers—the man in the Clapham omnibus. He might also be called the right-minded man. For my purpose I should like to call him the man in the jury box, for the moral judgement of society must be something about which any twelve men or women drawn at random might after discussion be expected to be unanimous. This was the standard the judges applied in the days before Parliament was as active as it is now and when they laid down rules of public policy. They did not think of themselves as making law but simply as stating principles which every right-minded person would accept as valid. It is what Pollock called 'practical morality', which is based not on theological or philosophical foundations but 'in the mass of continuous experience half-consciously or unconsciously accumulated and embodied in the morality of common sense'. He called it also 'a certain way of thinking on questions of morality which we expect to find in a reasonable civilized man or a reasonable Englishman, taken at random'.

Immorality then, for the purpose of the law, is what every right-minded person is presumed to consider to be immoral. Any immorality is capable of affecting society injuriously and in effect to a greater or lesser extent it usually does; this is what gives the law its *locus standi*. It cannot be shut out. But—and this brings me to the third question—the individual has a *locus standi* too; he cannot be expected to surrender to the judgement of society the whole conduct of his life. It is the old and familiar question of striking a balance between the rights and interests of society and those of the individual. . . . It is possible to make general statements of principle which it may be thought the legislature should bear in mind when it is considering the enactment of laws enforcing morals.

I believe that most people would agree upon the chief of these elastic principles. There must be toleration of the maximum individual freedom that is consistent with the integrity of society. It cannot be said that this is a principle that runs all through the criminal law. Much of the criminal law that is regulatory in character is based upon the opposite principle, that is, that the choice of the individual must give way to the convenience of the many. But in all matters of conscience the principle I have stated is generally held to prevail. It is not confined to thought and speech; it extends to action, as is shown by the recognition of the right to conscientious objection in war-time; this example shows also that conscience will be respected even in times of national danger. The principle appears to me to be peculiarly appropriate to all questions of morals. Nothing should be punished by the law that does not lie beyond the limits of tolerance. It is not nearly enough to say that a majority dislike a practice; there must be a real feeling of reprobation. Those who are dissatisfied with the present law on homosexuality often say that the opponents of reform are swayed simply by disgust. If that were so it would be wrong, but I do not think one can ignore disgust if it is deeply felt and not manufactured. Its presence is a good indication that the bounds of toleration are being reached. Not everything is to be tolerated. No society can do without intolerance, indignation, and disgust; they are the forces behind the moral law, and indeed it can be argued that if they or something like them are not present, the feelings of society cannot be weighty enough to deprive the individual of freedom of choice. I suppose that there is hardly anyone nowadays who would not be disgusted by the thought of deliberate cruelty to animals. No one proposes to relegate that or any other form of sadism to the realm of private morality or to allow it to be practised in public or in private. It would be possible no doubt to point out that until a comparatively short while ago nobody thought very much of cruelty to animals and also that pity and kindliness and the unwillingness to inflict pain are virtues more generally esteemed now than they have ever been in the past. But matters of this sort are not determined by rational argument. Every moral judgement, unless it claims a divine source, is simply a feeling that no right-minded man could behave in any other way without admitting that he was doing wrong. It is the power of a common sense and not the power of reason that is behind the judgements of society. But before a society can put a practice beyond the limits of tolerance there must be a deliberate judgement that the practice is injurious to society. There is, for example, a general abhorrence of homosexuality. We should ask ourselves in the first instance whether, looking at it calmly and dispassionately, we regard it as a vice so abominable that its mere presence is an offence. If that is the genuine feeling of the society in which we live, I do not see how society can be denied the right to eradicate it. Our feeling may not be so intense as that. We may feel about it that, if confined, it is tolerable, but that if it spread it might be gravely injurious; it is in this way that most societies look upon fornication, seeing it as a natural weakness which must be kept within bounds but which cannot be rooted out. It becomes then a question of balance, the danger to society in one scale and the extent of the restriction in the other. . . .

The limits of tolerance shift. This is supplementary to what I have been saying but of sufficient importance in itself to deserve statement as a separate principle which law-makers have to bear in mind. I suppose that moral standards do not shift; so far as they come from divine revelation they do not, and I am willing to assume that the moral judgements made by a society always remain good for that society. But the extent to which society will tolerate—I mean tolerate, not approve—departures from moral standards varies from generation to generation. . . . Laws, especially those which are based on morals, are less easily moved. It follows as another good working principle that in any new matter of morals the law should be slow to act. By the next generation the swell of indignation may have abated and the law be left without the strong backing which it needs. But it is then difficult to alter the law without giving the impression that moral judgement is being weakened. This is now one of the factors that is strongly militating against any alteration to the law on homosexuality.

A third elastic principle must be advanced more tentatively. It is that as far as possible privacy should be respected. This is not an idea that has ever been made explicit in the criminal law. Acts or words done or said in public or in private are all brought within its scope without distinction in principle. But there goes with this a strong reluctance on the part of judges and legislators to sanction invasions of privacy in the detection of crime. The police have no more right to trespass than the ordinary citizen has; there is no general right of search; to this extent an Englishman's home is still his castle. The Government is extremely careful in the exercise even of those powers which it claims to be undisputed. Telephone tapping and interference with the mails afford a good illustration of this. . . .

This indicates a general sentiment that the right to privacy is something to be put in the balance against the enforcement of the law. Ought the same sort of consideration to play any part in the formation of the law? Clearly only in a very limited number of cases. When the help of the law is invoked by an injured citizen, privacy must be irrelevant; the individual cannot ask that his right to privacy should be measured against injury criminally done to another. But when all who are involved in the deed are consenting parties and the injury is done to morals, the public interest in the moral order can be balanced against the claims of privacy. The restriction on police powers of investigation goes further than the affording of a parallel; it means that the detection of crime committed in private and when there is no complaint is bound to be rather haphazard and this is an additional reason for moderation. These considerations do not justify the exclusion of all private immorality from the scope of the law. I think that, as I have already suggested, the test of 'private behaviour' should be substituted for 'private morality' and the influence of the factor should be reduced from that of a definite limitation to that of a matter to be taken into account. Since the gravity of the crime is also a proper consideration, a distinction might well be made in the case of homosexuality between the lesser acts of indecency and the full offence, which on the principles of the Wolfenden Report it would be illogical to do.

The last and the biggest thing to be remembered is that the law is concerned with the minimum and not with the maximum; there is much in the Sermon on the Mount that would be out of place in the Ten Commandments. We all recognize the gap between the moral law and the law of the land. No man is worth much who regulates his conduct with the sole object of escaping punishment, and every worthy society sets for its members standards which are above those of the law. We recognize the existence of such higher standards when we use expressions such as 'moral obligation' and 'morally bound'. The distinction was well put in the judgement of African elders in a family dispute: 'We have power to make you divide the crops, for this is our law, and we will see this is done. But we have not power to make you behave like an upright man.'

It can only be because this point is so obvious that it is so frequently ignored. Discussion among law-makers, both professional and amateur, is too often limited to what is right or wrong and good or bad for society. There is a failure to keep separate the two questions I have earlier posed—the question of society's right to pass a moral judgement and the question of whether the arm of the law should be used to enforce the judgement. The criminal law is not a statement of how people ought to behave; it is a statement of what will happen to them if they do not behave; good citizens are not expected to come within reach of it or to set their sights by it, and every enactment should be framed accordingly.

The arm of the law is an instrument to be used by society, and the decision about what particular cases it should be used in is essentially a practical one. . . . The part that the jury plays in the enforcement of the criminal law, the fact that no grave offence against morals is punishable without their verdict, these are of great importance in relation to the statements of principle that I have been making. They turn what might otherwise be pure exhortation to the legislature into something like rules that the law-makers cannot safely ignore. The man in the jury box is not just an expression; he is an active reality. It will not in the long run work to make laws about morality that are not acceptable to him.

This then is how I believe my third interrogatory should be answered—not by the formulation of hard and fast rules, but by a judgement in each case taking into account the sort of factors I have been mentioning. The line that divides the criminal law from the moral is not determinable by the application of any clear-cut principle. It is like a line that divides land and sea, a coastline of irregularities and indentations. There are gaps and promontories, such as adultery and fornication, which the law has for centuries left substantially untouched. Adultery of the sort that breaks up marriage seems to me to be just as harmful to the social fabric as homosexuality or bigamy. The only ground for putting it outside the criminal law is that a law which made it a crime would be too difficult to enforce; it is too generally regarded as a human weakness not suitably punished by imprisonment. All that the law can do with fornication is to act against its worst manifestations; there is a general abhorrence of the commercialization of vice, and that sentiment gives strength to the law against brothels and immoral earnings. There is no logic to be found in this. The boundary between the criminal law and the moral law is fixed by balancing in the case of each particular crime the pros and cons of legal enforcement in accordance with the sort of considerations I have been outlining. The fact that adultery, fornication, and lesbianism are untouched by the criminal law does not prove that homosexuality ought not to be touched. The error of jurisprudence in the Wolfenden Report is caused by the search for some single principle to explain the division between crime and sin. The Report finds it in the principle that the criminal law exists for the protection of individuals; on this principle fornication in private between consenting adults is outside the law and thus it becomes logically indefensible to bring homosexuality between consenting adults in private within it. But the true principle is that the law exists for the protection of society. It does not discharge its function by protecting the individual from injury, annoyance, corruption, and exploitation; the law must protect also the institutions and the community of ideas, political and moral, without which people cannot live together. Society cannot ignore the morality of the individual any more than it can his loyalty; it flourishes on both and without either it dies.

I have said that the morals which underly the law must be derived from the sense of right and wrong which resides in the community as a whole; it does not matter whence the community of thought comes, whether from one body of doctrine or another or from the knowledge of good and evil which no man is without. If the reasonable man believes that a practice is immoral and believes also—no matter whether the belief is right or wrong, so be it that it is honest and dispassionate—that no right-minded member of his society could think otherwise, then for the purpose of the law it is immoral.

This brings me back in the end to a question I posed at the beginning. . . . I have spoken of the criminal law as dealing with the minimum standards of human conduct and the moral law with the maximum. The instrument of the criminal law is punishment; those of the moral law are teaching, training, and exhortation. If the whole dead weight of sin were ever to be allowed to fall upon the law, it could not take the strain. If at any point there is a lack of clear and convincing moral teaching, the administration of the law suffers. . . .

I return now to the main thread of my argument and summarize it. Society cannot live without morals. Its morals are those standards of conduct which the reasonable man approves. A rational man, who is also a good man, may have other standards. If he has no standards at all he is not a good man and need not be further considered. If he has standards, they may be very different; he may, for example, not disapprove of homosexuality or abortion. In that case he will not share in the common morality; but that should not make him deny that it is a social necessity. A rebel may be rational in thinking that he is right but he is irrational if he thinks that society can leave him free to rebel.

A man who concedes that morality is necessary to society must support the use of those instruments without which morality cannot be maintained. The two instruments are those of teaching, which is doctrine, and of enforcement, which is the law.

LAW, LIBERTY AND MORALITY

H. L. A. Hart

A renowned scholar in the philosophy of law, H. L. A. Hart is Professor of Jurisprudence in Oxford University and fellow of University College, Oxford. He has also taught at Harvard, the University of California at Los Angeles, and Stanford University. He was named a 1966 recipient of the distinguished Ames Prize for legal scholarship by the Faculty of the Harvard Law School for his Concept of Law *(1961). Among his other works are* Law, Liberty and Morality *(1963) and* Punishment and Responsibility *(1968), a collection of essays dealing with the theory of punishment and legal criteria of responsibility.*

Much dissatisfaction has for long been felt in England with the criminal law relating to both prostitution and homosexuality, and in 1954 the committee well known as the Wolfenden Committee was appointed to consider the state of the law. This committee reported in September 1957 and recommended certain changes in the law on both topics. As to homosexuality they recommended by a majority of 12 to 1 that homosexual practices between consenting adults in private should no longer be a crime . . .

What concerns us here is less the fate of the Wolfenden Committee's recommendations than the principles by which these were supported. These are strikingly similar to those expounded by Mill in his essay *On Liberty*. Thus section 13 of the Committee's Report reads:

> [The] function [of the criminal law], as we see it, is to preserve public order and decency, to protect the citizen from what is offensive or injurious and to provide sufficient safeguards against exploitation or corruption of others, particularly those who are specially vulnerable because they are young, weak in body or mind or inexperienced. . . .

This conception of the positive functions of the criminal law was the

Committee's main ground for its recommendation concerning prostitution that legislation should be passed to suppress the offensive public manifestations of prostitution, but not to make prostitution itself illegal. Its recommendation that the law against homosexual practices between consenting adults in private should be relaxed was based on the principle stated simply in section 61 of the Report as follows: "There must remain a realm of private morality and immorality which is, in brief and crude terms, not the law's business."

It is of some interest that these developments in England have had near counterparts in America. In 1955 the American Law Institute published with its draft Model Penal Code a recommendation that all consensual relations between adults in private should be excluded from the scope of the criminal law. Its grounds were (*inter alia*) that "no harm to the secular interests of the community is involved in atypical sex practice in private between consenting adult partners"; and "there is the fundamental question of the protection to which every individual is entitled against state interference in his personal affairs when he is not hurting others." This recommendation had been approved by the Advisory Committee of the Institute but rejected by a majority vote of its Council. The issue was therefore referred to the annual meeting of the Institute at Washington in May 1955, and the recommendation, supported by an eloquent speech of the late Justice Learned Hand, was, after a hot debate, accepted by a majority of 35 to 24.

It is perhaps clear from the foregoing that Mill's principles are still very much alive in the criticism of law, whatever their theoretical deficiencies may be. But twice in one hundred years they have been challenged by two masters of the Common Law. The first of these was the great Victorian judge and historian of the Criminal Law, James Fitzjames Stephen. His criticism of Mill is to be found in the sombre and impressive book *Liberty, Equality, Fraternity,* which he wrote as a direct reply to Mill's essay *On Liberty.* It is evident from the tone of this book that Stephen thought he had found crushing arguments against Mill and had demonstrated that the law might justifiably enforce morality as such or, as he said, that the law should be "a persecution of the grosser forms of vice." Nearly a century later, on the publication of the Wolfenden Committee's report, Lord Devlin, now a member of the House of Lords and a most distinguished writer on the criminal law, in his essay on *The Enforcement of Morals* took as his target the Report's contention "that there must be a realm of morality and immorality which is not the law's business" and argued in opposition to it that "the suppression of vice is as much the law's business as the suppression of subversive activities."

Though a century divides these two legal writers, the similarity in the general tone and sometimes in the detail of their arguments is very great. . . . though their arguments are at points confused, they certainly still deserve the compliment of rational opposition. They are not only admirably stocked with concrete examples, but they express the considered views of skilled, sophisticated lawyers experienced in the administration of the criminal law. Views such as theirs are still quite widely held especially by lawyers both in England and in this country; it may indeed be that they are more popular, in both countries, than Mill's doctrine of Liberty.

Before we consider the detail of these arguments, it is, I think, necessary to appreciate three different but connected features of the question with which we are concerned.

. . . it is plain that the question is one *about* morality, but it is important to observe that it is also itself a question *of* morality. It is the question whether the enforcement of morality is morally justified; so morality enters into the question in two ways. The importance of this feature of the question is that it would plainly be no sufficient answer to show that in fact in some society—our own or others—it was widely regarded as morally quite right and proper to enforce, by legal punishment, compliance with the accepted morality. No one who seriously debates this question would regard Mill as refuted by the simple demonstration that there are some societies in which the generally shared morality endorses its own enforcement by law, and does so even in those cases where the immorality was thought harmless to others. The existence of societies which condemn association between white and coloured persons as immoral and punish it by law still leaves our question to be argued. It is true that Mill's critics have often made much of the fact that English law does in several instances, apparently with the support of popular morality, punish immorality as such, especially in sexual matters; but they have usually admitted that this is where the argument begins, not where it ends. I shall indeed later claim that the play made by some legal writers with what they treat as examples of the legal enforcement of morality "as such" is sometimes confused. But they do not, at any rate, put forward their case as simply proved by pointing to these social facts. Instead they attempt to base their own conclusion that it is morally justifiable to use the criminal law in this way on principles which they believe to be universally applicable, and which they think are either quite obviously rational or will be seen to be so after discussion.

Thus Lord Devlin bases his affirmative answer to the question on the quite general principle that it is permissible for any society to take the steps needed to preserve its own existence as an organized society, and he thinks that immorality—even private sexual immorality—may, like treason, be something which jeopardizes a society's existence. Of course many of us may doubt this general principle, and not merely the suggested analogy with treason. We might wish to argue that whether or not a society is justified in taking steps to preserve itself must depend both on what sort of society it is and what the steps to be taken are. If a society were mainly devoted to the cruel persecution of a racial or religious minority, or if the steps to be taken included hideous tortures, it is arguable that what Lord Devlin terms the "disintegration" of such a society would be morally better than its continued existence, and steps ought not to be taken to preserve it. Nonetheless Lord Devlin's principle that a society may take the steps required to preserve its organized existence is not itself tendered as an item of English popular morality, deriving its cogency from its status as part of our institutions. He puts it forward as a principle, rationally acceptable, to be used in the evaluation or criticism of social institutions generally. And it is surely clear that anyone who holds the question whether a society has the "right" to enforce morality, or whether it is morally permissible for any society to enforce its morality by law, to be discussable at all, must be prepared to deploy some such general principles of critical morality. In asking the question, we are assuming the legitimacy of a standpoint which permits criticism of the institutions of any society, in the light of general principles and knowledge of the facts.

To make this point clear, I would revive the terminology much favoured by the Utilitarians of the last century, which distinguished "positive morality," the morality actually accepted and shared by a given social group, from the general moral principles used in the criticism of actual social institutions including positive morality. We may call such general principles "critical morality" and say that our question is one of critical morality about the legal enforcement of positive morality.

A second feature of our question worth attention is simply that it is a question of *justification*. In asking it we are committed at least to the general critical principle that the use of legal coercion by any society calls for justification as something *prima facie* objectionable to be tolerated only for the sake of some countervailing good. For where there is no *prima facie* objection, wrong, or evil, men do not ask for or give *justifications* of social practices, though they may ask for and give *explanations* of these practices or may attempt to demonstrate their value.

It is salutary to inquire precisely what it is that is *prima facie* objectionable in the legal enforcement of morality; for the idea of legal enforcement is in fact less simple than is often assumed. It has two different but related aspects. One is the actual punishment of the offender. This characteristically involves depriving him of liberty of movement or of property or of association with family or friends, or the infliction upon him of physical pain or even death. All these are things which are assumed to be wrong to inflict on others without special justification, and in fact they are so regarded by the law and morality of all developed societies. To put it as a lawyer would, these are things which, if they are not justified as sanctions, are delicts or wrongs.

The second aspect of legal enforcement bears on those who may never offend against the law, but are coerced into obedience by the threat of legal punishment. This rather than physical restrictions is what is normally meant in the discussion of political arrangements by restrictions on liberty. Such restrictions, it is to be noted, may be thought of as calling for justification for several quite distinct reasons. The unimpeded exercise by individuals of free choice may be held a value in itself with which it is *prima facie* wrong to interfere; or it may be thought valuable because it enables individuals to experiment—even with living—and to discover things valuable both to themselves and to others. But interference with individual liberty may be thought an evil requiring justification for simpler, utilitarian reasons; for it is itself the infliction of a special form of suffering —often very acute—on those whose desires are frustrated by the fear of punishment. This is of particular importance in the case of laws enforcing a sexual morality. They may create misery of a quite special degree. For both the difficulties involved in the repression of sexual impulses and the consequences of repression are quite different from those involved in the abstention from "ordinary" crime. Unlike sexual impulses, the impulse to steal or to wound or even kill is not, except in a minority of mentally abnormal cases, a recurrent and insistent part of daily life. Resistance to the temptation to commit these crimes is not often, as the suppression of sexual impulses generally is, something which affects the development or balance of the individual's emotional life, happiness, and personality.

Thirdly, the distinction already made, between positive morality and principles of critical morality, may serve to dissipate a certain misunderstanding of the question and to clarify its central point. It is sometimes said that the question is not whether it is morally justifiable to enforce morality as such, but only *which* morality may be enforced. Is it only a utilitarian morality condemning activities which are harmful to others? Or is it a morality which also condemns certain activities whether they are harmful or not? This way of regarding the question misrepresents the character of, at any rate, modern controversy. A utilitarian who insists that the law should only punish activities which are harmful adopts this as a critical principle, and, in so doing, he is quite unconcerned with the question whether a utilitarian morality is or is not already accepted as the positive morality of the society to which he applies his critical principles. If it is so accepted, that is not, in his view, the reason why it should be enforced. It is true that if he is successful in preaching his message to a given society, members of it will then be compelled to behave as utilitarians in certain ways, but these facts do not mean that the vital difference between him and his opponent is only as to the content of the morality to be enforced. For as may be seen from the main criticisms of Mill, the Utilitarian's opponent, who insists that it is morally permissible to enforce morality as such, believes that the mere fact that certain rules or standards of behaviour enjoy the status of a society's positive morality is the reason—or at least part of the reason—which justifies their enforcement by law. No doubt in older controversies the opposed positions were different: the question may have been whether the state could punish only activities causing secular harm or also acts of disobedience to what were believed to be divine commands or prescriptions of Natural Law. But what is crucial to the dispute in its modern form is the significance to be attached to the historical fact that certain conduct, no matter what, is prohibited by a positive morality. The utilitarian denies that this has any significance sufficient to justify its enforcement; his opponent asserts that it has. These are divergent critical principles which do not differ merely over the content of the morality to be enforced, but over a more fundamental and, surely, more interesting issue.

Part Three

Racial
Discrimination

The domination in a society with strong egalitarian traditions of one race over another has produced moral problems which are unique to the American experience. A Martian astronaut, contemplating us for the first time and ignorant of our history, might well conclude that we are a people perversely intent on making unnecessary trouble for ourselves. He would no doubt report back about a so-called "race problem" that was pointless, gratuitous, and quite senseless. And so might we consider it. But this would not be to banish it. For there the problem is, haunting the national conscience, filling us with anxiety and anguish.

On December 5, 1946, events did indeed appear to take a turn for the better. The date is a significant one in the Negroes' struggle for civil rights. On that day President Truman, by executive order, created a Committee on Civil Rights. The now famous report of the Committee, entitled "To Secure These Rights," was issued in 1947.

The Commitee's report provided the basis for President Truman's "civil-rights" message to Congress in February 1948, in which he urged legislation creating a National Fair Employment Practices Commission and passage of federal laws prohibiting lynching, racial segregation, and the poll tax. Civil-rights legislation was one of the major issues in the presidential election that followed. Both major parties included a "civil-rights" plank in their platform. Despite major defections in the South (not to mention Henry Wallace's abortive third-party movement in the North) Truman scored the now historical upset victory over Dewey. It appeared that a new era might be opening for the victims of race prejudice.

Much has happened since. We have witnessed the Supreme Court's unanimous 1954 decision outlawing segregation in the schools (Brown v. Board of Education of Topeka), the use of federal troops to enforce that decision, and the gradual capitulation of the border states followed by the slower erosion of resistance in the deep South. A new generation of Southern Negroes, committed to nonviolent resistance and helped by the unspeakable brutalities of Selma and Birmingham and Neshoba County, succeeded in enlisting the active sympathy of the North. The great March on Washington not only prodded Congress into action, it also dramatized the essential dignity of the Negro protest. A breakthrough occurred when for the first time the Senate ended a filibuster on a civil rights bill by invoking cloture, thereby making possible the passage of the Civil Rights Act of 1964.

The 1964 law was designed to enforce the constitutional right to vote. It gave U.S. district courts the power to enjoin against discrimination in public accommodations; a Commission on Equal Employment Opportunity to prevent unfair employment practices was established; and the Commission on Civil Rights charged with preventing discrimination in federally assisted programs was given a new lease on life. It was followed shortly by the Economic Opportunity Act of 1964 and, in 1965, by a voting rights law which suspends all literacy, knowledge and character tests for voters in all states and counties where less than 50 percent of the population of voter age was registered or voted in November, 1964. The same law provides for Federal registrars to qualify voters when the Attorney General finds it necessary to enforce the 15th Amendment's guarantee of the right to vote. A new 1967 civil rights bill before the 90th Congress was threatened as usual with a filibuster on the issue of open housing. The Senate invoked cloture in the spring of 1968 to end the filibuster and pass a new civil rights bill which, among other things, establishes a precedent for prohibiting discrimination in the sale and rental of housing. It is difficult to say whether the measure as written would have passed the House if Martin Luther King had not been assassinated on April 4, 1968—an event which provoked rioting in more than sixty American cities. The bill was signed by the President on April 11, and by 1970 an estimated 80 percent of the nation's housing was affected.

Southern blacks are now voting in growing numbers; they are enrolled increasingly in schools and colleges from which they had been barred; segregation in public places has virtually broken down. For the first time we witness the appearance of a sizeable black middle class, and blacks are being appointed and elected to high public office. The election in 1973 of a black mayor in America's third largest city with a comparatively small black population (about 18 percent)—that same city in which the Watts riots erupted only a few years earlier—was a signal that no pessimistic black separatist can ignore. The widow of Medgar Evers, returning to Mississippi in 1973 exactly ten years after the slaying of her husband, one of the black leaders of the civil rights movement, was greeted by a biracial crowd of nine thousand gathered to honor her dead husband. The Governor of Mississippi had officially declared the occasion Medgar Evers Day—an act that would have led to his impeachment ten years earlier—and was commended by Medgar's brother, now mayor of Fayette. A decade ago hundreds of blacks had been herded into a makeshift jail because they had marched peacefully for the right to vote.

But the "American Dilemma," as Myrdal taught us to call it, stubbornly persists. Although we have not recently had a "long hot summer" with its harvest of mass violence, there is always real danger that some small grievance will be fanned into furious flame and some minor altercation escalated into a destructive holocaust. Carl Rowan and David Mazie, widely read reporters, refer with alarm to "thousands" of ugly racial incidents and the racial polarization which resentful blacks have joined segregationist whites in encouraging. As the following articles will show, we are still far from a solution to our most serious problem.

Attention here has necessarily been limited to one racial minority. The needs and problems of other minorities are, of course, equally worthy of attention. It seemed to the editor preferable to treat the problems of our largest minority in greater (albeit still limited) depth than merely to skim for the sake of appearances over the problems of Americans of Asian origin, Indians, and our large Spanish-speaking population.

9

Pessimism or Optimism?

Progress always seems more rapid to those who act to correct an abuse than to those who suffer from it. Thus, the optimism of the controversial Wattenberg-Scammon article reprinted below and the statistics on which it is based (reenforced by Harvard economist Richard B. Freeman's 1973 Brookings Institution study) are bitterly challenged in the pages of *Crisis* (official organ of the NAACP), leaving us to wonder whether these are differences over facts or fundamental values. Is Father Hesburgh, whose comments below hardly justify self-congratulation on the progress we have made, guilty of the kind of "liberal rhetoric" to which Wattenberg and Scammon refer? As late as 1969 he likened the implementation of civil rights legislation to "putting a Band-Aid on a cancer." Reality or rhetoric?

A PROGRAM FOR RACIAL JUSTICE

Theodore M. Hesburgh

The Reverend Theodore Hesburgh became president of Notre Dame at the age of 33. The university has undergone a spectacular growth since he assumed his post in 1945. The

*speech at Union Theological Seminary on which the following
article is based was delivered on the occasion of his receiving
the Reinhold Niebuhr Award. At that time he held the chair-
manship of the United States Commission on Civil Rights to
which he had been named by Richard Nixon in 1969. Chosen,
reportedly, because of his firm line on student dissidents, he
fell out of favor after his bipartisan commission characterized
the policies and programs of the Nixon administration as a
"major retreat."*

Because of our failure to cope with color differences, as we did with
differences of religion and nationality, we now have uniquely complicated
domestic problems. I speak frankly as a white man to the white majority.
Equally frank talk will be needed between and among the colored minority
groups.

Most of our domestic problems are exacerbated by our problem
with color. In fact, until we recognize this and begin to understand that failing to cope with color means inevitably failing to cope with the other
domestic problems, we are condemning ourselves as a nation to a constant
lowering of our quality of life, to a continual negation of the hopes of an
increasing number of Americans who are now without much hope of real
equality. Moreover, while this is very much a minority problem in its pinch,
it must be very much a majority problem in its solution. The white majority
does not like to face the real cost of the solution.

Few white Americans have taken time to study the real dimensions
of the color problem, except insofar as it touches them personally as whites.
In the context of our segregated society, it touches all too few very acutely.
First, look at the numbers. About one out of every six Americans is colored.
Twenty-two million are black, about 12 million are brown, about a million
are yellow, somewhat less than a million are red, and then there are variations of all these colors—for a total of 36 million Americans. This means
that there are more blacks in America than whites in Canada, more browns
in America than white Australians in Australia. A problem of this dimension cannot be ignored or Band-aided over. It should be noted parentheti-
cally that not all of these colors are equally unequal. Generally, reds are at
the bottom of the totem pole of inequality, browns are in the middle and
blacks, whose problem is larger and has, because of visibility, received more
attention in recent years, are on top. Yellows are a very special case.

All of these, whatever their nonwhite color, are people, Americans
and citizens, and they are probably growing in numbers faster than the white
majority. Consequently, the longer this problem remains unsolved, the
larger and more complicated it becomes. Also, the more intractable become
most of our other domestic problems, which are so enmeshed with the problem of color. The time for solutions is now—it should have been yesterday,
when the problem was smaller. . . .

I believe that we are at a historic crossroads today, much more momentous than that of a century ago. We have witnessed enormous progress for colored Americans, especially blacks, in the sixties. The whole upward thrust may be reversed in the days ahead as white Americans tire of the effort, or are impatient with the tenacity of the problem, the price it really demands of whites everywhere, not only in the South. Never was Santayana's famous dictum truer: Those who ignore history are condemned to repeat its mistakes.

Consider for a moment how the problem of color complicates some of the domestic problems mentioned above. Education is the best issue to begin with, *the* real issue hidden under the phony issue of busing. As an N.A.A.C.P. pamphlet on the matter was entitled: "It Ain't the Busing; It's the Niggers." The title comes from a remark made by a white woman.

When one tries to find an effective approach to the total problem of racial justice, education is by all odds the best. View the vicious circle: A black youngster is generally born into an atmosphere of poverty and failure. He grows up in a poor house in a poor neighborhood. He has a 30 per cent chance of not having a father at home to guide him, and, if so, his mother must often work to support him, which deprives him of the parental education that most white youngsters take for granted. Then he must go to a dismal ghetto school which resembles a jail more than a school and, often enough, functions as a custodial rather than an educational institution. All around him the atmosphere is polluted, not just bad air and water, but a bad human situation in which to grow up: failure, violence, drugs, prostitution, stealing, unemployment, aimlessness, hopelessness.

Our black youngster may be bright, but no matter. Many of our eager politicians of both parties, lusting for office, obliterate whatever hope he might have of leaving this impossible situation. Even if busing is the only way out, and the courts find that he is indeed being deprived of his 14th Amendment rights to equal opportunity in education, busing will not be available to him as a means of redressing his inequality, if these politicians have their way. If good white neighborhood schools are good for whites in the suburbs, then bad black neighborhood schools are in no way good for blacks in the ghetto. But no matter: Blacks should not be allowed to contaminate our nice white schools, or neighborhoods, or businesses, and they don't have enough political power to challenge the white majority anyway. So prejudice speaks.

Mind you, I am not proposing that white children go to bad ghetto schools. I am making the opposite point: that unless black children are given a chance to get out of, and away from, these schools we now finally see as so bad (since white children might have to attend them), then we have destroyed the last bridge out of the ghetto, which we also created by prejudice and often by Government-financed housing policies.

Without a real educational opportunity (which for a black often means a non-ghetto school), the black youngster will never eventually matriculate at a first-rate college or university, will never qualify for a profession or even a decent job, will never be able to support his family, will often drop out of the only dismal school available and become a troublesome, costly and nonproductive member of society. This isn't much fun for him either, so he will also often be frustrated, aggressive, violent.

There is no escape in trying to put the blame for such educational deprivation on inherent lack of talent or virtue. There are too many telling examples of those few given an equal chance measuring up and even excelling. It would be like accusing blacks of lack of physical courage to compete when they were excluded from competition in professional sports, as they were excluded during our apartheid years. Once allowed to compete, they not only excelled, they dominated, despite their being a minority. The same is true in other fields.

There will always be inequality of performance among men and women of every country. Some will be more virtuous, work harder, accomplish more. But it is in the nature of *our* national commitment that here in America all will start equal, all will have equality of opportunity. As long as equality of opportunity is not a reality for all, we have no right to criticize bad performance. And it is not a reality today.

I am not saying here that blacks can get a good education only in the company of whites, but I am saying that most predominantly white schools are much better than most predominantly black schools in a society where the majority is white and the political power of the purse is white, where most whites live in good neighborhoods and most blacks in the worst neighborhoods—those discarded by whites. I am saying that in America, North and South, East and West, white children educated in predominantly white schools have historically had a better education than black children educated in predominantly black schools. There have been ample studies to document this.

Some say improve the ghetto schools, but for long decades we whites have been unconcerned about black education and blacks are rightly dubious about another empty promise. Meanwhile, another generation of young blacks and other colored minorities is condemned to another round of human hopelessness.

One final point: Ever since there have been buses, white parents have been busing their children to where the best education was—as black children were bused only to inferior schools, away from whites. It was only when it looked as if the process might be reversed that the furor began.

It has been rightly observed that the educational and busing crisis is fundamentally created by housing patterns, and that the problem will remain with us until open housing becomes a reality. No segment of American life is more completely ruled by prejudice and white superiority than housing. It is a simple fact that an underworld gangster or a white call girl can more easily rent or buy a house in most white neighborhoods than a black

professional man or woman. A very short time ago, prejudice was so institutionalized that it could be written into leases. The lily-white arrangement
was preserved by Federal housing agencies. Even after World War II,
houses foreclosed on white veterans would not be shown to black veterans.

Thus we have created the ghettos that blight all of our large cities
in every part of the country. Now begins a new and more subtle development. Those with education, employment and social acceptance—mainly
white—move to the suburbs. Businesses and employment follow them. So
the blacks are ringed by the white noose of the suburbs. If some people try
to build low- and moderate-income housing there, so blacks can escape the
ghettos and be closer to better schools and jobs, suddenly there are new
zoning laws requiring multiple-acre tracts for each dwelling. The suburbs
are willing to enjoy every possible Federal subsidy for roads, sewerage,
schools and so on, but do nothing that would mean sharing their better
living conditions with colored minorities. Even improvements in public
transportation come about largely because of the demands of the affluent,
who must get into the city to work and back to the safe and secure suburbs
at night.

No one person is responsible for this pattern of prejudice, but
everyone white is responsible; we and our white institutions, our white housing contractors, our white real-estate agents, our white financial and lending
entities—all maintain the myth that one black family, no matter how nice,
inevitably ruins the neighborhood. This is a self-fulfilling prophecy, and the
real-estate agents have made it a profitable myth by their block-busting
techniques.

Why do we have bad neighborhoods in the world's most affluent
country? Even in some less affluent European countries there are no neighborhoods as bad as ours. Again, we face the problem of color and the total
failure to integrate one-sixth of our population with the other five-sixths.
There are relatively few blacks who live in good neighborhoods. Those who
do are well-educated and well-employed—and they are the proof of what is
possible in America, as well as the exception to the present rule of prejudice
that has given us our ghettos.

As far back as present memories go, and further beyond to slavery and
Reconstruction days, it was unthinkable for most whites to live next door to
blacks, since blacks were thought to be inferior—simply because of their
color—and, therefore, a superior white should not socialize with an inferior
black. It was all right for blacks to take care of white children and nurse
them, clean the house, wash the clothes, tend the sick, build the buildings,
cook and serve the meals and clean up afterward, even sleep with lecherous
whites who so desired, but even after all that association, they must be kept
in their place. That meant until a decade ago there were many places in
America where blacks could not get a drink of water or a Coke, a meal or
a room, a seat up front on a bus, a swim, a place to pray, a bed in a hospital

or, God help us, a place to be buried—if doing any of this involved associating with whites. It is part of my real hope for America that all, or most, of this daily affront to the human dignity of blacks was outlawed in one day by the Civil Rights Act of 1964. But there is no known way of outlawing prejudice, and all of us whites must confess that the sense of white superiority is still deeply rooted within us. As a Catholic priest I should certainly know better, but I catch myself thinking and judging unjustly almost every day.

If problems of housing and education are organically linked, there is a third link in the chain—employment. If you have equal access to jobs, you have access to what are called the good things in life: education, housing, health, food and drink. Now the simple fact is that most Americans of color have unequal access to the better jobs because of a variety of reasons growing out of other inequalities—mainly educational. Ninety-six per cent of the jobs paying above $15,000 annually in America are held by *white men,* which says something about women's inequality, too. There are always twice as many unemployed blacks as whites, and black teen-agers are about 25 per cent unemployed and often unemployable, mainly because they went to ghetto schools or dropped out of them. Those blacks who are employed make on the average about half as much as whites. Most black mothers of families must also work to supplement the family income. Even those liberal white institutions for the working man—the labor unions in the construction trades—have had a miserable record in granting equal access to work.

Because of the numbers involved and the available facts, I have mainly spoken here of blacks, but we learned a few years ago in a Southwest Chicano hearing of the Civil Rights Commission that the average *family* income of Chicano migrant farm workers in Texas was $1,400 a year. The condition of their housing, educational, health and social services was far worse than that of most blacks. American Indians, we are learning, are equally far below the miserably low scale of Chicano farm workers.

I have never been deeply concerned about the wealthy or powerful of this land being deprived of their rights. Only the poor and powerless have these problems in any real sense. And even here, the beginnings of Federal help—for legal services, for example—are now under attack by insensitive legislators and executives on both the Federal and state levels. New York contractors have been let off the hook for two years on their "affirmative-action" minority-employment programs. Pressure on the Federal Civil Service Commission to hire more minority-group employees has been relaxed, just when the commission had finally begun to move forward on this problem. Again, it's the old vicious circle: Deny equal opportunity to become qualified and then deny employment on the basis of nonqualification.

Americans have traditionally tried to solve problems with money, except when it comes to our own poor. I am willing to concede that the present welfare situation is a mess and should be totally reorganized. However, 75 per cent of present welfare goes to the poor who, as the good Lord reminded us, will always be with us: children without parents, the physically disabled, the blind and the halt, the old, the wounded veterans, the mentally deficient. Even some wealthy people who are so ready to criticize welfare costs cannot want this group to starve or be homeless.

As for the "welfare loafers," it makes little sense to criticize anyone willing to work if there are no jobs available or no training available to qualify for work. I believe that everyone who can work, should work—but this does mean both creating enough jobs and opening job training for those now denied it because of color.

It would be interesting to compare welfare with other forms of American governmental subsidization as to cost and human justification. For openers, in nonwelfare costs, we subsidized others to the tune of $43-billion last year.

For example, we subsidize wealthy farmers; we subsidize railroads and airlines, and roads for those who have cars; we subsidize those looking for oil and gas, those investing in tax-free bonds, those sending heavy mail in huge quantities for commercial purposes; we subsidize military dictatorships, foreign investments, trips to the moon, travel by Congressmen and Government executives, everywhere for practically any purpose. We subsidize grain for the Russians and Chinese, even though it raises the cost of bread for our poor. We subsidize most poor countries while we gripe about a miserable subsidy to the poor of our own country, and cannot face the obvious solution: federalizing the program, providing work for those who can work and providing a minimal annual income for decent human living in America.

All this is tied up with tax reform, which would tend to lighten the burden of Middle Americans, whether colored or not. They now bear a disproportionate share of the financing of dubious governmental programs, and it is their sons who disproportionately paid with their lives and limbs for the Vietnam debacle. If America is verging toward populism today, it is precisely because the numerous lower- and middle-class Americans, the former made up chiefly of colored Americans and the latter of white ethnic Americans, are beginning to take equality of opportunity seriously, and justice and fairness, too.

The price of solving our domestic problems, especially the problem of color inherent in most of them, is very high. The price of delay is ever larger problems and ultimately a larger human cost. No nation will have true civil peace—and freedom—unless it expends every possible effort to achieve justice for everyone and, most of all, for the poor and powerless. . . . We might take some direct and simple steps: . . .

 • Eliminate *all* inferior schools. In America, there are too many whites, as well as colored children, in inexcusably poor schools. Recognize also that the school is the mirror of the neighborhood, that if the neighborhood is deteriorated, so the school will be.

● Accommodate in our already good schools—and they are the majority—as many of those children who are now being only barely educated, or not educated at all, as we can. If the only way to get students from bad schools is by busing, then bus them. Keep in mind the standards on busing established by the Supreme Court—not to bus in a way that will harm the child's health or his education. Also keep in mind that some minority parents would be willing to have their children take a reasonably long bus ride—as is done in most rural areas—if there is a vastly improved educational opportunity at the end of the ride.

● Give top priority to Federal and state assistance to experiment with new approaches to the educational problem and with integration of minority colored children into the improved mainstream of American education. Majority white students will cope better with the persistent American problem of color, I expect, if they have some acquaintance with black, brown, red and yellow American children, wherever possible, and on all levels of education—even at play. Only in this way will American white youngsters begin to see children of other colors as persons, as human beings who are different, yet alike, in their human loneliness, hope, fear and love. Children are not born with prejudice; they have to acquire it. An important prerequisite for living in a pluralistic society is education in a milieu free of prejudiced, stereotyped judgments about people who are different. Classroom instruction in the democratic goals of tolerance and understanding affirms and strengthens what is learned in the living integrated context.

● Do not confuse the educational problems of enormous black ghettos, like those in New York, Chicago, Washington, D.C., and Detroit, with the normal educational scene in America, where quiet progress was being made, North and South, before the retrogressive interference of vote-seeking politicians who needlessly muddied the waters.

● In very special problem areas, like those of urban ghettos, experiment with large-scale educational parks that create their own physical environment—much like some great Midwestern state universities that accommodate and educate 50,000 to 60,000 students at once. In such parks, we could provide both education and recreation for minority and majority children, as well as all the special classes needed, health and nutritional services, and room for all the private agencies and social services. Teachers would work with both talented and slow children there, in an atmosphere free of fear. All the physical hazards of the ghetto school could be eliminated, and there would be economy of size. All parents should be involved. They, too, might begin to learn how the presence of Americans of color can enrich both the educational process and the quality of life, as other groups of immigrants who were "different" have enriched American life.

● Vocational training and adult education must be an important element among our educational priorities. . . .

● Make buying a house, anywhere, for any American who can afford it, as simple as it is now to buy anything else.

● Rebuild the central city and eliminate the ghetto by bulldozing all condemned and dilapidated housing, replacing it with low, moderate- and high-income housing *throughout* the metropolitan area, on the pattern of the new cities of Reston, Va., and Columbia, Md. Bring more jobs, parks, cultural and recreational centers and pedestrian streets to the inner city. Re-establish, by total community effort, a sense of security in the city, a sense of belonging, pride and caring.

● Plan new satellite towns like Columbia and Reston that are linked to central cities by rapid transit and integrate people of different racial and economic groups. Shift the highway program to rapid transit plans that are fairer for all, more efficient, and less polluting. . . .

● Make equal access to employment a reality, not a fiction. Promote new legislation to insure that any business, including government, any trade, any association, any profession that discriminates in any way in hiring and promoting qualified people will be cut off from any participation whatever in public funds, directly or indirectly. The same for communities that tolerate only what maintains their lily-white situation. Public funds are for all the public and their expenditures and benefits must be color-blind.

So much of the social criticism one hears these days—even apart from campaign oratory—sounds dismal, threatening and depressing. I suppose that what I have written is also guilty of the same grayness. So I would like to conclude by suggesting that remaking our beloved America in its professed image can be adventurous, inspiring, exciting, even fun. We must be willing to shuck the status quo when it is retrogressive, unjust and going nowhere. We have to be open to change and alert to the great values that inspired this land's beginning and led it to greatness. We cannot do all that I have proposed without leadership to inspire us, agreement of all our people and the will to do it together. We must put an end to the expedient political compromises that stifle progress to gain votes. Many will enjoy more justice and a fuller life if we do what we must. A few Americans will be somewhat reduced materially, but enlarged spiritually, if they can see the justice of it all.

The consequences of not changing would be far worse. We could become, as we are now becoming, a polarized, divided nation, separated into hating groups of white and colored, rich and poor, educated and uneducated, employed and unemployed, secure and insecure, healthy and unhealthy, well-housed and poorly housed, hopeful and hopeless. Such a nation would be a breeding ground for disaster, for continual crisis, for fear and hatefulness, for constant social strife. . . .

BLACK PROGRESS AND LIBERAL RHETORIC

Ben J. Wattenberg and Richard M. Scammon

Some may find in the results reported by Wattenberg and Scammon a reason for smugness and self-congratulation. The authors clearly do not intend such a result. Surprising as their reports of progress may be, they caution that the situation is by no means uniformly good, that parity is a still unrealized goal, and that there is no cause for complacency.

B. J. Wattenberg was an aide to President Lyndon Johnson and was associated with the government's publication in 1967 and 1968 of Social and Economic Conditions of Negroes in the United States. *He has also been a political aide to Senators Hubert Humphrey and Henry Jackson. R. M. Scammon was director of the U.S. Census Bureau from 1961 to 1965 and is now director of the Elections Research Center in Washington. He was also a consultant to the U.S. Civil Rights Commission. He and Wattenberg are coauthors of* This is U.S.A. *(1965) and* The Real Majority *(1972).*

A remarkable development has taken place in America over the last dozen years: for the first time in the history of the republic, truly large and growing numbers of American blacks have been moving into the middle class, so that by now these numbers can reasonably be said to add up to a *majority* of black Americans—a slender majority, but a majority neverthe-less.

This development, which has occurred against a historical back-drop of social and economic discrimination, is nothing short of revolution-ary. Despite the fact that Southern blacks are economically still significantly worse off than Northern, and older blacks than younger, and despite the fact too that the economic and social gap separating whites and blacks is still a national disgrace, "middle class" has now become an accurate term to describe the social and economic condition of somewhat more than half of black Americans.

What does "middle class" mean in this context? Obviously any line that is drawn in the sociological sand must have about it something of the arbitrary and the artificial, yet there are a number of statistical criteria—notably in the areas of income, job patterns, and education—that serve to measure the relative standing of groups (as well, of course, as individuals) in society, and these indices have an unambiguous tale to tell about the recent economic and social movement of American blacks. Obviously, too, "middle class" as used here does not refer to a condition of affluence, to a black population made up of doctors, lawyers, and businessmen with cabin cruisers (although such blacks certainly do exist). It refers rather to the condition of that vast majority of working-class Americans who, although often hard-pressed, have safely put poverty behind them and are now looking ahead, no longer back; it refers not only to engineers and teachers, but also to plasterers, painters, bus drivers, lathe operators, secretaries, bank tellers, and automobile assembly-line workers: the kinds of people who, when they are white, are described as "Middle Americans" or members of the silent, real, or new American majorities. It refers, in the words of the economist Thomas Sowell, who is himself black, to "black men and women who go to work five days a week, pay their bills, try to find some happiness for themselves, and raise their children to be decent people with better prospects than they had. . . ."

To belong to this "middle class" means, first, to have enough to eat, to have adequate, if not necessarily expensive, clothes to wear, and to be able to afford housing that is safe and sanitary. But that is only the beginning. The advent of a majority of blacks into the middle-income class has triggered a domino-like movement throughout American society. Once the necessities of food, shelter, and clothing are provided for, a vast flow of secondary desires follows. A middle-income family wants not only a house that is safe and sanitary but one in a safe and sanitary neighborhood. Middle-income parents want their children to go to good schools, to stay in high school and graduate and, they hope, then go on to college. The young adults who come out of high school and college want better jobs than those their parents have held, the kinds of jobs that have always been available to whites in an equivalent socioeconomic position.

The middle-income blacks, as we shall see, have made much headway toward satisfying all these traditional middle-class desires. Their progress has hardly been trouble-free; as is the case with all forms of sharp economic movement, it has been accompanied by considerable social turbulence, much of it occasioned by race prejudice, and it has had a tremendous impact on the political life of the nation at large. But it is real progress, a massive achievement; and to all appearances it is here to stay.

This is a phenomenon of enormous portent for the future of American society. That it should have come about, as it has, at a time when many civil-rights leaders and liberals alike have insisted that conditions for American blacks are not improving at all, but actually deteriorating, is not the least astonishing aspect of the entire episode. It will be a great and tragic irony if this insistence on failure should in the end prove a hindrance to the continued upward progress of American blacks.

The first and most basic index of status in American life is money, and it is therefore to comparative income statistics that we must turn first to show the broad outlines of black upward mobility in the 1960's. According to the 1970 census figures, income for white families in America went up by 69 per cent in the 1960's, while income for black families[1] went up by 99.6 per cent. If we round off the 99.6 per cent figure it can be stated that black family income actually doubled during a single decade![2]

The *ratio* of black family income to white family income also changed dramatically in the period, climbing from 53 per cent in 1961 to 63 per cent in 1971. It might be argued—and rightly—that 63 per cent is a long way from 100 per cent and still scandalously low, but what is open to little argument is that there has been sharp progress—a catching up—during recent years which was not at all apparent during the previous decade (the ratio of black to white family incomes was the same in 1961 as it had been in 1951). And the changing percentage of black families earning above $10,000 is even more startling, jumping from 13 per cent in 1961 to 30 per cent in 1971 (from 1951 to 1961 the percentage had increased from 3 to 13); these figures are in 1971 constant dollars, the effects of inflation having been factored out.

The median family income in the United States in 1971 was $10,-285; today, it can be estimated at $11,000. This figure represents the middle-of-the-middle of family income distribution. Some lower figure—say, $8,000 outside the South—may be said to represent the bottom-of-the-middle or the beginning of middle-income status in America. In the South, where median income averages almost $2,000 lower, and where a disproportionate number of blacks still lives, the bottom-of-the-middle line may be drawn at $6,000. By these criteria, and again adjusting for recent income increases, just over half of black families in the United States are by now economically in the middle class (about 52 per cent).

The march of blacks across the invisible line into the lower-middle and middle classes may be seen even more clearly by looking at the data on the regional rather than on the national level, and by breaking down the figures by age and family characteristics. Thus, there is a sharp difference between black income in the South and black income elsewhere. Whereas in 1970 black family income in the South was 57 per cent of white family income, outside the South the corresponding figure was 74 per cent. A second variable affecting black-white income ratios is family status. As we shall note later, black families are much more likely than white families to be "female-headed," but when they are *not*—when the families are "husband-

---

[1] These figures are for "Negroes and other races." Throughout this essay the data used are either for "Negroes" or, when not available, for "Negroes and Other Races" as defined by the Census Bureau. Since "Negroes" comprise 90 per cent of this latter category, the index may be considered relatively reliable for American blacks as a whole.

[2] The statement, however, would be accurate only if inflation had not eroded *everyone's* income. Taking inflation into account we find that the actual income increases come out to 34 per cent for whites and 59 per cent for blacks.

wife" families—income is much likelier to approach equality with comparable white family incomes. Among black husband-wife families all over America in 1970, income was 73 per cent of white family income. Outside the South it was 88 per cent. But perhaps the most encouraging, and most significant, cross-tabulation of the income data concerns the economic status of young blacks. These young men and women have made striking educational gains in recent years; they have made gains in "occupation" as well, i.e., in the sorts of jobs they hold; and they have made gains in the amounts of money they earn. Black males aged 25–34, for example, earn 80 per cent of white levels of income on a national basis.

When one combines all these factors—youth, non-Southern residence, and an unbroken family—a truly striking statistic emerges. The median income of black husband-wife families, in the North and West, with the head of family under 35 years of age, rose from 78 per cent of white income in 1959 to 96 per cent in 1970. There is a word to describe that figure: parity. And if we add a fourth variable to the equation, and examine families in which both the husband and wife work, the figures come out to 85 per cent in 1959, and in 1970—104 per cent! For such families, parity has not only been achieved, it has even been surpassed: young, married blacks, outside of the South, with husband and wife both working, earn as much as or a trifle more than comparable whites.[3]

If income statistics are the most basic index of economic mobility in the United States, employment patterns follow closely behind. For the last two decades the reality of the black-white employment situation can be summed up, bleakly, as follows: black unemployment rates have been twice as high as white rates. But in recent years a massive shift has occurred in the identity of the black unemployed. A cross-tabulation of married men over age 20 reveals a far sharper *drop* in unemployment among blacks than for the population as a whole, as is shown by this comparison of two early years of the 60's with two early years of the 70's:

Unemployment Rate and Black-to-White
Ratio for Married Men, 20 Years and Over,
with Spouse Present, 1962 to 1972

	Negro & Other Races %	*White* %	*Ratio*
1962	7.9	3.1	2.5 to 1
1963	6.8	3.0	2.3 to 1
1971	4.9	3.0	1.6 to 1
1972	4.4	2.6	1.7 to 1

---

[3] Some, but by no means all, of these remarkable husband-wife family gains are due to the fact that young black wives outside of the South are somewhat more likely to work year 'round than young white wives (52 per cent versus 36 per cent).

The drop in the ratio from 1962 to 1972 is 53 per cent (from 2.5 to 1, to 1.7 to 1—with 1 to 1 representing parity). Here, too, then, we see a steady and powerful movement into the middle class. Black family men are, like white family men, "at work," that is, at least 95 out of 100 of them are, even during recessionary times.

At the same time, teen-age unemployment has gone up. Among the 1.9 million black teen-agers (age 16–19), unemployment rates in 1960 were 24 per cent; by 1970, the rate had climbed to 29 per cent, and by 1971 to 32 per cent. The rate for white teen-agers fluctuated between 13 and 15 per cent in the same years. These comparative data are discouraging, but there is something to be said about them that is not generally understood. In 1971, of the 1.9 million black teenagers, 1.25 million were "not in the labor force" at all (about a million were students, most of the rest housewives). They were neither "at work" nor "looking for work," and thus not tabulated in unemployment statistics. Of the 650,000 remaining black teen-agers, that is, those actually "in the labor force," more than two-thirds —about 450,000—were "at work." That left about 200,000 actually unemployed, i.e., "looking for work." The fraction 200,000 over 650,000 is what yielded the high "unemployment" rate—the percentage without jobs actively looking for work. But the fact is that even of these 200,000 unemployed black teen-agers, more than half—about 110,000—were *in school,* and about 90 per cent of these were looking for part-time work. That left about 100,000 black teen-agers—male and female—who were both out of work and out of school; this element represented not much more than 5 per cent of the total number of black teen-agers.

In other words, in 1971 about 70 per cent of black teen-agers were in school, about another 25 per cent were at work or at home as housewives; the rest—about 5 per cent—may be called the hard-core, full-time unemployed.[4]

On balance, then: teen-age unemployment rates are up, adult male rates are down, particularly among married males. Black teen-agers are mostly in school, adults are mostly supporting families. The net result would seem to be an important social and economic plus, despite the unfortunately large and continuing disproportion in black-white unemployment rates.

However, it is important to note that in those same families the husbands were also making progress. They earned 76 per cent of comparable white husbands in 1959—and 90 per cent of comparable white husbands in 1970.

[4] To be sure, many of those who were in school or at home wanted, and needed, work, particularly part-time work, and could not get it. They needed money to help support themselves through school, to provide a second income to make ends meet, to help out their parents and siblings struggling at home with too little money and too many mouths to feed. But they were not the primary breadwinners, and their relative position has to be judged accordingly.

The overall employment pattern, of course, is made up of more than the statistics of who is at work and who is without work. Of equal significance is what *kinds* of jobs people hold. And here again we see major progress by blacks in gaining access to middle-class occupations, especially in the categories of "white-collar workers," "craftsmen," and "operatives":

Numbers of White-Collar Workers, Craftsmen, and Operatives, in Millions

	Negro	*White*
1960	2.9	46.1
1970	5.1	57.0
Percentage increase	*76*	*24*

Over the same decade the numbers of Negroes in "other" work— primarily low-paying jobs in private households, as service workers, farm workers, and laborers—decreased from 4 million to 3.5 million. Comparing, then, the balance of occupational status for blacks in America in 1960 and 1970, we find that in 1960 blacks in "good" jobs totaled 2.9 million while blacks in "not good" jobs totaled 4 million; by 1970 the number of blacks with "good" jobs totaled 5.1 million, while those with "not good" jobs totaled 3.4 million—in short, a reversal, and then some. In 1960, 42 per cent of blacks held "good" (i.e., middle-class) jobs—less than half. By 1970 the rate had climbed to 64 per cent—almost two-thirds. . . .

Along with higher incomes and better jobs the 1960's also saw a great breakthrough in the area of education. Thus in 1960 only 36 per cent of young black males finished four years of high school, the educational level that seems to separate Americans into "middle class" and "non-middle class." By 1970 the rate was more than half—54 per cent. Among young black women the increase was even greater—from 41 per cent in 1960 to 61 per cent in 1971.

. . . The leap into the educational middle class can be seen in college-enrollment statistics. In 1970, there were over half a million young blacks in college, slightly more than 9 per cent of the total. Over a short six-year period—from 1965 to 1971—the comparative figures are as follows:

Per Cent of Persons, Aged 18–24, Enrolled in College 1965–1971

	1965	*1971*
	%	*%*
Negro	10	18
White	26	27
"Gap"	16	9

Again, there is a gap and it is still large—but it has narrowed considerably.

By most of the standards by which Americans measure middle-class status, then, blacks in the last decade have made mighty strides—both absolutely and relative to whites—and the time has come for this fact to be recognized. The image of the black in America must be changed, from an earlier one of an uneducated, unemployed, poverty-stricken slum-dweller, to that of an individual earning a living wage at a decent job, with children who stay in school and aspire to still-better wages and still-better jobs, living not in a slum (but still in a ghetto), in a decent if unelaborate dwelling, still economically behind his white counterpart but catching up.

But to say all this, while indeed correct, is *not* to say that the situation is uniformly good; that all blacks are in the middle class; that blacks as a whole have achieved parity with whites; that poverty is largely a thing of the past; or, last but not least, that there is cause for complacency in the realm of social and economic policy. None of these conclusions, in fact, is valid.

The high incidence of broken families among blacks—regarded by some observers as the key to the pathology of the black slums—has increased substantially in recent years. . . . Today, close to a third of black families are headed by females; twenty-odd years ago it was about a sixth. The white rate has changed only marginally in the same period.

The phrase "black female-headed families" is too often interchangeable with a more succinct term: "poor." In 1971, more than half (54 per cent) of such families were living below what the government calls the "low-income level"; only 17 per cent of male-headed families could be so designated. And the brutal fact is that from 1959 to 1971 the number of male-headed families in poverty decreased by more than half, while the number of female-headed families in poverty increased by a third. Thus, by 1971, almost six in ten black families in poverty were female-headed. As male-headed families exited from the poverty class, female-headed families entered it in growing numbers.

As the numbers and relative percentages of black female-headed families soared, so too did the numbers and rates of blacks on welfare.[5] In 1960, there were 3.1 million total welfare recipients in the United States. Of that number it is estimated that 41 per cent—roughly 1.3 million—were black, or about 7 per cent of the 18.8 million Negroes in America in 1960. As the decade progressed, the overall figures rose precipitously. . . .

Of the 10.6 million on welfare in 1971, 45 per cent were black—4.8 million. Of the total black population of 23 million, 21 per cent were on AFDC—up from 7 per cent only eleven years earlier.

---

[5] "Welfare" as the term is generally used refers primarily to aid disbursed under the category "Aid to Families with Dependent Children" (AFDC)—and numbers for that program are the ones used here.

It would be blinding ourselves to reality to deny the seriousness of these figures. The rise in female-headed black families living in poverty, and the concomitant increase in the number of blacks on welfare, is a deplorable situation from whatever angle it is viewed. It is deplorable for the millions of black children who grow up without a father in the house. It is deplorable for the stigma it attaches to those receiving welfare, and for the scars it inflicts on their spirit. And it is deplorable because of all the other circumstances that poverty entails: bad diet, bad clothing, bad housing, inferior medical care, etc. It is deplorable for black mothers torn between the desire to devote time and care to their children—especially children of pre-school age—and the desire to earn a better living than what the often inadequate welfare payments provide. These "welfare mothers" are often trapped in deteriorating neighborhoods that are havens for addicts, criminals, drunks, prostitutes, vandals, rapists, and muggers; existence—indeed mere survival —under such circumstances is perilous and grim.

And the situation is also deplorable because of what it does to our politicians and our politics—particularly liberal politicians and liberal politics. Middle-class voters—including many black middle-class voters—don't want to pay the bill for families they believe are "shiftless," for families they believe ought to be cared for by the (absent) man of the house. They especially resent paying when they believe that the standard of living they are providing for families on welfare has begun to approach their own, a standard they have toiled long and hard to reach. Politicians with liberal instincts feel compassion for the poor and the needy, but they also feel the hot breath of the voters on their necks. Caught between compassion and self-interest, liberal politicians also face torment from more conservative candidates who are perfectly willing, even anxious, to exploit the situation further.

Yet the welfare figures alone, deplorable as they are, do not tell the full story. For the increase in the percentage of blacks on welfare has occurred during a time when the rate of blacks in poverty has sharply decreased. The meaning of this apparent paradox is simply that those blacks still in poverty are more likely than they once were to be receiving aid. The percentage of blacks in poverty has gone sharply down from 48 to 29 per cent in the years from 1959 to 1971. That is an enormous change. At the same time, as we have seen, the percentage of blacks on welfare has gone sharply up—by about three times, from 7 to 21 per cent: another enormous change. A black person in the poverty range, then, is far more likely to be receiving welfare now than in the early 60's, perhaps as much as five times as likely. And whatever may be said about the deficiencies of AFDC as a program, not to mention the panoply of other welfare services like food stamps and Medicaid, it seems an unequivocal gain that poor blacks are now getting welfare whereas at an earlier time they were getting nothing at all. . . .

What do all these figures on poverty and dependency tell us? First of all, there are fewer blacks in poverty. Secondly, those blacks in poverty are far more likely to be receiving help than was formerly the case. And finally, poor blacks are rising to levels closer to the line dividing poverty from nonpoverty than before. Now, however, two additional factors must be considered which bear upon the current situation, and these are the changing demographic characteristics of the black poor and the problem of crime.

By and large over the last decade, people engaged in full-time work have left the poverty class. Thus the poor today are disproportionately the elderly and those in female-headed families; this holds true for whites and blacks alike. From 1959 to 1971 the percentage of all those in poverty who were over age 65 *increased* from 14 to 17 per cent, and the percentage of those families in poverty that were female-headed went up from 23 to 40 per cent.

It has been said that this change in the characteristics of the black poor amounts only to exchanging male poverty for female-poverty-plus-dependency, and that its net effect has thus been an increase, not a decrease, in dependency, as well as the creation of a vicious circle—what has been called the "welfare mess"—that drives more and more men away from home. But there is another side to the picture as well. As long as the poor are to remain with us—a notion that has outlived necessity but not, unfortunately, fact—it can surely be argued that it is better, all things considered, that their numbers be made up of those unable to work. Such a situation may be—is—a social tragedy of the first order; but an alternative situation —in which a husband-wife family, with the husband fully employed, was still on welfare—would be intolerable, both for the recipients and for the body politic as a whole.

Moreover, it is simply wrong to view every instance of female-poverty-plus-dependency as a net social loss. The "welfare mess" has also offered the woman who faces a drunk and brutal husband the option—however unpleasant—of telling him to pack up and get out. It may put her family on welfare, but it also dissolves a destructive relationship; this, after all, is an option that the upper classes have had, and used, for a long time.

As for the problem of crime, it hardly needs repeating, and scarcely needs to be documented, that crime rates—particularly violent crime rates —are high among blacks. Blacks comprise only about a ninth of the U.S. population, yet more blacks were arrested for crimes of violence in 1970 than whites—105,000 versus 96,000. This means, essentially, that the rate of violent crimes among blacks is about ten times the rate among whites. Furthermore, the victims of crime are also disproportionately black. In 1965, blacks were two-and-a-half times more likely than whites to be the victims of rape, robbery, or aggravated assault. In 1970 more blacks than whites were murdered: 7,490 blacks compared with 5,999 whites.

But as with the issue of dependency, so with the issue of crime. The negative side is bleak—bleaker in this instance than in years past, bleak to the point of horror and social morbidity. Yet it is important to note that while the rates of violent crime among blacks have soared, they have not done so equally throughout the black community. As blacks make economic progress into the middle class they tend to leave their old inner-city slum neighborhoods for better, safer environments. The old neighborhoods, like Hough and Watts, have often actually lost population in recent years. As the upwardly mobile leave the slum, its character undergoes an important change. It used to be a generally unsafe and unpleasant neighborhood, but one with a sizable quotient of hard-working, law-abiding families that provided some sort of social leavening and stability. Now it has become a place made up disproportionately of the dependent poor—the female-headed families and the elderly—and social derelicts: winos, addicts, hustlers, pimps, prostitutes, criminals, and bums. And the crime rates are high beyond imagining.

Yet one of the most significant aspects of the inner-city slum neighborhoods may turn out to be not the people who live there, but the people who live there no longer, the increasing numbers of middle-class blacks who now live in neighborhoods where crime—while still an enormous problem —is one that can be borne. It would be barbaric to contend that the near-safety of the black middle class, even if it is now a slim majority, somehow justifies the continued fear and degradation of those remaining in the slum. But it would be merely demagogic to pretend that the progress of any group of people can be accomplished all at once and without class fragmentation. The history of group progress in America tells us otherwise—as the present condition of the poor Irish, the poor Jews, and the poor Wasps testifies. The point we make is a simple, if harsh, one: the fact that some blacks have been "left behind" does not in itself negate the fact of massive black success.

Judging progress is of necessity a cold and comparative discipline. We believe, however, that on the basis of the statistics we have examined, it is fair to say that for American blacks *generally* in the 1960's a huge amount of progress was made—although there is still a substantial and necessary distance to traverse before some rough level of parity is reached. . . .

But what of the future? Two scenarios seem plausible to us; a third —an unpleasant one—seems unlikely.

The first scenario envisages continued progress for American blacks, not only absolutely as the rest of the nation progresses, but 1960's-style, in the form of a continued march toward statistical parity with whites. At least two good sets of reasons can be adduced to confirm the likelihood of this taking place. There are, first, the structural reasons. Black income levels are lowest in the South, yet rising relatively fastest there (up 113 per cent from

1960 to 1970, versus rates of from 70 to 80 per cent in other regions). A majority of all blacks still live in the South (compared with 31 per cent of all Americans), yet out-migration has been substantial and seems to be continuing. Blacks outside the South make more money than blacks in the South. There is no basis for supposing that any of these trends will change: blacks will continue to live disproportionately in the South where black earnings are climbing fastest, and they will continue to leave the South, thus getting an automatic boost toward income parity. From a broad statistical point of view, then, the "Southern" situation argues favorably both for blacks in the South and for blacks leaving it.

Another structural consideration is the status of young blacks. As noted earlier, the sharpest relative gains in the last decade were made by black families under 35. If this pattern continues—and there is no reason to believe it will not—it will of its own weight continue to move the total black-white numbers closer to parity. Elderly blacks will leave the labor force and ultimately die, and will be replaced by the new cohorts of young blacks (who happen to be a disproportionately large group today). These new young black families will enter at the present close-to-parity rates now held by young black families as a whole. Further, it seems likely that the now-young but soon-to-be-middle-aged blacks will continue to retain some, most, or all of their present relatively high standing as they reach their late thirties and early forties. This seems especially plausible if one assumes that young black families have made income progress in large measure because of their greater educational attainments and because they hold better jobs than they used to; the same jobs and the same educational background will continue to serve them in good stead as they move into middle age. A black who enters the civil service, or a labor union, at age 25—because he had suitable education or apprentice training—will not only not lose ground as he ages, but will gain all the normal advantages of seniority. What this means, in effect, is that the progress that is now discernible is due not to the sheer youth of young blacks, but to the fact that something happened in America that opened up paths of mobility for young blacks. As the proportion of those able to take advantage of this new situation becomes an ever-greater share of the total black population, the black-white statistics will look better and better as the years go on.

Beyond the structural reasons for assuring continued progress are the political and psychic ones. Something did indeed happen in the 1960's: the logjam broke—politically, legally, socially, economically, even spiritually—and there is no going back. Not Richard Nixon, not Barry Goldwater, not even Strom Thurmond or James Eastland wants to return to Little Rock, to Birmingham, to Selma. The logjam having broken, according to the first scenario, things will never be the same; continued progress is inevitable.

In the second—less optimistic—scenario of the future, the broad structural factors just mentioned are taken into account, the broad political-cultural factors are minimized, and two other factors are introduced.

First, insofar as it can be measured sketchily over a short period of time, progress in the Nixon years of 1969, 1970, and 1971 was less dramatic than in the Kennedy-Johnson years. True, the slowdown was not aimed at blacks; there was a national economic recession, and if the sinking rate of blacks in poverty stopped sinking, so, roughly, did the rate for whites. The rates of black families earning $10,000 a year or more in fact continued to climb, although more slowly than earlier. Black income viewed as a fraction of white income seemed to reach a plateau. Unemployment rates climbed for both blacks and whites—somewhat more so for whites. On some fronts progress continued strong—very strong—despite the recession: high-school drop-out rates for black males fell markedly from 1970 to 1971 (for 18-year-olds the rate fell from 30 per cent to 23 per cent; for 19-year-olds from 44 to 29 per cent). . . .

Aside from the recent figures, as the second scenario would have it, there is further reason to be concerned about the new Nixon budget for fiscal 1974. That budget has been described as the death knell of the Great Society, and while the description is no doubt overly dramatic, it is clear that if the President has his way many of the Great Society programs will be cut back or cut out. If these programs were indeed what was responsible for the great progress made by blacks in the 1960's, it follows that progress will decrease as the programs are eliminated or starved. Doing away with the programs, in effect, will presumably do away with some if not all of the relative gains that are likely to accrue from structural forces alone. . . .

The third and final scenario of the future course of events asserts confidently that the Great Society programs were in fact so important that their partial demise will not only eliminate the projected structural gains, but insure an absolute retrogression. Things for blacks will get relatively worse in the 70's according to this scenario.

In our judgment this is an improbable prognosis. President Nixon neither wants to, nor could, undo all the progress of the 60's. No one, for instance, has proposed repealing the Voting Rights Act, which wields enormous political clout. No one has proposed repealing the Public Accommodations Law. Nor the new minimum wages. Nor Medicaid. Nor aid to higher education. In addition, while no one can accurately quantify the impact of the New Frontier and Great Society, we believe it a mistaken analysis that the programs alone were responsible for the progress of the 60's. A key anti-poverty remedy in the past, and one likely to remain so in the future, is a steadily strong economy. The Great Society programs were a central ingredient of progress, but not so central that repeal of some of them now would actually reverse the tide.

It has been our contention, and one which we have attempted to document, that enormous progress has been made by American blacks in the past decade, so much so that a thin majority of American blacks now belong to the middle class. But we noted early in this essay that a blanket of silence seems to envelop the liberal community on this point, so that the economic and social advances made by blacks, far from being trumpeted or even acknowledged, are simply ignored when they are not actually denied. In the face of all the evidence to the contrary, not a few liberal spokesmen and civil-rights activists have claimed that blacks are in fact worse off now than they were ten years ago.

In December of last year the Lyndon Baines Johnson Library in Austin was host to a Civil Rights Symposium on the occasion of the opening of the monumental collection of papers and documents concerned with civil rights during the LBJ era. It was a major event at an institution that had already become known as a first-rate center of scholarship, and it was attended by many of the great and the near-great, the famous and the near-famous, of the civil-rights movement. Among those on hand were Roy Wilkins, Earl Warren, Vernon Jordan, Burke Marshall, Julian Bond, Richard Hatcher, Barbara Jordan, Yvonne Braithwaite Burke, plus a host of panelists. Each had his moment before the microphones, each participated in this most recent collective attempt to evaluate the past, present, and future of the black man's struggle for equality in our time.

Two general themes emerged as the conference went on. The first was a celebration of Lyndon Johnson (a theme which, since his subsequent death, has been sounded as well by those who scant years before had proclaimed him a "honky" and a murderer of children). Homage was paid to Mr. Johnson for the Civil Rights Acts of 1958 and 1960, passed when he was Senate majority leader, for the Voting Rights Act of 1964, for the Public Accommodations Act of 1965, and for the Housing Act of 1968. All this legislation, it was correctly noted, broke the back of legalized discrimination in America. For the first time blacks could vote everywhere in the nation, could eat at a lunch counter, could legally buy a house in any neighborhood. For this great formal progress, LBJ and the civil-rights movement were to be awarded accolades.

Yet curiously the talk was exclusively of new *rights* gained by blacks in this period, not of any achievements made by them as a consequence.

The second theme of the conference was one of condemnation, and its object was the new President, Richard Nixon. Even before the new budget had been announced, it seemed clear to most of the participants at this conference that President Nixon's aim was to roll back progress, undo economic gains, and reduce blacks once again to their former status of servitude and poverty—all in the name of what the participants viewed as his infamous "Southern Strategy."

In a departure from the general chorus of voices Senator Hubert Humphrey addressed himself to new Congressional strategies, stressing that the next round of liberal legislation must be aimed at helping not just the poor or the black, but all Americans, including those, black and white, in the middle class. And the late former President Johnson himself, in his last public address, uttered a stirring plea for reconciliation and a new commitment to equality for all.

But, astonishingly enough, no one—*no one*—thought it necessary, wise, or advisable to take as a theme the remarkable progress—economic, educational, occupational, social—made by blacks over the last decade. Julian Bond, in noting the current statistical condition of blacks in America, said, incredibly:

> . . . We are no longer slaves. Secondly, we can sit at lunch counters, sit downstairs at movie theaters, ride in the front of buses, register, vote, work, and go to school where we once could not. But in a great many ways, we are constantly discovering that things have either not changed at all, or have become much worse. A quick look at all of the facts and figures that measure how well, or how poorly, a people are doing—the kinds of statistics that measure infant mortality, unemployment, median family income, life expectancy—demonstrates clearly that the average black American, while better off in comparison than his father was, is actually worse off when his statistics are measured against similar ones for white people. It is as though black Americans are climbing a molasses mountain in snowshoes, while the rest of the country rides a rather leisurely ski-lift to the top. It is these depressing figures, and the accompanying pathology which results from them, that causes so much discontent and depression in black communities today. The realization is that separately over the years the diverse strategies of Booker T. Washington and Dr. W. E. B. Du Bois and Marcus Garvey and Martin Luther King and Malcolm X have not appreciably improved the material lot of the masses of black folk.

Why have the data of black advancement been kept secret by those who presumably have an interest in making them known? After all, the black man-in-the-street is perfectly aware of the gains that have been made. A Potomac Associates/Gallup Poll taken in 1972, for instance, revealed that whereas whites on the whole said life in America had gotten worse in recent years, blacks said things were getting better (they were the only group of 31 sub-categories who thought so). The answer is of course that civil-rights leaders do know what has happened, and even acknowledge it in private; but they have elected as a matter of policy to mute any public acknowledgment or celebration of black accomplishments in order to maintain moral and political pressure on the administration and on public opinion.

This strategy, we submit, is a mistaken one, counterproductive of its goal; the only people who have been kept under pressure by it are liberals themselves. As has been the case with many aspects of the liberal agenda in the last half-century, civil rights leaders who refuse to claim credit for the successes they have earned only lend themselves to the purposes of those who declare the bankruptcy of liberalism altogether as a political strategy.

Here is the dilemma in which liberals find themselves. Forty years have passed since they became the driving force of American politics, frequently occupying the White House, always influential in the Congress. In this period of time a remarkable body of legislation has been placed on the statute books, as a result of which great economic and social progress has been made in the country at large, from which all Americans have benefited. And this progress liberals now deny, claiming that the programs for which they fought and lobbied have not worked (but at the same time denouncing Richard Nixon when *he* says they haven't worked).

In short, the liberal battle-cry has become, "We have failed; let us continue!" . . .

Now let us suppose that, instead of the institutionalized gloom pervading liberal thought today, a different analysis—an *accurate* analysis—were substituted, and a different rhetoric adopted to conform to it. Of what would it consist? It would begin, first of all, in the recognition that in 1960 and in 1964, the nation elected Presidents who were pledged to get America moving again, to give a better deal to the poor and the black, to break a decades-old legal, political, and social logjam. Thanks to these Presidents, thanks to a liberal impulse in the Congress in the mid-1960's, thanks to the tireless efforts of liberals all over America, the legislation was passed to fulfill that pledge: manpower programs, poverty programs, and a stunning array of health, education, and legal services. Now, more than a decade later, we can look back and see—results. The census and the other statistical indices of our time show success in many crucial areas; in particular, a better deal has been given to the poor and the black to the point where many of them are now in the middle class, just as the Presidential pledges and the legislation promised. The confirming data have been presented above. To be sure, we cannot say absolutely that the legislation was *totally* responsible for the progress made, but we can say absolutely that it was crucial. Liberalism worked.

Normally, given a situation such as the one we have described, the political burden of proof would be on him who wished to deny it, in this case a Republican President with an analysis and a strategy of his own to promote. He would be the one forced to show that life in America has deteriorated, or at least that liberal programs had failed. Instead—at a moment when history and data show victory for their ideas—liberals loudly compete with each other to do his work. Instead of proclaiming success, liberals can only assert that America is a failure, that things are as bad as ever and maybe worse. And President Nixon smiles in agreement.

The problem is more than just political in the narrow, partisan sense. At issue finally is the possibility of achieving a rational and peaceful resolution of the enduring racial problems of this country. By refusing to acknowledge the facts of success, liberals give further currency to the old stereotypes of black poverty—slums, rat-infested dwellings, a self-perpetuating welfare culture—and thereby help to confer legitimacy on the policies of those who would shirk the hard task of social and economic integration. It simply makes no sense to demand of white middle-class Americans that they welcome into their hearts, let alone into their neighborhoods, schools, or places of work, such stereotyped examples of human misery and degradation as liberals proclaim the majority of American blacks to be. It makes eminent sense, on the other hand, to demand of white middle-class Americans that they extend a fair and equal chance to those who have, like them, earned their way into the middle class, as well as to all those millions who stand ready to do so once given the chance. Integration, still the only realistic solution to the race problem, will proceed only as economic class gaps narrow, and are publicly acknowledged to be narrowing. Trumpeting failure, the best deal liberals are likely to get, from this or any other administration, is one that amounts to standpatism. Acknowledging those successes that have in fact been achieved, demanding the means and the money for the completion of the job, liberals might legitimately hope for action, and an extension of their political writ.

BLACK PROGRESS OR ILLIBERAL RHETORIC?

John A. Morsell

Dr. John Morsell, a sociologist, is assistant executive director of the NAACP. One may infer that the views expressed here reflect the position of this moderate organization. The article, written for Crisis, *the official organ of the NAACP, is a direct rejoinder to Wattenberg and Scammon.*

Commentary Magazine for April, 1973, contains an article by Ben J. Wattenberg and Richard M. Scammon entitled "Black Progress and Liberal Rhetoric." It is no accident that the article appears in *Commentary,* since it has seemed for some time that its editors are intent upon dampening the receptivity of liberal whites to the thesis that race is as critical an issue today as it ever was and that massive effort is required to produce genuine correctives. *Commentary* articles have questioned the validity of school de-segregation (using the code-word "busing") and have professed to see in government's halfhearted enforcement of equal employment affirmative action guidelines a revival of restrictive job quotas. The danger of a racially separate, "two-society" nation as envisioned by the Kerner Commission has been both explicitly and implicitly soft-pedalled in the pages of *Commentary,* and there have been explicit avowals by its editor of the change in his thinking from an integrationist to a neutralist position in matters of race.

Now come Wattenberg and Scammon to add another set of planks to the edifice of indifference to the Negro's plight. Their thesis has two parts, both simple: First, things are much better than we are letting on; and, second, Negro leaders and their liberal white supporters (a diminishing breed for some time now) are making a mistake when they insist that the problems are *real,* that the situation is in many respects a desperate one, and that solutions cannot safely be deferred or sought at snail's-pace.

An analysis of "Black Progress and Liberal Rhetoric" must therefore proceed in two directions. First, there is the basic question of how valid are the Wattenberg-Scammon conclusions regarding the near-millennium which Negroes have now attained; second, how cogent is their advice to Negro leadership, whether or not their premises are correct.

According to the authors, "A remarkable development has taken place" since 1961; this development "is nothing short of revolutionary." For the first time, a slender majority (52 per cent) of black Americans can be defined statistically as having crossed over into middle-class status. Middle-class status, while hedged by the authors with some necessary qualifications, is given a cash value—$8,000 or higher a year family income in the North, $6,000 or more a year in the South. Beyond the bare financial criterion, the definition is expanded to encompass those who, "although hard-pressed, have safely put poverty behind them and are now looking ahead, no longer back." It means "to have enough to eat, to have adequate, if not necessarily expensive, clothes to wear, and to be able to afford housing that is safe and sanitary." There is, moreover, a "domino" effect that follows achievement of this condition: The level of aspiration rises, better things are wanted for self and children, people want better jobs and positions than their parents had.

The authors see evidence of phenomenal progress wherever they look. They report, for example, that the ratio of black to white family income moved from 53 per cent in 1961 to 63 percent in 1971. One may question their 63 per cent figure, since the most recent statistics available to us put it at 61 per cent; but it is undeniably higher than it was ten years earlier. What we are not told, however, is that this ratio is, above all, a *fluctuating* figure, whose inconsistency renders it unreliable as an indicator of trend. In 1945, a quarter of a century earlier, the ratio was 57 per cent; it dropped thereafter, rose again to 57 in 1952, and has occupied other points between then and now. In any event when seen in adequate perspective, it appears that the ratio rose from 57 per cent in 1945 to 61 per cent in 1970 —a total of *four percentage points in 25 years!* At this rate of change, parity between Negroes and whites will be achieved somewhere around the year 2270, or about 300 years hence.

It is always possible to engage in selective statistics-hopping, and this Wattenberg-Scammon do with a vengeance. They consistently compare whites to the relatively small groups of blacks enjoying the most favorable conditions. Thus, they note that, among young married Negroes outside the South, with both husband and wife working, incomes even surpass those among young white couples. It hardly needs sophistication to understand what is being pulled here: It is the *combined* black husband-wife income which has attained parity with white family income derived from a single wage-earner. Similarly, black families with both parents are found to be better off and nearer to white families in income than are black families headed only by the mother. Also, black males age 25–34 earn about four-fifths of what their white counterpart earns on a nationwide basis.

But the authors say nothing about the black-white gap in cash terms. Dr. Vivian Henderson, one of the nation's leading economists and the president of Clark College in Atlanta, has noted: "People spend and save dollars. It is this dollar difference that counts. Pronouncements regarding economic progress which are confined to acceleration concepts and percentage change (i.e., the Wattenberg-Scammon approach) obscure the real predicament—Negroes are losing ground rapidly in gaining dollar parity with whites." Census data for 1970 confirmed the growing dollar gap between white and black family income. A joint report of the Bureau of the Census and the Bureau of Labor Statistics revealed that the differential in the median income between white and black families had grown and that "the dollar gap has increased from about $2,500 in 1947 to about $3,600 in 1969."

If one wishes to be similarly selective (and the authors do), a much more favorable showing can be made in unemployment than the stark facts, taken as a whole, could conceivably justify. Nothing could be more reprehensible than the way the authors go about demonstrating that the spectre of massive teenage unemployment is really only a bogeyman, amounting to a mere 5 per cent hard-core, full-time unemployed teenagers. No sources are given for the series of data by which the huge unemployed figure was bit-by-bit reduced (e.g., some are in school, looking only for part-time work, etc.). But when we reach a rock-bottom figure of 100,000 teenagers both out of school and out of work, *this figure is not compared with the 650,000 officially classed as "in the labor force."* Incomplete as that comparison would have been, it would have yielded an effective unemployment rate of over 15 per cent; instead Wattenberg-Scammon compare the 100,000 with the entire 1.9 million black teenagers throughout the country. This is what permits them to arrive at their comforting and reassuring—and patently false—"5 per cent."

But, even if the authors were beyond reproach in their handling of national data on income and employment, their failure to deal with the differential conditions to be found in the large urban ghettos is inexcusable. Here is where the misery is piled up, thick and toughly resistant. Here is where the social dynamite is packed away. Here is where, for example, Department of Labor figures show the deplorable situation among young Negro males in the 18–25 year-old category (an age-range to which Wattenberg-Scammon for some reason never make specific reference). Of these young men, the Labor Department estimates that *50 per cent have never worked and may well never in life enter the labor force.*

We hear nothing about the enormous percentages of Negro men who evade the census taker to begin with (four times as large as among white males, according to the Bureau of the Census), who never even make the unemployment record because they are never counted in the labor force. Thus, in 1966, the U.S. Labor Department conducted special surveys of "sub-employment" in selected non-white urban areas. ("Sub-employment" includes, in addition to the jobless, part-time workers seeking full-time work, marginal earners, and those either not defined in the labor force or missed in the regular surveys.) The average rate of "sub-employment" for ten major ghetto areas was 34 per cent. According to the *Manpower Report of the President* for 1967, "one out of every three slum residents who was already a worker, or should and could become one with suitable help, was either jobless or not earning enough for living above the poverty level."

Wattenberg-Scammon find much cause to rejoice in the figures for apprenticeship training and for educational attainment in general. No one would deny or denigrate the advances made along these lines and yet it must be said that here, too, the benefits to be measured from these factors are grossly overdrawn. It is true that 13 per cent of construction trade apprentices are non-white and that the proportion is growing. It is also true that about 80 per cent of all skilled workmen in construction trades achieved their positions by *other than the apprenticeship route* and that discrimination remains the principal barrier to equality of black representation in those lines of endeavor.

It is certainly a fact that more and more black Americans finish high school and that the college component is steeply on the upgrade. Yet the fact is that the income disparity between white and black *rises,* rather than falls, as they approach parity in educational attainment. In other words, the earnings disparity between a white and a Negro high school graduate is *less* than the disparity between a white and a Negro college graduate! Not too long ago, *The New York Times* reported government studies showing that Negro income lagged behind that of Spanish-speaking Americans. Not only is this disparity the product of the large Mexican-American population's relatively greater affluence, but the disparity prevails in spite of the fact that Negroes are substantially better educated than are Hispanics.

It does not help matters that, after painting their glowing portrait, the authors proceed to enter some caveats against letting optimism run away with us. Their disclaimer comes late in the day, after the primary points have been set forth and emphasized. They acknowledge that equality remains a distant goal and that there is no "cause for complacency in the realm of social and economic policy." They hasten to give us the sad facts about fatherless families, about welfare dependency, about crime. But they find comfort even in the welfare figures, because these mean that, at least, the poverty-stricken are not being ignored.

The Wattenberg-Scammon article is almost totally devoid of any consideration of the psychological impact of continuing disparities in employment, income, housing and general well-being upon the attitudes of black Americans who suffer from the disparities. To a very large extent, this flows from the authors' concentration on a line of comparison that is inherently irrelevant to assessments of how people feel about their condition in life. As we quoted Vivian Henderson above, "pronouncements . . . which are confined to acceleration concepts and percentage change obscure the real predicament." It does not necessarily lead to satisfaction to know that statistically Negroes are better off than they were ten years earlier; the *critical* comparison is how do they stand relative to their white counterparts *today?* And the best Wattenberg-Scammon can come up with here is of very little meaningful consequence. Even if it were otherwise, it is axiomatic psychology that the nearer one gets to a coveted goal, the more impatient he is to reach it and the more heavily bear upon him the constraints of his inferior position.

Not long ago, one used to hear it asserted that American Negroes were the most fortunate blacks in the world: Better treated, enjoying higher standards of living, more social and political freedom, more access to the good things of their world, and so on. All of this was doubtless true, but it was a meaningless comparison. The gauge to progress for American Negroes is where they stand relative to American whites at any given time and in any given place. Their status with respect to Zambians is irrelevant.

Another psychological element of prime importance is also ignored by Wattenberg-Scammon. The gains Negroes have made have been costly. Black people have labored and sacrificed long for them. They have spent their meager resources, they have sacrificed their homes, their jobs, their physical well-being and sometimes their lives in order to achieve the advances which our two authors emphasize. The high cost includes the similar sacrifices of many whites who joined fully in the common struggle. It is not strange that, at times, the price seems to have been excessive for what actually came out of the effort, especially since Negroes know that they should not have had to pay anything for what was theirs by right in the first place.

Let us grant that things are better in 1971 than they were in 1951. It is Wattenberg-Scammon's thesis that we do not stress these advances sufficiently, that we press ahead with protest and argument as though nothing had improved. This, they warn us, tends to be self-defeating and, in any case, does not accord sufficient credit to the methods we employed to arrive where we are today. Failure to assess adequately the results of our efforts will render us unable to distinguish what works from what does not work. But it is also demonstrable that things were better in 1951 than they were in 1931; if, beginning in 1951, we had followed the Wattenberg-Scammon prescription, we would not have embarked upon the course of protest, agitation, appeals to conscience and the courts, and hard day-to-day work with the Congress and the Executive that led, by the authors' own proclamation, to the gains they hail. Instead, we would in 1951 and thereafter have devoted ourselves to repetitions of praise for what the preceding twenty years had accomplished.

A final prime psychological element, which the authors note only to discount, is that of insecurity. They seek to be reassuring and to make a case for inevitable continuation of the progress they describe. But we have already noted how precarious a measure is the black-white income ratio, fluctuating as it has almost from year to year during the past quarter of a century. There is no guarantee that next year, or the year after, will not see the gap widen once again. There is no guarantee that the trend in employment will not again move in a direction unfavorable to black workers. Negroes have enjoyed even the Wattenberg-Scammon measure of progress for so short a time that they have no confidence in its necessary continuance. They simply do not believe that the clock cannot be turned back.

And they have ample reason in the present national administration to expect the worst rather than the best, particularly when it is seen to be catering to those elements of the white population responsible for the housing controversy in Forest Hills, the school integration controversies in Canarsie, N.Y., Detroit and elsewhere and the job exclusions on construction sites across the country. The authors confidently assure us that "no one, for instance, has proposed repealing the Voting Rights Act." But Nixon came close: One of the Administration's first legislative initiatives was its attempt to weaken that law by making it easier for southern legislatures to enact regulations cutting away its protections.

Negroes have witnessed the Administration's efforts to turn the clock back on school desegregation by ending the bus transportation of pupils, often the only method whereby schools can be desegregated. They have seen the attempted appointments of Judges Clement F. Haynsworth and G. Harrold Carswell to the United States Supreme Court, an effort they correctly interpreted as aimed at weakening the Court's line-up of staunch defenders of equal rights.

In other words, nothing has happened, either in real life or in Wattenberg-Scammon's pages, that would convince black Americans that such progress as they have experienced in the last 20 years is either inevitable or permanent. In this respect, their reactions are analogous to those of American Jews, who often react strongly to words and actions which, in themselves, might seem of relatively little weight, but which, experienced against the backdrop of centuries of European and Mideastern history, assume a profoundly menacing aspect.

No one who is really familiar with the pronouncements of Negro leaders—as they have actually been made, not as they are selectively and unrepresentatively encountered in the media—could be under the impression that we make light of our achievements or fail to give due and sincere credit to the good things that have taken place. But we must be honest, with ourselves and with our constituents, and the truth is that so much more remains that is evil that we cannot slacken the pace of our protest by the merest fraction. We are well aware that the efficacy of our strategies and our procedures is often questioned by the so-called militants in our ranks, but we are equally aware that simply asserting that they have worked is not going to make much difference.

Indeed, their implication that "saying it makes it so" tars the Wattenberg-Scammon prescription for liberals with the brush of naivete. They recapitulate the legislative and other accomplishments of the Kennedy-Johnson years in glowing terms of triumph, ending with the assertion that "Liberalism worked." It would be properly the role of a Nixon, they say, to deny these triumphs and to trumpet the failure of the liberal programs. Instead, they complain, it is the liberals who "loudly compete with each other to do his work. Instead of proclaiming success, liberals can only assert that America is a failure, that things are as bad as ever and maybe worse. And President Nixon smiles in agreement."

Well, probably not all the Wattenberg-Scammon "liberals" are straw men, but certainly a lot of them are—even allowing for the slippery undefinableness of the breed. Some of them, bearing names like Kristol, Glazer, Moynihan and Bell—to cite a few—have been essentially working the same side of the street as Wattenberg and Scammon. They, too, have been suggesting that it is time to call a halt to agitation in behalf of blacks and Puerto Ricans and give some thought to safeguarding the status and perquisites of those who already have it made. Nor is it true that President Nixon is smiling in agreement that things are bad and getting worse: On the contrary, he has already proclaimed to a nationwide audience that the crisis in the cities is over, that inflation is under control, and that we are licking crime and unemployment. It is hard to believe that he went to the same Pollyanna school as Wattenberg and Scammon, but there is no questioning his deep satisfaction with their thesis.

Those of us who know a hawk from a handsaw could not ask for better proof that Wattenberg-Scammon's counsel is faulty than the obvious fact that if we followed it we would be playing Richard Nixon's game.

10

Where Do We Go from Here?

"Whites are now rejected as vehemently and irrationally [by blacks] as whites have rejected blacks," write Carl Rowan and David Mazie, both—it is relevant here to note—blacks. They call black separatism a "national tragedy." If the rhetoric has cooled and the flirtation—even brief embrace—with violence has been found counter-productive, it is useful to be reminded of the kind of protest that crested in the Sixties among some of the most gifted black leaders. One casualty of that turbulent period seems to be the ideal of integration that had heretofore inspired both whites and blacks in the struggle for racial justice. Can it be and ought it to be revived? Is it incompatible with an authentic pluralism which reckons with the importance of preserving black identity and the black contribution to the larger culture? If it is, can pluralism be purged of the elements of friction and conflict that are latent in it? The problem is not peculiar to blacks. Some Jewish leaders mourn the vanishing identity of the Jew; others prefer it to humiliating discrimination and have no objection to an assimilation that is reciprocal and voluntary. The articles that follow will illuminate some of these issues.

Where do we go from here? We are all asking that question as Martin Luther King, Jr., did in his magisterial book, a selection from which concludes this section as a reminder of how badly we need his leadership.

WHAT WE WANT

Stokely Carmichael

Stokely Carmichael was born in Trinidad in 1941 and came from Port-of-Spain to live in New York in 1952. He was one of the first "freedom riders" to be arrested and has been jailed many times since. The treatment he encountered in Southern jails apparently embittered him against all whites. He was elected chairman of the Student Nonviolent Coordinating Committee (SNCC) in 1966. By 1967 he had become the most vocal exponent of black power among Negro militants. In acerbic language he expresses the frustration of young Negroes embittered by the humiliations of life in Northern ghettoes and the meager results in the South of the Civil Rights Act of 1965. His first book, Black Power, the Politics of Liberation in America, *was published in 1967.*

Carmichael is no longer head of SNCC; after a year he announced "I'm going back to the fields where I came from." The "fields" included Havana where, joining with Castro, he seemed quite willing to rekindle the flames that have already devastated a number of American cities by calling upon American blacks to take up arms for "total revolution." But surprisingly, in light of Carmichael's other utterances, he refrains from advocating violence in his book.

The slogan "black power" is notorious for its ambiguity. Some who shout it approve the use of violence to bring about reform. Others advocate the use of force only in self-protection against violence. Still others see it as a call for bloc voting to increase the Negro political strength. For many, black power is a frank avowal of Negro separatism mingled, as separatism generally is, with black chauvinism. Carmichael sees in the slogan a reflection of "the necessity to reclaim our history and our identity from . . . cultural terrorism . . ."[1]

One of the tragedies of the struggle against racism is that up to now there has been no national organization which could speak to the growing militancy of young black people in the urban ghetto. There has been only a civil rights movement whose tone of voice was adapted to an audience of liberal whites. It served as a sort of buffer zone between them

---

[1] *The Massachusetts Review*, Vol. VII, No. 4 (Autumn 1966).

and angry young blacks. None of its so-called leaders could go into a rioting community and be listened to. In a sense, I blame ourselves— together with the mass media—for what has happened in Watts, Harlem, Chicago, Cleveland, Omaha. Each time the people in those cities saw Martin Luther King get slapped, they became angry; when they saw four little black girls bombed to death, they were angrier; and when nothing happened, they were steaming. We had nothing to offer that they could see, except to go out and be beaten again. We helped to build their frustration.

For too many years, black Americans marched and had their heads broken and got shot. They were saying to the country, "Look, you guys are supposed to be nice guys and we are only going to do what we are supposed to do—why do you beat us up, why don't you give us what we ask, why don't you straighten yourselves out?" After years of this, we are at almost the same point—because we demonstrated from a position of weakness. We cannot be expected any longer to march and have our heads broken in order to say to whites: come on, you're nice guys. For you are not nice guys. We have found you out.

An organization which claims to speak for the needs of a community—as does the Student Nonviolent Coordinating Committee—must speak in the tone of that community, not as somebody else's buffer zone. This is the significance of black power as a slogan. For once, black people are going to use the words they want to use—not just the words whites want to hear. And they will do this no matter how often the press tries to stop the use of the slogan by equating it with racism or separatism.

An organization which claims to be working for the needs of a community—as SNCC does—must work to provide that community with a position of strength from which to make its voice heard. This is the significance of black power beyond the slogan.

Black power can be clearly defined for those who do not attach the fears of white America to their questions about it. We should begin with the basic fact that black Americans have two problems: they are poor and they are black. All other problems arise from this two-sided reality: lack of education, the so-called apathy of black men. Any program to end racism must address itself to that double reality.

Almost from its beginning, SNCC sought to address itself to both conditions with a program aimed at winning political power for impoverished Southern blacks. We had to begin with politics because black Americans are a propertyless people in a country where property is valued above all. We had to work for power, because this country does not function by morality, love, and nonviolence, but by power. Thus we determined to win political power, with the idea of moving on from there into activity that would have economic effects. With power, the masses could *make or participate in making* the decisions which govern their destinies, and thus create basic change in their day-to-day lives.

But if political power seemed to be the key to self-determination, it was also obvious that the key had been thrown down a deep well many years earlier. Disenfranchisement maintained by racist terror makes it impossible to talk about organizing for political power in 1960. The right to vote had to be won and SNCC workers devoted their energies to this from 1961 to 1965. They set up voter registration drives in the Deep South. They created pressure for the vote by holding mock elections in Mississippi in 1963 and by helping to establish the Mississippi Freedom Democratic Party (MFDP) in 1964. That struggle was eased, though not won, with the passage of the 1965 Voting Rights Act. SNCC workers could then address themselves to the question: "Who can we vote for, to have our needs met—how do we make our vote meaningful?"

SNCC had already gone to Atlantic City for recognition of the Mississippi Freedom Democratic Party by the Democratic convention and been rejected; it had gone with the MFDP to Washington for recognition by Congress and been rejected. In Arkansas, SNCC helped thirty Negroes to run for School Board elections; all but one were defeated, and there was evidence of fraud and intimidation sufficient to cause their defeat. In Atlanta, Julian Bond ran for the state legislature and was elected—twice— and unseated—twice. In several states black farmers ran in elections for agricultural committees which make crucial decisions concerning land use, loans, etc. Although they won places on a number of committees, they never gained the majorities needed to control them.

All of the efforts were attempts to win black power. Then, in Alabama, the opportunity came to see how blacks could be organized on an independent party basis. An unusual Alabama law provides that any group of citizens can nominate candidates for county office and, if they win 20 per cent of the vote, may be recognized as a county political party. The same then applies on a state level. SNCC went to organize in several counties such as Lowndes, where black people—who form 80 per cent of the population and have an average annual income of $943—felt they could accomplish nothing within the framework of the Alabama Democratic Party because of its racism and because the qualifying fee for this year's elections was raised from $50 to $500 in order to prevent most Negroes from becoming candidates. On May 3, five new county "freedom organizations" convened and nominated candidates for the offices of sheriff, tax assessor, members of the school boards. These men and women are up for election in November—if they live until then. Their ballot symbol is the black panther; a bold, beautiful animal, representing the strength and dignity of black demands today. A man needs a black panther on his side when he and his family must endure—as hundreds of Alabamians have endured—loss of job, eviction, starvation, and sometimes death, for political activity. He may also need a gun and SNCC reaffirms the right of black men everywhere to defend themselves when threatened or attacked. As for initiating the use of violence, we hope that such programs as ours will make that unnecessary; but it is not for us to tell black communities whether they can or cannot use any particular form of action to resolve their problems. Responsibility for the use of violence by black men, whether in self-defense or initiated by them, lies with the white community.

This is the specific historical experience from which SNCC's call for "black power" emerged on the Mississippi march last July. But the concept of "black power" is not a recent or isolated phenomenon: It has grown out of the ferment of agitation and activity by different people and organizations in many black communities over the years. Our last year of work in Alabama added a new concrete possibility. In Lowndes county, for example, black power will mean that if a Negro is elected sheriff, he can end police brutality. If a black man is elected tax assessor, he can collect and channel funds for the building of better roads and schools serving black people—thus advancing the move from political power into the economic arena. In such areas as Lowndes, where black men have a majority, they will attempt to use it to exercise control. This is what they seek: control. Where Negroes lack a majority, black power means proper representation and sharing of control. It means the creation of power bases from which black people can work to change statewide or nationwide patterns of oppression through pressure from strength—instead of weakness. Politically, black power means what it has always meant to SNCC: the coming-together of black people to elect representatives and *to force those representatives to speak to their needs.* It does not mean merely putting black faces into office. A man or woman who is black and from the slums cannot be automatically expected to speak to the needs of black people. Most of the black politicians we see around the country today are not what SNCC means by black power. The power must be that of a community, and emanate from there.

SNCC today is working in both North and South on programs of voter registration and independent political organizing. In some places, such as Alabama, Los Angeles, New York, Philadelphia, and New Jersey, independent organizing under the black panther symbol is in progress. The creation of a national "black panther party" must come about; it will take time to build, and it is much too early to predict its success. We have no infallible master plan and we make no claim to exclusive knowledge of how to end racism; different groups will work in their own different ways. SNCC cannot spell out the full logistics of self-determination but it can address itself to the problem by helping black communities define their needs, realize their strength, and go into action along a variety of lines which they must choose for themselves. Without knowing all the answers it can address itself to the basic problem of poverty; to the fact that in Lowndes County, 86 white families own 90 per cent of the land. What are black people in that county going to do for jobs, where are they going to get money? There must be reallocation of land, of money.

Ultimately, the economic foundations of this country must be shaken if black people are to control their lives.

The colonies of the United States—and this includes the black ghettoes within its borders, north and south—must be liberated. For a century, this nation has been like an octopus of exploitation, its tentacles stretching from Mississippi and Harlem to South America, the Middle East, southern Africa, and Vietnam; the form of exploitation varies from area to area but the essential result has been the same—a powerful few have been maintained and enriched at the expense of the poor and voiceless colored masses. This pattern must be broken. As its grip loosens here and there around the world, the hopes of black Americans become more realistic. For racism to die, a totally different America must be born.

This is what the white society does not wish to face; this is why that society prefers to talk about integration. But integration speaks not at all to the problem of poverty, only to the problem of blackness. Integration today means the man who "makes it," leaving his black brothers behind in the ghetto as fast as his new sports car will take him. It has no relevance to the Harlem wino or to the cotton-picker making three dollars a day. As a lady I know in Alabama once said, "the food that Ralph Bunche eats doesn't fill my stomach."

Integration, moreover, speaks to the problem of blackness in a despicable way. As a goal, it has been based on complete acceptance of the fact that *in order to have* a decent house or education, blacks must move into a white neighborhood or send their children to a white school. This reinforces, among both black and white, the idea that "white" is automatically better and "black" is by definition inferior. This is why integration is a subterfuge for the maintenance of white supremacy. It allows the nation to focus on a handful of Southern children who get into white schools, at great price, and to ignore the 94 per cent who are left behind in unimproved all-black schools. Such situations will not change until black people have power—to control their own school boards, in this case. Then Negroes become equal in a way that means something, and integration ceases to be a one-way street. Then integration doesn't mean draining skills and energies from the ghetto into white neighborhoods; then it can mean white people moving from Beverly Hills into Watts, white people joining the Lowndes County Freedom Organization. Then integration becomes relevant.

Last April, before the furor over black power, Christopher Jencks wrote in a *New Republic* article on white Mississippi's manipulation of the anti-poverty program:

The war on poverty has been predicated on the notion that there is such a thing as *a community* which can be defined geographically and mobilized for a collective effort to help the poor. This theory has no relationship to reality in the Deep South. In every Mississippi county there are *two* communities. Despite all the pious platitudes of the moderates on both sides, these two communities habitually see their interests in terms of conflict rather than co-operation. Only when the Negro community can muster enough political, economic and professional strength to compete on somewhat equal terms, will Negroes believe in the possibility of true cooperation and whites accept its necessity. En route to integration, the Negro community needs to develop greater independence —a chance to run its own affairs and not cave in whenever "the man" barks . . . Or so it seems to me, and to most of the knowledgeable people with whom I talked in Mississippi. To OEO, this judgment may sound like black nationalism . . .

Mr. Jencks, a white reporter, perceived the reason why America's anti-poverty program has been a sick farce in both North and South. In the South, it is clearly racism which prevents the poor from running their own programs; in the North, it more often seems to be politicking and bureaucracy. But the results are not so different: In the North, non-whites make up 42 per cent of all families in metropolitan "poverty areas" and only 6 per cent of families in areas classified as not poor. SNCC has been working with local residents in Arkansas, Alabama, and Mississippi to achieve control by the poor of the program and its funds; it has also been working with groups in the North, and the struggle is no less difficult. Behind it all is a federal government which cares far more about winning the war on the Vietnamese than the war on poverty; which has put the poverty program in the hands of self-serving politicians and bureaucrats rather than the poor themselves; which is unwilling to curb the misuse of white power but quick to condemn black power.

To most whites, black power seems to mean that the Mau Mau are coming to the suburbs at night. The Mau Mau are coming, and whites must stop them. Articles appear about plots to "get Whitey," creating an atmosphere in which "law and order must be maintained." Once again, responsibility is shifted from the oppressor to the oppressed. Other whites chide, "Don't forget—you're only 10 per cent of the population; if you get too smart, we'll wipe you out." If they are liberals, they complain, "what about me?—don't you want my help any more?" These are people supposedly concerned about black Americans, but today they think first of themselves, of their feelings of rejection. Or they admonish, "you can't get anywhere without coalitions," when there is in fact no group at present with whom to form a coalition in which blacks will not be absorbed and betrayed. Or they accuse us of "polarizing the races" by our calls for black unity, when the true responsibility for polarization lies with whites who will not accept their responsibility as the majority power for making the democratic process work.

White America will not face the problem of color, the reality of it. The well-intended say: "We're all human, everybody is really decent, we must forget color." But color cannot be "forgotten" until its weight is recognized and dealt with. White America will not acknowledge that the ways in which this country sees itself are contradicted by being black—and always have been. Whereas most of the people who settled this country came here for freedom or for economic opportunity, blacks were brought here to be slaves. When the Lowndes County Freedom Organization chose the black panther as its symbol, it was christened by the press "the Black Panther Party"—but the Alabama Democratic Party, whose symbol is a rooster has never been called the White Cock Party. No one ever talked about "white power" because power in this country is white. All this adds up to more than merely identifying a group phenomenon by some catchy name or adjective. The furor over that black panther reveals the problems that white America has with color and sex; the furor over "black power" reveals how deep racism runs and the great fear which is attached to it.

Whites will not see that I, for example, as a person oppressed because of my blackness, have common cause with other blacks who are oppressed because of blackness. This is not to say that there are no white people who see things as I do, but that it is black people I must speak to first. It must be the oppressed to whom SNCC addresses itself primarily, not to friends from the oppressing group.

From birth, black people are told a set of lies about themselves. We are told that we are lazy—yet I drive through the Delta area of Mississippi and watch black people picking cotton in the hot sun for fourteen hours. We are told, "If you work hard, you'll succeed"—but if that were true, black people would own this country. We are oppressed because we are black—not because we are ignorant, not because we are lazy, not because we're stupid (and got good rhythm), but because we're black.

I remember that when I was a boy, I used to go to see Tarzan movies on Saturday. White Tarzan used to beat up the black natives. I would sit there yelling, "Kill the beasts, kill the savages, kill 'em!" I was saying: Kill *me*. It was as if a Jewish boy watched Nazis taking Jews off to concentration camps and cheered them on. Today, I want the chief to beat hell out of Tarzan and send him back to Europe. But it takes time to become free of the lies and their shaming effect on black minds. It takes time to reject the most important lie; that black people inherently can't do the same things white people can do, unless white people help them.

The need for psychological equality is the reason why SNCC today believes that blacks must organize in the black community. Only black people can convey the revolutionary idea that black people are able to do things themselves. Only they can help create in the community an aroused and continuing black consciousness that will provide the basis for political strength. In the past, white allies have furthered white supremacy without the whites involved realizing it—or wanting it, I think. Black people must do things for themselves; they must get poverty money they will control and spend themselves, they must conduct tutorial programs themselves so that black children can identify with black people. This is one reason Africa has such importance: The reality of black men ruling their own natives gives blacks elsewhere a sense of possibility, of power, which they do not now have.

This does not mean we don't welcome help, or friends. But we want the right to decide whether anyone is, in fact, our friend. In the past, black Americans have been almost the only people whom everybody and his momma could jump up and call their friends. We have been tokens, symbols, objects—as I was in high school to many young whites, who liked having "a Negro friend." We want to decide who is our friend, and we will not accept someone who comes to us and says: "If you do X, Y, and Z, then I'll help you." We will not be told whom we should choose as allies. We will not be isolated from any group or nation except by our own choice. We cannot have the oppressors telling the oppressed how to rid themselves of the oppressor.

I have said that most liberal whites react to "black power" with the question, What about me? rather than saying: Tell me what you want me to do and I'll see if I can do it. There are answers to the right question. One of the most disturbing things about almost all white supporters of the movement has been that they are afraid to go into their own communities—which is where the racism exists—and work to get rid of it. They want to run from Berkeley to tell us what to do in Mississippi; let them look instead at Berkeley. They admonish blacks to be nonviolent; let them preach nonviolence in the white community. They come to teach me Negro history; let them go to the suburbs and open up freedom schools for whites. Let them work to stop America's racist foreign policy; let them press this government to cease supporting the economy of South Africa.

There is a vital job to be done among poor whites. We hope to see, eventually, a coalition between poor blacks and poor whites. That is the only coalition which seems acceptable to us, and we see such a coalition as the major internal instrument of change in American society. SNCC has tried several times to organize poor whites; we are trying again now, with an initial training program in Tennessee. It is purely academic today to talk about bringing poor blacks and whites together, but the job of creating a poor-white power bloc must be attempted. The main responsibility for it falls upon whites. Black and white can work together in the white community where possible; it is not possible, however, to go into a poor Southern town and talk about integration. Poor whites everywhere are becoming more hostile—not less—partly because they see the nation's attention focused on black poverty and nobody coming to them. Too many young middle-class Americans, like some sort of Pepsi generation, have wanted to come alive through the black community; they've wanted to be where the action is—and the action has been in the black community.

Black people do not want to "take over" this country. They don't want to "get whitey"; they just want to get him off their backs, as the saying goes. It was for example the exploitation by Jewish landlords and merchants which first created black resentment toward Jews—not Judaism. The white man is irrelevant to blacks, except as an oppressive force. Blacks want to be in his place, yes, but not in order to terrorize and lynch and starve him. They want to be in his place because that is where a decent life can be had.

But our vision is not merely of a society in which all black men have enough to buy the good things of life. When we urge that black money go into black pockets, we mean the communal pocket. We want to see money go back into the community and used to benefit it. We want to see the cooperative concept applied in business and banking. We want to see black ghetto residents demand that an exploiting store keeper sell them, at minimal cost, a building or a shop that they will own and improve co-operatively; they can back their demand with a rent strike, or a boycott, and a community so unified behind them that no one else will move into the building or buy at the store. The society we seek to build among black people, then, is not a capitalist one. It is a society in which the spirit of community and humanistic love prevail. The word love is suspect; black expectations of what it might produce have been betrayed too often. But those were expectations of a response from the white community, which failed us. The love we seek to encourage is within the black community, the only American community where men call each other "brother" when they meet. We can build a community of love only where we have the ability and power to do so: among blacks.

As for white America, perhaps it can stop crying out against "black supremacy," "black nationalism," "racism in reverse," and begin facing reality. The reality is that this nation, from top to bottom, is racist; that racism is not primarily a problem of "human relations" but of an exploitation maintained—either actively or through silence—by the society as a whole. Camus and Sartre have asked, can a man condemn himself? Can whites, particularly liberal whites, condemn themselves? Can they stop blaming us, and blame their own system? Are they capable of the shame which might become a revolutionary emotion?

We have found that they usually cannot condemn themselves, and so we have done it. But the rebuilding of this society, if at all possible, is basically the responsibility of whites—not blacks. We won't fight to save the present society, in Vietnam or anywhere else. We are just going to work, in the way *we* see fit, and on goals *we* define, not for civil rights but for all our human rights.

THE FAILURE OF BLACK SEPARATISM

Bayard Rustin

Bayard Rustin, executive director of the A. Philip Randolph Institute, is supremely qualified to comment on the grand strategy of the struggle for racial justice. He has dedicated his life to that struggle. If arrests qualify warriors in such combat to an equivalent of the Purple Heart, he is entitled to more than twenty of them. He was a youth organizer for Randolph, has been a field secretary for CORE, participated in the first Freedom Ride, helped Martin Luther King in the first (1955) boycott and served as his special assistant for seven years, organized the historic 1963 March on Washington, and led the massive demonstration that followed Dr. King's assassination.

We are living in an age of revolution—or so they tell us. The children of the affluent classes pay homage to their parents' values by rejecting them; this, they say, is a youth revolution. The discussion and display of sexuality increases—actors disrobe on stage, young women very nearly do on the street—and so we are in the midst of a sexual revolution. Tastes in music and clothing change, and each new fashion too is revolutionary. With every new social phenomenon now being dubbed a "revolution," the term has in fact become nothing more than a slogan which serves to take our minds off an unpleasant reality. For if we were not careful, we might easily forget that there is a conservative in the White House, that our country is racially polarized as never before, and that the forces of liberalism are in disarray. Whatever there is of revolution today, in any meaningful sense of the term, is coming from the Right.

But we are also told—and with far greater urgency and frequency —that there is a black revolution. If by revolution we mean a radical escalation of black aspirations and demands, this is surely the case. There is a new assertion of pride in the Negro race and its cultural heritage, and although the past summer was marked by the lack of any major disruptions, there is among blacks a tendency more pronounced than at any time in Negro history to engage in violence and the rhetoric of violence. Yet if we look closely at the situation of Negroes today, we find that there has been not the least revolutionary reallocation of political or economic power. There is, to be sure, an increase in the number of black elected officials throughout the United States and particularly in the South, but this has largely been the result of the 1965 Voting Rights Act, which was passed before the "revolution" reached its height and the renewal of which the present Administration has not advocated with any noticeable enthusiasm. Some reallocation of political power has indeed taken place since the Presidential election of 1964, but generally its beneficiaries have been the Republicans and the anti-Negro forces. Nor does this particular trend show much sign of abating. . . .

There has been, it is true, some moderate improvement in the economic condition of Negroes, but by no stretch of the imagination could it be called revolutionary. According to Andrew Brimmer of the Federal Reserve System, the median family income of Negroes between 1965 and 1967 rose from 54 per cent to 59 per cent of that for white families. Much of that gain reflected a decrease in the rate of Negro unemployment. But between February and June of 1969, Negro unemployment rose again by 1.3 per cent and should continue to rise as Nixon presses his crusade against inflation. The Council of Economic Advisers reports that in the past eight years the federal government has spent $10.3 billion on metropolitan problems while it has spent $39.9 billion on agriculture, not to mention, of course, $507.2 billion for defense. In the area of housing, for instance, New York City needs at the present time as many new subsidized apartments—780,000— as the federal housing program has constructed *nationally* in its entire thirty-four years. The appropriations for model cities, rent supplements, the Job Corps, the Neighborhood Youth Corps, and other programs have been drastically reduced, and the Office of Economic Opportunity is being transformed into a research agency. Nixon's welfare and revenue-sharing proposals, in addition to being economically stringent, so that they will have little or no effect on the condition of the Northern urban poor, are politically and philosophically conservative.

Any appearance that we are in the grip of a black revolution, then, is deceptive. The problem is not whether black aspirations are outpacing America's ability to respond but whether they have outpaced her willingness to do so. Lately it has been taken almost as axiomatic that with every increase in Negro demands, there must be a corresponding intensification of white resistance. This proposition implies that only black complacency can prevent racial polarization, that any political action by Negroes must of necessity produce a reaction. But such a notion ignores entirely the question of what *kind* of political action, guided by what *kind* of political strategy. One can almost assert as a law of American politics that if Negroes engage in violence as a tactic they will be met with repression, that if they follow a strategy of racial separatism they will be isolated, and that if they engage in anti-democratic activity, out of the deluded wish to skirt the democratic process, they will provoke a reaction. To the misguided, violence, separatism, and minority ultimatums may seem revolutionary, but in reality they issue only from the desperate strivings of the impotent. Certainly such tactics are not designed to enhance the achievement of progressive social change. Recent American political history has proved this point time and again with brutal clarity.

The irony of the revolutionary rhetoric uttered in behalf of Negroes is that it has helped in fact to promote conservatism. On the other hand, of course, the reverse is also true: the failure of America to respond to the demands of Negroes has fostered in the minds of the latter a sense of futility and has thus seemed to legitimize a strategy of withdrawal and violence. Other things have been operating as well. The fifteen years since *Brown vs. Topeka* have been for Negroes a period of enormous dislocation. The modernization of farming in the South forced hundreds of thousands of Negroes to migrate to the North where they were confronted by a second technological affliction, automation. Without jobs, living in cities equipped to serve neither their material nor spiritual needs, these modern-day immigrants responded to their brutal new world with despair and hostility. The civil-rights movement created an even more fundamental social dislocation, for it destroyed not simply the legal structure of segregation but also the psychological assumptions of racism. Young Negroes who matured during this period witnessed a basic challenge to the system of values and social relations which had presumed the inferiority of the Negro. They have totally rejected this system, but in doing so have often substituted for it an exaggerated and distorted perception both of themselves and of the society. As if to obliterate the trace of racial shame that might be lurking in their souls they have embraced racial chauvinism. And as if in reply to past exclusions (and often in response to present insecurities), they have created their own patterns of exclusiveness.

The various frustrations and upheavals experienced recently by the Negro community account in large part for the present political orientation of some of its most vocal members: seeing their immediate self-interest more in the terms of emotional release than in those of economic and political advancement. One is supposed to think black, dress black, eat black, and buy black without reference to the question of what such a program actually contributes to advancing the cause of social justice. Since real victories are thought to be unattainable, issues become important in so far as they can provide symbolic victories. Dramatic confrontations are staged which serve as outlets for radical energy but which in no way further the achievement of radical social goals. So that, for instance, members of the black community are mobilized to pursue the "victory" of halting construction of a state office building in Harlem, even though it is hard to see what actual economic or social benefit will be conferred on the impoverished residents of that community by their success in doing so.

Such actions constitute a politics of escape rooted in hopelessness and further reinforced by government inaction. Deracinated liberals may romanticize this politics, nihilistic New Leftists may imitate it, but it is ordinary Negroes who will be the victims of its powerlessness to work any genuine change in their condition.

The call for Black Power is now over three years old, yet to this day no one knows what Black Power is supposed to mean and therefore how its proponents are to unite and rally behind it. If one is a member of CORE, Black Power posits the need for a separate black economy based upon traditional forms of capitalist relations. For SNCC the term refers to a politically united black community. US would emphasize the unity of black culture, while the Black Panthers wish to impose upon black nationalism the philosophies of Marx, Lenin, Stalin, and Chairman Mao. Nor do these exhaust all the possible shades and gradations of meaning. If there is one common theme uniting the various demands for Black Power, it is simply that blacks must be guided in their actions by a consciousness of themselves as a separate race.

Now, philosophies of racial solidarity have never been unduly concerned with the realities that operate outside the category of race. The adherents of these philosophies are generally romantics, steeped in the traditions of their own particular clans and preoccupied with the simple biological verities of blood and racial survival. Almost invariably their rallying cry is racial self-determination, and they tend to ignore those aspects of the material world which point up divisions within the racially defined group.

But the world of black Americans is full of divisions. Only the most supine of optimists would dream of building a political movement without reference to them. Indeed, nothing better illustrates the existence of such divisions within the black community than the fact that the separatists themselves represent a distinct minority among Negroes. No reliable poll has ever identified more than 15 per cent of Negroes as separatists; usually the percentage is a good deal lower. Nor, as I have already indicated, are the separatists unified among themselves, the differences among them at times being so intense as to lead to violent conflict. The notion of the undifferentiated black community is the intellectual creation of both whites—liberals as well as racists to whom all Negroes are the same—and of certain small groups of blacks who illegitimately claim to speak for the majority.

The fact is that like every other racial or ethnic group in America, Negroes are divided by age, class, and geography. Young Negroes are at least as hostile toward their elders as white New Leftists are toward their liberal parents. They are in addition separated by vast gaps in experience, Northern from Southern, urban from rural. And even more profound are the disparities in wealth among them. In contrast to the white community, where the spread of income has in recent years remained unchanged or has narrowed slightly, economic differentials among blacks have increased. In

1965, for example, the wealthiest 5 per cent of white and non-white families each received 15.5 per cent of the total income in their respective communities. In 1967, however, the percentage of white income received by the top 5 per cent of white families had dropped to 14.9 per cent while among non-whites the share of income of the top 5 per cent of the families had risen to 17.5 per cent. This trend probably reflects the new opportunities which are available to black professionals in industry, government, and academia, but have not touched the condition of lower-class and lower-middle-class Negroes.

To Negroes for whom race is the major criterion, however, divisions by wealth and status are irrelevant. Consider, for instance, the proposals for black economic advancement put forth by the various groups of black nationalists. These proposals are all remarkably similar. For regardless of one's particular persuasion—whether a revolutionary or a cultural nationalist or an unabashed black capitalist—once one confines one's analysis to the ghetto, no proposal can extend beyond a strategy for ghetto development and black enterprise. This explains in part the recent popularity of black capitalism and, to a lesser degree, black cooperatives: once both the economic strategy and goal are defined in terms of black self-determination, there is simply not much else available in the way of ideas.

There are other reasons for the popularity of black capitalism, reasons having to do with material and psychological self-interest. E. Franklin Frazier has written that Negro business is "a social myth" first formulated toward the end of the nineteenth century when the legal structure of segregation was established and Negro hopes for equality destroyed. History has often shown us that oppression can sometimes lead to a rationalization of the unjust conditions on the part of the oppressed and following on this, to an opportunistic competition among them for whatever meager advantages are available. This is, according to Frazier, exactly what happened among American Negroes. The myth of Negro business was created and tied to a belief in the possibility of a separate Negro economy. "Of course," wrote Frazier, "behind the idea of the separate Negro economy is the hope of the black bourgeoisie that they will have the monopoly of the Negro market." He added that they also desire "a privileged status within the isolated Negro community."

Nor are certain Negro businessmen the only ones who stand to gain from a black economy protected by the tariff of separatism. There are also those among the white upper class for whom such an arrangement is at least as beneficial. In the first place, self-help projects for the ghetto, of which black capitalism is but one variety, are inexpensive. They involve no large-scale redistribution of resources, no "inflationary" government expenditures, and above all, no responsibility on the part of whites. These same upper-class whites may have been major exploiters of black workers in the past, they may have been responsible for policies which helped to create ghetto poverty, but now, under the new dispensations of black separatism, they are being asked to do little more by way of reparation than provide a bit of seed money for a few small ghetto enterprises.

Moreover, a separate black economy appears to offer hope for what Roy Innis has called "a new social contract." According to Innis's theory, the black community is essentially a colony ruled by outsiders; there can be no peace between the colony and the "mother country" until the former is ruled by some of its own. When the colony is finally "liberated" in this way, all conflicts can be resolved through negotiation between the black ruling class and the white ruling class. Any difficulties within the black community, that is, would become the responsibility of the black elite. But since self-determination in the ghetto, necessitating as it would the expansion of a propertied black middle class, offers the advantage of social stability, such difficulties would be minimal. How could many whites fail to grasp the obvious benefit to themselves in a program that promises social peace without the social inconvenience of integration and especially without the burden of a huge expenditure of money? Even if one were to accept the colonial analogy—and it is in many ways an uninformed and extremely foolish one—the strategy implied by it is fatuous and unworkable. Most of the experiments in black capitalism thus far have been total failures. As, given the odds, they should continue to be. For one thing, small businesses owned and run by blacks will, exactly like their white counterparts, suffer a high rate of failure. In fact, they will face even greater problems than white small businesses because they will be operating in predominantly low income areas where the clientele will be poor, the crime rate and taxes high, and the cost of land, labor, and insurance expensive. They will have to charge higher prices than the large chains, a circumstance against which "Buy Black" campaigns will in the long or even the short run have little force. On the other hand, to create large-scale black industry in the ghetto is unthinkable. The capital is not available, and even if it were, there is no vacant land. In Los Angeles, for example, the area in which four-fifths of the Negroes and Mexican-Americans live contains only 0.5 per cent of all the vacant land in the city, and the problem is similar elsewhere. Overcrowding is severe enough in the ghetto without building up any industry there.

Another current axiom of black self-determination is the necessity for community control. Questions of ideology aside, black community control is as futile a program as black capitalism. Assuming that there were a cohesive, clearly identifiable black community (which, judging by the factionalism in neighborhoods like Harlem and Ocean Hill-Brownsville, is a far from safe assumption), and assuming that the community were empowered to control the ghetto, it would still find itself without the money needed in order to be socially creative. The ghetto would still be faced with the same poverty, deteriorated housing, unemployment, terrible health services, and inferior schools—and this time perhaps with the exacerbation of their being entailed in local struggles for power. Furthermore, the control would ultimately be illusory and would do no more than provide psychological comfort to those who exercise it. For in a complex technological society there is no such thing as an autonomous community within a large metropolitan area. Neighborhoods, particularly poor neighborhoods, will remain dependent upon outside suppliers for manufactured goods, transportation, utilities, and other services. There is, for instance, unemployment in the ghetto while the vast majority of new jobs are being created in the suburbs. If black people are to have access to those jobs, there must be a metropolitan transportation system that can carry them to the suburbs cheaply and quickly. Control over the ghetto cannot build such a system nor can it provide jobs within the ghetto.

The truth of the matter is that community control as an idea is provincial and as a program is extremely conservative. It appears radical to some people because it has become the demand around which the frustrations of the Negro community have coalesced. In terms of its capacity to deal with the social and economic causes of black unrest, however, its potential is strikingly limited. The call for community control in fact represents an adjustment to inequality rather than a protest against it. Fundamentally, it is a demand for a change in the racial composition of the personnel who administer community institutions: that is, for schools, institutions of public and social service, and political organizations—as all of these are presently constituted—to be put into the keeping of a new class of black officials. Thus in a very real sense, the notion of community control bespeaks a fervent hope that the poverty-stricken ghetto, once thought to be a social problem crying for rectification, might now be deemed a social good worthy of acceptance. Hosea Williams of SCLC, speaking once of community control, unwittingly revealed the way in which passionate self-assertion can be a mask for accommodation: "I'm now at the position Booker T. Washington was about sixty or seventy years ago," Williams said. "I say to my brothers, 'Cast down your buckets where you are'—and that means there in the slums and ghettos."

There is indeed profound truth in the observation that people who seek social change will, in the absence of real substantive victories, often seize upon stylistic substitutes as an outlet for their frustrations.

A case in point is the relation of Negroes to the trade-union movement. In their study *The Black Worker,* published in 1930, Sterling D. Spero and Abraham L. Harris describe the resistance to separatism among economically satisfied workers during the heyday of Marcus Garvey:

> . . . spokesmen of the Garvey movement went among the faction-torn workers preaching the doctrine of race consciousness. Despite the fact that Garveyism won a following everywhere at this time, the Negro longshoremen of Philadelphia were deaf to its pleas, for

their labor movement had won them industrial equality such as colored workers nowhere else in the industry enjoyed.

The inverse relation of black separatism and anti-unionism to the quality of employment available to Negroes holds true today also. In the May 1969 UAW elections, for example, black candidates won the presidency and vice-presidency of a number of locals. Some of the most interesting election victories were won at the Chrysler Eldon Gear and Axle Local 961 and at Dodge #3 in Hamtramck where the separatist Eldon Revolutionary Union Movement (ELRUM) and Dodge Revolutionary Union Movement (DRUM) have been active. At both locals the DRUM and ELRUM candidates were handily defeated by black trade unionists who campaigned on a program of militant integrationism and economic justice.

This is not to say that there are not problems within the unions which have given impetus to the separatist movements. There are, but in the past decade unions have taken significant steps toward eliminating discrimination against Negroes. As Peter Henle, the chief economist of the Bureau of Labor Statistics, has observed:

> Action has been taken to eliminate barriers to admission, abolish discrimination in hiring practices, and negotiate changes in seniority arrangements which had been blocking Negro advances to higher-paying jobs. At the same time, unions have given strong support to governmental efforts in this same direction.

Certainly a good deal is left to be done in this regard, but just as certainly the only effective pressure on the unions is that which can be brought by blacks pressing for a greater role *within* the trade-union movement. Not only is separatism not a feasible program, but its major effect will be to injure black workers economically by undermining the strength of their union. It is here that ignorance of the economic dimension of racial injustice is most dangerous, for a Negro, whether he be labeled a moderate or a militant, has but two alternatives open to him. If he defines the problem as primarily one of race, he will inevitably find himself the ally of the white capitalist against the white worker. But if, though always conscious of the play of racial discrimination, he defines the problem as one of poverty, he will be aligned with the white worker against management. If he chooses the former alternative, he will become no more than a pawn in the game of divide-and-conquer played by, and for the benefit of, management—the result of which will hardly be self-determination but rather the depression of wages for all workers. This path was followed by the "moderate" Booker T. Washington who disliked unions because they were "founded on a sort of enmity to the man by whom he [the Negro] is employed" and by the "militant" Marcus Garvey who wrote:

> It seems strange and a paradox, but the only convenient friend the Negro worker or laborer has in America at the present time is the white capitalist. The capitalist being selfish—seeking only the largest profit out of labor—is willing and glad to use Negro labor wherever possible on a scale reasonably below the standard union wage . . . but if the Negro unionizes himself to the level of the white worker, the choice and preference of employment is given to the white worker.

And it is being followed today by CORE, which collaborated with the National Right to Work Committee in setting up the Black Workers Alliance.

If the Negro chooses to follow the path of interracial alliances on the basis of class, as almost two million have done today, he can achieve a certain degree of economic dignity, which in turn offers a genuine, if not the only, opportunity for self-determination. It was this course which A. Philip Randolph chose in his long struggle to build a Negro-labor alliance, and it was also chosen by the black sanitation workers of Memphis, Tennessee, and the black hospital workers of Charleston, South Carolina.

Not that I mean here to exonerate the unions of their responsibility for discrimination. Nevertheless, it is essential to deal with the situation of the black worker in terms of American economic reality. And as long as the structure of this reality is determined by the competing institutions of capital and labor (or government and labor, as in the growing public sector of the economy), Negroes must place themselves on one side or the other. The idea of racial self-determination within this context is a delusion.

There are, to be sure, sources beyond that of economic discrimination for black separatism within the unions. DRUM, ELRUM, and similar groups are composed primarily of young Negroes who, like whites their age, are not as loyal to the union as are older members, and who are also affected by the new militancy which is now pervasive among black youth generally. This militancy has today found its most potent form of expression on campus, particularly in the predominantly white universities outside of the South. The confusion which the movement for programs in black studies has created on campus almost defies description. The extremes in absurdity were reached this past academic year at Cornell, where, on the one hand, enraged black students were demanding a program in black studies which included Course 300c, Physical Education: "Theory and practice in the use of small arms and hand combat. Discussion sessions in the proper use of force," and where, on the other hand, a masochistic and pusillanimous university president placed his airplane at the disposal of two black students so that they could go to New York City and purchase, with $2,000 in university funds, some bongo drums for Malcolm X Day. The foolishness of the students was surpassed only by the public-relations manipulativeness of the president.

The real tragedy of the dispute over black studies is that whatever truly creative opportunities such a program could offer have been either ignored or destroyed. There is, first, the opportunity for a vastly expanded scholastic inquiry into the contribution of Negroes to the American experience. The history of the black man in America has been scandalously distorted in the past, and as a field of study it has been relegated to a second-class status, isolated from the main themes of American history and omitted in the historical education of American youth. Yet now black students are preparing to repeat the errors of their white predecessors. They are proposing to study black history in isolation from the mainstream of American history; they are demanding separate black-studies programs that will not be open to whites, who could benefit at least as much as they from a knowledge of Negro history; and they hope to permit only blacks (and perhaps some whites who toe the line) to teach in these programs. Unwittingly they are conceding what racist whites all along have professed to believe, namely, that black history is irrelevant to American history.

In other ways black students have displayed contempt for black studies as an academic discipline. Many of them, in fact, view black studies as not an academic subject at all, but as an ideological and political one. They propose to use black-studies programs to create a mythologized history and a system of assertive ideas that will facilitate the political mobilization of the black community. In addition, they hope to educate a cadre of activists whose present training is conceived of as a preparation for organizational work in the ghetto. The Cornell students made this very clear when they defined the purpose of black-studies programs as enabling "black people to use the knowledge gained in the classroom and the community to formulate new ideologies and philosophies which will contribute to the development of the black nation."

Thus faculty members will be chosen on the basis of race, ideological purity, and political commitment—not academic competence. Under such conditions, few qualified black professors will want to teach in black-studies programs, not simply because their academic freedom will be curtailed by their obligation to adhere to the revolutionary "line" of the moment, but because their professional status will be threatened by their association with programs of such inferior quality.

Black students are also forsaking the opportunity to get an education. They appear to be giving little thought to the problem of teaching or learning those technical skills that all students must acquire if they are to be effective in their careers. We have here simply another example of the pursuit of symbolic victory where a real victory seems too difficult to achieve. It is easier for a student to alter his behavior and appearance than to improve the quality of his mind. If engineering requires too much concentration, then why not a course in soul music? If Plato is both "irrelevant" and difficult, the student can read Malcolm X instead. Class will be a soothing, comfortable experience, somewhat like watching television. Moreover, one's image will be militant and, therefore, acceptable by current college standards. Yet one will have learned nothing, and the fragile sense of security developed in the protective environment of college will be cracked when exposed to the reality of competition in the world.

Nelson Taylor, a young Negro graduate of Morehouse College, recently observed that many black students "feel it is useless to try to compete. In order to avoid this competition, they build themselves a little cave to hide in." This "little cave," he added, is black studies. Furthermore, black students are encouraged in this escapism by guilt-ridden New Leftists and faculty members who despise themselves and their advantaged lives and enjoy seeing young Negroes reject "white middle-class values" and disrupt the university. They are encouraged by university administrators who prefer political accommodation to an effort at serious education. But beyond the momentary titillation some may experience from being the center of attention, it is difficult to see how Negroes can in the end benefit from being patronized and manipulated in this way. Ultimately, their only permanent satisfaction can come from the certainty that they have acquired the technical and intellectual skills that will enable them upon graduation to perform significant jobs competently and with confidence. If they fail to acquire these skills, their frustration will persist and find expression in ever-newer forms of antisocial and self-destructive behavior.

The conflict over black studies, as over other issues, raises the question of the function in general served by black protest today. Some black demands, such as that for a larger university enrollment of minority students, are entirely legitimate; but the major purpose of the protest through which these demands are pressed would seem to be not so much to pursue an end as to establish in the minds of the protesters, as well as in the minds of whites, the reality of their rebellion. Protest, therefore, becomes an end in itself and not a means toward social change. In this sense, the black rebellion is an enormously *expressive* phenomenon which is releasing the pent-up resentments of generations of oppressed Negroes. But expressiveness that is oblivious to political reality and not structured by instrumental goals is mere bombast.

James Forman's *Black Manifesto,* for instance, provides a nearly perfect sample of this kind of bombast combined with positive delusions of grandeur.

"We shall liberate all the people in the U.S., and we will be instrumental in the liberation of colored people the world around. . . . We are the most humane people within the U.S. . . . Racism in the U.S. is so pervasive in the mentality of whites that only an armed, well-disciplined, black-controlled government can insure the stamping out of racism in this country. . . . We say think in terms of the total control of the U.S."

One might never imagine from reading the *Manifesto* that Forman's organization, the National Black Economic Development Conference, is politically powerless, or that the institution it has chosen for assault is not the government or the corporations, but the church. Indeed, the exaggeration of language in the *Black Manifesto* is directly proportional to the isolation and impotence of those who drafted it. And their actual achievements provide an accurate measure of their strength. Three billion dollars in reparations was demanded—and $20,000 received. More important, the effect of this demand upon the Protestant churches has been to precipitate among them a conservative reaction against the activities of the liberal national denominations and the National Council of Churches. Forman's failure, of course, was to be expected: the only effect of an attack upon so organizationally diffuse and nonpolitical an institution as the church can be the deflection of pressure away from the society's major political and economic institutions and, consequently, the weakening of the black movement for equality.

The possibility that his *Manifesto* might have exactly the opposite effect from that intended, however, was clearly not a problem to Forman, because the demands he was making upon white people were more moral than political or economic. His concern was to purge white guilt far more than to seek social justice for Negroes. It was in part for this reason that he chose to direct his attack at the church, which, as the institutional embodiment of our society's religious pretensions, is vulnerable to moral condemnation.

Yet there is something corrupting in the wholesale release of aggressive moral energy, particularly when it is in response to the demand for reparations for blacks. The difficulty is not only that as a purely racial demand its effect must be to isolate blacks from the white poor with whom they have common economic interests. The call for three billion dollars in reparations demeans the integrity of blacks and exploits the self-demeaning guilt of whites. It is insulting to Negroes to offer them reparations for past generations of suffering, as if the balance of an irreparable past could be set straight with a handout. In a recent poll, *Newsweek* reported that "today's proud Negroes, by an overwhelming 84 to 10 per cent, reject the idea of preferential treatment in hiring or college admissions in reparation for past injustices." There are few controversial issues that can call forth greater uniformity of opinion than this in the Negro community.

I also question both the efficacy and the social utility of an attack that impels the attacked to applaud and debase themselves. I am not certain whether or not self-flagellation can have a beneficial effect on the sinner (I tend to doubt that it can), but I am absolutely certain it can never produce anything politically creative. It will not improve the lot of the unemployed and the ill-housed. On the other hand, it could well happen that the guilty party, in order to lighten his uncomfortable moral burden, will finally begin to rationalize his sins and affirm them as virtues. And by such a process, today's ally can become tomorrow's enemy. Lasting political alliances are not built on the shifting sands of moral suasion.

On his part, the breast-beating white makes the same error as the Negro who swears that "black is beautiful." Both are seeking refuge in psychological solutions to social questions. And both are reluctant to confront the real cause of racial injustice, which is not bad attitudes but bad social conditions. The Negro creates a new psychology to avoid the reality of social stagnation, and the white—be he ever so liberal—professes his guilt precisely so as to create the illusion of social change, all the while preserving his economic advantages.

The response of guilt and pity to social problems is by no means new. It is, in fact, as old as man's capacity to rationalize or his reluctance to make real sacrifices for his fellow man. Two hundred years ago, Samuel Johnson, in an exchange with Boswell, analyzed the phenomenon of sentimentality:

> Boswell: "I have often blamed myself, Sir, for not feeling for others, as sensibly as many say they do."
> Johnson: "Sir, don't be duped by them any more. You will find these very feeling people are not very ready to do you good. They *pay* you by *feeling*."

Today, payments from the rich to the poor take the form of "Giving a Damn" or some other kind of moral philanthropy. At the same time, of course, some of those who so passionately "Give a Damn" are likely to argue that full employment is inflationary.

We are living in a time of great social confusion—not only about the strategies we must adopt but about the very goals these strategies are to bring us to. Only recently whites and Negroes of good will were pretty much in agreement that racial and economic justice required an end to segregation and the expansion of the role of the federal government. Now it is a mark of "advancement," not only among "progressive" whites but among the black militants as well, to believe that integration is passé. Unintentionally (or as the Marxists used to say, objectively), they are lending aid and comfort to traditional segregationists like Senators Eastland and Thurmond. Another "advanced" idea is the notion that government has gotten too big and that what is needed to make the society more humane and livable is an enormous new move toward local participation and decentralization. One cannot question the value or importance of democratic participation in the government, but just as misplaced sympathy for Negroes is being put to use by segregationists, the liberal preoccupation with localism is serving the cause of conservatism. Two years of liberal encomiums to decentralization have intellectually legitimized the concept, if not the name, of states' rights and have set the stage for the widespread acceptance of Nixon's "New Federalism."

The new anti-integrationism and localism may have been motivated by sincere moral conviction, but hardly by intelligent political thinking. It should be obvious that what is needed today more than ever is a political strategy that offers the real possibility of economically uplifting millions of impoverished individuals, black and white. Such a strategy must of necessity give low priority to the various forms of economic and psychological experimentation that I have discussed, which at best deal with issues peripheral to the central problem and at worst embody a frenetic escapism. These experiments are based on the assumption that the black community can be transformed from within when, in fact, any such transformation must depend on structural changes in the entire society. Negro poverty, for example, will not be eliminated in the absence of a total war on poverty. We need, therefore, a new national economic policy. We also need new policies in housing, education, and health care which can deal with these problems as they relate to Negroes within the context of a national solution. A successful strategy, therefore, must rest upon an identification of those central institutions which, if altered sufficiently, would transform the social and economic relations in our society; and it must provide a politically viable means of achieving such an alteration.

Surely the church is not a central institution in this sense. Nor is Roy Innis's notion of dealing with the banking establishment a useful one. For the banks will find no extra profit—quite the contrary—in the kind of fundamental structural change in society that is required.[1]

Moreover, the recent flurry of excitement over the role of private industry in the slums seems to have subsided. A study done for the Urban Coalition has called the National Alliance of Businessmen's claim to have hired more than 100,000 hard-core unemployed a "phony numbers game." . . . Yet even if private industry were fully committed to attack the problem of unemployment, it is not in an ideal position to do so. Private enterprise, for example, accounted for only one out of every ten new jobs created in the economy between 1950 and 1960. Most of the remainder were created as the result of expansion of public employment.

While the church, private enterprise, and other institutions can, if properly motivated, play an important role, finally it is the trade-union

---

[1] Innis's demand that the white banks deposit $6 billion in black banks as reparations for past injustices should meet with even less success than Forman's illfated enterprise. At least Forman had the benefit of the white churchman's guilt, an emotion not known to be popular among bankers.

movement and the Democratic party which offer the greatest leverage to the black struggle. The serious objective of Negroes must be to strengthen and liberalize these. The trade-union movement is essential to the black struggle because it is the only institution in the society capable of organizing the working poor, so many of whom are Negroes. It is only through an organized movement that these workers, who are now condemned to the margin of the economy, can achieve a measure of dignity and economic security. I must confess I find it difficult to understand the prejudice against the labor movement currently fashionable among so many liberals. These people, somehow for reasons of their own, seem to believe that white workers are affluent members of the Establishment (a rather questionable belief, to put it mildly, especially when held by people earning over $25,000 a year) and are now trying to keep the Negroes down. The only grain of truth here is that there *is* competition between black and white workers which derives from a scarcity of jobs and resources. But rather than propose an expansion of those resources, our stylish liberals underwrite that competition by endorsing the myth that the unions are the worst enemy of the Negro.

In fact it is the program of the labor movement that represents a genuine means for reducing racial competition and hostility. Not out of a greater tenderness of feeling for black suffering—but that is just the point. Unions organize workers on the basis of common economic interests, not by virtue of racial affinity. Labor's legislative program for full employment, housing, urban reconstruction, tax reform, improved health care, and expanded educational opportunities is designed specifically to aid both whites and blacks in the lower- and lower-middle classes where the potential for racial polarization is most severe. And only a program of this kind can deal simultaneously and creatively with the interrelated problems of black rage and white fear. It does not placate black rage at the expense of whites, thereby increasing white fear and political reaction. Nor does it exploit white fear by repressing blacks. Either of these courses strengthens the demagogues among both races who prey upon frustration and racial antagonism. Both of them help to strengthen conservative forces—the forces that stand to benefit from the fact that hostility between black and white workers keeps them from uniting effectively around issues of common economic interest. . . .

If the Republican ascendancy is to be but a passing phenomenon, it must once more come to be clearly understood among those who favor social progress that the Democratic party is still the only mass-based political organization in the country with the potential to become a majority movement for social change. And anything calling itself by the name of political activity must be concerned with building precisely such a majority movement. In addition, Negroes must abandon once and for all the false assumption that as 10 per cent of the population they can by themselves effect basic changes in the structure of American life. They must, in other words, accept the necessity of coalition politics. As a result of our fascination with novelty and with the "new" revolutionary forces that have emerged in recent years, it seems to some the height of conservatism to propose a strategy that was effective in the past. Yet the political reality is that without a coalition of Negroes and other minorities with the trade-union movement and with liberal groups, the shift of power to the Right will persist and the democratic Left in America will have to content itself with a well-nigh permanent minority status.

The bitterness of many young Negroes today has led them to be unsympathetic to a program based on the principles of trade unionism and electoral politics. Their protest represents a refusal to accept the condition of inequality, and in that sense, it is part of the long, and I think, magnificent black struggle for freedom. But with no comprehensive strategy to replace the one I have suggested, their protest, though militant in rhetoric and intention, may be reactionary in effect.

The strategy I have outlined must stand or fall by its capacity to achieve political and economic results. It is not intended to provide some new wave of intellectual excitement. It is not intended to suggest a new style of life or a means to personal salvation for disaffected members of the middle class. Nor is either of these the proper role of politics. My strategy is not meant to appeal to the fears of threatened whites, though it would calm those fears and increase the likelihood that some day we shall have a truly integrated society. It is not meant to serve as an outlet for the terrible frustrations of Negroes, though it would reduce those frustrations and point a way to dignity for an oppressed people. It is simply a vehicle by which the wealth of this nation can be redistributed and some of its more grievous social problems solved. This in itself would be quite enough to be getting on with. In fact, if I may risk a slight exaggeration, by normal standards of human society I think it would constitute a revolution.

STRIDE TOWARD FREEDOM

Martin Luther King, Jr.

Of all those who have fought racial injustice Dr. Martin Luther King, Jr. is easily the best known. Born in the South and educated in the North, he first came to national prominence as leader of the boycott of segregated buses in Mont-

gomery, Alabama. His work was recognized by the award in 1964 of the Nobel Peace Prize. An eloquent and tireless crusader for equality for his people, he became embroiled not only in a struggle against racist whites, but in controversies with black leaders who preach a different gospel of resistance.

The following selection was written before protesting marchers began chanting "black power" as they trudged across the state of Mississippi. Of this slogan Dr. King had later observed, even before the Newark and Detroit riots, that it "was an unwise choice at the outset. With the violent connotations that now attach to the words it has become dangerous and injurious. . . . Black supremacy or aggressive black violence is as invested with evil as white supremacy or white violence."[1] Later, however, in an effort to contain the "black power" movement, the Southern Christian Leadership Conference (SCLC), which he headed, adopted new phrases such as "sense of negritude" and "Afro-American unity" to reckon with the Negro identity crisis.

The selection should be read primarily for its bearing on the issue of civil disobedience. However, it will be clear that Dr. King was concerning himself with more than a defense of the duty to disobey an unjust law and with more than a commentary on the technique of nonviolent resistance; included is an examination of such more general moral phenomena as the spiritual invigoration that comes from selfless dedication to a common purpose.

. . . Violence as a way of achieving racial justice is both impractical and immoral. It is impractical because it is a descending spiral ending in destruction for all. The old law of an eye for an eye leaves everybody blind. It is immoral because it seeks to humiliate the opponent rather than win his understanding; it seeks to annihilate rather than to convert. Violence is immoral because it thrives on hatred rather than love. It destroys community and makes brotherhood impossible. It leaves society in monologue rather than dialogue. Violence ends by defeating itself. It creates bitterness in the survivors and brutality in the destroyers. A voice echoes through time saying to every potential Peter, "Put up your sword." History is cluttered with the wreckage of nations that failed to follow this command.

If the American Negro and other victims of oppression succumb to the temptation of using violence in the struggle for freedom, future generations will be the recipients of a desolate night of bitterness, and our chief legacy to them will be an endless reign of meaningless chaos. Violence is not the way.

---

[1] "Black Power," The Progressive, XXX (November 1966), 15–16.

[Another] way open to oppressed people in their quest for freedom is the way of nonviolent resistance. Like the synthesis in Hegelian philosophy, the principle of nonviolent resistance seeks to reconcile the truths of two opposites—acquiescence and violence—while avoiding the extremes and immoralities of both. The nonviolent resister agrees with the person who acquiesces that one should not be physically aggressive toward his opponent; but he balances the equation by agreeing with the person of violence that evil must be resisted. He avoids the nonresistance of the former and the violent resistance of the latter. With nonviolent resistance, no individual or group need submit to any wrong, nor need anyone resort to violence in order to right a wrong.

It seems to me that this is the method that must guide the actions of the Negro in the present crisis in race relations. Through nonviolent resistance the Negro will be able to rise to the noble height of opposing the unjust system while loving the perpetrators of the system. The Negro must work passionately and unrelentingly for full stature as a citizen, but he must not use inferior methods to gain it. He must never come to terms with falsehood, malice, hate, or destruction.

Nonviolent resistance makes it possible for the Negro to remain in the South and struggle for his rights. The Negro's problem will not be solved by running away. He cannot listen to the glib suggestion of those who would urge him to migrate en masse to other sections of the country. By grasping his great opportunity in the South he can make a lasting contribution to the moral strength of the nation and set a sublime example of courage for generations yet unborn.

By nonviolent resistance, the Negro can also enlist all men of good will in his struggle for equality. The problem is not a purely racial one, with Negroes set against whites. In the end, it is not a struggle between people at all, but a tension between justice and injustice. Nonviolent resistance is not aimed against oppressors but against oppression. Under its banner consciences, not racial groups, are enlisted.

If the Negro is to achieve the goal of integration, he must organize himself into a militant and nonviolent mass movement. All three elements are indispensable. The movement for equality and justice can only be a success if it has both a mass and militant character; the barriers to be overcome require both. Nonviolence is an imperative in order to bring about ultimate community.

A mass movement of a militant quality that is not at the same time committed to nonviolence tends to generate conflict, which in turn breeds anarchy. The support of the participants and the sympathy of the uncommitted are both inhibited by the threat that bloodshed will engulf the community. This reaction in turn encourages the opposition to threaten and resort to force. When, however, the mass movement repudiates violence while moving resolutely toward its goal, its opponents are revealed as the instigators and practitioners of violence if it occurs. Then public support is magnetically attracted to the advocates of nonviolence, while those who employ violence are literally disarmed by overwhelming sentiment against their stand.

Only through a nonviolent approach can the fears of the white community be mitigated. A guilt-ridden white minority lives in fear that if the Negro should ever attain power, he would act without restraint or pity to revenge the injustice and brutality of the years. It is something like a parent who continually mistreats a son. One day that parent raises his hand to strike the son, only to discover that the son is now as tall as he is. The parent is suddenly afraid—fearful that the son will use his new physical power to repay his parent for all the blows of the past.

The Negro, once a helpless child, has now grown up politically, culturally, and economically. Many white men fear retaliation. The job of the Negro is to show them that they have nothing to fear, that the Negro understands and forgives and is ready to forget the past. He must convince the white man that all he seeks is justice, *for both himself and the white man.* A mass movement exercising nonviolence is an object lesson in power under discipline, a demonstration to the white community that if such a movement attained a degree of strength, it would use its power creatively and not vengefully.

Nonviolence can touch men where the law cannot reach them. When the law regulates behavior it plays an indirect part in molding public sentiment. The enforcement of the law is itself a form of peaceful persuasion. But the law needs help. The courts can order desegregation of the public schools. But what can be done to mitigate the fears, to disperse the hatred, violence, and irrationality gathered around school integration, to take the initiative out of the hands of racial demagogues, to release respect for the law? In the end, for laws to be obeyed, men must believe they are right.

Here nonviolence comes in as the ultimate form of persuasion. It is the method which seeks to implement the just law by appealing to the conscience of the great decent majority who through blindness, fear, pride, or irrationality have allowed their consciences to sleep.

The nonviolent resisters can summarize their message in the following simple terms: We will take direct action against injustice without waiting for other agencies to act. We will not obey unjust laws or submit to unjust practices. We will do this peacefully, openly, cheerfully because our aim is to persuade. We adopt the means of nonviolence because our end is a community at peace with itself. We will try to persuade with our words, but if our words fail, we will try to persuade with our acts. We will always be willing to talk and seek fair compromise, but we are ready to suffer when necessary and even risk our lives to become witnesses to the truth as we see it.

The way of nonviolence means a willingness to suffer and sacrifice. It may mean going to jail. If such is the case the resister must be willing to fill the jail houses of the South. It may even mean physical death. But if physical death is the price that a man must pay to free his children and his white brethren from a permanent death of the spirit, then nothing could be more redemptive.

What is the Negro's best defense against acts of violence inflicted upon him? As Dr. Kenneth Clark has said so eloquently, "His only defense is to meet every act of barbarity, illegality, cruelty and injustice toward an individual Negro with the fact that 100 more Negroes will present themselves in his place as potential victims." Every time one Negro school teacher is fired for believing in integration, a thousand others should be ready to take the same stand. If the oppressors bomb the home of one Negro for his protest, they must be made to realize that to press back the rising tide of the Negro's courage they will have to bomb hundreds more, and even then they will fail.

Faced with this dynamic unity, this amazing self-respect, this willingness to suffer, and this refusal to hit back, the oppressor will find, as oppressors have always found, that he is glutted with his own barbarity. Forced to stand before the world and his God splattered with the blood of his brother, he will call an end to his self-defeating massacre.

American Negroes must come to the point where they can say to their white brothers, paraphrasing the words of Gandhi: "We will match your capacity to inflict suffering with our capacity to endure suffering. We will meet your physical force with soul force. We will not hate you, but we cannot in all good conscience obey your unjust laws. Do to us what you will and we will still love you. Bomb our homes and threaten our children; send your hooded perpetrators of violence into our communities and drag us out on some wayside road, beating us and leaving us half dead, and we will still love you. But we will soon wear you down by our capacity to suffer. And in winning our freedom we will so appeal to your heart and conscience that we will win you in the process."

Realism impels me to admit that many Negroes will find it difficult to follow the path of nonviolence. Some will consider it senseless; some will argue that they have neither the strength nor the courage to join in such a mass demonstration of nonviolent action. As E. Franklin Frazier points out in *Black Bourgeoisie,* many Negroes are occupied in a middle-class struggle for status and prestige. They are more concerned about "conspicuous consumption" than about the cause of justice, and are probably not prepared for the ordeals and sacrifices involved in nonviolent action. Fortunately, however, the success of this method is not dependent on its unanimous acceptance. A few Negroes in every community, unswervingly committed to the nonviolent way, can persuade hundreds of others at least to use nonviolence as a technique and serve as the moral force to awaken the slumbering national conscience. Thoreau was thinking of such a creative minority when he said: "I know this well, that if one thousand, if one hundred, if ten men whom I could name—if ten honest men only—aye, if one honest man, in the state of Massachusetts, ceasing to hold slaves, were actually to withdraw from the copartnership, and be locked up in the county jail therefore, it would be the abolition of slavery in America. For it matters not how small the beginning may seem to be, what is once well done is done forever."

Mahatma Gandhi never had more than one hundred persons absolutely committed to his philosophy. But with this small group of devoted followers, he galvanized the whole of India, and through a magnificent feat of nonviolence challenged the might of the British Empire and won freedom for his people.

This method of nonviolence will not work miracles overnight. Men are not easily moved from their mental ruts, their prejudiced and irrational feelings. When the underprivileged demand freedom, the privileged first react with bitterness and resistance. Even when the demands are couched in nonviolent terms, the initial response is the same. Nehru once remarked that the British were never so angry as when the Indians resisted them with nonviolence, that he never saw eyes so full of hate as those of the British troops to whom he turned the other cheek when they beat him with lathis. But nonviolent resistance at least changed the minds and hearts of the Indians, however impervious the British may have appeared. "We cast away our fear," says Nehru. And in the end the British not only granted freedom to India but came to have a new respect for the Indians. Today a mutual friendship based on complete equality exists between these two peoples within the Commonwealth.

In the South too, the initial white reaction to Negro resistance has been bitter. I do not predict that a similar happy ending will come to Montgomery in a few months, because integration is more complicated than independence. But I know that the Negroes of Montgomery are already walking straighter because of the protest. And I expect that this generation of Negro children throughout the United States will grow up stronger and better because of the courage, the dignity, and the suffering of the nine children of Little Rock, and their counterparts in Nashville, Clinton, and Sturges. And I believe that the white people of this country are being affected too, that beneath the surface this nation's conscience is being stirred.

The nonviolent approach does not immediately change the heart of the oppressor. It first does something to the hearts and souls of those committed to it. It gives them new self-respect; it calls up resources of strength and courage that they did not know they had. Finally it reaches the opponent and so stirs his conscience that reconciliation becomes a reality.

I suggest this approach because I think it is the only way to re-establish the broken community. Court orders and federal enforcement agencies will be of inestimable value in achieving desegregation. But desegregation is only a partial, though necessary, step toward the ultimate goal which we seek to realize. Desegregation will break down the legal barriers, and bring men together physically. But something must happen so to touch the hearts and souls of men that they will come together, not because the law says it, but because it is natural and right. In other words, our ultimate goal is integration which is genuine intergroup and inter-personal living. Only through nonviolence can this goal be attained, for the aftermath of nonviolence is reconciliation and the creation of the beloved community.

It is becoming clear that the Negro is in for a season of suffering. As victories for civil rights mount in the federal courts, angry passions and deep prejudices are further aroused. The mountain of state and local segregation laws still stands. Negro leaders continue to be arrested and harassed under city ordinances, and their homes continue to be bombed. State laws continue to be enacted to circumvent integration. I pray that, recognizing the necessity of suffering, the Negro will make it a virtue. To suffer in a righteous cause is to grow to our humanity's full stature. If only to save himself from bitterness, the Negro needs the vision to see the ordeals of this generation as the opportunity to transfigure himself and American society. If he has to go to jail for the cause of freedom, let him enter it in the fashion Gandhi urged his countrymen, "as the bridegroom enters the bride's chamber"—that is, with a little trepidation but with a great expectation.

Nonviolence is a way of humility and self-restraint. We Negroes talk a great deal about our rights, and rightly so. We proudly proclaim that three-fourths of the people of the world are colored. We have the privilege of watching in our generation the great drama of freedom and independence as it unfolds in Asia and Africa. All of these things are in line with the work of providence. We must be sure, however, that we accept them in the right spirit. In an effort to achieve freedom in America, Asia, and Africa we must not try to leap from a position of disadvantage to one of advantage, thus subverting justice. We must seek democracy and not the substitution of one tyranny for another. Our aim must never be to defeat or humiliate the white man. We must not become victimized with a philosophy of black supremacy. God is not interested merely in the freedom of black men, and brown men, and yellow men; God is interested in the freedom of the whole human race.

The nonviolent approach provides an answer to the long debated question of gradualism *versus* immediacy. On the one hand it prevents one from falling into the sort of patience which is an excuse for do-nothingism and escapism, ending up in standstillism. On the other hand it saves one from the irresponsible words which estrange without reconciling and the hasty judgment which is blind to the necessities of social process. It recognizes the need for moving toward the goal of justice with wise restraint and calm reasonableness. But it also recognizes the immorality of slowing up in the move toward justice and capitulating to the guardians of an unjust status quo. It recognizes that social change cannot come overnight. But it causes one to work as if it were a possibility the next morning.

Through nonviolence we avoid the temptation of taking on the psychology of victors. Thanks largely to the noble and invaluable work of the NAACP, we have won great victories in the federal courts. But we must not be self-satisfied. We must respond to every decision with an understanding of those who have opposed us, and with acceptance of the new adjustments that the court orders pose for them. We must act in such a way that our victories will be triumphs for good will in all men, white and Negro.

Nonviolence is essentially a positive concept. Its corollary must always be growth. On the one hand nonviolence requires noncoöperation with evil; on the other hand it requires coöperation with the constructive forces of good. Without this constructive aspect noncoöperation ends where it begins. Therefore, the Negro must get to work on a program with a broad range of positive goals.

One point in the Negro's program should be a plan to improve his own economic lot. Through the establishment of credit unions, savings and loan associations, and coöperative enterprises the Negro can greatly improve his economic status. He must develop habits of thrift and techniques of wise investment. He must not wait for the end of segregation that lies at the basis of his economic deprivation; he must act now to lift himself up by his own bootstraps.

The constructive program ahead must include a campaign to get Negroes to register and vote. Certainly they face many external barriers. All types of underhand methods are still being used in the South to prevent the Negroes from voting, and the success of these efforts is not only unjust, it is a real embarrassment to the nation we love and must protect. The advocacy of free elections in Europe by American officials is hypocrisy when free elections are not held in great sections of America.

But external resistance is not the only present barrier to Negro voting. Apathy among the Negroes themselves is also a factor. Even where the polls are open to all, Negroes have shown themselves too slow to exercise their voting privileges. There must be a concerted effort on the part of Negro leaders to arouse their people from their apathetic indifference to this obligation of citizenship. In the past, apathy was a moral failure. Today, it is a form of moral and political suicide.

The constructive program ahead must include a vigorous attempt to improve the Negro's personal standards. It must be reiterated that the standards of the Negro as a group lag behind not because of an inherent inferiority, but because of the fact that segregation does exist. The "behavior deviants" within the Negro community stem from the economic deprivation, emotional frustration, and social isolation which are the inevitable concomitants of segregation. When the white man argues that segregation should continue because of the Negro's lagging standards, he fails to see that the standards lag because of segregation.

Yet Negroes must be honest enough to admit that our standards do often fall short. One of the sure signs of maturity is the ability to rise to the point of self-criticism. Whenever we are objects of criticism from white men, even though the criticisms are maliciously directed and mixed with half-truths, we must pick out the elements of truth and make them the basis of creative reconstruction. We must not let the fact that we are the victims of injustice lull us into abrogating responsibility for our own lives.

Our crime rate is far too high. Our level of cleanliness is frequently far too low. Too often those of us who are in the middle class live above our means, spend money on nonessentials and frivolities, and fail to give to serious causes, organizations, and educational institutions that so desperately need funds. We are too often loud and boisterous, and spend far too much on drink. Even the most poverty-stricken among us can purchase a ten-cent bar of soap; even the most uneducated among us can have high morals. Through community agencies and religious institutions Negro leaders must develop a positive program through which Negro youth can become adjusted to urban living and improve their general level of behavior. Since crime often grows out of a sense of futility and despair, Negro parents must be urged to give their children the love, attention, and sense of belonging that a segregated society deprives them of. By improving our standards here and now we will go a long way toward breaking down the arguments of the segregationist.

This then must be our present program: Nonviolent resistance to all forms of racial injustice, including state and local laws and practices, even when this means going to jail; and imaginative, bold, constructive action to end the demoralization caused by the legacy of slavery and segregation, inferior schools, slums, and second-class citizenship. The nonviolent struggle, if conducted with the dignity and courage already shown by the people of Montgomery and the children of Little Rock, will in itself help end the demoralization; but a new frontal assault on the poverty, disease, and ignorance of a people too long ignored by America's conscience will make victory more certain.

In short, we must work on two fronts. On the one hand, we must continue to resist the system of segregation which is the basic cause of our lagging standards; on the other hand we must work constructively to improve the standards themselves. There must be a rhythmic alternation between attacking the causes and healing the effects.

This is a great hour for the Negro. The challenge is here. To become the instruments of a great idea is a privilege that history gives only occasionally. Arnold Toynbee says in *A Study of History* that it may be the Negro who will give the new spiritual dynamic to Western civilization that it so desperately needs to survive. I hope this is possible. The spiritual power that the Negro can radiate to the world comes from love, understanding, good will, and nonviolence. It may even be possible for the Negro, through adherence to nonviolence, so to challenge the nations of the world that they will seriously seek an alternative to war and destruction. In a day when Sputniks and Explorers dash through outer space and guided ballistic missiles are carving highways of death through the stratosphere, nobody can win a war. Today the choice is no longer between violence and nonviolence. It is either nonviolence or nonexistence. The Negro may be God's appeal to this age—an age drifting rapidly to its doom. The eternal appeal takes the form of a warning: "All who take the sword will perish by the sword."

Part Four

The Values of a
Business Society

"The business of America is business." Thus did Calvin Coolidge, a man not given to prolixity, sum up America's ideals and aspirations. In this he seemed to confirm Dickens' harsh impeachment of Americans in *Martin Chuzzlewit:* "All their cares, hopes, joys, affections, virtues, and associations, seemed to be melted down into dollars. . . . Men were weighed by their dollars; life was auctioneered, appraised, put up and knocked down for its dollars."

The image of Americans and America that such statements perpetuate is of a materialist civilization exclusively preoccupied with the accumulation of wealth and physical goods,[1] an image inspired these days, one suspects, as much by secret envy of our wealth as by an accurate estimate of the difference in taste and refinement between Europeans and Americans. Our European cousins are prone to such an appraisal of us, and they have succeeded in converting some American intellectuals to the same view. In truth, now that prosperity has come to the West Europeans, they generally display that same regard for mechanical gadgets that overwhelmed many of us;[2] they pursue wealth just as

---

[1] For some, Coca-Cola has unaccountably become the symbol of our degradation. Thus, in a letter to the editor of *The New York Times* (June 14, 1962) a prominent British historian, A. R. Burns, refers to the "Coca-Cola-vization of the American way of life" and adds that "if the only way to keep Europe from Communism were to have it completely Americanized, I should have my doubts about the merits of the bargain." It is reassuring to learn in the same letter that some of historian Burns' best friends are Americans.

[2] Peter Viereck's comment is surely apt: "Old world disdainers of us soulless American vulgarians still engage in heated debates about the rival aesthetics of the 'Cinquecents' and 'Seicents.' These two Italian labels, however, no longer refer to Renaissance art but to Fiat automobiles. Soon it may be necessary for left-bank sensitive plants to flee from modern, rootless, gadget-giddy Europe to ancient, medieval, traditionalist America." (*The Unadjusted Man*, p. 69.)

avidly, and, if public benefactions and tax avoidance are measures, their capitalists are far more grasping.

We often find in others the faults that are most conspicuous in ourselves—the psychological mechanism involved may aptly be called a disowning projection—and the European in stigmatizing Americans as materialistic may well be guilty of this rationalization. The libel is compounded when critics ignore the growing concern in America for scholarship and the fine arts. However, once all this is said and we have expressed our righteous indignation over what is an unfair caricature of American culture, the question may well be raised: ought not our concern for the arts and letters and sciences to be greater? Is it not true that, however overstated by unfair critics, profoundly important values are overshadowed and obscured by the emphasis in our society on the pursuit of wealth? Is it not the case that the motives of the marketplace invade the church, the school, government, the professions, the arts, deflecting them from their proper mission? In particular, how has the profit motive affected the quality of the so-called mass media to which we give so many of our leisure hours? May it not be said that business monopolizes too much of our lives? Many years ago De Tocqueville, most perceptive of foreign observers of American life, spoke of "the business-like qualities" of the Americans and of their "trading passions." The question is, have we carried these passions too far?

There is another aspect to the problem. A society that emphasizes pecuniary motives is organized about the satisfaction of *individual* needs and interests. Must this result in a neglect of national or community goals and purposes? Our cities, for example, have been called by Lewis Mumford a "crystallization of chaos." The rich and moderately well-to-do of the most affluent country in all history are engaged in an ignominious evacuation of their cities, leaving them—except for well-guarded islands of high commerce and plush living—to ethnic minorities, to marginal members of the majority group, and to the superannuated. In the past this occurred because there was an invader at the gates; today it occurs because our cities are less and less viable as communities. Does this suggest, as many have charged, that in our quest for consumer goods we have starved our social services, neglected public amenities, ignored national goals?

A major reason for our preoccupation with consumer goods is that the talents and energies of a great many able people are concentrated on promotion and salesmanship, which in effect bias the outlay we make as a people in favor of consumption to the neglect of such social needs as urban redevelopment, education, recreation, and conservation. Quite apart from the fact that supersalesmanship may—by persuading people to buy what they would not in ordinary circumstances want—lead to such neglect and to a misdirection of resources, how are we morally to evaluate the main manifestation of such promotion in the form of advertising? Is the effect desirable? Without reference to the tastelessness of the average commercial message on television or radio, or the influence of advertisers on newspaper or program content, how shall we morally assess the deception that characterizes most advertising? Is it discounted by the listener or viewer and therefore innocuous and morally irrelevant, or are we so institutionalizing mendacity that we dull our capacity to be morally discriminating?

Such a line of inquiry leads to two issues of increasing concern to responsible business leaders and to the community at large. Both issues involve the ethics of the business community. Private enterprise in this country, according to a number of its most distinguished leaders, is facing a moral crisis. The issue quite simply is honesty—honesty as commonly defined and understood. To what extent are businessmen honest with each other, honest with their government, honest with the public? The same question may of course be put to labor leaders, clergymen, and educators. But businessmen are leaders of the larger community as well as of their own enterprises in a sense in which leaders in other areas are not. The answer of businessmen to this question is therefore crucially important. Quite probably if they are dishonest—the reference here is not to marginal businessmen or even to an occasional Robert Vescoe but to the respected and established businessman—we as a people will be dishonest, with ourselves and with others. The power of businessmen to corrupt government was demonstrated in the Watergate scandals which, as everyone knows, began as a revelation of the willingness of some politicians to use illegal means in worsting their opponents and culminated as a disclosure of the way in which vast sums of money are secretly made available by important members of the business community to a government that serves their purposes.

The second question is more difficult and the answer more controversial. It involves much more than considerations of simple honesty. What are the responsibilities of the business community to the larger community of which it is a part? In recent years we have heard much of "corporate citizenship." It is said by many that the robber-baron days are over and that business executives have a new sense of the larger social responsibilities of the corporations over which they preside. Large-scale financial aid to colleges and universities is often cited as an example. Others will argue that the stewardship of private ownership and management has degraded our mass media, that the action of the management of basic industries in initiating price increases has indicated an obliviousness to the impact such action would have on the nation's economy, that industry (as in the case of automobile manufacture) is more concerned with a saleable appearance than with basic quality (and safety), that industrialists with rare exceptions have been oblivious of the harm they do to the environment and in general of the social costs incurred by their undertakings, that—in sum—the ideal of corporate citizenship is a veneer and a pretense. Clearly, such questions are of profound interest to every American.

It is all too easy to come up with simple answers and sweeping generalizations. All of them, including many of the adverse judgments implied above, must be weighed against the achievements of an open society in which, uniquely in man's history, vast strides towards banishing want and suffering have been made and in which—to borrow from Pericles—"Although only a few may originate a policy, we are all able to judge it." Such a judgment is made in the challenging comments that follow.

11

The Acquisitive Ideal

The acquisitive impulse is as old as man and has manifested itself wherever men have lived, but what R. H. Tawney has called the Acquisitive Society hardly antedates the third quarter of the eighteenth century. For a large part of this period its ambit was limited to England, the United States, and a small part of the continent of Europe. Max Weber was referring to a period not too long before the eighteenth century, when he wrote: "That anyone should be able to make it the sole purpose of his life-work, to sink into the grave weighed down with a great material load of money and goods, seems to him [pre-capitalist man] explicable only as the product of a perverse instinct, the *aura sacra fames.*"[1]

The acquisitive society institutionalized the profit motive, gave it a central role, made it the driving force that transformed the static and stable economies of an earlier era. This was, as Tawney has said, its "whole tendency and interest and preoccupation."[2] An acquisitive society is one in which the means of production are privately owned and in which the motives of the market, that is to say, the calculated interests of buyers and sellers, determine the allocation of productive resources and the distribution of incomes. Such a society, as Joseph Schumpeter has written, "has been cast in a purely economic mold: its foundations, beams and beacons are all made of economic material. The

---

[1] *The Protestant Ethic and the Spirit of Capitalism,* translated by Talcott Parsons (London: George Allen & Unwin, Ltd., 1930), pp. 71–72.

[2] *The Acquisitive Society* (New York: Harcourt, Brace and World, Inc.), p. 29.

building faces toward the economic side of life. Prizes and penalties are measured in pecuniary terms. Going up and down means making and losing money."[3]

For a long time such a society felt no need to examine its basic premises, including its economic bias and the central place it accorded economic man—viewed always, in Veblen's famous phrase, as a "lightning calculator." In recent years, however, such a review has been going on. Not only did the acquisitive society develop unexpected weaknesses; it had to meet the challenge of competing systems and ideologies. The resulting reexamination has gone far beyond economic analysis to a reappraisal of the basic values of a good society. If the society emerging from appraisals such as those that follow would be unrecognizable to Mr. Gladstone or Mr. Coolidge, there is good reason to believe that it will prove more durable in the end.

---

[3] *Capitalism, Socialism, and Democracy* (New York: Harper & Row, Inc., 1942), p. 73.

THE HOUSE DIVIDED AGAINST ITSELF

John Dewey

Although not so widely read as during the first third of this century, John Dewey remains the towering eminence among American philosophers. In 1952, when he died at the age of 93, he left behind him a prodigious legacy of provocative and important books and articles such as few other men have encompassed in a lifetime. It is safe to say that he influenced our thinking more than any other American. His greatest works in the field of general philosophy are Experience and Nature *(1925) and* The Quest for Certainty *(1929). In ethical theory he waged a long war not only against absolutism, but against the kind of relativism which asserts that judgments of value are not, like judgments of fact, demonstrable and are therefore merely "emotive." Dewey believed that judgments of value are susceptible of validation and hence meaningful, even though this is not accomplished by referring them to or deriving them from moral absolutes. Much of what he said on this subject is intended for the professional philosopher, but his* Ethics (*1938*) (*especially Part II, which he wrote without his collaborator, James Tufts*) *will reward the general reader, as will* Human Nature and Conduct (*1922*) *and* Reconstruction in Philosophy (*1920*).

Dewey was an ardent social reformer. In this sense he was a philosophe *as well as a philosopher, if we agree with Carl Becker's view of the former as interested not only in ideas but in the impact of ideas on events. Dewey's interest was a logical outcome of his "instrumentalism," to use the term he preferred for his version of the pragmatic philosophy of which he was the leading exponent. But it was also an outcome of his recoil as an individual from what he regarded as the less wholesome features of a pecuniary culture.*

Although Individualism, Old and New *appeared in 1930, much recent social criticism bears a striking resemblance to it. When the book was first published, relatively few students were moved by Dewey's criticism of business. Today student attitudes have changed drastically enough to affect recruitment and concern business leaders. The* Los Angeles Times, *in an article about a weekend seminar of businessmen and students at Pomona College with the headline "Students Tell Why They Shun Business," reported that the two groups are "not on the same beam." Typical student comment, according to the* Times, *stressed that money is not the prime objective of today's students and that students want to do something that is "socially useful."*

Dewey's work is a severe impeachment of patterns of conduct prevalent during the first quarter of this century. We need now to ask ourselves to what extent these patterns still prevail.

. . . Anthropologically speaking, we are living in a money culture. Its cult and rites dominate. "The money medium of exchange and the cluster of activities associated with its acquisition drastically condition the other activities of the people." This, of course, is as it should be; people have to make a living, do they not? And for what should they work if not for money, and how should they get goods and enjoyments if not by buying them with money—thus enabling someone else to make more money, and in the end to start shops and factories to give employment to still others, so that they can make more money to enable other people to make more money by selling goods—and so on indefinitely. So far, all is for the best in the best of all possible cultures: our rugged—or is it ragged?—individualism.

And if the culture pattern works out so that society is divided into two classes, the working group and the business (including professional) group, with two and a half times as many in the former as in the latter, and with the chief ambition of parents in the former class that their children should climb into the latter, that is doubtless because American life offers such unparalleled opportunities for each individual to prosper according to his virtues. If few workers know what they are making or the meaning of what they do, and still fewer know what becomes of the work of their hands . . . this is doubtless because we have so perfected our system of distribution that the whole country is one. And if the mass of workers live in constant fear of loss of their jobs, this is doubtless because our spirit of progress, manifest in change of fashions, invention of new machines and power of overproduction, keeps everything on the move. Our reward of industry and thrift is so accurately adjusted to individual ability that it is natural and proper that the workers should look forward with dread to the age of fifty or fifty-five, when they will be laid on the shelf.

All this we take for granted; it is treated as an inevitable part of our social system. To dwell on the dark side of it is to blaspheme against our religion of prosperity. But it is a system that calls for a hard and strenuous philosophy. If one looks at what we do and what happens, and then expects to find a theory of life that harmonizes with the actual situation, he will be shocked by the contradiction he comes upon. For the situation calls for assertion of complete economic determinism. We live as if economic forces determined the growth and decay of institutions and settled the fate of individuals. Liberty becomes a well-nigh obsolete term; we start, go, and stop at the signal of a vast industrial machine. Again, the actual system would seem to imply a pretty definitely materialistic scheme of value. Worth is measured by ability to hold one's own or to get ahead in a competitive pecuniary race. . . . The philosophy appropriate to such a situation is that of struggle for existence and survival of the economically fit. One would expect the current theory of life, if it reflects the actual situation, to be the most drastic Darwinism. And, finally, one would anticipate that the personal traits most prized would be clear-sighted vision of personal advantage and resolute ambition to secure it at any human cost. Sentiment and sympathy would be at the lowest discount.

It is unnecessary to say that the current view of life in Middletown, in Anytown, is nothing of this sort. Nothing gives us Americans the horrors more than to hear that some misguided creature in some low part of the earth preaches what we practice—and practice much more efficiently than anyone else—namely, economic determinism. Our whole theory is that man plans and uses machines for his own humane and moral purposes, instead of being borne wherever the machine carries him. Instead of materialism, our idealism is probably the loudest and most frequently professed philosophy the world has ever heard. We praise even our most successful men, not for their ruthless and self-centered energy in getting ahead, but because of their love of flowers, children, and dogs, or their kindness to aged relatives. Anyone who frankly urges a selfish creed of life is everywhere frowned upon. . . . We are surcharged with altruism and bursting with the desire to "serve" others.

These are only a few of the obvious contradictions between our institutions and practice on one hand, and our creeds and theories on the other, contradictions which a survey of any of our Middletowns reveals. It is not surprising that the inhabitants of these towns are bewildered, uneasy, restless, always seeking something new and different, only to find, as a rule, the same old thing in a new dress. It may all be summed up, perhaps, by saying that nowhere in the world at any time has religion been so thoroughly respectable as with us, and so nearly totally disconnected from life. . . .

It makes little difference whether one selects important or trivial aspects of the contradiction between our life as we outwardly live it and our thoughts and feelings—or what we at least say are our beliefs and sentiments. The significant question is: What is the cause of this split and contradiction? . . . It is evident enough that the rapid industrialization of our civilization took us unawares. Being mentally and morally unprepared, our older creeds have become ingrowing; the more we depart from them in fact, the more loudly we proclaim them. In effect we treat them as magic formulae. By repeating them often enough we hope to ward off the evils of the new situation, or at least to prevent ourselves from seeing them—and this latter function is ably performed by our nominal beliefs.

With an enormous command of instrumentalities, with possession of a secure technology, we glorify the past, and legalize and idealize the *status quo,* instead of seriously asking how we are to employ the means at our disposal so as to form an equitable and stable society. This is our great abdication. It explains how and why we are a house divided against itself. Our tradition, our heritage, is itself double. It contains in itself the ideal of equality of opportunity and of freedom for all, without regard to birth and status, as a condition for the effective realization of that equality. This ideal and endeavor in its behalf once constituted our essential Americanism; that which was prized as the note of a new world. It is the genuinely spiritual element of our tradition. No one can truthfully say that it has entirely disappeared. But its promise of a new moral and religious outlook has not been attained. It has not become the well-spring of a new intellectual consensus; it is not (even unconsciously) the vital source of any distinctive and shared philosophy. It directs our politics only spasmodically, and while it has generously provided schools it does not control their aims or their methods.

Meanwhile our institutions embody another and older tradition. Industry and business conducted for money profit are nothing new; they are not the product of our own age and culture; they come to us from a long past. But the invention of the machine has given them a power and scope they never had in the past from which they derive. Our law and politics and the incidents of human association depend upon a novel combination of the machine and money, and the result is the pecuniary culture characteristic of our civilization. The spiritual factor of our tradition, equal opportunity and free association and intercommunication, is obscured and crowded out. Instead of the development of individualities which is prophetically set forth, there is a perversion of the whole idea of individualism to conform to the practices of a pecuniary culture. It has become the source and justification of inequalities and oppressions. Hence our compromises, and the conflicts in which aims and standards are confused beyond recognition. . . .

The marks and signs of [the] "impersonalization" of the human soul are quantification of life, with its attendant disregard of quality; its mechanization and the almost universal habit of esteeming technique as an end, not as a means, so that organic and intellectual life is also "rationalized"; and, finally, standardization. Differences and distinctions are ignored and overridden; agreement, similarity, is the ideal. There is not only absence of social discrimination but of intellectual; critical thinking is conspicuous by its absence. Our pronounced trait is mass suggestibility. The adaptability and flexibility that we display in our practical intelligence when dealing with external conditions have found their way into our souls. Homogeneity of thought and emotion has become an ideal.

Quantification, mechanization and standardization: these are then the marks of the Americanization that is conquering the world. They have their good side; external conditions and the standard of living are undoubtedly improved. But their effects are not limited to these matters; they have invaded mind and character, and subdued the soul to their own dye. The criticism is familiar; it is so much the burden of our own critics that one is never quite sure how much of the picture of foreign critics is drawn from direct observation and how much from native novels and essays that are not complacent with the American scene. This fact does not detract from the force of the indictment; it rather adds to it, and raises the more insistently the question of what our life means.

. . . the impoverishment of the individual is accompanied, even now, by an enrichment of community resources. Collectively, present society . . . is marked by a power over nature and by intellectual resource and power exceeding that of the classic Athenian and the man of the Renaissance. Why is it that this collective enrichment does not operate to elevate correspondingly the life of the individual? . . . Failure to consider [this question] constitutes to my mind the chief failure of critics whether foreign or native. Our materialism, our devotion to money making and to having a good time, are not things by themselves. They are the product of the fact that we live in a money culture; of the fact that our technique and technology are controlled by interest in private profit. There lies the serious and fundamental defect of our civilization, the source of the secondary and induced evils to which so much attention is given. Critics are dealing with symptoms and effects. The evasion of fundamental economic causes by critics both foreign and native seems to me to be an indication of the prevalence of the old European tradition, with its disregard for the body, material things, and practical concerns. The development of the American type, in the sense of the critics, is an expression of the fact that we have retained this tradition and the economic system of private gain on which it is based, while at the same time we have made an independent development of industry and technology that is nothing short of revolutionary. When our critics deal with this issue instead of avoiding it there will be something really doing.

Until the issue is met, the confusion of a civilization divided against itself will persist. The mass development, which our European critics tell us has submerged individuality, *is* the product of a machine age; in some form it will follow in all countries from the extension of a machine technology. Its immediate effect has been, without doubt, a subjection of certain types of individuality. As far as individuality is associated with aristocracy of the historic type, the extension of the machine age will presumably be hostile to individuality in its traditional sense all over the world. . . . The problem of constructing a new individuality consonant with the objective conditions under which we live is the deepest problem of our times. . . .

Assured and integrated individuality is the product of definite social relationships and publicly acknowledged functions. Judged by this standard, even those who seem to be in control and to carry the expression of their special individual abilities to a high pitch, are submerged. They may be captains of finance and industry, but until there is some consensus of belief as to the meaning of finance and industry in civilization as a whole, they cannot be captains of their own souls—their beliefs and aims. They exercise leadership surreptitiously and, as it were, absentmindedly. They lead, but it is under cover of impersonal and socially undirected economic forces. Their reward is found not in what they do, in their social office and function, but in a deflection of social consequences to private gain. They receive the acclaim and command the envy and admiration of the crowd, but the crowd is also composed of private individuals who are equally lost to a sense of social bearings and uses.

The explanation is found in the fact that while the actions promote corporate and collective results, these results are outside their intent and irrelevant to that reward of satisfaction which comes from a sense of social fulfillment. To themselves and to others, their business is private and its outcome is private profit. No complete satisfaction is possible where such a split exists. Hence the absence of a sense of social value is made up for by an exacerbated acceleration of the activities that increase private advantage and power. One cannot look into the inner consciousness of his fellows; but if there is any general degree of inner contentment on the part of those who form our pecuniary oligarchy, the evidence is sadly lacking. As for the many, they are impelled hither and yon by forces beyond their control. . . .

The unrest, impatience, irritation and hurry that are so marked in American life are inevitable accompaniments of a situation in which individuals do not find support and contentment in the fact that they are sustaining and sustained members of a social whole. They are evidence, psychologically, of abnormality, and it is as idle to seek for their explanation within the deliberate intent of individuals as it is futile to think that they can be got rid of by hortatory moral appeal. Only an acute maladjustment between individuals and the social conditions under which they live can account for such widespread pathological phenomena. Feverish love of anything as long as it is a change which is distracting, impatience, unsettlement, nervous discontentment, and desire for excitement, are not native to human nature. They are so abnormal as to demand explanation in some deep-seated cause.

I should explain a seeming hypocrisy on the same ground. We are not consciously insincere in our professions of devotion to ideals of "service"; they mean something. Neither the Rotarian nor the big business enterprise uses the term merely as a cloak for "putting something over" which makes for pecuniary gain. But the lady doth protest too much. The wide currency of such professions testifies to a sense of a social function of business which is expressed in words because it is so lacking in fact, and yet which is felt to be rightfully there. If our external combinations in industrial activity were reflected in organic integrations of the desires, purposes and satisfactions of individuals, the verbal protestations would disappear, because social utility would be a matter of course.

THE PROFIT MOTIVE

Peter Drucker

Peter Drucker is a well-known authority on the corporation as a social institution. He is both a teacher and management consultant and the author of a number of widely read books, including The End of Economic Man *(1939),* The Future of Industrial Man *(1941),* The New Society *(1950),* Landmarks of Tomorrow *(1959), and* Age of Discontinuity *(1969). For eighteen months he served as outside consultant to General Motors Corporation, which asked him to study and report on its managerial policies and organization. The volume from which the following selection is taken is a result of this study. While rejecting the hedonistic preconceptions of orthodox economics as a basis on which to plead that the profit motive is inherent in human nature, he argues that the profit motive is nevertheless indispensable to a viable economy and a free society.*

Profit and profitability are objective criteria of economic action. They have nothing to do with the beliefs of a given society or with particular institutions but apply to any society however organized. Essentially profit and profitability are nothing but reformulations of the law of the conservation of energy in economic terms.

The "profit motive" on the other hand pertains to man's actions and reactions. In capitalist society, moreover, it is institutionalized in special institutions, and behavior according to the "profit motive" receives social sanctions and rewards. It is this "profit motive," the socially sanctioned behavior of the individual to obtain the maximum material gain, which is under attack as "unnatural" and "antisocial." And since the corporation in a free-enterprise economy is directed by, and dedicated to, the satisfaction of this "profit motive," the question arises whether the "profit motive" is indeed incompatible with a stable, functioning and good society.

The attack on the profit motive as "unnatural" and conflicting with socially and individually more beneficial and more fundamental human motives is, like the attack on profitability, partly the result of an excessive reaction against the wrong psychology of the utilitarian economists. They had proclaimed that man has a natural instinct to "truck and bargain," and they deduced from this instinct the laws of classical economics. We know today that there is no such thing as a natural instinct to "truck and bargain." If we ever needed proof of the fallacy of the utilitarian concept, it has been abundantly supplied by modern cultural anthropology and modern psychology. We also know that in most human activities, motives are thoroughly mixed, and that we will never find anybody acting on the basis of that "simple and clear calculation" of possible gain against possible effort on which the classical economists based their theories of economic behavior. Finally, we know that the orthodox economists were completely mistaken when they used the utilitarian "pleasure-pain calculus" to equate "work" with "pain." The psychological and social ravages of unemployment have certainly shown that idleness, far from being pleasing, is destructive, and that work, far from being disagreeable, is a necessity of human existence and self-respect and in itself a source of pride and satisfaction. There is little left today of that psychology from which the profit motive emerged as the controller of human destinies and as the natural law of human behavior.

To say that the profit motive is not inborn in man and the expression of his true nature is, however, something very different from asserting that it is vicious, unnatural and socially undesirable. This assertion rests on two beliefs which are both as untenable and as fallacious psychologically as the dogma of the preordained profit motive which they tried to replace. The first of these is the belief that man's "creative instinct" is not only good in itself but alone sufficient to make man socially constructive—the belief which is expressed in Veblen's famous juxtaposition of "industry" and "business." The second of these beliefs asserts that, but for the profit motive, human society would be one of equality and peace, and that all drive for power and privilege, all conflict and all inequality are the result of the lust for gain. In other words, both beliefs see in the profit motive the one, or at least the main, obstacle to the millennium.

It cannot be said too emphatically that no society can be based on man's "creative instincts." In order to make social life possible there must always be a principle of organization which reduces individual fulfillment and individual drive to a social purpose. Otherwise that co-ordinated human effort on which social life rests becomes impossible. If we do not use profit and profitability as the reduction gear, we would have to work out some other social mechanism to convert the subjective drive of the individual into the objective performance of society.

If we take, for instance, the people employed in the production of an automobile, we shall find that the "instinct of workmanship" leads in totally different directions, depending upon whether we look at the engineer, the production man or the sales manager. For the engineer the highest standard of achievement and craftsmanship lies in the most functional and most up-to-date car embodying the best and newest in engineering research, in materials and in design. He may be inclined to regard as alien and as in conflict with his ideas of workmanship such considerations as cheapness and ease of production, habits of automobile users, their comfort, etc.; and he would want to change his design all the time in order to·incorporate the latest engineering improvements. The standards by which the production man will measure his workmanship and achievement would be above all cheapness, speed and ease of production. His ideal is an engineering design that will never change. His attitude towards the consumer's preference and desires was summed up perfectly in the epigram attributed to that prince of production men, Henry Ford, when he said that "the customer can have any color as long as it's black." The sales manager finally—or anybody whose business it is to distribute cars—sees maximum achievement in the most salable car, a cheap car that "looks like a million dollars" and satisfies the consumer's desire to keep up with the Joneses—however unreasonable this may appear to the engineer or to the production man. Each has "instincts of workmanship" which are creative. But the instinct of the one can find free rein only at the expense of the instinct of another. If society wants automobiles, it must be able to subordinate the instincts of each man to an objective principle of social satisfaction. However much such an objective principle "violates" individual integrity—a point mooted since the dawn of history—society must have it.

The profit motive may not be the best reduction gear. It certainly is not the only possible one. But to denounce it because it is a reduction gear—Veblen's procedure—begs the question. What we have to answer is not whether the profit motive is good or bad, but whether it is efficient or inefficient as a principle of social integration of individual motives and desires.

In a society which accepts economic advancement and economic goals as socially efficient and as socially desirable the profit motive is socially the most efficient device. In any other society, it is not an efficient mechanism. In the Middle Ages, for instance, the profit motive was clearly socially inefficient from the point of view of an order which regarded economic goals—beyond mere physical survival—as socially irrelevant and as morally suspect. In a society which believes in the desirability of economic progress, as has ours for the last two hundred years, the profit motive is an efficient mechanism of integration, because it relates individual motives and drives directly to accepted social purposes. Obviously, this creates problems in those spheres of social life to which economic rationality is not applicable, such as the arts. But these problems are no greater than those faced by the Middle Ages in applying their noneconomic objective principle of social integration to the economic sphere with its necessarily economic rationality. In other words, while no society and no principle of social integration can be perfect or automatic, the profit motive is the most efficient and the simplest mechanism for the conversion of individual drives into social purpose and action under the given conditions and beliefs of *our* society. It is, perhaps, the best commentary on this conclusion that the Soviet Union has gone as far as any capitalist country —and further—in using economic rewards and incentives in industry. For however different its social tenets and institutions, Russia shares with the West the belief in economic goals.

What about the second count in the popular indictment of the profit motive: that it is the cause of the lust for power and dominance and the sole or main obstacle to peace and equality? Certainly the "profit motive" is not necessarily inherent in human nature. But inherent in human nature there is a drive for power and distinction of which the profit motive is only one possible form. If we eliminate the profit motive, the result will not be the equal and peaceful society of the millennium but the emergence of some other outlet for men's basic lust for power.

The weakness of the traditional argument is beautifully illustrated by the first great sermon on the profit motive as the original sin, and on its abolition as the key to the earthly paradise—Thomas More's *Utopia*. More's ideal society is perfect, peaceful, free of strife and ambition simply because property and gain have been eliminated. At the same time—almost on the same page—More proposes an elaborate system of honors and preferments as the basis for social power and political rulership. And he never sees the obvious: that the competition for these honors and preferments would at once bring back the ambition, the strife, the factionalism and the lust for power and prestige which he had just driven out by banishing the profit motive. Plato—and More was a Platonist—knew better. But his proposal in the *Republic* not to admit anyone to rulership until he be old enough to be past ambition is hardly more realistic; is there an age limit on ambition and pride? Wherever in history a man was kept out of power until very late, his lust for power, his ambition, his dominance and factiousness increased, often to the point of pathological exaggeration.

If I may again point to the findings of modern anthropology: the sentimental concept of "primitive equality" popularized by Rousseau and Marx has been exploded completely. There are many primitive tribes which do not know individual property in the sense in which we use the term. There are however no examples of real communism among primitive tribes; communism is far too complicated a social arrangement to be attainable for a primitive society. And in every single culture we know of, there is a socially accepted motive of advancement to power and prestige around which the social organization is built.

Actually, we should not have needed anthropology to teach us that society is based on man's innate drive for power and social recognition. We have known for thousands of years that Pride is an essentially human quality. We may, with the ancient Greeks and the Renaissance, accept Pride as a virtue. Or we may with the Christian doctrine regard Pride as both cause and result of man's fall from grace and as the center of his corruption. But we can never hope to have a society without it. The statesman may, as a Christian, deplore the weakness of man and strive to overcome it in himself. As a statesman, however, he has to accept the fact that Pride and its manifestations are both the reason for the existence of society, and a constant in any social organization. The problem of the statesman is not to suppress or to overcome the drive for power; that is the concern of philosopher and saint. The political problem is how to direct the drive for power into the socially most constructive or least destructive channels.

To say, as is customary, that the profit motive is bad because all drive for power is bad, evades the issue; it may be good theology but it certainly is not relevant to politics. To say that the profit motive is bad because without it there would be no drive for power, is not even bad theology; it is nonsense. The only relevant and meaningful question is whether the profit motive is the socially most efficient one of the available directions in which the drive for power can be channeled.

I do not think that anyone can give a dogmatic answer; the absolutely best lies in the field of religion or philosophy, not in that of politics or social organization. But we can say that of the channels available and known to us, the profit motive has a very high, if not the highest, social efficiency. All the other known forms in which the lust for power can be expressed, offer satisfaction by giving the ambitious man direct power and domination over his fellow man. The profit motive alone gives fulfillment through power over things. It is an old truth that the richest and most overbearing millionaire in a capitalist society has less power over the individual worker than the worst paid official in a collectivist state, who can grant or withhold a license to do business or a work card. Certainly there is the danger that the power over things may develop into a power over men. But it is not an inevitable danger, and it can be checked by social action. . . .

The profit motive is the one way known to us to divert ambition from the socially destructive goal of power over men, into a socially constructive channel, that of economic production. This, though not by itself sufficient, is a protection against the danger that the lives and the livelihood of the individual citizen will become pawns in the game of human ambition and fair prey for the drive for power. It is no accident that the great villains of history are not found among the "economic royalists" but among the "incorruptibles," whose aim was power and power alone. Neither Robespierre nor Hitler could have been bought off by money; they lacked economic acquisitiveness entirely. But this hardly made them any more beneficial for mankind; their indifference to anything but naked power over men only heightened their inhumanity. . . .

To have a free society we must make it possible for man to act and to live in society without destroying himself or enslaving his fellow men. We must harness the lust for power to a social purpose. This, in a society accepting economic goals, the profit motive can do.

We do not have to regard the drive for gain as noble or as the best man is capable of. But noble or base, it directs the drive for power into the least dangerous channel. Of course the profit motive does not bring about a free society; the identification of capitalism with democracy, so current today, is utterly superficial and is the result of a truly shocking confusion. But while the profit motive by itself leads to a free society as little as any other human drive, it is more compatible with it than the other forms in which the lust for power may manifest itself socially. A free society is not based on man's drive but on his reason; it always has to guard against the danger of its perversion by the drive for power or by any other drive. The profit motive contains potential threats like all other manifestations of human pride. But unlike the other forms in which the drive for power may become socially effective, the profit motive of a free-enterprise society also contains powerful safeguards against the politically most dangerous consequence of human pride, the tyranny of the power-drunk.

12

The Problem of Priorities

The foregoing discussions have dealt in general terms with the way in which the profit motive has shaped our culture and influenced our ideals and aspirations as a people. Traditionally in our country the profit motive operates through the market and ours is known as a "market economy." The alternative to a market economy is some form of planning, either private or public, partial or total. In truth, ours is a "mixed economy" in which private planning and public planning combine with the conventional forces of the market to determine the way in which we allocate our human and physical resources. In this mix, the movements of the market are influenced significantly by the decisions of those who own or manage the private sector of the economy. In recent times the beneficence of this influence on our scale of preferences as these are reflected in public and private expenditures has become a subject of much controversy.

It will become evident that the problem of priorities, as we have come to know it, is a special one, touched upon, to be sure, in the preceding selections but not in its own terms. Thus, if an individual were to spend a disproportionate amount of his income on luxuries—flashy automobiles, sports, liquor, etc.—at the same time that his family was badly housed and without adequate medical care, and his children inadequately educated, our moral appraisal of him would be a severe one. The contention is that collectively as a people we dispose of our resources in some analogous fashion.

The disposition of our resources, to repeat, is determined either by the market or by government. According to conservatives, the market reflects the multitudinous decisions of individuals, each one the best judge of his own interest and each choosing freely and rationally[1] within the limitations of his income and thereby guiding the flow of resources into the uses that coincide most nearly with his demands. Government is generally thought of as consisting of potentially tyrannous individuals arbitrarily imposing their judgment on others. Is this an accurate description of the alternatives? And does the kind of market economy that prevails in the United States bias the allocation of resources in favor of frivolous expenditures to the neglect of fundamental needs? The question has come increasingly into the forefront of our thinking. Although it is generally discussed in economic and political terms, moral issues are clearly involved.

Many would say that, except at the margins, we need not stumble over the difficulty of distinguishing between what is extravagant and frivolous and what is basic and fundamental. Oversized cars, rapid changes of fashion in attire, and built-in obsolescence would appear to fall into the first category; water purification, housing, medical care, and education, into the latter. Even so, some will ask who is to determine what is good or bad in the way we spend our money? Others will answer that the consumer should, but under conditions that enable him to exercise his best judgment. This, then, is the problem of priorities: Do our economic institutions as they now operate make for a wise or foolish allocation of our resources? Two contrasting views are presented in the selections that appear below.

---

[1] To be rational in this sense is to know what one wants and to choose the means most likely to get it and least likely to interfere with the satisfaction of stronger wants.

THE THEORY OF SOCIAL BALANCE

John Kenneth Galbraith

John Kenneth Galbraith, well-known economist, was appointed by President Kennedy as ambassador to India. He later returned to his professorship at Harvard. As an economist he has generally preferred novel and arresting insights and generalizations to detailed statistical analyses, a preference no doubt abetted by a biting epigrammatic style that has been lacking in the literature of political economy since the days of England's R. H. Tawney and America's Thorstein Veblen. More than any recent book, Galbraith's volume from which the following selection is taken focused attention on the contrast between what he has called "private opulence and public squalor." He has also written Modern Competition and Business Policy (*1938*), American Capitalism: The Concept of Countervailing Power (*1952*), The Liberal Hour (*1960*), *and* The New Industrial State (*1967*). *His most recent book is* Economics and the Public Purpose (*1973*).

The final problem of the productive society is what it produces. This manifests itself in an implacable tendency to provide an opulent supply of some things and a niggardly yield of others. This disparity carries to the point where it is a cause of social discomfort and social unhealth. The line which divides our area of wealth from our area of poverty is roughly that which divides privately produced and marketed goods and services from publicly rendered services. Our wealth in the first is not only in startling contrast with the meagerness of the latter, but our wealth in privately produced goods is, to a marked degree, the cause of crisis in the supply of public services. For we have failed to see the importance, indeed the urgent need, of maintaining a balance between the two.

This disparity between our flow of private and public goods and services is no matter of subjective judgment. On the contrary, it is the source of the most extensive comment which only stops short of the direct contrast being made here. In the years following World War II, the papers of any major city—those of New York were an excellent example—told daily of the shortages and shortcomings in the elementary municipal and metropolitan services. The schools were old and overcrowded. The police force was under strength and underpaid. The parks and playgrounds were insufficient. Streets and empty lots were filthy, and the sanitation staff was underequipped and in need of men. Access to the city by those who work there was uncertain and painful and becoming more so. Internal transportation was overcrowded, unhealthful, and dirty. So was the air. Parking on the streets had to be prohibited, and there was no place elsewhere. The deficiencies were not in new and novel services but in old and established ones. Cities have long swept their streets, helped their people move around, educated them, kept order, and provided horse rails for vehicles which sought to pause. That their residents should have a nontoxic supply of air suggests no revolutionary dalliance with socialism.

The discussion of this public poverty competed, on the whole successfully, with the stories of ever-increasing opulence in privately produced goods. The Gross National Product was rising. So were retail sales. So was personal income. Labor productivity had also advanced. The automobiles that could not be parked were being produced at an expanded rate. The children, though without schools, subject in the playgrounds to the affectionate interest of adults with odd tastes, and disposed to increasingly imaginative forms of delinquency, were admirably equipped with television sets. We had difficulty finding storage space for the great surpluses of food despite a national disposition to obesity. Food was grown and packaged under private auspices. The care and refreshment of the mind, in contrast with the stomach, was principally in the public domain. Our colleges and universities were severely overcrowded and underprovided, and the same was true of the mental hospitals.

The contrast was and remains evident not alone to those who read. The family which takes its mauve and cerise, air-conditioned, power-steered, and power-braked automobile out for a tour passes through cities that are badly paved, made hideous by litter, blighted buildings, billboards, and posts for wires that should long since have been put underground. They pass on into a countryside that has been rendered largely invisible by commercial art. (The goods which the latter advertise have an absolute priority in our value system. Such aesthetic considerations as a view of the countryside accordingly come second. On such matters we are consistent.) They picnic on exquisitely packaged food from a portable icebox by a polluted stream and go on to spend the night at a park which is a menace to public health and morals. Just before dozing off on an air mattress, beneath a nylon tent, amid the stench of decaying refuse, they may reflect vaguely on the curious unevenness of their blessings. Is this, indeed, the American genius?

In the production of goods within the private economy it has long been recognized that a tolerably close relationship must be maintained between the production of various kinds of products. The output of steel and oil and machine tools is related to the production of automobiles. Investment in transportation must keep abreast of the output of goods to be transported. The supply of power must be abreast of the growth of industries requiring it. The existence of these relationships—coefficients to the economist—has made possible the construction of the input-output table which shows how changes in the production in one industry will increase or diminish the demands on other industries. To this table, and more especially to its ingenious author, Professor Wassily Leontief, the world is indebted for one of its most important of modern insights into economic relationships. If expansion in one part of the economy were not matched by the requisite expansion in other parts—were the need for balance not respected—then bottlenecks and shortages, speculative hoarding of scarce supplies, and sharply increasing costs would ensue. Fortunately in peacetime the market system operates easily and effectively to maintain this balance, and this, together with the existence of stocks and some flexibility in the coefficients as a result of substitution, insures that no serious difficulties will arise. We are reminded of the existence of the problem only by noticing how serious it is for those countries—Poland or, in a somewhat different form, India—which seek to solve the problem by planned measures and with a much smaller supply of resources.

Just as there must be balance in what a community produces, so there must also be balance in what the community consumes. An increase in the use of one product creates, ineluctably, a requirement for others. If we are to consume more automobiles, we must have more gasoline. There must be more insurance as well as more space on which to operate them. Beyond a certain point more and better food appears to mean increased need for medical services. This is the certain result of the increased consumption of tobacco and alcohol. More vacations require more hotels and more fishing rods. And so forth. With rare exceptions—shortages of doctors are an exception which suggests the rule—this balance is also maintained quite effortlessly so far as goods for private sale and consumption are concerned. The price system plus a rounded condition of opulence is again the agency.

However, the relationships we are here discussing are not confined to the private economy. They operate comprehensively over the whole span of private and public services. As surely as an increase in the output of automobiles puts new demands on the steel industry so, also, it places new demands on public services. Similarly, every increase in the consumption of private goods will normally mean some facilitating or protective step by the state. In all cases if these services are not forthcoming, the consequences will be in some degree ill. It will be convenient to have a term which suggests a satisfactory relationship between the supply of privately produced goods and services and those of the state, and we may call it social balance.

The problem of social balance is ubiquitous, and frequently it is obtrusive. As noted, an increase in the consumption of automobiles requires a facilitating supply of streets, highways, traffic control, and parking space. The protective services of the police and the highway patrols must also be available, as must those of the hospitals. Although the need for balance here is extraordinarily clear, our use of privately produced vehicles has, on occasion, got far out of line with the supply of the related public services. The result has been hideous road congestion, an annual massacre of impressive proportions, and chronic colitis in the cities. As on the ground, so also in the air. Planes are endlessly delayed or collide in the air with disquieting consequences for passengers when the public provision for air traffic control fails to keep pace with private use of the airways.

But the auto and the airplane, versus the space to use them, are merely an exceptionally visible example of a requirement that is pervasive. The more goods people procure, the more packages they discard and the more trash that must be carried away. If the appropriate sanitation services are not provided, the counterpart of increasing opulence will be deepening filth. The greater the wealth the thicker will be the dirt. This indubitably describes a tendency of our time. As more goods are produced and owned, the greater are the opportunities for fraud and the more property that must be protected. If the provision of public law enforcement services do not keep pace, the counterpart of increased well-being will, we may be certain, be increased crime.

The city of Los Angeles, in modern times, is a near-classic study in the problem of social balance. Magnificently efficient factories and oil refineries, a lavish supply of automobiles, a vast consumption of handsomely packaged products, coupled for many years with the absence of a municipal trash collection service which forced the use of home incinerators, made the air nearly unbreathable for an appreciable part of each year. Air pollution could be controlled only by a complex and highly developed set of public services—by better knowledge of causes stemming from more public research, better policing, a municipal trash collection service, and possibly the assertion of the priority of clean air over the production of goods. These were long in coming. The agony of a city without usable air was the result.

The issue of social balance can be identified in many other current problems. Thus an aspect of increasing private production is the appearance of an extraordinary number of things which lay claim to the interest of the young. Motion pictures, television, automobiles, and the vast opportunities which go with the mobility, together with such less enchanting merchandise as narcotics, comic books, and pornographia, are all included in an advancing Gross National Product. The child of a less opulent as well as a technologically more primitive age had far fewer such diversions. The red schoolhouse is remembered mainly because it had a paramount position in the lives of those who attended it that no modern school can hope to attain.

In a well-run and well-regulated community, with a sound school system, good recreational opportunities, and a good police force—in short a community where public services have kept pace with private production —the diversionary forces operating on the modern juvenile may do no great damage. Television and the violent mores of Hollywood and Madison Avenue must contend with the intellectual discipline of the school. The social, athletic, dramatic, and like attractions of the school also claim the attention of the child. These, together with the other recreational opportunities of the community, minimize the tendency to delinquency. Experiments with violence and immorality are checked by an effective law enforcement system before they become epidemic.

In a community where public services have failed to keep abreast of private consumption things are very different. Here, in an atmosphere of private opulence and public squalor, the private goods have full sway. Schools do not compete with television and the movies. The dubious heroes of the latter, not Miss Jones, become the idols of the young. The hot rod and the wild ride take the place of more sedentary sports for which there are inadequate facilities or provision. Comic books, alcohol, narcotics, and switchblade knives are, as noted, part of the increased flow of goods, and there is nothing to dispute their enjoyment. There is an ample supply of private wealth to be appropriated and not much to be feared from the police. An austere community is free from temptation. It can be austere in its public services. Not so a rich one.

Moreover, in a society which sets large store by production, and which has highly effective machinery for synthesizing private wants, there are strong pressures to have as many wage earners in the family as possible. As always all social behavior is part of a piece. If both parents are engaged in private production, the burden on the public services is further increased. Children, in effect, become the charge of the community for an appreciable part of the time. If the services of the community do not keep pace, this will be another source of disorder.

Residential housing also illustrates the problem of the social balance, although in a somewhat complex form. Few would wish to contend that, in the lower or even the middle income brackets, Americans are munificently supplied with housing. A great many families would like better located or merely more houseroom, and no advertising is necessary to persuade them of their wish. And the provision of housing is in the private domain. At first glance at least, the line we draw between private and public seems not to be preventing a satisfactory allocation of resources to housing.

On closer examination, however, the problem turns out to be not greatly different from that of education. It is improbable that the housing industry is greatly more incompetent or inefficient in the United States than in those countries—Scandinavia, Holland, or (for the most part) England—where slums have been largely eliminated and where *minimum* standards of cleanliness and comfort are well above our own. As the experience of these countries shows, and as we have also been learning, the housing industry functions well only in combination with a large, complex, and costly array of public services. These include land purchase and clearance for redevelopment; good neighborhood and city planning, and effective and well-enforced zoning; a variety of financing and other aids to the housebuilder and owner; publicly supported research and architectural services for an industry which, by its nature, is equipped to do little on its own; and a considerable amount of direct or assisted public construction for families in the lowest income brackets. The quality of the housing depends not on the industry, which is given, but on what is invested in these supplements and supports.

The case for social balance has, so far, been put negatively. Failure to keep public services in minimal relation to private production and use of goods is a cause of social disorder or impairs economic performance. The matter may now be put affirmatively. By failing to exploit the opportunity to expand public production we are missing opportunities for enjoyment which otherwise we might have had. Presumably a community can be as well rewarded by buying better schools or better parks as by buying bigger automobiles. By concentrating on the latter rather than the former it is failing to maximize its satisfactions. As with schools in the community, so with public services over the country at large. It is scarcely sensible that we should satisfy our wants in private goods with reckless abundance, while in the case of public goods, on the evidence of the eye, we practice extreme self-denial. So, far from systematically exploiting the opportunities to derive use and pleasure from these services, we do not supply what would keep us out of trouble.

The conventional wisdom holds that the community, large or small, makes a decision as to how much it will devote to its public services. This decision is arrived at by democratic process. Subject to the imperfections and uncertainties of democracy, people decide how much of their private income and goods they will surrender in order to have public services of which they are in greater need. Thus there is a balance, however rough, in the enjoyments to be had from private goods and services and those rendered by public authority.

It will be obvious, however, that this view depends on the notion of independently determined consumer wants. In such a world one could with some reason defend the doctrine that the consumer, as a voter, makes an independent choice between public and private goods. But given the dependence effect—given that consumer wants are created by the process by which they are satisfied—the consumer makes no such choice. He is subject to the forces of advertising and emulation by which production creates its own demand. Advertising operates exclusively, and emulation mainly, on behalf of privately produced goods and services. Since management and emulative effects operate on behalf of private production, public services will have an inherent tendency to lag behind. Automobile demand which is expensively synthesized will inevitably have a much larger claim on income than parks or public health or even roads where no such influence operates. The engines of mass communication, in their highest state of development, assail the eyes and ears of the community on behalf of more beer but not of more schools. Even in the conventional wisdom it will scarcely be contended that this leads to an equal choice between the two.

The competition is especially unequal for new products and services. Every corner of the public psyche is canvassed by some of the nation's most talented citizens to see if the desire for some merchantable product can be cultivated. No similar process operates on behalf of the non-merchantable services of the state. Indeed, while we take the cultivation of new private wants for granted we would be measurably shocked to see it applied to public services. The scientist or engineer or advertising man who devotes himself to developing a new carburetor, cleanser, or depilatory for which the public recognizes no need and will feel none until an advertising campaign arouses it, is one of the valued members of our society. A politician or a public servant who dreams up a new public service is a wastrel. Few public offenses are more reprehensible.

So much for the influences which operate on the decision between public and private production. The calm decision between public and private consumption pictured by the conventional wisdom is, in fact, a remarkable example of the error which arises from viewing social behavior out of context. The inherent tendency will always be for public services to fall behind private production. . . .

Social balance is also the victim of . . . the truce on inequality . . . With rare exceptions such as the post office, public services do not carry a price ticket to be paid for by the individual user. By their nature they must, ordinarily, be available to all. As a result, when they are improved or new services are initiated, there is the ancient and troublesome question of who is to pay. This, in turn, provokes to life the collateral but irrelevant debate over inequality. As with the use of taxation as an instrument of fiscal policy, the truce on inequality is broken. Liberals are obliged to argue that the services be paid for by progressive taxation which will reduce inequality. Committed as they are to the urgency of goods . . . they must oppose sales and excise taxes. Conservatives rally to the defense of inequality—although without ever quite committing themselves in such uncouth terms—and oppose the use of income taxes. They, in effect, oppose the expenditure not on the merits of the service but on the demerits of the tax system. Since the debate over inequality cannot be resolved, the money is frequently not appropriated and the services not performed. . . .

In practice matters are better as well as worse than this statement of the basic forces suggests. Given the tax structure, the revenues of all levels of government grow with the growth of the economy. Services can be maintained and sometimes even improved out of this automatic accretion.

However, this effect is highly unequal. The revenues of the federal government, because of its heavy reliance on income taxes, increase more than proportionately with private economic growth. In addition, although the conventional wisdom greatly deplores the fact, federal appropriations have only an indirect bearing on taxation. Public services are considered and voted on in accordance with their seeming urgency. Initiation or improvement of a particular service is rarely, except for purposes of oratory, set against the specific effect on taxes. Tax policy, in turn, is decided on the basis of the level of economic activity, the resulting revenues, expediency, and other considerations. Among these the total of the thousands of individually considered appropriations is but one factor. In this process the ultimate tax consequence of any individual appropriation is *de minimus,* and the tendency to ignore it reflects the simple mathematics of the situation. Thus it is possible for the Congress to make decisions affecting the social balance without invoking the question of inequality.

Things are made worse, however, by the fact that a large proportion of the federal revenues are pre-empted by defense. The increase in defense costs has also tended to absorb a large share of the normal increase in tax revenues. The position of the federal government for improving the social balance has also been weakened since World War II by the strong, although receding, conviction that its taxes were at artificial wartime levels and that a tacit commitment exists to reduce taxes at the earliest opportunity.

In the states and localities the problem of social balance is much more severe. Here tax revenues—this is especially true of the General Property Tax—increase less than proportionately with increased private production. Budgeting too is far more closely circumscribed than in the case of the federal government—only the monetary authority enjoys the pleasant privilege of underwriting its own loans. Because of this, increased services for states and localities regularly pose the question of more revenues and more taxes. And here, with great regularity, the question of social balance is lost in the debate over equality and social equity.

Thus we currently find by far the most serious social imbalance in the services performed by local governments. The F.B.I. comes much more easily by funds than the city police force. The Department of Agriculture can more easily keep its pest control abreast of expanding agricultural output than the average city health service can keep up with the needs of an expanding industrial population. One consequence is that the federal government remains under constant and highly desirable pressure to use its superior revenue position to help redress the balance at the lower levels of government. . . .

A feature of the years immediately following World War II was a remarkable attack on the notion of expanding and improving public services. During the depression years such services had been elaborated and improved partly in order to fill some small part of the vacuum left by the shrinkage of private production. During the war years the role of government was vastly expanded. After that came the reaction. Much of it, unquestionably, was motivated by a desire to rehabilitate the prestige of private production and therewith of producers. No doubt some who joined the attack hoped, at least tacitly, that it might be possible to sidestep the truce on taxation vis-à-vis equality by having less taxation of all kinds. For a time the notion that our public services had somehow become inflated and excessive was all but axiomatic. Even liberal politicians did not seriously protest. They found it necessary to aver that they were in favor of public economy too.

In this discussion a certain mystique was attributed to the satisfaction of privately supplied wants. A community decision to have a new school means that the individual surrenders the necessary amount, willy-nilly, in his taxes. But if he is left with that income, he is a free man. He can decide between a better car or a television set. This was advanced with some solemnity as an argument for the TV set. The difficulty is that this argument leaves the community with no way of preferring the school. All private wants, where the individual can choose, are inherently superior to all public desires which must be paid for by taxation and with an inevitable component of compulsion.

The cost of public services was also held to be a desolating burden on private production, although this was at a time when the private production was burgeoning. Urgent warnings were issued of the unfavorable effects of taxation on investment—"I don't know of a surer way of killing off the incentive to invest than by imposing taxes which are regarded by people as punitive." This was at a time when the inflationary effect of a very high level of investment was causing concern. The same individuals who were warning about the inimical effects of taxes were strongly advocating a monetary policy designed to reduce investment. However, an understanding of our economic discourse requires an appreciation of one of its basic rules: men of high position are allowed, by a special act of grace, to accommodate their reasoning to the answer they need. Logic is only required in those of lesser rank.

Finally it was argued, with no little vigor, that expanding government posed a grave threat to individual liberties. "Where distinction and rank are achieved almost exclusively by becoming a civil servant of the state . . . it is too much to expect that many will long prefer freedom to security."

With time this attack on public services has somewhat subsided. The disorder associated with social imbalance has become visible even if the need for balance between private and public services is still imperfectly appreciated.

Freedom also seemed to be surviving. Perhaps it was realized that all organized activity requires concessions by the individual to the group. This is true of the policeman who joins the police force, the teacher who gets a job at the high school, and the executive who makes his way up the hierarchy of General Motors. If there are differences between public and private organizations, they are of kind rather than of degree. As this is written the pendulum has in fact swung back. Our liberties are now menaced by the conformity exacted by the large corporation and its impulse to create, for its own purposes, the organization man.

Nonetheless, the postwar onslaught on the public services left a lasting imprint. To suggest that we canvass our public wants to see where happiness can be improved by more and better services has a sharply radical tone. Even public services to avoid disorder must be defended. By contrast the man who devises a nostrum for a nonexistent need and then successfully promotes both remains one of nature's noblemen.

PRIVATE VS. PUBLIC

Henry E. Wallich

Among academic economists, Henry E. Wallich might be described as belonging to the "conservative" school. He is Professor of Economics at Yale and author of Mainsprings of the German Revival *(1955) and* The Cost of Freedom: A New Look at Capitalism *(1960). He was a member of President Eisenhower's Council of Economic Advisers between 1959 and 1961.*

. . . It is one thing to be irritated by certain manifestations of our contemporary civilization—the gadgets, the chrome, . . . and the activities that go with them. It is quite another—and something of a *non sequitur*—to conclude from this that the only alternative to foolish private spending is public spending. Better private spending is just as much of a possibility. My contention here will be that to talk in terms of "public vs. private" is to confuse the issue. More than that, it is to confuse means and ends. The choice between public and private money is primarily a choice of means. The sensible approach for those who are dissatisfied with some of the ends to which private money is being spent, is to specify first what other ends are important and why. Having determined the ends, the next step is to look to the means. That is the order in which I propose to proceed here.

One may share the irritation of the new social critics as they look upon some of the fluff and the floss on our standard of living. . . . The critics may want to bear in mind, however, that not all the money in this country is spent by people for whom life begins at $25,000. The median family income is $5,600.[1] Would these critics of the affluent society want to try living on much less than that? When Galbraith inveighs eloquently against switchblades, narcotics, and other phases of juvenile delinquency, he deserves the support of all right-thinking representatives of what he calls the "conventional wisdom." But are the sources of these aberrations more intimately tied to affluence or to poverty? The exponents of the new social criticism may also want to remember the outcome of that "noble experiment," Prohibition. It should have taught us that it is futile to become our brother's dietitian. I hope that it has also imbued us with wholesome doubt about the moral right of some members of the community to regulate the lives of the rest.

Irritation with the poor judgment of other people who fail to appreciate one's own more advanced tastes is not new. It was a familiar situation during the 1920s. The critics then quoted T. S. Eliot's *The Waste Land,* and some went off to Paris in search of greener cultural pastures. The feeling behind the new social criticism is not dissimilar. Hence one might suppose that the reaction would likewise turn in a cultural direction. One might expect the critics of contemporary materialism to plead for more intensive preoccupation with things of the mind. Some fits and starts in that direction there have been, to be sure. But they have not been in the main stream of the movement. The principal alternative to private materialism that has been offered to us has been public materialism.

Obviously, the quality of our culture could be greatly improved by public expenditures for education and support of the arts. The sales of good paperbacks and LPs are encouraging signs. But if contemporary materialism is to be leavened by such pursuits, it will be principally because large numbers of individuals make private decisions to that end. Social criticism is constructive if it helps precipitate these decisions. It obstructs a desirable evolution if it suggests that public creature comforts are the only alternative to private.

But while emphasis on nonmaterial ends seems sadly lacking in the new social criticism, the critics are right in pointing out that new material needs also have been carried to the fore by social and economic evolution—even though they mislabel them as public needs. In the good old days, when this was still a nation of farmers, most people had no serious retirement worries, there was no industrial unemployment problem, good jobs could be had without a college degree, most diseases were still incurable—in short, social security, education, and health care found primitive and natural solutions within the family and among the resources of the neighborhood. Today, these solutions are neither adequate nor usually even possible.

Meanwhile mounting wealth and advancing technology have brought within reach the means of meeting these needs. We can afford to

---

[1] Editor's note: The 1973 median family income was about $11,000.

live better in every way—more creature comforts, more leisure, more attention to matters of the mind and the spirit. At the same time we can take better care of retirement, of unemployment, of illness, of education, of the possibilities opened by research, than ever before.

There are indeed new needs. The citizen-taxpayer has his choice of meeting them, as well as all his other needs, in one of two ways. He can buy the goods or services he wants privately, for cash or credit. Or he can buy them from the government, for taxes.

The nation as a whole pays taxes to buy public services as it pays grocery bills to buy groceries. The tax burden may be heavier for some individuals than for others. But the nation as a whole has no more reason to complain about the "burden" of taxes than about the "burden" of grocery bills—and no more reason to hope for relief.

Of the two stores, the private store today still is much the bigger. The public store is smaller, but it is growing faster.

Each store has some exclusive items. The private store sells most of the necessities and all of the luxuries of life, and in most of these has no competition from the government side. The public store has some specialties of its own: defense, public order and justice, and numerous local services that the private organization has not found profitable. But there is a wide range of items featured by both stores: provision for old age, health services, education, housing, development of natural resources.

The bulk of the new needs are in this competitive area. The fashionable notion is to claim them all for the public store and to label them public needs. The statistics say otherwise. They say in fact two things: First, the supply of this group of goods and services has expanded very rapidly in recent years; and second, they are being offered, in varying degrees, both by the private and the public suppliers. Let us run down the list.

Provision for old age is predominantly private. The average American family, realizing that while old age may be a burden, it is the only known way to achieve a long life, takes care of the matter in three ways: (1) by private individual savings—home ownership, savings deposits, securities; (2) by private collective savings—life insurance, corporate pension funds; and (3) by public collective savings through social security. Statisticians report that the two collective forms are advancing faster than the individual. The increases far exceed the rise in the Gross National Product of almost 80 per cent (in current prices) over the past ten years; they do not indicate either that these needs are neglected or that they are necessarily public in character.

Education: the bulk of it is public; but a good part, particularly of higher education, is private. Total expenditures for all education have advanced in the last ten years from $9.3 billion to $24.6 billion ($19.3 billion of it public). Education's share in the national income has advanced from

3.8 per cent to 5.8 per cent. The silly story that we spend more on advertising than on education is a canard, though with its gross of over $10 billion, advertising does take a lot of money.

Health expenditures are still mainly private. At considerable expense, it is now possible to live longer and be sick less frequently or at least less dangerously. In the past, most people paid their own doctors' bills, although health care for the indigent has always been provided by public action or private philanthropy. Since the war, the proliferation of health insurance has given some form of collective but private insurance to three-quarters of our 182 million people. This has greatly reduced pressure for a national health service along British lines. For the aging, whose health-care needs stand in inverse proportion to their capacity to pay or insure, public insurance has finally been initiated and needs to be expanded. The total annual expenditure on health is estimated at over $25 billion, a little more than on education. Of this, about $6 billion is public.

So much for the allegation that the "new needs" are all public needs. Now for some further statistics on the public store, which is said to have been neglected. Some of them could make an investor in private growth stocks envious. Research expenditures (mainly for defense and atomic energy) have gone from about $1 billion to over $8 billion in the last ten years. Federal grants to the states have advanced from $2.2 billion to $7 billion during the same period. Social-security benefits rose from $1 billion to over $10 billion. All in all, public cash outlays (federal and state) advanced from $61 billion to $134 billion over ten years, 57 per cent faster than the GNP.

For those who feel about public spending the way Mark Twain felt about whiskey, these figures may still look slim. (Mark Twain thought that while too much of anything was bad, too much whiskey was barely enough.) To others, the data may suggest that the advocates of more public spending have already had their way. Could their present discontent be the result of not keeping their statistics up-to-date? In one of his recent pamphlets, Arthur M. Schlesinger, Jr. claims that the sum of the many neglects he observes (including defense) could be mended by raising public expenditures by $10 to $12 billion. That is well below the increase in public cash outlays that actually did take place in one single fiscal year, from $118.2 billion in 1958 to $132.7 billion in 1959. In the three fiscal years 1957–59, these outlays went up more than $31 billion, though the advance slowed down in 1960. More facts and less indignation might help to attain better perspective.

Some parts of federal, state, and local budgets have expanded less rapidly than those cited—in many cases fortunately. The massive buildup in defense expenditures from the late 'forties to the 'fifties has squeezed other programs. Unfortunately, on the other hand, some programs that both political parties have favored—including aid to education, to depressed areas, for urban renewal—have been delayed unduly by the vicissitudes of politics. But the figures as a whole lend little support to the thesis that politicians don't spend enough, and that the government store is not expanding fast enough.

The two stores—private and public—work very hard these days to capture the business of the citizen-taxpayer. Here is what he hears as he walks into the private store.

"The principal advantage of this store," the private businessman says, "is that you can shop around and buy exactly what you want. If I don't have it I'll order it. You, the consumer, are the boss here. To be sure, I'm not in business for charity but for profit. But my profit comes from giving you what you want. And with competition as fierce as it is, you can be sure the profit won't be excessive."

If the proprietor has been to Harvard Business School, he will perhaps remember to add something about the invisible hand which in a free economy causes the self-seeking of competitors to work for the common good. He will also, even without benefit of business school, remember to drop a word about the danger of letting the public store across the street get too big. It might endanger freedom.

As the citizen turns this sales talk over in his mind, several points occur to him. Without denying the broad validity of the argument, he will note that quite often he has been induced to buy things he did not really need, and possibly to neglect other, more serious needs. Snob appeal and built-in obsolescence promoted by expensive advertising don't seem to him to fit in with the notion that the consumer is king. Looking at the brand names and patents and trademarks, he wonders whether most products are produced and priced competitively instead of under monopoly conditions. The invisible hand at times seems to be invisible mainly because it is so deep in his pocket.

Bothered by these doubts, the citizen walks across the street and enters the public store.

"Let me explain to you," says the politician who runs it—with the aid of a horde of hard-working bureaucrats doing the chores. "The principles on which the store is run are known as the political process, and if you happen to be familiar with private merchandising they may seem unusual, but I assure you they work. First of all, almost everything in this store is free. We simply assess our customers a lump sum in the form of taxes. These, however, are based largely on each customer's ability to pay, rather than on what he gets from the store. We have a show of hands from the customers once a year, and the majority decides what merchandise the store is to have in stock. The majority, incidentally, also decides how much everybody, including particularly the minority, is to be assessed in taxes.

"You will observe," the politician continues, "that this store is not run for profit. It is like a co-operative, run for the welfare of the members.

I myself, to be sure, am not in politics for charity, but for re-election. But that means that I must be interested in your needs, or you would not vote for me. Moreover, there are some useful things that only I can do, with the help of the political process, and in which you and every citizen have an interest. For instance, everybody ought to go to school. I can make them go. Everybody ought to have old-age insurance. I can make that compulsory too. And because I don't charge the full cost of the service, I can help even up a little the inequalities of life.

"By the way," the politician concludes, "if there is any special little thing you want, I may be able to get it for you, and of course it won't cost you a nickel."

The citizen has some fault to find with the political process too. He notes that there is not even a theoretical claim to the benefits of an invisible hand. Majority rule may produce benefits for the majority, but how about the other 49 per cent? Nor is there the discipline of competition, or the need for profits, to test economy of operation. There is no way, in the public store, of adjusting individual costs and benefits. And the promise to get him some small favor, while tempting, worries him, because he wonders what the politician may have promised to others. The political process, he is led to suspect, may be a little haphazard.

He asks himself how political decisions get to be made. Sometimes, obviously, it is not the majority that really makes a decision, but a small pressure group that is getting away with something. He will remember that—after payments for major national security and public debt interest—the largest single expenditure in the federal budget is for agriculture, and the next for veterans. He may also recall that one of the first budgetary actions of the new Administration was to increase funds for agriculture by $3 billion.

Next, the citizen might consider the paralyzing "balance-of-forces" effect that often blocks a desirable reshuffling of expenditures. The allocation of public funds reflects the bargaining power of their sponsors, inside or outside the government. A classical example was the division of funds that prevailed in the Defense Department during the late 'forties. Army, Navy, and Air Force were to share in total resources in a way that would maximize military potential. By some strange coincidence, maximum potential was always achieved by giving each service the same amount of money. It took the Korean War to break this stalemate.

What is the consequence of the balance-of-forces effect? If the proponents of one kind of expenditure want to get more money for their projects, they must concede an increase also to the advocates of others. More education means more highways, instead of less; more air power means more ground forces. To increase a budget in one direction only is as difficult as letting out one's belt only on one side. The expansion tends to go all around. What this comes down to is that politicians are not very

good at setting priorities. Increases in good expenditures are burdened with
a political surcharge of less good ones.

The last-ditch survival power of federal programs is a specially
illuminating instance of the balance of forces. If a monument were built in
Washington in memory of each major federal program that has been dis-
continued, the appearance of the city would not be greatly altered. In
contrast, when the Edsel doesn't sell, production stops. But the government
is still reclaiming land to raise more farm surpluses and training fishermen
to enter an occupation that needs subsidies to keep alive. Old federal
programs never die, they don't even fade away—they just go on.

The citizen will remember also the ancient and honorable practice
of logrolling. The unhappy fate of the Area Development bill illustrates it
admirably. As originally proposed, the bill sought to aid a limited number
of industrial areas where new jobs were badly needed. It got nowhere in the
Congress. Only when it was extended to a large number of areas with less
urgent or quite different problems were enough legislators brought aboard
to pass it. Because of the heavy political surcharge with which it had
become loaded, President Eisenhower vetoed the bill. A bill was finally
enacted early this year, long after aid should have been brought to the
areas that needed it.

Finally, the citizen might discover in some dark corner of his mind
a nagging thought: Any particular government program may be a blessing,
but could their cumulative effect be a threat to freedom? He has heard
businessmen say this so often that he has almost ceased to pay attention to
it. He rather resents businessmen acting the dog in the manger, trying to
stop useful things from being done unless they can do them. He is irritated
when he hears a man talk about freedom who obviously is thinking about
profit. And yet—is there any conclusive rebuttal?

The citizen would be quite wrong, however, if he blamed the
politician for the defects of the political process. The fault lies with the
process, or better with the way in which the process, the politician, and the
citizen interact. The citizen therefore would do well to examine some of his
own reactions and attitudes.

First, when he thinks about taxes, he tends to think of them as a
burden instead of as a price he pays for a service. As a body, the nation's
taxpayers are like a group of neighbors who decide to establish a fire
department. Because none is quite sure how much good it will do him, and
because each hopes to benefit from the contribution of the rest, all are
prudent in their contributions. In the end they are likely to wind up with a
bucket brigade.

But when it comes to accepting benefits, the citizen-taxpayers act
like a group of men who sit down at a restaurant table knowing that they
will split the check evenly. In this situation everybody orders generously; it
adds little to one's own share of the bill, and for the extravagance of his

friends he will have to pay anyhow. What happens at the restaurant table explains—though it does not excuse—what happens at the public trough.

Finally, in his reaction to public or free services, the citizen takes a great deal for granted, and seldom thinks of the cost. Public beaches mistreated, unmetered parking space permanently occupied, veterans' adjustment benefits continued without need—as well as abuses of unemployment compensation and public assistance—are some examples. This applies also, of course, to privately offered benefits, under health insurance, for instance. The kindly nurse in the hospital—"Why don't you stay another day, dearie, it won't cost you anything, it's all paid for by Blue Cross"—makes the point.

By removing the link between costs and benefits, the political process also reduces the citizen's interest in earning money. The citizen works to live. If some of his living comes to him without working, he would be less than rational if he did not respond with a demand for shorter hours. If these public benefits increase his tax burden so that his over-all standard of living remains unchanged, the higher taxes will reduce his work incentive. Why work hard, if much of it is for the government?

These various defects of the political process add up to an obvious conclusion: the dollar spent by even the most honest and scrupulous of politicians is not always a full-bodied dollar. It often is subject to a discount. It buys less than it should because of the attrition it suffers as it goes through the process, and so may be worth only 90 cents or 80 cents and sometimes perhaps less. The private dollar, in too many cases, may also be worth less than 100 per cent. But here each man can form his own judgment, can pick and choose or refuse altogether. In the political process, all he can do is say Yes or No once a year in November.

The discount on the public dollar may be compensated by the other advantages of government—its ability to compel, to subsidize, to do things on a big scale and at a low interest cost. Whether that is the case needs to be studied in each instance. Where these advantages do not apply, the private market will give better service than the political process. For many services, there is at least some leeway for choice between the private and public store—health and retirement, housing, research, higher education, natural-resource development. Defense, on the other hand, as well as public administration, public works of all kinds, and the great bulk of education—while perhaps made rather expensive by the political process—leave no realistic alternative to public action.

The argument I have offered is no plea to spend more or less on any particular function. It is a plea for doing whatever we do in the most effective way.

13

Conscience and the Corporation

Private ownership of the means of production in a highly industrialized economy has produced the modern corporation, through which the financial resources of large numbers of people are pooled, ownership and management are separated, and vast enterprises launched and operated. Given the central place of the private corporation in our institutional life, the ideals and standards of management, in particular management's conception of the social obligations of the corporation, will have a great deal to do with the kind of society in which we live. In recent times, the strategic place of the corporation has presented management with a new problem: whether to construe the role of the corporation narrowly as a strictly amoral business enterprise organized to maximize profits, or to accept a broader, socially oriented interpretation of the responsibilities of the corporation that would include the welfare of the community.

However, welfare of the community is ambiguous. It may mean compensation to the community for costs incurred in correcting specific damages suffered as a result of the operations of an enterprise or increasing the cost of production to end the nuisance, as in the case of pollutants that are poured into streams, lakes, and air. Such damage to the environment is really part of the cost of production—the social cost—which has not heretofore been included in the price at which a commodity sells. For the most part industry has not only ignored such costs but has fought legislation that would compel it to pay them. Welfare of the community might also embrace fair employment practices even if at some immediate sacrifice of efficiency.[1] However, there is a great and rarely noted difference between the assumption of such responsibilities and the gifts to schools, churches, etc. which Dr. Eells defends and Theodore Levitt criticizes in the following pages. Readers pondering the implications of this difference will be led to this basic question: Are there ways in which corporations can assume important social responsibilities without a dangerous extension of already formidable managerial power? The late Albert Carr, whose comments are reprinted below, believed that there are, contending that the corporation must exhibit a social conscience if it is to enjoy its rightful place in a free society. His words are echoed by many corporation executives these days, although one wonders if theirs are the real views of the business community.

One cannot invoke a corporate social conscience without raising a fundamental issue that is glossed over in most discussions of this subject and therefore calls for more extended attention in these introductory comments.

The issue of honesty is related to, yet nevertheless distinct from, a discussion of the social obligations of the business community. The area of social responsibility embraces much terra incognita: should business acknowledge responsibility (as few businesses have) for the employment of workers during slack periods and off-seasons; should a large corporation shut down a marginal plant in a community completely dependent on its operation; should corporations (as distinguished from individuals) give aid to churches and institutions of higher learning; should the steel industry reckon with the impact of its pricing policies on the economy as a whole? The nature of obligation is not clearly defined in these areas, and standards are in flux.

On the other hand, the question of honesty involves no comparable perplexities, not even concerning certain practices permitted by law. Normal people generally know when they are dishonest. At issue here is adherence to precepts that the business community itself accepts. Quite simply, honesty is opposed to lying, cheating, bribing, or stealing. Also, it involves practicing what we preach, especially when we preach with moral fervor.

---

[1] What can be accomplished is strikingly exemplified by the jeans manufacturer, Levi Strauss, one of the most successful corporations in this country. Minorities make up 33 percent of its American labor force, 10 percent of its officials and managers, and 15 percent of its professionals. Also, its board of directors includes a black member. In an unrelated area, a Norton Simon enterprise has announced that it will no longer call attention to irrelevant or fictitious differences in its advertising.

Are incidents of illegal or unethical business conduct isolated and unrepresentative, or do they indicate the presence of widespread dishonesty and moral obtuseness in the business community?[2] In the case of the General Electric and Westinghouse executives who were jailed a few years ago for conspiring to fix prices, the defense pleaded in extenuation that the violations were part of the "prevailing business morality." Was counsel exaggerating to help his client or was he describing a true state of affairs? His plea was almost identical with the more recent words of the head of American Airlines who, confessing to a large illegal contribution of the corporation's funds to the Nixon campaign, declared that this is common practice.[3] Most heads of corporations, to be sure, when they engage in such practices, are less obvious in violating the law; they have their colleagues make personal contributions and then reimburse them through padded (and tax deducted) expense accounts.

Again, the business community affirms its dedication to the ideal of consumer "sovereignty" with moral fervor and great vigor.[4] But it has a long record of fierce opposition to compulsory grade-labeling and other legal requirements that would enable

---

[2] For example, in 1961 a federal judge upheld the conviction of eleven major oil firms on gasoline price-fixing charges. In 1962, five steel corporations were fined a total of $44,000 on their plea of no contest to charges of conspiracy to fix prices and rig bids in steel sales. In 1964 six of the nation's largest aluminum firms were accused by the Justice Department of submitting rigged bids and overcharging government agencies for aluminum conductor cable. They settled out of court, paying the U.S. Government $563,000. In 1967, it was the turn of the drug industry. For another kind of example, shipments of General Foods' Maxwell House instant coffee were seized recently by the Food and Drug Administration because the giant "economy" size was costing the consumer more per ounce than the small jar. Instances can be multiplied.

[3] By way of confirmation he was soon followed (July 20, 1973) by the chairman of the board of Ashland Oil Company, a giant petrochemical corporation, who confessed that he had made an illegal (and therefore cash) gift of $100,000 of the corporation's funds to the Nixon campaign. He in turn has been followed by B. R. Dorsey, board chairman of Gulf Oil Corporation who tapped his corporation for $100,000; and Russell Deyoung of Goodyear Tire and Rubber Co., who turned over $40,000 of his company's funds. Others lured by the promise of clemency will no doubt come forward.

[4] "Within the market society the working of the price mechanism makes the consumer supreme. . . . In that endless rotating mechanism the entrepreneurs and capitalists are servants of the consumer. The consumers are the masters. . . . The market is a democracy in which every penny gives a right to vote . . ." Ludwig Von Mises, *Omnipotent Government* (New Haven: Yale University Press, 1944), pp. 49–50. So, too, John Chamberlain, whose book *The Roots of Capitalism* is one of a series designed to promote understanding of prevailing business practices, writes: "The test of an economic system lies in the choices it offers. . . ." In a free system such as ours "the consumer directs production, forcing or luring energy, brains, and capital to obey his will" (New York: D. Van Nostrand Co., 1959), p. 165.

otherwise uninformed consumers to know what they are buying. The "Truth in Lending" bill, authored by former Senator Paul H. Douglas, which required disclosure of simple annual interest rates and the actual cost in dollars of buying on the installment plan, was bitterly opposed by retailers and lenders and required seven years for a compromise version to pass the Senate before going to the House in July 1967. One revealing compromise was the exclusion of first mortgages on houses because (according to the AP report) the "industry" said disclosure of full dollar cost of the financing might discourage home buyers! (The exemption was removed from a somewhat stricter House bill reported out of committee on December 13, 1967.) Quite apart from the ethics of calling, say, a 14 percent interest rate 7 percent, is it honest to call the consumer sovereign while energetically opposing a measure intended to let him know what he is doing?

Above all, issues of honesty are involved, as the Watergate scandals have reminded us, in the relation of business and government. That relationship is crucial since, in the absence of a business community composed of angels, government is our only source of protection. The issue raised here does not concern the right or propriety of business openly to oppose or favor legislation affecting it, that is, to lobby. Its position on any given legislation may or may not be honest or ethical; that could be difficult (though not impossible) to determine because of differences in the value judgments of the several parties involved. Can there be a comparable difference of opinion concerning the morality of providing lobbyists with funds so generous that they are obviously intended to *buy* legislative support? Again, when the services of an obscure small town law firm are sought out by major corporations from distant cities, can there be any debate concerning the dishonesty of thus rewarding one of the most powerful members of the U.S. Senate who is one of the senior partners of the firm?

What are we to think when major American corporations such as United Air Lines, Atlantic Richfield, Pacific Lighting, Music Corporation of America, Dart Industries, and the Marriott Corporation shift their business after President Nixon's 1968 victory to Nixon's personal attorney? To what extent are such practices general? Only a few such questions can be explored here. Until they are answered, claims concerning the decency and integrity of most businessmen will continue to evoke the kind of skepticism exhibited by Ralph Nader and Mark Green in the following pages.

It must be emphasized that reference here is not to isolated examples of human weakness or spectacular single-shot capers such as Equity Funding Life Insurance Company's forgery of more than two billion dollars in nonexistent insurance policies—one of history's biggest swindles that failed to receive the attention it deserved during the year of the more spectacular Watergate scandals. It is unfair to demand perfection of any community or institution. Concern here is with practices that appear to be endemic to the business community such as those recited below by Ralph Nader and Mark Green when they write about "Crime in the Suites."

A caveat. We must be on guard against regarding dishonesty as an exclusive monopoly of the business community. We are helped in this by the Teamsters Union and similarly managed labor organizations, by the refusal of Congress to pass a "conflict of interest" law applicable to its own members, and by the precautions that must be taken even in the rarefied atmosphere of a college campus against book thefts and cheating on examinations. In a more inclusive survey these would deserve close attention. Even so, one may still ask whether such evidences of widespread dishonesty suggest an inherent depravity in human nature or reflect the influence of the acquisitive ideal in our society.

It is unlikely that business management, whatever the prevailing practice, would disagree significantly with what has been said here about honesty. Disagreement occurs between those who believe that dishonesty is built into the business system as Albert Carr's remarks often seem to suggest, and those who, like the late Clarence Randall, believe that business leaders "can and must set off a moral and spiritual reawakening."

CORPORATION GIVING IN A FREE SOCIETY

Richard Eells

Richard Eells is Public Policy Research Consultant for the General Electric Company and Adjunct Professor in Business of the Graduate School of Business, Columbia University. He is the author of The Meaning of Modern Business *(1960) and* The Government of Corporations *(1962) and co-author of* Conceptual Foundations of Business *(1961). His most recent book is* Global Corporations *(1972).*

A searching question facing the corporations of today is: Should business corporations make gifts for scientific, educational, and charitable purposes; and if they do, what principles and policies should they adopt as a guide to their philanthropic programs? . . .

We have reached a stage in the evolution of corporate enterprise and the development of philanthropy where the two are meeting. The corporation has become a philanthropic force in the sheer bulk of its contributions.

Most Americans have an awareness of the constructive contributions to society of such private philanthropic work as that done by Carnegie, Rockefeller, Ford, Guggenheim, Harkness, and others, and of the magnitude and significance of their support. But the American corporation is in a position to reduce previous philanthropy to pioneering efforts. . . .

The basic justification for corporate giving is a philosophy of enlightened self-interest. For if a company merely engages in "charity *qua* charity," it reflects an altruism more laudable than defensible as an exercise of corporate authority. Yet, if its gifts fail to serve the broader interests of mankind, they cease to qualify as philanthropy, with implications that will concern the tax collector. Corporation philanthropy, in short, must get in between the horns of a rather difficult dilemma.

It is hardly surprising that public policy deliberately encourages corporate boards to develop aggressive solutions for this dilemma. Public law invites the business corporation to benefit mankind through tax-deductible gifts. The trend of judicial decision is to widen corporate authority to engage in philanthropic pursuits, even though the benefits accruing to the corporate donor and its share owners may appear to be incommensurable when noted on a company's financial balance sheet. . . . A significant result is a strengthening of the American faith in the autonomy of private sectors.

The concept of private sectors is of key importance to a philosophy of corporation philanthropy in a country engaged in an epochal struggle to defend free institutions. The higher duty of corporate giving is to defend and preserve these sectors. It is the private sectors that constitute the foundations of a society of free men. The private sectors constitute all the areas of meaningful human activity apart from public government: the multifold activities of the family; the local community; the indigenous welfare groups of the local community; the private schools, the colleges, and the universities; the churches; the healers of body and soul; the associations of scholars, scientists, writers, and artists; the labor unions; the business enterprises—indeed, the whole spectrum of voluntary associations through which men hope in their own ways to achieve their goals, mundane and divine.

The constitution of a society of free men must preserve the vital private sectors as a counterpoise to tyranny. If they were to be progressively absorbed into the State, the corporate environment of free enterprise for industry would rapidly disappear.

No denial of the legitimate regulative powers of national, state, and local governments is necessarily implicit in the vigorous defense of private sectors. Corporate philanthropy will not patronize any pluralistic renunciation of state sovereignty. The controlling consideration . . . is not the negative one of forestalling government intervention into these private sectors. Stated affirmatively, the objective must always be to strengthen a balanced multigroup social structure that makes intervention unnecessary. More, the social structure to be preserved must be one that lends vitality to American values of individual freedom and human dignity.

What specific objectives should a donor company set for itself in the light of the philosophy of corporation philanthropy which has as its goal the strengthening of the private sectors in society? The bases for a policy of giving in a given company will depend upon a considered view of its enlightened self-interest. How should the donor proceed in the task of appraising the wider social responsibilities as they relate to the more immediate economic interests a corporate board is obligated to preserve and protect?

One function of corporate management, in the years ahead, will be to open up new avenues of social and economic research with support comparable to the financial resources thrown hitherto into technological research.

It is a truism that our social sciences have lagged dangerously behind our physical sciences and engineering skills. A major responsibility of corporation philanthropy today is to throw its weight on the side of developing the social sciences, with courage to withstand the assaults that are being made, and will be made, upon studies of the structure and dynamics of a free society. Business has such a large stake in the outcome of such research that it must stand resolutely against the anti-intellectualism and obscurantism now rising in powerful quarters aimed at thwarting scientific analysis of human relations. It would seem that economists, political scientists, jurists, anthropologists, and social psychologists still require a common language and terminology through which a frontal attack can be made upon the broad problem of maintaining a free society in which private enterprise can prosper. Corporation philanthropy will advance both corporate interests and the interests of the nation as a whole if it supports such collaborative research.

Despite the deep concern of businessmen with the constant encroachment of government into business, there is a growing fear that corporations dare not give any money for "scientific, educational, and charitable" purposes that have anything to do with politics, or even with studies of the governmental process. There are even those who would shy away from any projects in the "dubious" area of the social sciences.

One reason for this reluctance to give corporate support to the necessary study—and action—in the whole field of social and governmental forces that play upon business enterprise is the fear of political retaliation. The path of caution is to steer clear of such corporation giving as may rouse the least suspicion that tax-exempt funds are being used for any "political" purpose, however remote the political implication may be. Yet, what will the result be if this rule of caution is adhered to? It will mean that no funds will be allocated even for membership in an organization that undertakes in any way to influence the direction of public policy, unless such payments come from other than tax-exempt funds.

Business might elect to withdraw completely from any support—whether by tax-exempt funds or otherwise—of efforts to influence legislation directly or indirectly. To do so, of course, would be to abdicate an elementary right of corporate citizenship and to avoid clear responsibilities to the stockholders of the corporation. The corporation is, and must be, concerned with the governmental process at all levels. This does not imply that corporation foundations will have to engage in "politics," in the popular sense of that term; it does mean that business leaders must accept the responsibilities of corporate citizenship by concerning themselves in an enlightened way with the health of the body politic.

Corporate management faces the general problem of effective restraints upon the power of both public and private government. Through the selective disbursal of gifts and grants, it should attempt to implant throughout the private sectors of American organized life a lively appreciation of our constitutional tradition, with its emphasis on the limitation of both public and private governmental powers. . . .

This goal is not a doctrinaire stand against public education, public health measures, or social legislation in general. One always assumes that public efforts may be required where private efforts fail. But in a constitutional system such as ours there is a presumption against restraint when freedom of action can produce the desired results. . . .

Requirements for philanthropic support of education, and especially of private educational institutions, [have] been mentioned. A recent survey of educational philanthropy published by the Council for Financial Aid to Education indicated the nation's colleges and universities will need new funds for buildings, facilities and operations, in addition to present support, averaging at least $500 million a year for the next ten years. Corporation philanthropy should aim toward continuous support in one form or another for a much longer time, in fact indefinitely, not as charity but as a sound and indispensable investment in the future of our human resources. Further, we must provide a more solid educational base at the primary and secondary school level. The "fourth level" of adult education requires increasing attention. And finally at the highest level of education—the production of scientists and scholars—we face, as a nation, grave shortages.

Corporate support of education should not necessarily be confined to private institutions. The design of a company's plan of educational support may cut across both public and private schools and colleges. Corporation philanthropy has to set for itself, and for others, high standards of nonencroachment upon the "academic republic." The principle involved here is not academic freedom in any narrow sense. In mankind's pursuit and cultivation of knowledge, it is the business, not of outsiders, but of scholars, academic and nonacademic, to find the best organizational and procedural means.

Other major categories of private sectors deserve corporate support. Among the more important of these are the religious sectors. Corporate donors have too often shied away from contributions for any religious purposes whatever. Such gifts are frequently regarded as being "dangerous" or "dubious." Since the "danger" does not lie in religiousness as such this trepidation is comparable to the self-defeating fears about philanthropic work in the social sciences.

But is not the pursuit of the religious way of life at least as important as the pursuit of knowledge in the physical sciences, engineering, and the social sciences? Is it not as important to survival of the free society in which corporate enterprise hopes to live? Is there valid justification for the neglect of churches as objects of corporation philanthropy?

It is a strange argument to say that corporations ought to support the *welfare* and *educational* work of religious groups but avoid like a plague any support of the centers of religion—the churches themselves.

There is no sound ground for excluding gifts for the construction and maintenance of places of worship themselves, if it be conceded that a pervasive and pluralistic religious life is basic to American constitutionalism.

Corporation philanthropy can with good reason also lend support to the creative arts, libraries, museums, recreation, and to fraternal groups. Activities that now seem remote from managerial interests in the immediate business operation will assume more important proportions as our understanding of social, cultural, and political processes widens and deepens.

It may well turn out to be far more fruitful, for example, in combating subversive trends in our political system, to strengthen the "primary groups" in society—groups that provide cohesion in close and personal grounds—than to engage in the more dramatic political struggle on the domestic national level. The cohesive force of nonpolitical groupings, where people are intent upon creative endeavor, provides a community with resistive powers against disintegration more effectively than outright propagandistic indoctrination. . . .

Today, corporate managers find themselves at the core of a "twentieth-century capitalist revolution"—a humane movement that stands in contrast to inhumane collectivist drives in some other parts of the world. Many business leaders will take in their stride the responsibilities inherent in this position at the heart of our "capitalist revolution." The rise of philanthropy as a facet of corporate action relates directly to the central position of business leadership. In the years just ahead many executives will strive to do a bigger job at the higher levels of human aspiration as well as at the economic level. Many will succeed; and one of their instruments is certain to be corporation philanthropy.

The defense of our way of life is predicated upon the preservation of individual dignity and freedom. If we are able to link the future affairs of the corporation to these human values we will succeed in laying a secure foundation both for the corporation and our Western culture.

THE DANGERS OF SOCIAL RESPONSIBILITY

Theodore Levitt

Theodore Levitt is a consultant to big business. He has been adviser to the top management of Standard Oil Company (Indiana) on long-range marketing policy, strategy, and organization and has served as consultant to the Ohio Industrial Council.

Concern with management's social responsibility has become more than a Philistinic form of self-flattery practiced at an occasional community chest banquet or at a news conference celebrating a "selfless example of corporate giving" to some undeserving little college in Podunk. It has become more than merely intoning the pious declarations of Christian brotherhood which some hotshot public relations man has pressed into the outstretched hands of the company president who is rushing from an executive committee meeting to a League of Women Voters luncheon. It has become a deadly serious occupation—the self-conscious, soul-searching preoccupation with the social responsibilities of business, with business statesmanship, employee welfare, public trust, and with all the other lofty causes that get such prominent play in the public press.

Contrary to what some uncharitable critics may say, this preoccupation is not an attitudinizing pose. Self-conscious dedication to social responsibility may have started as a purely defensive maneuver against strident attacks on big corporations and on the moral efficacy of the profit system. But defense alone no longer explains the motive.

The Nonprofit Motive

When outnumbered by its critics at the polls, business launched a counterattack via the communications front. Without really listening to what the critics alleged, business simply denied all that they were saying. But a few executives did listen and began to take a second look at themselves. Perhaps this criticism was not all captious. And so they began to preach to their brethren.

Before long something new was added to the ideological stockpile of capitalism. "Social responsibility" was what business needed, its own leaders announced. It needed to take society more seriously. It needed to participate in community affairs—and not just to take from the community but to give to it. Gradually business became more concerned about the needs of its employees, about schools, hospitals, welfare agencies, and even aesthetics. Moreover, it became increasingly clear that if business and the local governments failed to provide some of the routine social-economic amenities which people seemed clearly intent on getting, then that Brobdingnagian freewheeling monster in far-off Washington would.

So what started out as the sincere personal viewpoints of a few selfless businessmen became the prevailing vogue for them all. Today pronouncements about social responsibility issue forth so abundantly from the corporations that it is hard for one to get a decent play in the press. Everybody is in on the act, and nearly all of them actually mean what they say! Dedication reverberates throughout the upper reaches of corporate officialdom.

This, it is widely felt, is good. Business will raise itself in the public's esteem and thereby scuttle the political attacks against it. If the public likes big business, nobody can make capital by attacking it. Thus social responsibility will prolong the lifetime of free enterprise. Meanwhile, the profit motive is compromised in both word and deed. It now shares its royal throne with a multitude of noncommercial motives that aspire to loftier and more satisfying values. Today's profits must be merely adequate, not maximum. If they are big, it is cause for apologetic rationalization (for example, that they are needed to expand the company's ability to "serve" the public even better) rather than for boastful celebration. It is not fashionable for the corporation to take gleeful pride in making money. What *is* fashionable is for the corporation to show that it is a great innovator; more specifically, a great public benefactor; and, very particularly, that it exists "to serve the public."

The mythical visitor from Mars would be astonished that such a happy tableau of cooperative enterprise can create such vast material abundance. "People's Capitalism" is a resounding success. The primitive principle of aggrandizing selfishness which the Marxists mistakenly contend activates capitalism does not count at all. What we have instead is a voluntary association of selfless entrepreneurs singularly dedicated to creating munificence for one and all—an almost spiritually blissful state of cooperative and responsible enterprise. We are approaching a jet-propelled utopia. And, unlike some other periods in the short and turbulent history of capitalism, today has its practicing philosophers. These are the men busily engaged in the canonistic exposition of a new orthodoxy—the era of "socially responsible enterprise."

Occasionally some big business representative does speak less sanctimoniously and more forthrightly about what capitalism is really all about. Occasionally somebody exhumes the apparently antique notion that the business of business is profits; that virtue lies in the vigorous, undiluted assertion of the corporation's profit-making function. But these people get no embossed invitations to speak at the big, prestigeful, and splashy business conferences—where social responsibility echoes as a new tyranny of fad and fancy. . . .

The fact is, the profit motive is simply not fashionable today among emancipated conferees of the Committee for Economic Development or even in the National Association of Manufacturers. It has been dying a lingering, unmourned death for ten years. Rarely can a big business leader eulogize it today without being snubbed by his self-consciously frowning peers. . . .

There is nothing mysterious about the social responsibility syndrome. It does not reflect a change in businessmen's nature or the decay of self-interest. Quite to the contrary, often it is viewed as a way of maximizing the lifetime of capitalism by taking the wind out of its critics' sails. Under direct questioning it will be confessed that activities such as supporting company intramural athletic programs, hiring a paid director for a company choral society, or underwriting employee dramatic performances (even on company time) are not charity. They are hardheaded tactics of survival against the onslaught of politicians and professional detractors. Moreoever, they build morale, improve efficiency, and yield returns in hard cash.

In other words, it pays to play. If it does not pay, there is no game. For instance, when it comes to choosing between the small Arkansas supplier whose town would be ruined if orders stopped and the Minneapolis supplier who can make it cheaper, there is no doubt that even the most socially responsible corporation will take the latter. It can always fall back on responsibility to its employees, stockholders, or customers, and still pretend it is being fashionable.

In some respects, therefore, all this talk *is* merely talk. It stops at the pocketbook. How, then, can it be dangerous? I think the answer is very simple: what people say, they ultimately come to believe if they say it enough, and what they believe affects what they do. . . .

The talk about social responsibility is already more than talk. It is leading into the believing stage; it has become a design for change. I hope to show why this change is likely to be for the worse, and why no man or institution can escape its debilitating consequences. . . .

A New Feudalism

The function of business is to produce sustained high-level profits. The essence of free enterprise is to go after profit in any way that is consistent with its own survival as an economic system. The catch, someone will quickly say, is "consistent with." This is true. In addition, lack of profits is not the only thing that can destroy business. Bureaucratic ossification, hostile legislation, and revolution can do it much better. Let me examine the matter further. Capitalism as we like it can thrive only in an environment of political democracy and personal freedom. These require a pluralistic society—where there is division, not centralization, of power; variety, not unanimity, of opinion; and separation, not unification, of workaday economic, political, social, and spiritual functions.

We all fear an omnipotent state because it creates a dull and frightening conformity—a monolithic society. We do not want a society with one locus of power, one authority, one arbiter of propriety. We want and need variety, diversity, spontaneity, competition—in short, pluralism. We do not want our lives shaped by a single viewpoint or by a single way of doing things, even if the material consequences are bountiful and the intentions are honorable. Mussolini, Stalin, Hitler, Franco, Trujillo, Peron, all show what happens when power is consolidated into a single, unopposed, and unopposable force.

We are against the all-embracing welfare state not because we are against welfare but because we are against centralized power and the harsh social discipline it so ineluctably produces. We do not want a pervasive welfare state in government, and we do not want it in unions. And for the same reasons we should not want it in corporations.

But at the rate we are going there is more than a contingent probability that, with all its resounding good intentions, business statesmanship may create the corporate equivalent of the unitary state. Its proliferating employee welfare programs, its serpentine involvement in community, government, charitable, and educational affairs, its prodigious currying of political and public favor through hundreds of peripheral preoccupations, all these well-intended but insidious contrivances are greasing the rails for our collective descent into a social order that would be as repugnant to the corporations themselves as to their critics. The danger is that all these things will turn the corporation into a twentieth-century equivalent of the medieval Church. The corporation would eventually invest itself with all-embracing duties, obligations, and finally powers—ministering to the whole man and molding him and society in the image of the corporation's narrow ambitions and its essentially unsocial needs.

Now there is nothing wrong as such with the corporation's narrow ambitions or needs. Indeed, if there is anything wrong today, it is that the corporation conceives its ambitions and needs much too broadly. The trouble is not that it is too narrowly profit-oriented, but that it is not narrowly profit-oriented *enough*. In its guilt-driven urge to transcend the narrow limits of derived standards, the modern corporation is reshaping not simply the economic but also the institutional, social, cultural, and political topography of society.

And there's the rub. For while the corporation also transforms itself in the process, at bottom its outlook will always remain narrowly materialistic. What we have, then, is the frightening spectacle of a powerful economic functional group whose future and perception are shaped in a tight materialistic context of money and things but which imposes its narrow ideas about a broad spectrum of unrelated noneconomic subjects on the mass of man and society.

Even if its outlook were the purest kind of good will, that would not recommend the corporation as an arbiter of our lives. What is bad for this or any other country is for society to be consciously and aggressively shaped by a single functional group or a single ideology, whatever it may be.

If the corporation believes its long-run profitability to be strengthened by these peripheral involvements—if it believes that they are not charity but self-interest—then that much the worse. For, if this is so, it puts much more apparent justification and impulse behind activities which are essentially bad for man, bad for society, and ultimately bad for the corporation itself.

The belief that one institution should encompass the complete lives of its members is by no means new to American society. One example can be taken from the history of unionism:

In the latter part of the nineteenth century America's budding labor unions were shaken by a monumental internal struggle for power. On the one side were the unctuous advocates of the "whole man" idea of the union's function. For them the union was to be an encompassing social institution, operating on all conceivable fronts as the protector and spokesman of the workingman at large. In the process they acknowledged that the union would have to help shape and direct the aspirations, ideas, recreations, and even tastes—in short, the lives—of the members and the society in which they functioned.

Opposing this view were the more pragmatic "horny-handed sons of toil," the "bread and butter" unionists. All they wanted, in the words of Samuel Gompers, was "more, more, more." At the time it was widely believed that this made Gompers a dangerous man. Lots of pious heads shook on the sidelines as they viewed the stark contrast between the dedicated "uplifters" and Gompers' materialistic opportunism. Who would not side with the "uplifters"? Yet Gompers won, and happily so, for he put American unionism on the path of pure-and-simple on-the-job demands, free of the fanciful ideological projects and petty intellectualism that drain the vitality of European unions.

As late as the early 1930's the American Federation of Labor remained true to Gompers' narrow rules by opposing proposed Social Security legislation. And when, in the 1930's, the communists and the pseudo humanitarians pushed the "whole man" concept of unionism, they also lost. Today, however, without ideologically sustained or conscious direction, the more "progressive" unions have won the battle for what the nineteenth century ideologists lost. With all their vast might and organizational skill, these unions are now indeed ministering to the whole man:

> Walter Reuther's United Auto Workers runs night schools, "drop-in" centers for retired members, recreation halls; supports grocery cooperatives; publishes and broadcasts household hints, recipes, and fashion news; and runs dozens of social, recreational, political, and action programs that provide something for every member of the family every hour of the day.
> David Dubinsky's International Ladies' Garment Workers' Union has health centers, citizenship and hobby classes, low-cost apartment buildings, and a palatial summer resort in the Poconos.
> A Toledo union promotes "respectability" in clothes and hair styles among teenagers. . . .

Thus, the union is transformed in such cases from an important and desirable economic functional group into an all-knowing, all-doing, all-wise father on whom millions become directly dependent for womb-to-tomb ministration.

This is the kind of monolithic influence the corporation will eventually have if it becomes so preoccupied with its social burden, with employee welfare, and with the body politic. Only, when the corporation does this, it will do a much more thorough job than the union. For it is more protean and potentially more powerful than any democratic union ever dreamed of being. It is a self-made incubator and instrument of strength, more stable and better able to draw and hold a following than is the union. It creates its own capital and its own power by the sheer accident of doing what it is expected to do. . . .

If the corporate ministry of man turns out to be only half as pervasive as it seems destined to be, it will turn into a simonist enterprise of Byzantine proportions. There is a name for this kind of encircling business ministry, and it pains me to use it. The name is fascism. It may not be the insidious, amoral, surrealistic fascism over which we fought World War II, or the corrupt and aggrandizing Latin American version, but the consequence will be a monolithic society in which the essentially narrow ethos of the business corporation is malignantly extended over everyone and everything.

This feudalistic phantasmagoria may sound alarmist, farfetched, or even patently ridiculous. For one thing, it will be said, not all corporations see alike on all things. At the very least there will be the pluralism of differences arising out of corporate differences in productive functions and their differences as competitors. But look at it this way: When it comes to present-day corporate educational, recreational, welfare, political, social, and public relations programs, attitudes, ideas, promotions, and preferences, how much difference is there? Are they more alike or more unlike? Are they growing more similar or more dissimilar?

It may also be protested, "What is wrong with the corporate ideology, anyway? Who will deny the material abundance, the leisure, and even the aesthetic values it has created and fostered in the United States? Nobody!" But that is irrelevant. The point is: we do not want a monolithic society, even if its intentions are the best. Moreoever, a group's behavior in the pluralistic, competitive past is no guarantee of its behavior once it reaches complete ascendance. . . .

There is nothing more dangerous than the sincere, self-righteous, dedicated proselyte sustained by the mighty machinery of a powerful institution—particularly an economic institution. The reformer whose only aim is personal aggrandizement and whose tactics are a vulgar combination of compulsive demagoguery and opportunistic cynicism is much less dangerous than the social evangelist who, to borrow from Nietzsche, thinks of himself as "God's ventriloquist." As Greek tragedies show, there is nothing more corrupting than self-righteousness and nothing more intolerant than an ardent man who is convinced he is on the side of the angels.

When the spokesmen for such causes begin to make speeches and write books about their holy mission, to canonize their beliefs into faith, conviction, and doctrine, and to develop ways of thinking by which their particular institutional ambitions are ideologically sustained—that is the time for us to begin trembling. They will then have baptized their mission with a book—still the most powerful instrument of change devised by man. . . .

So far the movement is a young and rather unassuming one. But when it really gathers momentum, when its forms become crystallized and its primal innocence becomes more professionalized, its success should amaze us. The corporation is not handicapped by the cumbersome authority that has always characterized the church and the state. It can make its authority sweet as honey by making itself the embodiment of material welfare, of unbounded security, of decorous comfort, amusing diversion, healthful recreation, and palatable ideology. It can far surpass even the medieval Church in efficiency and power.

It may have no intention of doing this (and I firmly believe that this is the last thing that the apostles of corporate humanity want), but what we get is seldom what we want. History is fortuitous. It does not move on tracks made by rational social engineers.

Business wants to survive. It wants security from attack and restriction; it wants to minimize what it believes is its greatest potential enemy—the state. So it takes the steam out of the state's lumbering engines by employing numerous schemes to win its employees and the general public to its side. It is felt that these are the best possible investments it can make for its own survival. And that is precisely where the reasoning has gone wrong. These investments are only superficially *easy* solutions, not the best.

Welfare and society are not the corporation's business. Its business is making money, not sweet music. The same goes for unions. Their business is "bread and butter" and job rights. In a free enterprise system, welfare is supposed to be automatic; and where it is not, it becomes government's job. This is the concept of pluralism. Government's job is not business, and business's job is not government. And unless these functions are resolutely separated in all respects, they are eventually combined in every respect. In the end the danger is not that government will run business, or that business will run government, but rather that the two of them will coalesce, as we saw, into a single power, unopposed and unopposable.

The only political function of business, labor, and agriculture is to fight each other so that none becomes or remains dominant for long. When one does reach overwhelming power and control, at the very best the state will eventually take over on the pretense of protecting everybody else. At that point the big business executives, claiming possession of the tools of large-scale management, will come in, as they do in war, to become the bureaucrats who run the state.

The final victor then is neither government, as the representative of the people, nor the people, as represented by government. The new leviathan will be the professional corporate bureaucrat operating at a more engrossing and exalted level than the architects of capitalism ever dreamed possible.

The functions of the four main groups in our economy—government, business, labor, agriculture—must be kept separate and separable. As soon as they become amalgamated and indistinguishable, they likewise become monstrous and restrictive.

Tending to Business

If businessmen do not preach and practice social responsibility, welfare, and self-restraint, how can management effectively deal with its critics, the political attacks, the confining legislation—that is, the things which have induced it to create its own private welfare state? The answer is fairly simple: to perform its main task so well that critics cannot make their charges stick, and then to assert forthrightly its function and accomplishments with the same aroused spirit that made nineteenth-century capitalism as great as it was extreme.

It seems clear that today's practices fall far short of this prescription. When it comes to material things, the accomplishments of American capitalism are spectacular. But the slate is not clean. American capitalism also creates, fosters, and acquiesces in enormous social and economic cancers. Indeed, it fights against the achievement of certain forms of economic and social progress, pouring millions into campaigns against things which people have a right to expect from their government and which they seem to want their government to provide. For example:

> Business motives helped to create slums, and now business seems all too frequently to fight their abolition. The free operation of the profit motive has not abolished them. Indeed, it sustains them. But if abolishing slums is not a sound business proposition, business should cease its campaign against government doing a job which nobody in his right mind can deny should be done. If supporting state and federal efforts at urban renewal does not raise the public's esteem of business's good intentions, few things will. Certainly self-righteous claims of good intentions are not enough.
> The same is true of health insurance, pensions, school construction, and other proposals for activities which are best handled by government (for reasons of administration as well as of ability to meet the commitments) and are therefore logical government functions. Businessmen will simply have to accept the fact that the state can be a powerful auxiliary to the attainment of the good life. This is particularly so in a free enterprise economy where

there is a natural division of social and economic functions, and where this division is fortified by countervailing institutional checks and balances.

Yet in both word and deed business constantly denies the potentially beneficial role of the state. Where it does not fight the public interest, it often adopts a placid air of indifference or a vapid neutrality. . . .

I am not arguing that management should ignore its critics. Some of them have made a good case from time to time against business's social delinquencies and against its shortsightedness in fighting practically all of Washington's efforts to provide security. (Indeed, if business had not always fought federal welfare measures, perhaps the unions would not have demanded them from business itself.) . . .

In the end business has only two responsibilities—to obey the elementary canons of everyday face-to-face civility (honesty, good faith, and so on) and to seek material gain. The fact that it is the butt of demagogical critics is no reason for management to lose its nerve—to buckle under to reformers—lest more severe restrictions emerge to throttle business completely. Few people will man the barricades against capitalism if it is a good provider, minds its own business, and supports government in the things which are properly government's.

CAN AN EXECUTIVE AFFORD A CONSCIENCE?

Albert Z. Carr

The late Albert Carr wrote extensively about corporate ethics. He was a consultant, an entrepreneur, and a government official as well as a writer. An earlier article in the Harvard Business Review, *"Is Business Bluffing Ethical?", attracted much attention. Most of the article reprinted below appears in his 1971 book,* The Executive Conscience.

Ask a business executive whether his company employs child labor, and he will either think you are joking or be angered by the implied slur on his ethical standards. In the 1970's the employment of children in factories is clearly considered morally wrong as well as illegal.

Yet it was not until comparatively recently (1941) that the U.S. Supreme Court finally sustained the constitutionality of the long-contested Child Labor Act, which Congress had passed four years earlier. During most of the previous eight decades, the fact that children 10 years old worked at manual jobs for an average of 11 hours a day under conditions of virtual slavery had aroused little indignation in business circles.

To be sure, only a few industries found the practice profitable, and the majority of businessmen would doubtless have been glad to see it stopped. But in order to stop it the government had to act, and any interference with business by government was regarded as a crime against God, Nature, and Respectability. If a company sought to hold down production costs by employing children in factories where the work did not demand adult skills or muscle, that was surely a matter to be settled between the employer and the child's parents or the orphanage.

To permit legitimate private enterprise to be balked by unrealistic do-gooders was to open the gate to socialism and anarchy—such was the prevailing sentiment of businessmen, as shown in the business press, from the 1860's to the 1930's.

Every important advance in business ethics has been achieved through a long history of pain and protest. The process of change begins when a previously accepted practice arouses misgivings among sensitive observers. Their efforts at moral suasion are usually ignored, however, until changes in economic conditions or new technology make the practice seem increasingly undesirable.

Businessmen who profit by the practice defend it heatedly, and a long period of public controversy ensues, climaxed at last by the adoption of laws forbidding it. After another 20 or 30 years, the new generation of businessmen regard the practice with retrospective moral indignation and wonder why it was ever tolerated.

A century of increasingly violent debate culminating in civil war had to be lived through before black slavery, long regarded as an excellent business proposition, was declared unlawful in the United States. To achieve laws forbidding racial discrimination in hiring practices required another century. It took 80 years of often bloody labor disputes to win acceptance of the principle of collective bargaining, and the country endured about 110 years of flagrant financial abuses before enactment of effective measures regulating banks and stock exchanges.

In time, all of these forward steps, once bitterly opposed by most businessmen, came to be accepted as part of the ethical foundation of the American private enterprise economy.

In the second half of the twentieth century, with the population, money supply, military power, and industrial technology of the United States expanding rapidly at the same time, serious new ethical issues have arisen for businessmen—notably the pollution of the biosphere, the concentration of economic power in a relatively few vast corporations, increasing military domination of the economy, and the complex interrelationship between business interests and the threat of war. These issues are the more formidable because they demand swift response; they will not wait a century or even a generation for a change in corporate ethics that will stimulate businessmen to act.

The problems they present to business and our society as a whole are immediate, critical, and worsening. If they are not promptly dealt with by farsighted and effective measures, they could even bring down political democracy and the entrepreneurial system together.

In fact, given the close relationship between our domestic economic situation and our military commitments abroad, and the perils implicit in the worldwide armaments buildup, it is not extreme to say that the extent to which businessmen are able to open their minds to new ethical imperatives in the decade ahead may have decisive influence in this century on the future of the human species.

Considering the magnitude of these rapidly developing issues, old standards of ethical judgment seem almost irrelevant. It is of course desirable that a businessman be honest in his accountings and faithful to his contracts—that he should not advertise misleadingly, rig prices, deceive stockholders, deny workers their due, cheat customers, spread false rumors about competitors, or stab associates in the back. Such a person has in the past qualified as "highly ethical," and he could feel morally superior to many of those he saw around him—the chiselers, the connivers, the betrayers of trust.

But standards of personal conduct in themselves are no longer an adequate index of business ethics. Everyone knows that a minority of businessmen commit commercial mayhem on each other and on the public with practices ranging from subtle conflicts of interest to the sale of injurious drugs and unsafe automobiles, but in the moral crisis through which we are living such tales of executive wrongdoing, like nudity in motion pictures, have lost their power to shock.

The public shrugs at the company president who conspires with his peers to fix prices. It grins at the vice president in charge of sales who provides call girls for a customer. After we have heard a few such stories, they become monotonous.

We cannot shrug or grin, however, at the refusal of powerful corporations to take vigorous action against great dangers threatening the society, and to which they contribute. Compared with such a corporation or with the executive who is willing to jeopardize the health and well-being of an entire people in order to add something to current earnings, the man who merely embezzles company funds is as insignificant in the annals of morality as Jesse James is compared with Nero.

The moral position of the executive who works for a company that fails in the ethics of social responsibility is ambiguous. The fact that he does not control company policy cannot entirely exonerate him from blame. He is guilty, so to speak, by employment.

If he is aware that the company's factories pollute the environment or its products injure the consumer and he does not exert himself to change the related company policies, he becomes morally suspect. If he lends himself to devious evasions of laws against racial discrimination in hiring practices, he adds to the probability of destructive racial confrontations and is in some degree an agent of social disruption. If he knows that his company is involved in the bribery of legislators or government officials, or makes under-the-table deals with labor union officials, or uses the services of companies known to be controlled by criminal syndicates, he contributes through his work to disrespect for law and the spread of crime.

If his company, in its desire for military contracts, lobbies to oppose justifiable cuts in the government's enormous military budget, he bears some share of responsibility for the constriction of the civilian economy; for price inflation, urban decay, and shortage of housing, transportation, and schools; and for failure to mitigate the hardships of the poor.

From this standpoint, the carefully correct executive who never violates a law or fails to observe the canons of gentlemanly behavior may be as open to ethical challenge as the crooks and the cheaters.

The practical question arises: If a man in a responsible corporate position finds that certain policies of his company are socially injurious, what can he do about it without jeopardizing his job?

Contrary to common opinion, he is not necessarily without recourse. The nature of that recourse I shall discuss in the final section of this article. Here, I want to point out that unless the executive's sense of social responsibility is accompanied by a high degree of realism about tactics, then he is likely to end in frustration or cynicism.

One executive of my acquaintance who wrote several memoranda to his chief, detailing instances of serious environmental contamination for which the company was responsible and which called for early remedy, was sharply rebuked for a "negative attitude."

Another, a successful executive of a large corporation, said to me quite seriously in a confidential moment that he did not think a man in a job like his could afford the luxury of a conscience in the office. He was frank to say that he had become unhappy about certain policies of his company. He could no longer deny to himself that the company was not living up to its social responsibilities and was engaged in some political practices that smacked of corruption.

But what were his options? He had only three that he could see, and he told me he disliked them all:

• If he argued for a change in policies that were helping to keep net earnings high, he might be branded by his superiors as "unrealistic" or "idealistic"—adjectives that could check his career and might, if he pushed too hard, compel his resignation.

● Continued silence not only would spoil his enjoyment of his work, but might cause him to lose respect for himself.

● If he moved to one of the other companies in his industry, he would merely be exchanging one set of moral misgivings for another.

He added with a sigh that he envied his associates whose consciences had never developed beyond the Neanderthal stage and who had no difficulty in accepting things as they were. He said he wondered whether he ought not to try to discipline himself to be as indifferent as they to the social implications of policies which, after all, were common in business.

Perhaps he made this effort and succeeded in it, for he remained with the company and forged ahead. He may even have fancied that he had killed his conscience—as the narrator in Mark Twain's symbolic story did when he gradually reached the point where he could blithely murder the tramps who came to his door asking for handouts.

But conscience is never killed; when ignored, it merely goes underground, where it manufactures the toxins of suppressed guilt, often with serious psychological and physical consequences. The hard fact is that the executive who has a well-developed contemporary conscience is at an increasing disadvantage in business unless he is able to find some personal policy by which he can maintain his drive for success without serious moral reservations.

The problem faced by the ethically motivated man in corporate life is compounded by growing public distrust of business morality.

The corporation executive is popularly envied for his relative affluence and respected for his powers of achievement, but many people deeply suspect his ethics—as not a few successful businessmen have been informed by their children. Surveys made in a number of universities across the country indicate that a large majority of students aiming at college degrees are convinced that business is a dog-eat-dog proposition, with which most of them do not want to be connected.

This low opinion is by no means confined to youngsters; a poll of 2,000 representative Americans brought to light the belief of nearly half of them that "most businessmen would try anything, honest or not, for a buck."[1] The unfairness of the notion does not make it less significant as a clue to public opinion. (This poll also showed that most Americans are aware of the notable contributions of business to the material satisfactions of their lives; the two opinions are not inconsistent.)

---

[1] Louis B. Harris and Associates, in a survey reported at a National Industrial Conference Board meeting, April 21, 1966.

Many businessmen, too, are deeply disturbed by the level of executive morality in their sphere of observation. Although about 90% of executives in another survey stated that they regarded themselves as "ethical," 80% affirmed "the presence of numerous generally accepted practices in their industry which they consider unethical," such as bribery of government officials, rigging of prices, and collusion in contract bidding.[2]

The public is by no means unaware of such practices. In conversations about business ethics with a cross-section sampling of citizens in a New England town, I found that they mentioned kickbacks and industrial espionage as often as embezzlement and fraud. One man pointed out that the kickback is now taken so much for granted in corporations that the Internal Revenue Service provides detailed instructions for businessmen on how to report income from this source on their tax returns.

The indifference of many companies to consumers' health and safety was a major source of criticism. Several of the persons interviewed spoke of conflicts of interest among corporation heads, accounts of which had been featured not long before in the press. Others had learned from television dramas about the ruthlessness of the struggle for survival and the hail-fellow hypocrisy that is common in executive offices.

Housewives drew on their shopping experience to denounce the decline in the quality of necessities for which they had to pay ever-higher prices. Two or three had read in *Consumer Reports* about "planned obsolescence."

I came to the conclusion that if my sample is at all representative— and I think it is—the public has learned more about the ways of men in corporate life than most boards of directors yet realize.

These opinions were voiced by people who for the most part had not yet given much thought to the part played by industrial wastes in the condition of the environment, or to the inroads made on their economic well-being by the influence of corporation lobbyists on military decision makers. It is to be expected that if, as a result of deteriorating social and economic conditions, these and other major concerns take on more meaning for the public, criticism of business ethics will widen and become sharper.

If the threats of widespread water shortage in the 1970's and of regional clean air shortages in the 1980's are allowed to materialize, and military expenditures continue to constrict civilian life, popular resentment may well be translated into active protest directed against many corporations as well as against the government. In that event, the moral pressure on individual executives will become increasingly acute.

Regard for public opinion certainly helped to influence many companies in the 1950's and 1960's to pledge to reduce their waste discharges

---

[2] Raymond C. Baumhart, S.J., "How Ethical Are Businessmen?" HBR July-August 1961, p. 6.

into the air and water and to hire more people with dark skins. Such declarations were balm for the sore business conscience.

The vogue for "social responsibility" has now grown until, as one commentator put it, "pronouncements about social responsibility issue forth so abundantly from the corporations that it is hard for one to get a decent play in the press. Everybody is in on the act, and nearly all of them actually mean what they say!"[3] More than a few companies have spent considerable sums to advertise their efforts to protect a stream, clean up smokestack emissions, or train "hard-core unemployables."

These are worthy undertakings, as far as they have gone, but for the most part they have not gone very far. In 1970 it has become obvious that the performance of U.S. corporations in the area of social responsibility has generally been trivial, considering the scope of their operations.

No company that I have ever heard of employs a vice president in charge of ethical standards; and sooner or later the conscientious executive is likely to come up against a stone wall of corporate indifference to private moral values.

When the men who hold the real power in the company come together to decide policy, they may give lip service to the moral element in the issue, but not much more. The decision-making process at top-management levels has little room for social responsibilities not definitely required by law or public opinion.

Proposals that fail to promise an early payoff for the company and that involve substantial expense are accepted only if they represent a means of escaping drastic penalties, such as might be inflicted by a government suit, a labor strike, or a consumer boycott. To invest heavily in antipollution equipment or in programs for hiring and training workers on the fringe of employability, or to accept higher taxation in the interest of better education for the children of a community—for some distant, intangible return in a cloudy future—normally goes against the grain of every profit-minded management.

It could hardly be otherwise. In the prevailing concept of corporate efficiency, a continual lowering of costs relative to sales is cardinal. For low costs are a key not only to higher profits but to corporate maneuverability, to advantage in recruiting the best men, and to the ability to at least hold a share of a competitive market.

Of the savings accruing to a company from lowered costs, the fraction that finds its way into the area of social responsibility is usually miniscule. To expend such savings on nonremunerative activities is regarded as weakening the corporate structure.

The late Chester A. Barnard, one of the more enlightened business leaders of the previous generation and a man deeply concerned with ethics,

---

[3] Editor's note: See above, pp. 303.

voiced the position of management in the form of a question: "To what extent is one morally justified in loading a productive undertaking with heavy charges in the attempt to protect against a remote possibility, or even one not so remote?"[4] Speaking of accident prevention in plants, which he favored in principle, he warned that if the outlay for such a purpose weakened the company's finances, "the community might lose a service and the entrepreneur an opportunity."

Corporate managers apply the same line of reasoning to proposals for expenditure in the area of social responsibility. "We can't afford to sink that amount of money in nonproductive uses," they say, and, "We need all our cash for expansion."

The entrepreneur who is willing to accept some reduction of his income—the type is not unknown—may be able to operate his enterprise in a way that satisfies an active conscience; but a company with a competitive team of managers, a board of directors, and a pride of stockholders cannot harbor such an unbusinesslike intention.

Occasionally, statesmen, writers, and even some high-minded executives, such as the late Clarence B. Randall, have made the appeal of conscience to corporations. They have argued that, since the managers and directors of companies are for the most part men of goodwill in their private lives, their corporate decisions also should be guided by conscience.

Even the distinguished economist A. A. Berle, Jr. has expressed the view that the healthy development of our society requires "the growth of conscience" in the corporation of our time.[5] But if by "conscience" he meant a sense of right and wrong transcending the economic, he was asking the impossible.

A business that defined "right" and "wrong" in terms that would satisfy a well-developed contemporary conscience could not survive. No company can be expected to serve the social interest unless its self-interest is also served, either by the expectation of profit or by the avoidance of punishment.

Before responsibility to the public can properly be brought into the framework of a top-management decision, it must have an economic justification. For instance, executives might say:

- "We'd better install the new safety feature because, if we don't, we'll have the government on our necks, and the bad publicity will cost us more than we are now saving in production."

- "We should spend the money for equipment to take the sulfides out of our smokestacks at the plant. Otherwise we'll have trouble recruiting

---

[4] *Elementary Conditions of Business Morals* (Berkeley, Committee on the Barbara Weinstock Lectures, University of California, 1958).

[5] *The Twentieth Century Capitalist Revolution* (New York, Harcourt, Brace & Company, 1954), pp. 113–114.

labor and have a costly PR problem in the community."

It is worth noting that Henry Ford II felt constrained to explain to stockholders of the Ford Motor Company that his earnest and socially aware effort to recruit workers from Detroit's "hard-core unemployed" was a preventive measure against the recurrence of ghetto riots carrying a threat to the company.

In another situation, when a number of life insurance companies agreed to invest money in slum reconstruction at interest rates somewhat below the market, their executives were quick to forestall possible complaints from stockholders by pointing out that they were opening up future markets for life insurance. Rationally, the successful corporate manager can contemplate expense for the benefit of society only if failure to spend points to an eventual loss of security or opportunity that exceeds the cost.

There can be no conscience without a sense of personal responsibility, and the corporation, as Ambrose Bierce remarked, is "an ingenious device for obtaining individual profit without individual responsibility." When the directors and managers of a corporation enter the boardroom to debate policy, they park their private consciences outside.

If they did not subordinate their inner scruples to considerations of profitability and growth, they would fail in their responsibility to the company that pays them. A kind of Gresham's Law of ethics operates here; the ethic of corporate advantage invariably silences and drives out the ethic of individual self-restraint.

(This, incidentally, is true at every level of the corporate structure. An executive who adheres to ethical standards disregarded by his associates is asking for trouble. No one, for example, is so much hated in a purchasing department where graft is rife as the man who refuses to take kickbacks from suppliers, for he threatens the security of the others. Unless he conforms, they are all too likely to "get him.")

The crucial question in boardroom meetings where social responsibility is discussed is not, "Are we morally obligated to do it?" but, rather, "What will happen if we don't do it?" or, perhaps, "How will this affect the rate of return on investment?"

If the house counsel assures management that there will be no serious punishment under the law if the company does not take on the added expense, and the marketing man sees no danger to sales, and the public relations man is confident he can avoid injury to the corporate image, then the money, if it amounts to any considerable sum, will not be spent—social responsibility or no social responsibility.

Even the compulsion of law is often regarded in corporate thinking as an element in a contest between government and the corporation, rather than as a description of "right" and "wrong." The files of the Federal Trade Commission, the Food and Drug Administration, and other government agencies are filled with records of respectable companies that have not hesitated to break or stretch the law when they believed they could get away with it.

It is not unusual for company managements to break a law, even when they expect to be caught, if they calculate that the fine they eventually must pay represents only a fraction of the profits that the violation will enable them to collect in the meantime. More than one corporate merger has been announced to permit insiders to make stock-market killings even though the companies concerned recognized that the antitrust laws would probably compel their eventual separation.

One can dream of a big-business community that considers it sound economics to sacrifice a portion of short-term profits in order to protect the environment and reduce social tensions.

It is theoretically conceivable that top managers as a class may come to perceive the profound dangers, for the free-enterprise system and for themselves, in the trend toward the militarization of our society, and will press the government to resist the demand for nonessential military orders and overpermissive contracts from sections of industry and elements in the Armed Services. At the same level of wishfulness, we can imagine the federal government making it clear to U.S. companies investing abroad that protection of their investments is not the government's responsibility.

We can even envisage a time when the bonds of a corporation that is responsive to social needs will command a higher rating by Moody's than those of a company that neglects such values, since the latter is more vulnerable to public condemnation; and a time when a powerful Executive League for Social Responsibility will come into being to stimulate and assist top managements in formulating long-range economic policies that embrace social issues. In such a private-enterprise utopia the executive with a social conscience would be able to work without weakening qualms.

In the real world of today's business, however, he is almost sure to be a troubled man. Perhaps there are some executives who are so strongly positioned that they can afford to urge their managements to accept a reduced rate of return on investment for the sake of the society of which they are a part. But for the large majority of corporate employees who want to keep their jobs and win their superiors' approbation, to propose such a thing would be inviting oneself to the corporate guillotine.

But this does not necessarily mean that the ethically motivated executive can do nothing. In fact, if he does nothing, he may so bleach his conception of himself as a man of conviction as to reduce his personal force and value to the company. His situation calls for sagacity as well as courage. Whatever ideas he advocates to express his sense of social responsibility must be shaped to the company's interests.

Asking management flatly to place social values ahead of profits would be foolhardy, but if he can demonstrate that, on the basis of long-range profitability, the concept of corporate efficiency needs to be broadened to include social values, he may be able to make his point without injury—indeed, with benefit—to his status in the company. A man respected for competence in his job, who knows how to justify ethically-based programs in economic terms and to overcome elements of resistance in the psychology of top management, may well be demonstrating his own qualifications for top management.

In essence, any ethically oriented proposal made to a manager is a proposal to take a longer-range view of his problems—to lift his sights. Nonethical practice is shortsighted almost by definition, if for no other reason than that it exposes the company to eventual reprisals.

The longer range a realistic business projection is, the more likely it is to find a sound, ethical footing. I would go so far as to say that almost anything an executive does, on whatever level, to extend the range of thinking of his superiors tends to effect an ethical advance.

The hope and the opportunity of the individual executive with a contemporary conscience lies in the constructive connection of the long economic view with the socially aware outlook. He must show convincingly a net advantage for the corporation in accelerating expenditures or accepting other costs in the sphere of social responsibility.

I was recently able to observe an instance in which an executive persuaded his company's management to make a major advance in its anti-pollution policy. His presentation of the alternatives, on which he had spent weeks of careful preparation, showed in essence that, under his plan, costs which would have to be absorbed over a three-year period would within six years prove to be substantially less than the potential costs of less vigorous action.

When he finished his statement, no man among his listeners, not even his most active rivals, chose to resist him. He had done more than serve his company and satisfy his own ethical urge; he had shown that the gap between the corporate decision and the private conscience is not unbridgeable if a person is strong enough, able enough, and brave enough to do what needs to be done.

It may be that the future of our enterprise system will depend on the emergence of a sufficient number of men of this breed who believe that in order to save itself business will be impelled to help save the society.

CRIME IN THE SUITES

Ralph Nader and Mark Green

Ralph Nader, consumers' shield and scourge of corporations, hardly needs introduction. He is the David who worsted Goliath (General Motors) and who, more than anyone, has given life to the virtually dormant consumers' movement in this country. Perhaps more significantly, his extraordinary career demonstrates what single individuals can still accomplish in a world largely taken over by organizations. Mark Green is the director of the Corporate Accountability Research Group and the author of the Nader report, The Closed Enterprise System, *published in 1972.*

The following selection might well have been included in the discussion in Part One on law and order by way of questioning the extent to which those who call for law and order are willing to impose it impartially on all. It is included here as bearing crucially on the general problem of honesty in business.

As defined by sociologist Edwin Sutherland in the late 1940s, white collar crime is committed by businessmen, government officials and professionals in their occupational roles. The culprits look like respectable citizens, not shifty-eyed mobsters, which makes it so hard for many to accept what they do as "crime." White collar crime has never made it into Richard Nixon's "law and order" lexicon.

Even more difficult to establish is *corporate crime,* involving premeditated business predations. Sutherland found that slightly over 97 percent of the corporations studied were "recidivists," with at least two convictions each. He concluded that "practically all large corporations engage in illegal restraint of trade, and . . . from half to three-fourths of them engage in such practices so continuously that they may properly be called 'habitual criminals.' "

In 1961 the *Harvard Business Review* surveyed its subscribers on the issue of business ethics. About four out of seven respondents to one question believed that businessmen "would violate a code of ethics whenever they thought they could avoid detection." When asked, "In your industry, are there any [accepted business] practices which you regard as unethical?" four-fifths responded affirmatively. That same year, a General Electric executive sentenced to jail for conspiring to fix prices asserted, "Sure collusion was illegal, but it wasn't unethical."

But what's unethical often *is* illegal. Take antitrust crime, the sabotage of economic competition. Antitrust offenses include price-fixing, market divisions, and exclusionary boycotts—all of which result in inflated consumer prices, inflated corporate returns and often rewarded inefficiencies. The possible penalties according to the Sherman Antitrust Act: up to a year in jail and/or a $50,000 fine per violation.

Although the number of criminal antitrust cases prosecuted each year by the Justice Department is small (due largely to their meager resources)—averaging 25 a year from 1960 to 1964, and 11 a year from 1965 to 1970—the total number of industries involved in criminal antitrust acts in the past 30 years is quite large. Nearly every conceivable industry has been affected, from milk and bread to heavy electrical equipment, from lobster fishing and the cranberry industry to steel sheets and plumbing fixtures. This large volume, plus the fact that the industries implicated are in no significant way unlike others, lead some analysts to conclude that their illegal acts are practiced elsewhere—without detection.

The vast scale of the electrical manufacturing conspiracy of 1961, involving nearly every firm in that industry, startled many complacent antitrust watchers who had intoned that price-fixing was nonexistent, even unnecessary, in an oligopolistic industry. The comment by a defendant in that case, that "conspiracy is just as much 'a way of life' in other fields as it was in electrical equipment," made observers wonder how many other industries were price-rigged. Our antitrust study *The Closed Enterprise System* asked the presidents of *Fortune*'s top 1000 firms how many agreed with this assertion. Nearly *60 percent* of those answering (100) concurred that "many . . . price fix." And the only scholarly attempt to estimate the extent of price-fixing concluded in the *Northwestern Law Review* that "it is apparent that price fixing is quite prevalent in American business."

While antitrust crime may seem only remotely relevant—esoterica to be unraveled by economists but surely not consumers—its impact on corporations and the public is direct and vast. An international quinine cartel cornered the world market in the early sixties, raising the price of quinine from 37¢ an ounce to $2.13, and thereby pricing it beyond the means of patients who needed it to restore natural heart rhythm. "I cannot continue to pay these high prices for quinine," complained one elder citizen to a Senate subcommittee, "yet my doctor tells me I cannot live without it." Between 1953 and 1961, 100 tablets of the antibiotic tetracycline cost as little as $1.52 to manufacture but retailed for about $51; ten years later, after congressional hearings and a criminal indictment exposed a conspiracy among some of the nation's largest drug houses, the retail price for the same quantity was approximately $5. While the average American paid about 20¢ for a loaf of bread in 1964, the Seattle consumer was paying 24¢, or 20 percent more, due to a local price-fixing conspiracy, which was finally ended by a Federal Trade Commission ruling; it was estimated that consumers in the Seattle area were overcharged by $35 million. The electrical price-fixing cases of 1961 saw seven corporate officials sent to jail (20 others got suspended sentences). Seven billion dollars of equipment sales were implicated during the conspiracy, and more money was stolen by this one suite crime than all the street crime for that year combined. Summarized one unindicted official, "the boys could resist everything but temptation." Or as Woody Guthrie sang in "Pretty Boy Floyd," "As through this world I've rambled/I've seen lots of funny men/Some rob you with a six gun/And some with a fountain pen."

What are the countervailing costs which could dissuade such business crime? There are four basic sanctions—imprisonment, criminal fines, treble damages and loss of good will. Yet cushioning their sting is an effective combination of official impediments: the pattern of Justice Department enforcement, the frequent settlement of criminal cases by so-called "no-contest pleas," and general judicial hostility.

The antitrust budget of the Justice Department is slender ($11.5 million for 1971, or $1/20$th of Procter & Gamble's advertising budget), and the percentage of criminal cases it files, as opposed to civil, is declining: for 1940–1949, 59 percent of all cases were criminal; in 1950–1959, 48 percent; and in 1960–1969, 31 percent. In 1970, Attorney General John Mitchell filed a total of *five* criminal antitrust cases, or nine percent of all cases brought.

No-contest pleas (also known as *nolo contendere*) account for 79 percent of all antitrust convictions over the last decade. By it a defendant admits without trial that he committed the alleged offense. For this plea judges often sentence more leniently, later private suits are made more difficult, and public trials are avoided. All erode the deterrence of antitrust sanctions. Legal philosopher Lon Fuller has argued that "the public trial and condemnation of the criminal serves the symbolic function of reinforcing the public sense that there are certain acts that are fundamentally wrong, that must not be done." This view seems particularly applicable when many violate the law and few consider the action as wrong. "In such a moral atmosphere," Fuller continues, "it may be argued, men need to have their sense of guilt restored."

Judges rarely refuse the offer of no-contest pleas, even when the government objects to them. And they show their hostility to antitrust in ways other than accepting such sanctionless settlements. Maximum fines or jail sentences are rarely imposed; defense counsel are treated cordially, government counsel with dispatch and disdain. For many judges, a business defendant looks like the judge, may belong to the same country club, or at the very least, is the kind of client he represented in his former law practice. (One lawyer said in an interview that "it is best to find the judge's friend or law partner to defend an antitrust client—which we have done.") For others antitrust is unimportant. One district court judge proudly admitted that "antitrust laws are a part of America's romantic dream, which can never be realized . . . in a modern industrial system."

While enforcement patterns, no-contest pleas and antagonistic judges reduce the deterrent potential of the four basic antitrust sanctions, each one is already perforated with problems:

Imprisonment   The likelihood of a white collar antitrust criminal spending time in prison is near nil. Even in the 1940s, which included Thurman Arnold's widely admired tenure and involved a record number of criminal cases filed, there was not one case where a defendant was actually incarcerated. Since 1890, there have been a total of 461 individual defendants *sentenced* to prison. Most were labor racketeers or individuals who mixed violence with a labor or management scheme. In almost all cases the sentences were immediately suspended. In the more than 80-year history of the Sherman Act, there have been only *three* occasions when businessmen have actually gone to jail for a criminal violation.

Juries are one reason why. Even when the evidence is strong, a form of jury nullification can occur. How can the jurors send that well-dressed, white, wealthy, articulate father of three to jail with unkempt, non-white, poor, uneducated street criminals?

The fundamental reason why the Sherman Act has not been effective, however, is again the judicial bench. Judges simply do not like to send businessmen to jail. District Court Judge John Lord, when sentencing convicted school suppliers in an early 1960s antitrust case, said, "All are God-fearing men, highly civic-minded, who have spent lifetimes of sincere and honest dedication and service to their families, their churches, their country and their communities. . . . I could never send Mr. Kurtz to jail." When judges were asked "Why do so few convicted Sherman Act violators ever serve jail sentences?" in a recent questionnaire sent by the writers to all district court judges, some of the typical replies were: "recidivism is unlikely," "violators are *not* hardened criminals," "defendants are victims of economic forces," and "not clear in corporate case that guilty ones are in court."

This leniency toward corporate criminality contrasts with the often sadistic sentences imposed on street criminals. A year after seven electrical manufacturers were sent to jail for 30 days apiece, a man in Asbury Park, New Jersey stole a $2.98 pair of sunglasses and a $1 box of soap and was sent to jail for four months. A George Jackson is sent to prison for ten years to life for stealing $70 from a gas station, his third minor offense; and in Dallas one Joseph Sills received a 1000-year sentence for stealing $73.10. Many states send young students who are marijuana first offenders to jail for five to ten year terms. But the *total* amount of time spent in jail by all businessmen who have ever violated the antitrust laws is a little under two years.

Criminal Fines From 1890 to 1955 the maximum Sherman Act fine was $5000 per violation; in 1955 it was increased to $50,000 per violation. Both are insignificant, dwarfed by the $49 million average net income for each of the top 500 industrial firms in 1969. Moreover, the *actual* fines levied are usually far below the maximum possible. Between 1946 and 1953, for example, the average Sherman Act fine was $2600. Despite the tenfold increase in possible penalties in 1955, between 1955 and 1965 corporate fines averaged only $13,420 and individual fines $3,365. (The $50,000 fine is even small by white collar standards. For example, the Nixon Environmental Program, if passed, would allow court-imposed fines as high as $50,000 *per day* for a second violation of water quality standards.) Lee Loevinger, former antitrust division chief, has described GE's $437,500 total fine in the electrical cases as "no more severe than a $3 ticket for overtime parking for a man with a $15,000 income." While some court-imposed fines achieve compensation and others seek deterrence, antitrust fines do neither.

Treble Damage Suits Such actions could be a great deterrent to price-fixing. The theory is that any person who can prove damages from the illegal antitrust conspiracy can then recover three times his damages from the corporate defendant. The multi-fold return was intended to spur the bringing of such private suits, which would both penalize the violator and indemnify the victim. But for a number of reasons—the high rate of no-contest pleas, the difficulty of proving actual damage, the reluctance of many harmed companies to sue a brother firm, and procedural obstacles—private treble damage suits have never realized their potential.

Goodwill A potentially powerful deterrent occurs when a corporation's goodwill is damaged by an antitrust conviction. Corporations may not mind paying minor sums out of their profits but do object if their reputation is besmirched in consumers' minds. Lack of interest by the news media eases the pain of this informal stigma. And, as already stressed, *"nolo"* does not ring in peoples' minds as does "guilty." Therefore, business firms and law firms try to perpetuate the fiction that a *nolo* plea, while legally an admission of guilt, really concedes nothing at all, or even that a *guilty plea* doesn't mean quite that. Former Attorney General Herbert Brownell represented Westinghouse during the 1961 courtroom proceedings. Upon pleading his client guilty to seven counts, he had the pluck to assert that Westinghouse "does not admit the allegation of any of these indictments, but is simply changing its pleas for the purpose of promptly disposing of pending litigation."

In sum, the network of sanctions that aim to deter antitrust criminality does not outweigh the possible benefits to the violator. The meager fines imposed, and even treble damage payments, become merely costs of doing business. Based on six case studies, including offending firms who had their damage payments trebled, a study by the Law Department of New York City concluded: "Indictment by a federal grand jury, punishment inflicted through criminal action, the payment of trebled damages resulting from civil trials, all legal costs incurred in the process, *none of these nor any combination of them succeeds today in denying the price fixer a profit realization at least double a normal level.*" (emphasis supplied)

In America, Inc., crime pays.

A combination of new measures should ease antitrust crimes into extinction. All are predicated on an obvious fact about this genre of crime: violations are neither spontaneous nor *ad hoc,* but are carefully planned out by intelligent people balancing risks and benefits; it is with just such calculating individuals that strong penalties can be successful deterrents.

The long-standing judicial failure to impose penal and monetary sanctions compels the need for minimum penalties. When a defendant admits to or is found guilty of a knowing and willful violation, there should be a minimum prison term of four months for the first offense and one year for the second. A minimum fine of one percent of the corporation's sales receipts for the years of the conspiracy (subsidiaries taken separately) would help make the punishment fit the crime. Within the judge's discretion, it could go up to 10 percent. Since it has been estimated that a price fixing conspiracy can, on the average, inflate prices by 25 percent, it does not seem unreasonable to insist that convicted firms divest themselves of at least a minimal portion of their illegally acquired proceeds. With serious financial penalties built into the fabric of enforcement, the profit motive itself should be adequate incentive to self-regulate the system into compliance.

Just as the Landrum-Griffin Act ousts labor leaders from their positions for criminal convictions, any member of management who obtains a criminal record relating to his corporate duties should take a permanent vacation. So that individuals not be relieved of the bite of liability for their personal wrongs, federal law should forbid the corporate indemnification of criminal, individual fines—which is permitted by some states today. A corporate agent in a supervisory capacity should be held criminally liable if he has specific knowledge of an antitrust violation within his area of supervision, and if he willfully fails to report or end it; the intentional disregard of a duty should entail legal accountability. Also, corporations should be compelled to inform the public of their criminal convictions—as suggested by the National Commission on the Reform of Federal Criminal Laws—as the only way to counteract massive publicity which projects them as concerned and magnanimous citizens.

Finally, corporations should voluntarily stop putting impossible demands and pressures on middle rank executives, the kind which can only compel them to fix prices in order to reach projected profit margins. What did lead John H. Chiles—a division manager at Westinghouse, 57 years old, a senior warden of his local Episcopal church, vice president of his United Fund drive, and according to his lawyer, "the benefactor of charities for crippled children and cancer victims"—to meet illegally with his competition? No doubt there was a breakdown of personal morality, but, as Chiles's lawyer also argued, "There is such a thing as business compulsion . . . there is such a thing as atmosphere; there is such a thing as knowing acquiescence in a situation." The top executives in the electrical firms were never indicted or convicted. Instead, just two months before sentencing of his subordinates began, chairman Ralph Cordiner was selected as the National Association of Manufacturers' man of the year.

14

The Ethics of Persuasion

The question of business and morality and corporate citizenship is hardly separable from the more specific issue of how private enterprise conducts one of its two most important activities. As every commercial on television reminds us, it is engaged in *selling* as well as producing—and this involves making representations to the buying public. Are these representations, whether through advertisements, labels, or simple statements concerning the rate of interest charged for a loan, honest or dishonest? This question should focus not on marginal practices that are illegal, or universally characterized as shady even by those who engage in them, but on the more or less general conduct of selling as it prevails in our economy.

THE ARTS OF SELLING

Aldous Huxley

Aldous Huxley was one of the noted writers of our time. Novelist, essayist, poet, dramatist, he was also justly called a humanist because he was interested in people and what happens to them. This interest extended from (quite literally) improving their sight (The Art of Seeing) to improving their vision (The Perennial Philosophy). *Of his many works the best known are no doubt* Point Counter Point *and* Brave New World. *In* Brave New World, *written in 1931, he prophesied for the sixth or seventh century* "A.F. *(After Ford)" the coming of a completely organized society with, in his summary words, a "scientific caste system, the abolition of free will by methodical conditioning, servitude made acceptable by regular doses of chemically induced happiness, . . . orthodoxies drummed in by nightly courses of sleep-teaching. . . ." The depression-ridden world of the 1930's was, he said, "a nightmare of too little order," the world of the seventh century,* A.F., *of too much. He had hoped that during the long interval in between the more fortunate third of the human race would make the best of both worlds. Later he was no longer so sure, and in* Brave New World Revisited, *from which the selection below is taken, he tells us why. Among the uncontrolled impersonal forces that he finds accelerating the speed with which his depressing prophecies are being brought to pass is modern advertising.*

The survival of democracy depends on the ability of large numbers of people to make realistic choices in the light of adequate information. A dictatorship, on the other hand, maintains itself by censoring or distorting the facts, and by appealing, not to reason, not to enlightened self-interest, but to passion and prejudice, to the powerful "hidden forces," as Hitler called them, present in the unconscious depths of every human mind.

In the West, democratic principles are proclaimed and many able and conscientious publicists do their best to supply electors with adequate information and to persuade them, by rational argument, to make realistic choices in the light of that information. All this is greatly to the good. But unfortunately propaganda in the Western democracies, above all in America, has two faces and a divided personality. In charge of the editorial department there is often a democratic Dr. Jekyll—a propagandist who would be very happy to prove that John Dewey had been right about the ability of human nature to respond to truth and reason. But this worthy man controls only a part of the machinery of mass communication. In charge of advertising we find an anti-democratic, because anti-rational, Mr. Hyde—or rather a Dr. Hyde, for Hyde is now a Ph.D. in psychology and has a master's degree as well in the social sciences. This Dr. Hyde would be very unhappy indeed if everybody always lived up to John Dewey's faith in human nature. Truth and reason are Jekyll's affair, not his. Hyde is a motivation analyst, and his business is to study human weaknesses and failings, to investigate those unconscious desires and fears by which so much of men's conscious thinking and overt doing is determined. And he does this, not in the spirit of the moralist who would like to make people better, or of the physician who would like to improve their health, but

simply in order to find out the best way to take advantage of their ignorance and to exploit their irrationality for the pecuniary benefit of his
employers. But after all, it may be argued, "capitalism is dead, consumerism is king"—and consumerism requires the services of expert salesmen
versed in all the arts (including the more insidious arts) of persuasion.
Under a free enterprise system commercial propaganda by any and every
means is absolutely indispensable. But the indispensable is not necessarily
the desirable. What is demonstrably good in the sphere of economics may
be far from good for men and women as voters or even as human beings.
An earlier, more moralistic generation would have been profoundly
shocked by the bland cynicism of the motivation analysts. Today we read a
book like Mr. Vance Packard's *The Hidden Persuaders,* and are more
amazed than horrified, more resigned than indignant. Given Freud, given
Behaviorism, given the mass producer's chronically desperate need for
mass consumption, this is the sort of thing that is only to be expected. But
what, we may ask, is the sort of thing that is to be expected in the future?
Are Hyde's activities compatible in the long run with Jekyll's? Can a
campaign in favor of rationality be successful in the teeth of another and
even more vigorous campaign in favor of irrationality? These are questions
which, for the moment, I shall not attempt to answer, but shall leave
hanging, so to speak, as a backdrop to our discussion of the methods of
mass persuasion in a technologically advanced democratic society.

The task of the commercial propagandist in a democracy is in
some ways easier and in some ways more difficult than that of a political
propagandist employed by an established dictator or a dictator in the
making. It is easier inasmuch as almost everyone starts out with a prejudice
in favor of beer, cigarettes and iceboxes, whereas almost nobody starts out
with a prejudice in favor of tyrants. It is more difficult inasmuch as the
commercial propagandist is not permitted, by the rules of his particular
game, to appeal to the more savage instincts of his public. The advertiser
of dairy products would dearly love to tell his readers and listeners that all
their troubles are caused by the machinations of a gang of godless international margarine manufacturers, and that it is their patriotic duty to
march out and burn the oppressors' factories. This sort of thing, however,
is ruled out, and he must be content with a milder approach. But the mild
approach is less exciting than the approach through verbal or physical
violence. In the long run, anger and hatred are self-defeating emotions. But
in the short run they pay high dividends in the form of psychological and
even (since they release large quantities of adrenalin and noradrenalin)
physiological satisfaction People may start out with an initial prejudice
against tyrants; but when tyrants or would-be tyrants treat them to
adrenalin-releasing propaganda about the wickedness of their enemies—
particularly of enemies weak enough to be persecuted—they are ready to
follow him with enthusiasm. In his speeches Hitler kept repeating such

words as "hatred," "force," "ruthless," "crush," "smash"; and he would accompany these violent words with even more violent gestures. He would yell, he would scream, his veins would swell, his face would turn purple. Strong emotion (as every actor and dramatist knows) is in the highest degree contagious. Infected by the malignant frenzy of the orator, the audience would groan and sob and scream in an orgy of uninhibited passion. And these orgies were so enjoyable that most of those who had experienced them eagerly came back for more. Almost all of us long for peace and freedom; but very few of us have much enthusiasm for the thoughts, feelings and actions that make for peace and freedom. Conversely almost nobody wants war or tyranny; but a great many people find an intense pleasure in the thoughts, feelings and actions that make for war and tyranny. These thoughts, feelings and actions are too dangerous to be exploited for commercial purposes. Accepting this handicap, the advertising man must do the best he can with the less intoxicating emotions, the quieter forms of irrationality.

Effective rational propaganda becomes possible only when there is a clear understanding, on the part of all concerned, of the nature of symbols and of their relations to the things and events symbolized. Irrational propaganda depends for its effectiveness on a general failure to understand the nature of symbols. Simple-minded people tend to equate the symbol with what it stands for, to attribute to things and events some of the qualities expressed by the words in terms of which the propagandist has chosen, for his own purposes, to talk about them. Consider a simple example. Most cosmetics are made of lanolin, which is a mixture of purified wool fat and water beaten up into an emulsion. This emulsion has many valuable properties: it penetrates the skin, it does not become rancid, it is mildly antiseptic and so forth. But the commercial propagandists do not speak about the genuine virtues of the emulsion. They give it some picturesquely voluptuous name, talk ecstatically and misleadingly about feminine beauty and show pictures of gorgeous blondes nourishing their tissues with skin food. "The cosmetic manufacturers," one of their number has written, "are not selling lanolin, they are selling hope." For this hope, this fraudulent implication of a promise that they will be transfigured, women will pay ten or twenty times the value of the emulsion which the propagandists have so skilfully related, by means of misleading symbols, to a deep-seated and almost universal feminine wish—the wish to be more attractive to members of the opposite sex. The principles underlying this kind of propaganda are extremely simple. Find some common desire, some widespread unconscious fear or anxiety; think out some way to relate this wish or fear to the product you have to sell; then build a bridge of verbal or pictorial symbols over which your customer can pass from fact to compensatory dream, and from the dream to the illusion that your product, when purchased, will make the dream come true. "We no longer buy

oranges, we buy vitality. We do not buy just an auto, we buy prestige."
And so with all the rest. In toothpaste, for example, we buy, not a mere
cleanser and antiseptic, but release from the fear of being sexually repul-
sive. In vodka and whisky we are not buying a protoplasmic poison which,
in small doses, may depress the nervous system in a psychologically
valuable way; we are buying friendliness and good fellowship, the warmth
of Dingley Dell and the brilliance of the Mermaid Tavern. With our
laxatives we buy the health of a Greek god, the radiance of one of Diana's
nymphs. With the monthly best seller we acquire culture, the envy of our
less literate neighbors and the respect of the sophisticated. In every case
the motivation analyst has found some deep-seated wish or fear, whose
energy can be used to move the consumer to part with cash and so,
indirectly, to turn the wheels of industry. Stored in the minds and bodies of
countless individuals, this potential energy is released by, and transmitted
along, a line of symbols carefully laid out so as to bypass rationality and
obscure the real issue.

Sometimes the symbols take effect by being disproportionately
impressive, haunting and fascinating in their own right. Of this kind are the
rites and pomps of religion. These "beauties of holiness" strengthen faith
where it already exists and, where there is no faith, contribute to conversion. Appealing, as they do, only to the aesthetic sense, they guarantee
neither the truth nor the ethical value of the doctrines with which they have
been, quite arbitrarily, associated. As a matter of plain historical fact, the
beauties of holiness have often been matched and indeed surpassed by the
beauties of unholiness. Under Hitler, for example, the yearly Nuremberg
rallies were masterpieces of ritual and theatrical art. "I had spent six years
in St. Petersburg before the war in the best days of the old Russian ballet,"
writes Sir Nevile Henderson, the British ambassador to Hitler's Germany,
"but for grandiose beauty I have never seen any ballet to compare with the
Nuremberg rally." One thinks of Keats—"Beauty is truth, truth beauty."
Alas, the identity exists only on some ultimate, supramundane level. On
the levels of politics and theology, beauty is perfectly compatible with
nonsense and tyranny. Which is very fortunate; for if beauty were incompatible with nonsense and tyranny, there would be precious little art in the
world. The masterpieces of painting, sculpture and architecture were
produced as religious or political propaganda, for the greater glory of a
god, a government or a priesthood. But most kings and priests have been
despotic and all religions have been riddled with superstition. Genius has
been the servant of tyranny and art has advertised the merits of the local
cult. Time, as it passes, separates the good art from the bad metaphysics.
Can we learn to make this separation, not after the event, but while it is
actually taking place? That is the question.

In commercial propaganda the principle of the disproportionately
fascinating symbol is clearly understood. Every propagandist has his Art

Department, and attempts are constantly being made to beautify the billboards with striking posters, the advertising pages of magazines with lively drawings and photographs. There are no masterpieces; for masterpieces appeal only to a limited audience, and the commercial propagandist is out to captivate the majority. For him, the ideal is a moderate excellence. Those who like this not too good, but sufficiently striking, art may be expected to like the products with which it has been associated and for which it symbolically stands.

Another disproportionately fascinating symbol is the Singing Commercial. Singing Commercials are a recent invention; but the Singing Theological and the Singing Devotional—the hymn and the psalm—are as old as religion itself. Singing Militaries, or marching songs, are coeval with war, and Singing Patriotics, the precursors of our national anthems, were doubtless used to promote group solidarity, to emphasize the distinction between "us" and "them," by the wandering bands of paleolithic hunters and food gatherers. To most people music is intrinsically attractive. Moreover, melodies tend to ingrain themselves in the listener's mind. A tune will haunt the memory during the whole of a lifetime. Here, for example, is a quite uninteresting statement or value judgment. As it stands nobody will pay attention to it. But now set the words to a catchy and easily remembered tune. Immediately they become words of power. Moreover, the words will tend automatically to repeat themselves every time the melody is heard or spontaneously remembered. Orpheus has entered into an alliance with Pavlov—the power of sound with the conditioned reflex. For the commercial propagandist, as for his colleagues in the fields of politics and religion, music possesses yet another advantage. Nonsense which it would be shameful for a reasonable being to write, speak or hear spoken can be sung or listened to by that same rational being with pleasure and even with a kind of intellectual conviction. Can we learn to separate the pleasure of singing or of listening to song from the all too human tendency to believe in the propaganda which the song is putting over? That again is the question.

Thanks to compulsory education and the rotary press, the propagandist has been able, for many years past, to convey his messages to virtually every adult in every civilized country. Today, thanks to radio and television, he is in the happy position of being able to communicate even with unschooled adults and not yet literate children.

Children, as might be expected, are highly susceptible to propaganda. They are ignorant of the world and its ways, and therefore completely unsuspecting. Their critical faculties are undeveloped. The youngest of them have not yet reached the age of reason and the older ones lack the experience on which their new-found rationality can effectively work. In Europe, conscripts used to be playfully referred to as "cannon fodder." Their little brothers and sisters have now become radio fodder and television fodder. In my childhood we were taught to sing nursery rhymes and, in pious households, hymns. Today the little ones warble the Singing Commercials. Which is better—"Rheingold is my beer, the dry beer," or "Hey diddle-diddle, the cat and the fiddle"? "Abide with me" or "You'll wonder where the yellow went, when you brush your teeth with Pepsodent"? Who knows?

"I don't say that children should be forced to harass their parents into buying products they've seen advertised on television, but at the same time I cannot close my eyes to the fact that it's being done every day." So writes the star of one of the many programs beamed to a juvenile audience. "Children," he adds, "are living, talking records of what we tell them every day." And in due course these living, talking records of television commercials will grow up, earn money and buy the products of industry. "Think," writes Mr. Clyde Miller ecstatically, "think of what it can mean to your firm in profits if you can condition a million or ten million children, who will grow up into adults trained to buy your product, as soldiers are trained in advance when they hear the trigger words, Forward March!" Yes, just think of it! And at the same time remember that the dictators and the would-be dictators have been thinking about this sort of thing for years, and that millions, tens of millions, hundreds of millions of children are in process of growing up to buy the local despot's ideological product and, like well-trained soldiers, to respond with appropriate behavior to the trigger words implanted in those young minds by the despot's propagandists.

Self-government is in inverse ratio to numbers. The larger the constituency, the less the value of any particular vote. When he is merely one of millions, the individual elector feels himself to be impotent, a negligible quantity. The candidates he has voted into office are far away, at the top of the pyramid of power. Theoretically they are the servants of the people; but in fact it is the servants who give orders and the people, far off at the base of the great pyramid, who must obey. Increasing population and advancing technology have resulted in an increase in the number and complexity of organizations, an increase in the amount of power concentrated in the hands of officials and a corresponding decrease in the amount of control exercised by electors, coupled with a decrease in the public's regard for democratic procedures. Already weakened by the vast impersonal forces at work in the modern world, democratic institutions are now being undermined from within by the politicians and their propagandists.

Human beings act in a great variety of irrational ways, but all of them seem to be capable, if given a fair chance, of making a reasonable choice in the light of available evidence. Democratic institutions can be made to work only if all concerned do their best to impart knowledge and to encourage rationality. But today, in the world's most powerful democracy, the politicians and their propagandists prefer to make nonsense of democratic procedures by appealing almost exclusively to the ignorance and irrationality of the electors. "Both parties," we were told in 1956 by the editor of a leading business journal, "will merchandise their candidates and issues by the same methods that business has developed to sell goods. These include scientific selection of appeals and planned repetition. . . . Radio spot announcements and ads will repeat phrases with a planned intensity. Billboards will push slogans of proven power. . . . Candidates need, in addition to rich voices and good diction, to be able to look 'sincerely' at the TV camera."

The political merchandisers appeal only to the weaknesses of voters, never to their potential strength. They make no attempt to educate the masses into becoming fit for self-government; they are content merely to manipulate and exploit them. For this purpose all the resources of psychology and the social sciences are mobilized and set to work. Carefully selected samples of the electorate are given "interviews in depth." These interviews in depth reveal the unconscious fears and wishes most prevalent in a given society at the time of an election. Phrases and images aimed at allaying or, if necessary, enhancing these fears, at satisfying these wishes, at least symbolically, are then chosen by the experts, tried out on readers and audiences, changed or improved in the light of the information thus obtained. After which the political campaign is ready for the mass communicators. All that is now needed is money and a candidate who can be coached to look "sincere." Under the new dispensation, political principles and plans for specific action have come to lose most of their importance. The personality of the candidate and the way he is projected by the advertising experts are the things that really matter.

In one way or another, as vigorous he-man or kindly father, the candidate must be glamorous. He must also be an entertainer who never bores his audience. Inured to television and radio, that audience is accustomed to being distracted and does not like to be asked to concentrate or make a prolonged intellectual effort. All speeches by the entertainer-candidate must therefore be short and snappy. The great issues of the day must be dealt with in five minutes at the most—and preferably (since the audience will be eager to pass on to something a little livelier than inflation or the H-bomb) in sixty seconds flat. The nature of oratory is such that there has always been a tendency among politicians and clergymen to oversimplify complex issues. From a pulpit or a platform even the most conscientious of speakers finds it very difficult to tell the whole truth. The methods now being used to merchandise the political candidate as though he were a deodorant positively guarantee the electorate against ever hearing the truth about anything.

WANTED: RESPONSIBLE
ADVERTISING CRITICS

James Webb Young

*The late James Webb Young was regarded as one of the
elder statesmen of the advertising industry. He helped build the
world's largest advertising agency and served as an advertising
consultant. He taught business history and advertising at the
University of Chicago.*

I learned my trade as a writer of advertisements in a religious
publishing house, selling books by mail to Methodist ministers. My first big
success was with a book called "Personal Evangelism," which had the
worthy purpose of telling these ministers how to increase the membership
of their church and, as the saying had it, to "bring more souls to Christ."

In such an activity I had no suspicion that I was entering upon
what—much later—President Angell of Yale told me was a *"déclassé*
profession." And I dare say the present writer of an effective series of
advertisements, now being published by the Knights of Columbus for the
Catholic faith, would have been as astonished as I was when I heard
this.

My first warning on the status of the advertising man came on
another campus. Early in the 1920s, in the midst of a busy advertising life,
I had undertaken to get a solid physiological base for the study of psychology. And the famous Anton J. Carlson at the University of Chicago
had agreed personally to give it to me in his laboratory.

One day Dr. Carlson introduced me to the late C. Judson Herrick,
notable for his researches on the brain and nervous system, whose latest
book I had been given to study. I said: "Dr. Herrick, it may surprise you to
know that an advertising man is finding your new book on the brain of the
greatest interest." Said Dr. Herrick, looking at me sourly over his glasses:
"I am not only surprised; I am chagrined. As far as I can see there is no
connection between brains and advertising."

Since then, through the years, in my notes on many kinds of
human behavior, I have recorded other equally sweeping generalizations
about advertising, made by faculty members of Harvard, Columbia, Prince-
ton, Cornell, Wisconsin, Johns Hopkins, and McGill.

But sweeping generalizations about advertising are not confined to
the academic groves, nor to recent times. A notable piece on the subject

came from the pen of Dr. Samuel Johnson, in the mid-eighteenth century. And currently . . . any number of people have gotten into the act. . . .

Note . . . the adverbs used by Father P. P. Harbrecht, S.J., in a . . . booklet issued by the Twentieth Century Fund on his excellent study "Toward the Paraproprietal Society." Speaking of such big corporations as General Motors, du Pont, U.S. Steel, Alcoa, and General Electric, he says (italics mine): "Their research and innovations transform our lives, *quietly* with home appliances or *dramatically* with atomics and space flight; *brashly* with TV advertising or *culturally* with subsidies to education." Is all the TV advertising of all these firms done "brashly"?

Now, let me say clearly that advertising needs, is entitled to, and can profit from criticism of the most public kind. It needs it more than ever today because advertising has become one of the most potent forces in our culture—ranking as an "institution" with the church and education, according to Professor Potter of Yale, in his book "People of Plenty."

But it needs that criticism in the form that the dictionary defines as "the act of passing judgment on the merits of anything"; that is, discriminating criticism, which applauds the good and damns the bad.

No one is more concerned about the misuses of advertising than the responsible people in advertising. And, in fact, they have been trying for a very long time to do something about these misuses. If any of the shoot-from-the-hip critics of this activity would take the same trouble to understand my specialty as I was taking to understand that of Dr. Herrick, these are some of the things they would find:

First, that the technical literature of advertising is currently filled with the kind of "good-and-bad" criticism advertising needs.

Second, that advertising people have promoted and secured the adoption of "Truth in Advertising" laws in over half our states, and have supported the work of Better Business Bureaus in policing these laws.

Third, that they have supported the purposes, if not always the methods, of the Federal Trade Commission, to prevent the use of advertising in ways unfair to competition.

Fourth, that in their various trade and professional organizations advertising men have drafted any number of codes of "ethical" practices—and have been busy reactivating these lately!

Fifth, that many important advertising media refuse to accept advertising for certain classifications of products; and that the largest advertising agency in the world has never undertaken advertising for "hard" liquors—all at a considerable cost to their revenues.

All these things have, in fact, brought improvements in the use of advertising, as a recent writer noted. "In front of us," he says, "is a 1913 advertisement pointing out the advantages of Postum over Brazilian coffee. Among the ills attributed to coffee: 'Sallow Complexions; Stomach Trouble; Bad Liver; Heart Palpitations; Shattered Nerves; Caffeine, a

Drug; Weakness from Drugging.' We doubt if the present owners of Postum would O.K. copy like this today. Even if they didn't own Maxwell House."

But all this is not enough, and nobody knows it better than those hard-working creators of much of our advertising, inaccurately stereotyped as "Madison Avenue."

The reason why it is not enough is that, as developed in America, the set of facilities and techniques called advertising has become the most powerful single means that the world has ever seen for informing, persuading, and inspiring a people to action. As such, it becomes vital that its potentialities for good or ill become fully recognized; that the responsibilities for its use be squarely shouldered; and that the magnificent opportunities for its use in the public service, as now amply demonstrated in the work of the Advertising Council, be fully exploited.

It is therefore my thesis that what advertising now needs is to be given, in public print, the same kind of continuing, knowing, responsible criticism as that given to the theatre, music, the arts, books, and other major aspects of our culture. It needs a "career critic," keeping a steady spotlight on both the good and the bad in the uses of advertising, and on its unexploited social potentialities.

What would be the qualifications for such a public critic of advertising—assuming the judicial temperament of the responsible man?

First, he should know that "advertising" is a set of facilities and techniques as impersonal as electricity or atomic energy, and thus equally usable for noble ends or shabby ones. Hence he will avoid the "pathetic fallacy" of animating the inanimate, into which so many critics of advertising fall. It is *advertisers* who need criticism—not advertising.

Second, he will understand clearly the economic necessities which brought advertising into existence, and still control its use. These were well stated in 1870 by Walter Bagehot in his classic work "Lombard Street." Said Bagehot:

> Our current political economy does not sufficiently take account of *time* as an element in trade operations. But as soon as the division of labour has once established itself in a community, two principles at once begin to be important, of which time is the very essence. These are—
> *First,* that as goods are produced to be exchanged, it is good that they should be exchanged as quickly as possible.
> *Secondly,* that as every producer is mainly occupied in producing what others want, and not what he wants himself, it is desirable that he should always be able to find, without effort, without delay, and without uncertainty, others who want what he can produce.

These words are even truer today than when Bagehot wrote them. To understand the workhorse job of advertising in a high production-consumption economy such as ours is primary for any intelligent criticism of its uses.

Third, he must understand that the methods by which advertising gets the workhorse job done in today's economy have been greatly developed since Bagehot's day; and why in these methods are to be found some of the roots of the criticisms of advertising.

. . . early in the expansion of the use of advertising it was discovered that the mere repetition of a name or trademark could produce a preference for one product over another. Remember "Gold Medal flour— Eventually, Why Not Now?" This sort of advertising worked because mere familiarity is a *value* to the human being. It satisfies one of his deepest needs: for a sense of "at-homeness" in this world. You can check this, perhaps, by recalling when, in a crowd of strangers, you have found yourself gravitating toward one familiar face—possibly even that of a person not well liked. Familiarity is a value, and no advertising works which does not, in some form, deliver a value to somebody.

Then it was discovered that there is a function for advertising merely as a "re-minder" of something we are already "minded" to do. For example, to "Say it with flowers!" when you have a wedding anniversary coming up. A service, surely, in the cause of domestic tranquillity!

After this, as railroads made a national market possible, came a development in the *news* use of advertising. Just as the Associated Press came into being to gather and transmit general news, so the advertising agency came into being to gather and transmit commercial news, thus making possible the announcement, say, of a new model automobile on the same day everywhere.

But there is also another kind of "news," in the advertising sense. It is the kind of news you pay no attention to until you need to know it. In our long march from the cradle to the grave we pass into, and out of, many areas of experience. And as we do, our receptivity to all sorts of news changes. Thus the young woman who ignores the infant-feeding advertisement of today may become its most eager reader next year.

Then, along the way, came the discovery that advertising could be used to overcome human inertia. Hell is indeed paved with many good intentions, toward such things as making a will, taking out adequate life insurance, seeing the dentist regularly, and so on. In all such things the reward for action taken, or the punishment for action postponed, is remote and delayed. Advertising, by making more vivid such rewards or punishments, can often overcome the inertia—to the profit of the reader or listener as well as the advertiser.

Religions have always had to deal with this problem in the training of ministers, and here it seems always to have been a moot question whether portrayal of the rewards of heaven or of the punishments of hell converted more sinners.

Then, finally, came the discovery that advertising could *add a value not in the product.* And because these values were subjective ones (such as status symbols; or, say, the luxury of bathing with the same soap the movie stars use; or what Edith Wharton once called "the utility of the useless"), here advertising really got into trouble. For in this area of subjective values, one man's meat is definitely another man's poison.

In this area, too, our critic will come face to face with one of his most difficult problems. Advertising, like editing, politics, and even to some extent education, always operates within the context of the culture of its day. One irony of its present situation is that some of the people who are most vocal in their negative attitudes toward advertising may themselves have contributed to some aspects of it which they most deplore. By supporting liberal policies for the wider distribution of wealth in this country, they have helped bring into existence a mammoth class of *nouveau riche,* whose incomes have improved faster than their tastes and subjective values.

In addition to such an understanding of the ways in which advertising works, our critic must grasp some of the trends in our economy which have major impacts on the creation of advertising.

The most important of these lie in our technology. Innovation has become an industry, as Dr. Sumner Slichter pointed out. Theoretically, our accelerated rate of innovation should produce more and more advertising news about distinction in products. But counter forces produce in some considerable degree an opposite effect.

One of these counter forces is governmental pressure for the preservation of competition. This tends to force a cross-licensing of patents which rapidly spreads any given innovation throughout an industry. Thus, for instance, when one manufacturer of television sets produces a more compact tube, soon many of his major competitors have the benefit of it.

Then, too, innovation often comes, not from the end-producer of the product or service, but from the supplier of an ingredient or part, whose interest is to gain its adoption by as many end-producers as possible. See, for example, the current jet plane advertising of our airlines.

Added to these we have, in this country, a widespread "free trade" in technological ideas, through such channels as the Society of Automotive Engineers and numerous trade and technical journals. The result is that innovating ideas get "in the air," and soon all our automobiles, for example, become more and more alike.

All these forces result in the reverse of a distinction between competitive products and services. But the advertising man is expected to present each of them as one with important differences, leading to the manufacture of mountains out of molehills in the advertising. Our critic must be knowledgeable about this problem, and about the constructive ways to deal with it.

Finally, and most importantly, our critic should be conscious of the still underdeveloped use of advertising as a social force outside the exchange of goods and services.

He must know of the remarkable results that the Advertising Council has produced over the last fifteen years for some fifty "good causes"—through the voluntary services of advertising men, and with contributions of some $180 million annually, in time and space, from advertisers and media.

And he should know, too, of the following-up of this lead in such fine corporation advertising campaigns as:

a. The striking campaign of the Standard Oil Company (N.J.) in the interest of international friendship.

b. The Weyerhaeuser Company's campaign for the preservation of our forests and for conservation through tree-farming.

c. The campaign for better schools, safer highways, forest fire prevention, and other useful purposes of the Caterpillar Tractor Co.

d. The campaign of the New York Life Insurance Company to help parents guide their children in career choices, or the notable campaign of the Metropolitan Life Insurance Company on behalf of better health.

e. The campaign for citizen responsibility of Nationwide Insurance.

An alert critic might see, too, in such uses of advertising, potentialities for our great foundations; for the use of some of their funds in the *distribution* of knowledge, through this most modern high-speed means of communication.

In all this let our critic be not only objective but specific. Let him deal, not with "advertising," but with its uses, good and bad. Let him examine:

Whether there is too much crowding of advertising in time and space—such as commercials per TV program, and billboards per scenic mile?

Whether there is too much stridency and bad manners in some advertising, now that it can project personal salesmanship into the living room?

Whether the paucity of real buying information, and the superfluity of adjectives in some advertising is, not a crime, but worse —a mistake?

Would such a critic have any real effect on the advertising scene? All I know is that the genius of advertising is reiteration, and that its prophet, Isaiah, said: "Whom shall he teach knowledge? and whom shall he make to understand doctrines? . . . For precept must be upon precept; precept upon precept; line upon line; line upon line; here a little, and there a little."

What I am looking for is a publisher or editor with the insight and courage to enter this new field of criticism—and for the competent critic to aid him. Such a publisher or editor will have to take some risks with his advertisers, yes. But he will, I believe, make a major contribution to the better and wiser use of advertising in our day; he will find himself attracting a surprising volume of mail from his readers; and, in the longer haul, profiting from the sharp attention given his publication by advertisers and advertising men.

Are there any takers in the house?

Part Five

Alienation in the Modern World

Although the term alienation as we now use it has a venerable history which goes back at least as far as Hegel, it has only recently acquired new prominence. We need it as we try to understand once subterranean moods and tendencies which seemed suddenly to surface in the 1960s. The title of one of Freud's best known works is "Civilization and Its Discontents." Were he alive today he might give us a sequel entitled "Modern Society and Its Discontents." We have been, indeed, in our winter of discontent; and alienation, for reasons now to be explored, is the condition which best explains it. The discontent is of a special kind, removed, if not entirely from war, then from storm, hunger, plague and the other immemorial disasters which have brought man grief. The object of the following pages is to examine the new alienation, especially as it prevails among young people, to note the forms it has taken and the recent changes it has undergone, and then to deal with the remedy, drugs, to which many of the discontented have turned.

15

Discontent and Disillusionment

Industrial capitalism has always had its bitter critics as well as its ardent apologists. Usually the criticism has been economic, emphasizing the way in which the profit motive results in exploiting workers and victimizing consumers with attendant breakdowns in the economy such as occurred in the 1930s. Sometimes the criticism has been ethical, concentrating on the corrupting influence of the profit motive. Sometimes, as with romanticists, criticism has concentrated on the mechanization of production and its dehumanization of the worker. Most such criticism was inspired by the sordid beginnings of industrial capitalism when unprotected workers, including women and children, were in fact cruelly overworked and underpaid and lived under indescribably wretched conditions; or by the period of *Hochcapitalismus* when the most predatory practices of businessmen and capitalists were almost completely uncontrolled.

Today, although there are still serious defects in the social system of which industrial capitalism is the foundation, most critics would concede that vast improvements have taken place. Democracy is no longer a utopian dream. Despite great and potentially dangerous concentrations of power, and the disclosures triggered by the Watergate scandal, democratic institutions do in fact function as they did not a century ago. An autonomous labor movement gives workers a strong voice they did not have before. Marx's prediction that they would undergo progressive degradation has not been confirmed. On the contrary, both the conditions and rewards of work have been vastly improved in the last century for the great majority of workers in Europe and America. If a sixty hour work week once made it difficult to distinguish between a free worker and a slave, the reduction of the work week, especially in the United States, is surely a spectacular achievement exceeded only by the elimination of poverty for four-fifths of our population. A substantial proportion of our people are still deprived of the basic necessities of life and in a society as affluent as ours this is scandalous, but it may fairly be argued that our failures should not obscure what has been accomplished for the other four-fifths. Also, education, even though it leaves much to be desired, has been made available to all. And the system provides ample opportunity for the able and talented even though ethnic prejudice mars the record. If provision for those who are not able and talented is still much too meager, it is in glaring contrast to the poorhouses and almshouses (not to mention the pesthouses) of another century.

To be sure, it is all too easy to exaggerate these accomplishments, as many do, and to use them as a pretext for ignoring the blighted condition of our cities or the predicament of our ethnic minorities. Only the smug and myopic will fail to recognize that much remains to be done. Nevertheless, enough has been achieved to render strikingly paradoxical the appearance in the 1960s, among many, of a mood of complete disenchantment and disillusionment. Even more mysteriously, this mood afflicted a considerable number who could hardly be described as economically disadvantaged. Perhaps most bewildering was the scope of their censure which went beyond such traditional grievances as poverty and inequality to totally fault a whole way of life. They were repelled by what they saw. Recitations of past accomplishments and encouraging trends completely failed to impress them. They were supported by many of our most highly regarded writers and artists who saw nothing worth recording in the world about them except the ugly and pathological. All felt trapped in a mechanized, depersonalized, regimented, over-organized society where, as they saw it, honesty was displaced by hypocrisy, venality triumphed over generosity, ambition was mistaken for self-realization, and beauty was driven out by ugliness. Their animadversions were directed not merely against capitalism, but against communism, at any rate communism of the variety subscribed to in the USSR. Both were seen as threatening the individual's sense of identity, as diminishing him, as manipulating him, as making him a pawn of forces external to him.

We were confronted by the protest of people, most of them young and therefore concentrated on college campuses, who felt isolated, displaced, rootless, lonely, estranged, in a word, alienated. Two major groupings are roughly distinguishable. Some took the way of retreat, exiling themselves from conventional society. Among these were the "hippies," who carried their protest to the point of adopting a new style of life. They became refugees from what they chose to call the rat-race. Their advice in the curious patois which has become a trademark was, "Do your own thing."

Although they may not have known it, the pedigree of the hippies goes back to Diogenes and the Greek Cynics who, like them, sought "honesty" and escape from artificial conventions by living doglike ("canine" and "cynical" have the same Latin and Greek roots), i.e., "natural," lives. It embraces Thoreau, and extends through Nietzsche, who likewise sought a transvaluation of all values, and the existentialists, with borrowings from the oriental mystics. Among the hippies a wholesale repudiation of middle-class values, whether related to propriety or property, manifested itself in sartorial and tonsorial eccentricity and sexual permissiveness and an attitude of complete disdain for status and wealth. It was difficult (for those who were not their troubled parents) to regard the hippies as more than impudent teen (or tween)-agers transiently intent on savoring complete freedom—including freedom from hard work —and shocking their elders. However, the hippies were only the more visible and quixotic vanguard of a much more numerous legion which embraces large numbers of artists, writers, students, and teachers. There was therefore good reason for taking this phenomenon seriously, although the real perils and sheer boredom of living in New York's East Village or San Francisco's Haight-Ashbury finally led to the dispersal of these and similar settlements. The extent to which the hippies and the counterculture they created survived this diaspora will be discussed in the following pages.

If there is the way of the yogi, there is also, to recall Koestler's useful distinction, the way of the commissar. Thus, some prefer rebellion to retreat, to change the world rather than to escape it. These became exponents of the so-called "new politics" and as the "New Left," not only denounced the profit system, but organization and discipline as well, and therefore regarded Communists and liberals with the same condescension reserved for all "Organization" men. New Leftists shared with their drug-oriented cousins a complete alienation from the "Establishment." However their estrangement led them not to beads and flowers and inner exploration but to picket lines, teach-ins, marches, demonstrations, and other forms of vehement social protest. Their pedigree goes back to the youthful Karl Marx, from whose early *Economic and Philosophic Manuscripts* (which he later repudiated) they took their notions of alienation. Many of them served their apprenticeship in the civil rights movement, bravely courting danger in Mississippi and other centers of southern hospitality. Later they earned their spurs demonstrating against a war in Vietnam which confirmed their severest criticism of American practices. Dedicated activists, they relished slogans such as "Black Power" and "Student Power." Since universities and colleges are peculiarly vulnerable to student activists, campus protests often prospered. These local successes led them to exaggerate the potentialities of militancy in other areas such as the Pentagon or a hotel (Century City, Los Angeles) where the President might be speaking. It should be added that, having repudiated what they regarded as the stale left-of-center formulas of the traditional liberal, Social-Democratic, or Communist varieties, they were as vague in defining program as they were valiant in protest.

As everyone knows, a dramatic change of climate occurred in the early 1970s brought about in part by the conclusion of the war in Vietnam and the ending of compulsory military service, in part by an extension of suffrage to include eighteen to twenty-one-year olds which provided a political outlet for activism, and in part because, as will be seen, the vehicles in which the alienated rode were too creaky to stay on the road very long. Nevertheless, it would be a mistake to conclude that the estrangement and hostility that found expression in political activism and the counterculture have disappeared. Jesus-freaks, oriental cultists, a new interest in pseudo-science, a "nothing makes sense" mood, and with it a rejection of reason and logic as associated with marketplace calculations or explorations by technology-mad squares of outer space—in sum, strong currents of irrationalism warn us against writing off the critics of the Sixties. So, too, does the continuing attractiveness of drugs. It is therefore highly relevant to ask how seriously we should take their protests and the value judgments on which these were based. Has youthful exhibitionism and exuberance been confused with authentic moral criticism? Why did alienation become acute in the 1960s instead of the 1940s or 1950s? Should we look for our answer to the family? The permissive antiauthoritarian middle-class parents of many of the new young protestors rarely invoked sanctions or imposed discipline; they preferred, especially if they were artists or intellectuals, to rely on reason and consensus. Is the total and often bitter rejection of American institutions and values by their children the result of a first, unaccustomed confrontation with extrafamilial authority and its institutional manifestations, an authority which often (like the university) wearies of explaining itself and says: "Do this, or else!"

Some answers will be found in the selections which follow, two of which are written by rueful participants—one in the es-

capist, the other in the revolutionary expression of the protest of
the Sixties—who are trying to understand what went wrong.

NEEDED: A COUNTER COUNTERCULTURE

David French

*David French is a former economics consultant and foreign
service officer. He is teaching at Johnson State College in Vermont. He writes from the point of view of one who has been
part of the counterculture.*

The counterculture is dying. Left behind are a thousand hopeful
articles about the New Consciousness, a thousand photographs of half-
naked, acid-rich bodies jumbled together in some urban pad in mockery of
the straights. Countless people still live their own versions of the old Haight-
Ashbury dream, but there it ends. Eaten away from within by its Establishment heritage, the movement has lost its energy, is left with nowhere to go.

The drugs were most obvious and the music, the dress, the hair.
But at its best, the movement came together first around a sense of community. Appalled by the isolation and barren privatism of their parents, the
young banded together in political collectives, urban crash pads, rural communes. And they shared: money, dope, beds, ideas. It seemed a revolution,
and a lot of us set out to take part in it. But it was a revolution *manqué*,
and we are left now with the long struggle to find what lies beyond.

We came to community, Elena and I, at the end of a long train of
thought. Together, we had done a tour of duty in the "real world": I as
Foreign Service officer and economic consultant, Elena as language teacher
and interpreter, both of us as graduate students and then college teachers.
We were good at what we did, and at first we liked it. But it was the sixties,
for us as for everyone else. We were in Ethiopia at the birth of a deep and
continuing anti-Americanism, fed by uncritical American support for the
corrupt and repressive imperial regime. We were in Nigeria for 11 months
of the civil war. We were teaching at a black college in Pennsylvania the
year Martin Luther King was murdered. We were in Cambridge for the first
great Harvard Square riot.

It was our very own prerevolutionary era, with the special twist that much of it was played out for us against an African backdrop. Some things seemed much clearer that way. The empty pretentiousness of our own technology-bound economic system, for example, was thrown into the most embarrassing relief. In Africa, stinking factories and tasteless high-rises in the Western mold came across most strikingly as defilements of the ageless villages across whose life they were beginning to sprawl. It was possible to grow very angry at those who would commit such violence for their own profit. In contrast to such barbarism were the extraordinary ways of traditional Africa. They could be seductive, those old ways: for many, the worst culture shock from overseas living involved coming home again.

The means of my own seduction was a young Ethiopian couple who lived in a small village 20 miles from Addis Ababa. As I got to know them, watched them struggle to survive on a monthly income of $40 or so, I came to realize that they were at least as humanly fulfilled as, and certainly more serene than, other friends making $4,000 a month in American suburbs. The damage to the great American assumption, Money Equals Happiness, was nearly total.

A straightforwardness unobstructed by the Western penchant for abstraction, characterized all of their relationships. They could be so direct, in fact, that they would become almost nonverbal, communicating by a kind of telepathy. And the same sense of involvement extended outward, to their families, their extended families, their tribal environments. In other dimensions, it went even beyond that: an almost mystical sense of spiritual full-ness seemed to entwine them with generations dead and yet unborn. It all seemed wondrously human, caring, spontaneous, clearly opposed to the world in which Elena and I spent most of our time. There, the choreographies were always designed to preserve people's apartness: interoffice memos, private property, cocktail parties, the nuclear family. For our Ethiopian friends, the equivalent patterns were all constructed to build community. We had to escape, to find this other, more human sort of consciousness, which seemed to be embodied in collective, tribalized social units.

Forgive us our flights of fancy; it was by no means that simple. But there was *something* special going on around us, something that a lot of people were finding then in Africa, in the cultures of the American Indians, or simply buried deep within themselves. And community seemed to be at the heart of it. We then were left to figure out what the communities *we* were going to build would look like, what they would do for us. For Elena and me, it had a lot to do with overcoming the David-and-Elena games, our own versions of the usual barriers to healthy man-woman relationships. We kept getting tangled up in these, both of us losing perspective, setting up defenses and indulging reflexes neither of us could see. In a community of people interested in human liberation, we could break out of these patterns, gaining new perspectives on them as we shared insights with others into the games we *all* were heir to.

If the first result of this process would be a deepening of our own relationship, the next step would be an extension of this closeness to others in the community, and beyond. As the community began to feel its own identity, it in turn would reach with new force into relationships with other communities. It all would build toward an experiencing of the organic unity of things. This would come back always to the particular people involved, to their sense of greater human completeness. But it supposed that individual completeness would not be achieved in isolation. Rather, individuals would realize their full capacities only as they saw the points of interpenetration between their own uniqueness and that of others.

These forces would work themselves out most fully through common work and shared experience across the full range of human activities. So it had been, at least, for us. We had been most whole, individually and together, during those periods when we were involved in things jointly: teaching at the same college, working together on a study of West African marketing systems. We had been least able to relate fully to ourselves, to each other, or to anyone else when we were doing wholly distinct things, seeing each other in the corners of time left over from work. If there were to be a revolution, it would express itself in revised life patterns that integrated people's lives instead of fragmenting them. And the basic social expression of this was community.

We came to rest at The Community, and we came to The Community through Martha's House. All was normal the afternoon we arrived: The House's five inhabitants were all there, and the pace of things was just shy of hysteria. Martha was cleaning up the debris left by a group that had been there earlier in the day to talk about radical economics. John was cooking dinner, with help from Cathy. George was bringing in firewood. Linda was on her way out to collect a woman referred to the House for a night's lodging by the local abortion counseling center. Through the evening, other members of The Community dropped in and out, exchanging tales of that day in The Community's life or partaking of the running discussion on Women's Liberation that lasted into the early hours of the next morning. For Elena and me, fresh from a too-private California life style and temporary jobs as waitress and school-bus driver, it all seemed an exciting change of pace.

It had been long in happening. For 18 months we had been transient, the world of consulting and teaching abandoned in a search for some elusive next step. We lived with various people, community never quite growing out of what we found to share. But we kept looking, talking with community builders in Europe, Canada, New England, Maryland and Virginia, the Midwest, California. And we read the magazines the movement has spun off: The Modern Utopian, Alternate Society, Mother Earth News, Vocations for Social Change, The Green Revolution. The disparity between what we knew and what we practiced became more and more awkward. When we found The Community, we felt we were finally home.

The Community was an urban group, founded in the Pacific Northwest by exiles—students and faculty—from a local college. When we arrived, it had more than 50 members, most of whom lived in a dozen houses like Martha's, clumped together on the edges of the city's black ghetto. The Community's academic background surfaced in highly informal "learning groups" reflecting the interests of various members: radical economics, Old English, dance, science fiction, woodworking. But most activities were less formal still, with people spending much of their time talking about ways to extricate themselves further from the straight environment. For some, this meant leaving the city, and The Community was negotiating for 80 acres of land half an hour's drive outside of town. It was financially well able to do this; in its early, earnest days as an alternative living-learning experiment, it had arranged a sizable foundation grant. This money, supplemented by voluntary contributions from members, also made it possible for food and shelter to be provided everyone from Community funds.

It was a dream come true—for a while. Then, during a marathon Women's Lib debate at Martha's, Elena and I began to find ourselves under siege. What we were doing with each other, it turned out, was "coupling" (images of dogs or railroad cars, and those were exactly the overtones). Coupling was a long-term relationship between two people; and it led to stagnation, parochialism, sexism, even worse. In vain did we try to talk of working out those things in the context of a relationship—maybe even a marriage! Knowing smiles informed us of our naiveté. For the women of the house, it was clear that to avoid the chauvinism required avoiding the males; better to be asexual, emotionally detached. And the men, grooving on their guilt, fell willingly into line. No relationships for them either, at least until they had purged themselves of their chauvinist tendencies.

It wasn't all quite that self-flagellating. For Martha, on the mend from a short-lived, highly traditional marriage, to keep these distances was part of a totally serious effort to work out her own sense of self. Ultimately, she would be able to re-enter with greater strength the social life of a world she justly saw as being male chauvinist to the gills. But the party line within The Community toward human attachments tended to be much more crude —and very cold. When one of the women in another house had an abortion, she and her partner in conception were joking about it the next day. Their attitude was consistent with the orthodoxy; for the liberated woman, abortions were nothing more momentous than cutting off a hangnail. In the same way, to stop sleeping with someone was no more serious than slipping off a jacket. It was a shock; where Elena and I had come to community to deepen our own relationship, extend it to others, we found the entire idea of serious relationship under fire.

The same was true of human intimacy in any form. Community members were constantly on the go, down to San Francisco, back East, moving in and out of The Community or from house to house within it. This mobility was guarded above all else: Martha, for example, held that her house would be a success if people living there could leave altogether without anyone feeling any special sense of emotional strain. The points of human reference became diluted, through both space and large numbers of people, by all this motion. At one point, I asked Linda how many people she could turn to if her head began to come unglued, how many people would understand what was happening to her. Dozens, she said, scattered all over the world; and I could not explain the difference between an understanding among dozens and one evolved over time with a single person, or two or three. Much less could I explain why I valued that more intimate sort of understanding. It was an awkward attempt at intercultural communication, and it did not succeed.

To guard against intimacy demands constant attention. Gradually, we began to see a brittleness in the ways Community members dealt with one another, in the set of their faces, in what they said. Compassion was held to be condescending. Favored instead as a basis for interpersonal style was a sort of brutal honesty that forced distances between people, stressed their apartness. Ideological confrontation was valued: "That's a male chauvinist thing to say"; "How can you have such a reactionary attitude?" People broke off conversations to analyze each other's neuroses: "You're just projecting when you say that"; "Why do you have so much self-hatred?" Someone wrote in The Community's weekly newsletter that "I hope you [his fellow Community members] curl up and die." Others laughed, pleased at the directness of it. It had to do again with preserving mobility. Compassion would have led to involvement, involvement to commitment, and commitment to chains on tomorrow.

The coupling phobia spilled over into attitudes toward work. With relationship not an objective, the idea of relationship around work became irrelevant. Instead, people sought activities that expressed their own special apartness. Crafts were in favor, since they were personal things, done alone. And writers, artists and other solitaries were overrepresented. As for the work that paid the bills, the same centrifugal forces applied. One person, for example, was economic consultant to a major health plan, someone else worked the graveyard shift as janitor at a local hotel, a third spent odd hours at a skid-row pawnshop. Most people didn't work at all, preferring to live off the foundation money or checks from home. There was no sense that any of this inhibited The Community's development in any way. It began to seem instead that "community" was not really a Community objective, was rather to be resisted, as if it were simply a multiperson version of coupling—as indeed it is.

It led people inward, to an indifference to the experiences of others. At one point, I found an excellent postmortem of a failed commune, the problems described hauntingly familiar in the Community context. Several people refused to read it. It was someone else's trip in some other place—what could it possibly have to say to them? Such an approach devalued the more extensive life experiences of The Community's adults to the point where they became almost ashamed to take positions on things. It seemed an unwritten law that they were never *never* to appear to know more about anything than the rawest escapee from some middle-class suburban home. On the other hand, they *were* allowed to do the tedious administrative work that those younger didn't care to do. The allowable role seemed to be that of the Token Adult, the ultimately permissive, useful-to-have-around parent, viewed with the sort of tolerant affection that shaded off into dismissal.

We came to realize that everyone was in flight, that The Community was bound together largely by its negativism. Traumatized by courses, assigned readings, tests, Community members would have learning groups where nobody had to read anything, or even come. Offended by the authoritarianism of their parents and teachers, members would create an environment where age and experience were disqualifications for being taken seriously. Antagonized beyond reason by the social pressures of the straight world, members would see to it that nobody was required to do anything for the group. Appalled by the empty possessiveness of their parents' marriages, members would ensure that nobody had any claims on anyone else. They were right to flee what they were fleeing; but in simply trying to turn it upside down, they largely were functions of it still.

It all took its toll. Signs: At any given moment, half The Community was sick, an illness level we had seen before only among the people we knew in Nigeria during the worst of the civil war. Or, animals being a sensitive index of environmental vibrations, take the Community dogs, a sobering assortment of freaked-out creatures howling and whining and snapping for attention. (The cats, having a greater instinct for self-preservation, simply ran away.) Or, worse still, the Community children, brittle, supercharged, alienated. One spoke of himself as "the computer": "The computer is ready to answer your question now." They were peripheral to the point where one 5-year-old called his own meeting to complain that The Community offered nothing in which he could participate. Where children and dogs are out of place, beware, beware.

We left The Community the same way we entered it—through Martha's House. One day, Elena and I went to the state prison to talk with a group of black inmates about Ethiopian culture. The people we saw were open and eager to communicate, reaching out to establish points of contact with us. We went back to Martha's. People were lying around on the floor as if paralyzed, talking with their customary detachment about Women's Liberation. It was shattering; *here* were the imprisoned. What we had originally thought of as The Community's ever-provocative dialogue was instead, we were finally realizing, an elaborate mechanism of self-defense. Alone behind their walls of words, people preserved distances between each other by ceaselessly talking. It had become compulsive. "There's too damned much verbiage around this place," someone once said to John. "You and I had better have a long talk about this," he replied.

It was too much to bear. We had come to The Community for intimacy, and none was wanted. We had come for communal work, and none was wanted. We had come to build a new culture, and what we found was as alienating as the old . . . we packed and left.

If some things about The Community were unusual (its affluence, age, range, size), it was in other ways typical of the movement as a whole (white, middle-class, well-educated). But those are just the demographic measures. In its inner life, The Community was strikingly representative of tendencies within the counterculture. Living in The Community had catalyzed for us a sense of the counterculture that we had not really wanted to see.

A warning: All generalizations are partially unfair to a movement containing within itself practically every conceivable variant of human living arrangement. What is true of communes in New York is only partly true of communes in Colorado, and the range within any given area is equally great. Still, there are patterns which cross many of these lines, which apply to the great majority of people within the counterculture, and which therefore give the movement its tone. The most destructive of these are a surprising number of basic attitudes borrowed from the straight world. In large measure, the counterculture has reached its current impasse through the extent to which its members are their parents' children.

The straight world, for example, has come to place a premium on physical and psychological transience. People are expected to move easily from place to place, job to job, product to product, person to person, fad to fad. It is the natural consequence of a growth economy run rampant. As workers or professionals, people respond through movement to the shifting requirements of their work, losing jobs, finding others, carrying out some short-term assignment here, transferring to a higher rung on some other corporate ladder there. As consumers, the same people are encouraged to change brands, discard all-but-new possessions in favor of others, support today's cause and forget yesterday's. The only constant is inconstancy, a state of mind that Elena and I were escaping in coming to the counterculture.

Or so we thought. We found instead that the counterculture has taken transience to the extreme. It is reflected in the language. People are "into" this or that. And what you get into, as opposed to what you take into yourself, you can also get out of—and preferably do. Someone once stuck into The Community's weekly newsletter a line from a Janis Joplin song: "Freedom's just another word for nothing left to lose." Their understanding of this was more clear than complete: You're free if you have nothing to lose, if nothing (or nobody) has you. It is curious. In Alvin Toffler's phrase, the counterculture is full of true "Men of the Future," mobile, eager for the new. The central message of the larger world has been absorbed: don't get involved; you'll be somewhere else tomorrow. . . .

The two worlds share also a surfeit of abstractions. In both, ever-larger parts of life consist of mental images of things taking place out of sight. The adults have The War, Communism, the Gross National Product, Problems of the Inner City; the young have The War, Cuba, Our Black Brothers, The Revolution. Such mental geometries are better able to process facts and theories than to deal with the elusive realities of direct experience; and in response, people depersonalize even their human contacts. . . . People in The Community asked Elena about the liberation movement in Ethiopia, where she was raised. Nobody wanted to know what it was like to grow up there. Barraged incessantly by information, most of it second-hand, people naturally come to deal with the data glut, and with each other, in formulas. What is surprising is the degree to which the counterculture has made this failing its own.

The triumph of these tendencies owes a great deal to self-indulgence. In the larger culture, people feed TV dinners to their children, push buttons on their cars instead of shifting gears (or even walking), pop pills to induce euphoria. In the counterculture, the search for the effortless takes the form of pills too; but its more basic expression comes in the insistence on "doing your own thing." One thing this means is not doing anything you don't want to do, which means in turn not doing anything that is too much work. Someone at The Community told me she'd given up yoga because it was "nonorganic"; that is, it involved motions that were not natural to the body. Similarly, the process of building personal relationships over time calls for stretching oneself in uncomfortable directions; and most people are unwilling to make the effort. In rejecting the distorting disciplines found in their schools and families, those in the counterculture have by and large rejected as well the idea that some disciplines can be liberating. "Do your own thing" has become a counsel of flabbiness, one which owes much to the value America as a whole places on the easy.

Finally, the counterculture has accepted, in its most atomistic form, the American view that fulfillment lies in serving one's narrow self-interest. During our early years of driving for national economic expansion, this was justified in material terms: If everyone pursued his own profit, the group as a whole would prosper. Now, liberated by enormous national wealth from such mundane preoccupations, we hasten to convert the old rationalizations for material greed into new ones for psychological self-seeking. In line with this, the straights have produced such doctrines as that of "self-actualization," while each member of the counterculture asserts his right to his own special "trip." According to these new versions of rugged individualism, everyone will be better off if each person seeks psychological completeness within himself, taking from his surroundings—or from others—whatever he needs to achieve this. There is little sense here of any obligation to the outside world. Even less is there any drive to know the great wholenesses of which we are a part, starting from the wholeness of intimate personal relationship and moving outward from there. Instead of developing a sense of the organic, each person is to become ever the more complete atom.

The counterculture may see more sharing of worldly treasures, but it joins the straight world in giving to others little of its inner self—and in then trying to make a cosmic principle of being apart. Ironically, it does this in communities, which its members enter to avoid both aloneness and involvement. By dispersing the claims on emotion through a large group of people, an even sense of good fellowship can prevail with minimal personal commitment. The group can be left, re-entered, abandoned with no particular sense of strain. Community has become the television of the counterculture, serving the same need that Americans of fewer radical pretensions fill by keeping the tube running, even when they're not watching, just to have "someone" around the house.

If the counterculture has rejected grades, authority, the nuclear family, it has thus carried over from the straight world psychological transience, the fragmentation of lives, immersion in abstractions, self-indulgence, and an atomistic version of individual growth. And it would face the greatest difficulty in trying to move beyond these. First, because a system has been constructed where the least prevails. No communal sharing of selves and work can rise far above the aspirations of the least willing to give, and the movement has been diluted by thousands of hustlers and media-struck newcomers with more interest in ripping off the counterculture than in salvaging its abortive moves to community. Second, the counterculture's mobility keeps any group from remaining together long enough to build the attitudes and learn the skills necessary for a true alternative. People will continue to move into the counterculture, savor its partial freedoms, and move out again; but the movement already shows signs of fatigue. And as an agent for radical transformation of people's lives, the counterculture is dead.

What this country needs is a good *counter* counterculture culture. The danger instead is of a reaction that would obliterate much of what the counterculture has done without moving beyond. If nothing else, the energies of the young could dissipate through a movement that cannot provide answers, leaving only a sense of hopelessness and apathy. We would be back where we were a decade ago. It would be a shame; for even in failing, those in the movement have given us much. Many of their negative insights into the straight world were correct, for example. Their parents *were* living a life of senseless frenzy, indiscriminately accumulating money and power and divorces and ulcers, doing untold violence along the way to their children, the blacks, the environment, the world. And if the counterculture forgot to leave behind the basic attitudes that made all this carnage possible, perhaps we will know better on the next attempt.

What should the next try be like? There is no blueprint, but here at least are some qualities that might be built in: Material sharing. Sharing of selves. Something of the African sense of the world as existing *here, now*. Something of the African sense of "here" being related to "there," of "now" being related to "then." A minimum of verbiage. Productive work, done together. Knowing the names of birds and trees. Things like that. And maybe work should be the starting point. Rather than innovate, those in the counterculture preferred to support themselves within the patterns allowed by the straight world: welfare, odd jobs, checks from parents. It is hardly surprising that they stayed so close to home psychologically as well. To build truly alternative communities, however, will require working units that are radically different from, and maybe even independent of, the straight economy.

Nobody knows how to do it yet, but we at least know some of the problems to be solved—problems the counterculture never even got around to posing. What kinds of work bring people together instead of forcing them apart? How can we adapt sophisticated technologies to relatively small groups of people working in community? Can the income from such work be distributed on the basis of need, rather than wealth or output? Can we develop principles for exchanging goods among producing units that do not simply copy the exploitative ones of the larger culture? What patterns of shared services, or cooperation generally, can be evolved between community groups? The list goes on and on, but it has to be tackled. Instead of being quite so self-congratulatory about alternatives in style (or even consciousness), we now need a commitment to explore alternatives in all of the areas that make up life.

The job is made all the harder by the lack of historical precedent. Early communal experiments in this country and elsewhere were based on simple methods of farming and small-scale industry; solutions will differ where a more advanced technology is available. Even the Israeli collectives, the closest existing parallel to what we seek, have been so distorted by more than half a century of nationalistic struggle against an external enemy that the relevance to us of what they have done is not clear. And the nearest thing to a theoretical framework for community-based development—anarchism—has always been far enough from being applied in practice that its specifics of social and economic organization are few. If there are invaluable lessons to be learned from all these sources (though not by the counterculture, which refuses as a matter of principle to examine them), we are ultimately confronted by the need to come up with new answers, relevant to the people and technology of America today. . .

LOOKING BACKWARD

Andrew Kopkind

Andrew Kopkind has been a frequent contributor to liberal and radical journals. His articles have appeared in the New Republic, *the* New York Review of Books, *and* Ramparts. *His own commitments were expressed when, hailing in 1969 the reality of a new culture of opposition, he wrote of the "disintegration of the old forms, the vinyl and aerosol institutions that carry all the inane and destructive values of privatism, competition, commercialism, profitability and elitism"* (Current, *p. 59, 1969). He is now a free-lance journalist.*

I have some scattered papers before me: "An Interracial Movement of the Poor," by Tom Hayden and Carl Wittman; "The Triple Revolution"; "Prospectus for Organizing Project in Boston Suburbs"; *The Port Huron Statement.* They've been buried near the bottom of a file of documents I used to save under the catch-all heading, "Movement." The file was in a cardboard box that turned up recently among possessions I had stored in some dark cellar three moves ago. Or was it four?

It may be that re-reading the accumulated verbal effluent of a decade of social upheaval and political movement will help me make sense of the times, draw a proper analysis, develop a basis for clear prediction. We need maps. What route connects Port Huron, Woodstock and Attica? Selma, Altamont and Eleventh Street? Orangeburg, Kent State and Columbia? Where do the roads start, and where are they leading? If I were so inclined, I could spend a lifetime burrowing through these papers. There is certainly enough to read. But movements composed largely of students and intellectuals employ the typewriter and mimeograph as other movements have used the gun and bomb—for defense as well as terror; and the menacing weight of written words deflects and intimidates me.

My own approach to understanding the decadal history is, at this late date, experiential, personal, self-analytical. It's true that there are immense perils in relying on one's own life and mind as a guide to the march of time. But history, after all, is a problem of consciousness (Hegel agrees with me), and the only consciousness I know personally sees with my eyes, touches with my hands, feels with my heart. I don't want to extrapolate from my *behavior;* the action of others is far more significant, worthy, far-reaching. But my experience of history is as valid as anyone's in this world, or the Second, Third or Fourth Worlds—no more, no less—and I'm compelled to take it from there.

These musings are prompted, in part, from a recent reading of Tom Hayden's interim memoirs in *Rolling Stone* (print freaks just cannot stop reading; we need help). Hayden's survey of the New Left—ten years after he co-wrote *Port Huron*—is most real when it grows out of his own experience: the "shambles" of the Left after Chicago 1968, the fantastic logic of Weatherman after the "failure" of unarmed struggle. Hayden is at his least convincing when he fails to connect ideas with his life; for example, he attempts to fit feminism and communalism into abstract categories of thought, rather than see the actuality of those ideas in his own history at the Red Family collective. It can't be that correct ideas come from social practice only *sometimes.*

Hayden's reminiscences mean a lot to me, because he was one of a few people by, with or against whom I was "radicalized" in the mid-'60s. We all have our war stories now. I was softened up in the South of the civil rights movement—at a safe but sensitive distance. Soon thereafter, I wandered into Hayden's ghetto organizing project in the Clinton Hill section of Newark. I blanch now (so to speak) at the memory of lily-white kids "organizing" the black poor for some elusive seizure, or creation, of community power. Whatever that project didn't do for the black people of Newark, it did a lot for the white youths who went through it, saw it, heard about it. I spent a short time at the Newark project, as a well-kempt liberal journalist, in the same way that I had visited sites of other political and social "stories" I was covering. But this was no simple story. I felt things in Newark that had a strange and disruptive effect on my life. There were people very much like myself working in ways that drastically shrunk the distance between themselves and "others"—their co-workers and their community. Their commitment to a common cause cut into the loneliness of work, which I had always assumed was inevitable. The isolation I thought I'd always feel from people in another class or another race was not, after all, immutable. I had a glimpse, from a corner of my mind's eye, of how things could be different. Liberals spend their lives looking for victims whom they can pity; here were people looking for soldiers with whom they could fight. In that intense mood, I fantasized an end to alienation, despair, emptiness. I wanted to shout out loud, never go home, hug people, love everybody in Clinton Hill.

At length, of course, I went home, backsliding all the way, but I could never return completely to the mind-set of liberal journalism. Clinton Hill was always there. For many of my friends in that generation, Tom Hayden remained a touchstone in our lives. . . . Years afterwards, when pondering a political or existential decision, I would flash on Hayden and guess what he'd say, or think, or do. . . .

It may be some kind of sin to personalize the process of political change; no doubt I was long ago consigned to that brim-stoned Hell where languish all bourgeois intellectuals who insist on reading history as the chronicle of their own exquisitely tortured and infinitely fascinating psyches. Would it be more correct to say that radicalization of certain middle-class youth in the '60s was occasioned by the interplay of contradictions in post-scarcity capitalist society? I've written that, and I believe it. But I have very narrow visions of history, too: fleeting shots of fears, faces, pain, insights, anger by which I can relate everyday experiences to social theory.

It took a while for "the New Left" to penetrate the popular political vocabulary, by which time it had lost most of its meaning. It's funny to hear Justice Department officials calling current radical specimens "New Leftists," in the way that stodgy newspapers still call hippy freaks "Beatniks." If the "New Left" had specific meaning as a political category, it referred to a rather small group of white and black students and post-students committed to radical Socialist reformism, who were working from about 1961 to 1966. . . .

The New Left then had half a dozen foci: race relations, industrial democracy, militarism and war, educational bureaucracy, and the welfare system. It grew alongside the Kennedy/Johnson programs of managerial liberalism, and while it always maintained a critical distance, it had springs in many of the same places. For instance, Michael Harrington, whose popular book, *The Other America,* promoted poverty as a problem, was a leading member—and later chief—of the League for Industrial Democracy, the biologic parent of SDS.

No one in the New Left in those days had much to say about class revolution, or Third World revolution, or black revolution. Indeed, we almost entirely avoided the word "revolution." I worked for the liberal weekly magazine *The New Republic* in the mid-'60s, and I had contacts with both intellectual and activist Leftists. During that period, there was a recognizable, upper-case M, identifiable "Movement": a single, if shadowy, integrated political consciousness that could embrace the ideas of blacks and whites, women and men, First and Third Worlds, straights and gays, students and non-students. Only later was it obvious that the terms of that consciousness were dominated by the First World-white-straight-male-students.

Although tensions had been building for years, the first overt break in the unitary New Left Movement came with the Black Power revolt in the spring and summer of 1966. Many whites had been working with "peace candidates" in Congressional primaries that spring, and had lost touch with the Southern branch of the Movement from where most had come. Then attention shifted to the "Meredith March" in Mississippi—and the SNCC people's clenched fists. It was a decisive, definitive trauma. Abbie Hoffman wrote a kiss-off letter to his wayward black Movement comrades and published it in the *Village Voice:* good-bye you ornery ingrates. The New York white "radicals" were angry, confused, hurt.

It's easy to smile now at the naïveté of Movement whites in those years, and condemn the racism. But it was genuinely painful for whites to see their comrades depart into the murky world of segregated revolution. "Stokely's Advice"—that white radicals should organize white America to destroy racism[1] was wise and correct, but it did not heal the pain of lost comradeship, a common cause fragmented. The amazing integration of the SDS community organizing projects—of the Clinton Hill "community union" —was an illusion, at last, perpetrated by white kids and believed by blacks.

Similar scenarios, involving women, Third World radicals, gays, workers—and later, Left factions and sects—were enacted scores of times after the Black Power split. In each case, the dominant sector registered pain, confusion, a sense of loss; the dominated sector replied with anger, pride, confidence. In that way, the Movement became many movements, the consequences of many perceptions of evil, different classes, separate needs. The coalitions that now form on one or another issue—the war, prisons, GIs—do not have the integrated consciousness of the New Left Movement, the unifying analysis of oppression, the assumed shape of reform that emerged from Mississippi and Port Huron.

It wasn't until 1967 that many white radicals began to speak of "revolution," or "the Revolution," and the press began to treat the notion seriously, if always incredulously. The rhetorical escalation preceded—or took the place of—the establishment of any conditions that could reasonably be called revolutionary. Not that it has been a flight of fancy; but the *shape* of "revolution" in America in the last few years has never been drawn. It remains an undefined idea. The rhetoric began, I think, in response to the increased militancy of the black movement and in relation to the ties binding American radicals to "the Vietnamese." . . .

Tom Hayden and Staughton Lynd were the first "non-Communist" political activists to be invited to wartime Hanoi—in 1965. After that, sporadic contacts between SDS and Our Friends in Vietnam took place in hospitable quarters of the globe. Then a full-scale, sit-down, dress-up conference between New Left and NLF/North Vietnamese delegations took place in Bratislava, Czechoslovakia, in September 1967. . . .

---

[1] Editor's note: See above, pp. 223–32.

The Bratislava Conference was a lopsided affair, with responsible, well-informed Vietnamese meeting 30 friends of Tom Hayden, chosen at random. *Their* side was led by Madame Binh and Mr. Vy, now negotiators in Paris; *our* side included the usual cross-section of the movements—a few blacks and women, one verifiable Welfare Mother, Dave Dellinger, and several stoned underground-newspaper editors. Since I was travelling in the right set for all the exotic junkets, I was invited too. But much of the conference seems to me now a dim blur. . . . The one indelible memory that remains is of a private meeting with Madame Binh. . . . We sat for an hour and talked, first in French for the small-talk, then in English and Vietnamese—interpreted—for the heavy stuff. But what was it all about? I remember only my fantasies: I was to be appointed a master spy, I was to visit the Liberated Zones, I was to receive the Revolutionary Word. None of the above happened. I did get one of those rings made of scrap aluminum from an American plane shot down over North Vietnam. But the result, of course, was that I was no longer merely "against the war," but struggling in solidarity with Vietnamese revolutionaries. Another flash: distance obliterated—struggle and liberation. Exaggerated or attenuated, that experience was replicated for many Americans in the years that followed—and reinforced for me by a visit to Hanoi in 1968. The one problem, of course, was what I, or anyone, was supposed to do with this new sense of revolutionary solidarity. Nothing that young Americans were doing (that is, nothing that seemed possible for me) seemed appropriate to the comradeship entrusted to us. And simply feeling guilty was, as people used to say, a stone drag.

With black revolution raging in America and world revolution directed against America, it was hardly possible for white radicals to think themselves anything less than revolutionaries. There was no broad base for revolution in America in the late '60s, but we acted as if there were. We still had no shape in mind: some examples, no models. But perhaps our apocalyptic prophecies would be self-fulfilling; wishing might make it so. The vast anomic suburbs, brimming with Marcusian contradictions, would explode any day now. Students would soon drop out of their schools and intellectuals would flee their professions *en masse* to join the revolution. Surely, someone must be organizing the working class, the blacks, the Chicanos; it would all come together.

Like many others who had experienced the history of the New Left from civil rights to community organizing to anti-war activism, I played out the last logical number on that set in Weatherland in 1969. I had missed the Chicago Democratic Days the previous year (I was in Prague again—as the Russian tanks rumbled into town), but had caught the act in Paris in May-June: a few nights in the streets, *continuez le combat,* then back to the USSA. In August there was Woodstock; in October, the Days of Rage. It seemed like two sides of the same coin. I went to Woodstock and got stoned, went to Chicago and got busted. When I had paid my fine and returned home, I joined with several other "older" political friends and formed what became known affectionately as a "geriatric Weather-symp" collective. We called ourselves the High Pressure Front. We ran in one big demonstration, performed the absolute minimum of trashing for a group of such revolutionary pretensions, and decided *not* to get any closer to the frightening center of the Weather machine.

As the organized Left split into bitterly antagonistic factions, we clung to what we felt to be the thematic heritage of the early '60s New Left, the idealistic, gentle, Dylan-singing friends who were in Newark, Cleveland's West Side project, Uptown in Chicago. . . . All journalistic milestones are suspect, but let one stand: the Greenwich Village "townhouse" explosion, which killed three Weatherpeople, signaled the end of the logical progression of "New Left" movements. There certainly have been actions and movements since, but they seem to belong to a different progression, like animal strains descending from different ancestors. The "Kent State/ Cambodia" strike, which came a few months after Eleventh Street, was enormous and somehow important, but not as a "Movement" event—rather, in spite of the movements. May Day in 1971 had overtones of the old numbers, but it was something different—a militant coalition without antecedents or consequences. Since Che uttered his famous phrase, "Dos, tres, muchos Vietnam!" the Left has suffered from repetition fallacy. Two, three, many Berkeleys; two, three, many Chicagos; two, three, many May Days. It doesn't work (Che's advice hasn't been followed very successfully, either).

The Weather Underground continued after the townhouse explosion, as active bombers for a year, then as "New Morning" culture freaks. I get excited when they pull off an action, I hope they keep at it, but I'm not sure why. I don't see where it will lead. Perhaps for everybody this is more or less a time to hold on. Coalitions form and dissolve; they make their gains, or losses, and serve to keep alive both the reality and the illusion of a Left, a movement in an ambulatory coma waiting for a revolutionary kiss to bring it to life again.

The mood I feel most often from people who think of themselves "in the movements" is entrenchment—not despair or surrender (although there's enough of that), but digging in. Digging into residential communities, into working places, into tolerable and tolerant jobs, into research, into hip media, into communal life, into self-understanding. Four or five years ago someone made up a series of titles for the predicament of the New Left: "From Lenin to Lennon," "From Kark Marx to Groucho," "From Base to Acid." Some of those jokes are being reversed. The generation of the '70s is not only post-Weatherman and post-Attica, but post-acid: after the Rock.

My own street fighting days were followed by total bafflement about the Left. I still went to "events," like May Day 1970 in New Haven, and the Washington "Honor America Day" Yippie freak-out and smoke-in. But I couldn't understand discussions about strategy and theory, and even the events ceased to make sense outside of the hours of action. Politics as exhilaration is nice until it ceases to be exhilarating. Soon I found myself reading mysticism instead of Marxism, breathing hallucinogenic fumes instead of tear gas, worrying about one-pointedness instead of political consciousness. Even an existence in an urban political environment became unbearable, and I slipped off to a commune in Vermont. . . .

Communal life-arrangements are probably as transitory as any others of this era, but they do push forward an aspect of the movements of the '60s that was neglected after Weatherman: the way in which people can understand the power they exert over their fellows. That had been a central issue in the crack-up of the New Left, but it was never successfully resolved. Weather collectives made a daring (and somewhat disastrous) attempt to reduce so radically the distance between their members that a group could operate as a single organism. When I first had seen Weatherpeople moving in a crowd—as the Chicago Conspiracy trial opened in late September 1969 —I was amazed at the obvious lines of unspoken communication that passed between members. It was as if they were carrying spirit walkie-talkies to keep in touch. As it turned out, much of that closeness was based on guilt-tripping, gut-checking and power-laying, and the Weather collectives fell under the weight of un-collectivized egos.

But from that time, less hectic communal and collective styles developed, in which the elements of power and the aspects of ego could be contested. At our rural commune there was as much talk about sex roles and life definitions as there was about farming. It snowed a great deal that first winter in Vermont (coldest in the century, the snowplow driver said) and we spent most of it talking around the woodstove: about who we were, and how we knew each other, and how we made our demands known and our needs felt. City folks would sometimes come up for R and R and after a few hours of chit-chat tell us we were immoral for isolating ourselves in woodland retreats while workers, black people, prisoners, Vietnamese . . . All true, but at that time beside the point. There *was* no point in running in circles for the wretched of the earth. That kind of course did nobody any good. It is useless to pretend that we can deal with social class if we do not comprehend the feelings engendered by privilege; or deal with sexism if we cannot feel the pain of sexual oppression; or organize others if we can only hear ourselves talk.

I find myself back in a city, going to demonstrations, writing, poking around organizing projects, hoping. The New Left and the movements that it spawned did not change America yet in most of the ways it would have wanted; but it did provide the groundwork for a culture in which its members could exist. Life in that culture is not entirely satisfactory, which encourages us to perfect it. There is an infrastructure of institutions based on Left consciousness which lets us do that work: media, political organizations, educational institutions, living places. We have our own Underground to enliven our dreary days with fantasies. We know we're real because we are being repressed, harassed, hounded. But not so much that we will disappear. People wait for a new organization, a pre-party, a party—to appear, as the strikers waited for Lefty, or as they waited for Godot.

Dialectics, at least, denies nostalgia: it's not the '50s, because it cannot be. It feels to me like a waiting time, and although suspension is a form of torture, there's not much to be done but to get into it. Having finished with the politics of fantasy and having rejected the politics of despair, the only prospect now is hope.

16

Drugs: The Magic Passkey

The catalyst in the transvaluation of bourgeois values essayed by large numbers of the discontented is the hallucinogenic drug, mild or strong. Drugs are, of course, an ancient device for escaping reality. However, we now confront the burgeoning use of such drugs, calling for new decisions about their use and abuse. Such decisions, including those we make about the sanctions to invoke against the use of drugs, can hardly be intelligent unless we know something about drugs.

In the case of the so-called "hard" drugs such as cocaine and the opium derivatives (e.g., heroin, morphine) there is no disagreement about their harmfulness. The hard drugs are admittedly addictive. This means, according to the World Health Organization: "(1) An overpowering desire or need (compulsion) to continue taking the drug and to obtain it by any means; (2) a tendency to increase the dose; (3) a psychic (psychological) and generally a physical dependence on the effects of the drug; (4) an effect detrimental to the individual and society."

On the other hand, the nature of the detrimental effect is subject to much misconception. For example, competent authorities agree that the heroin addict is not aroused by the drug he takes and transformed into the "dope fiend" and rapist-killer of popular folklore; opium is a depressant tending to dull sexual appetite and reduce violent behavior. Criminal behavior generally occurs when the addict is not under the influence of the drug but desperately needs money for a new dose. Contrary to popular opinion, there are no known organic diseases associated with opiate addiction as there are with heavy smoking and alcohol. The crucial question is how to curb addiction without encouraging the crime that occurs when drugs are bootlegged at artificially high prices.

Notable among the nonaddictive mind-altering drugs are marihuana, a mild hallucinogen derived from the hemp plant (cannabis sativa), and LSD-25 (lysergic acid diethylamide), which is now easily synthesized and is enormously potent. Marihuana (also variously called grass, pot, Mary Jane, tea, etc., and closely related to hashish, which is a stronger derivative of the same plant), while it may cause psychological dependency, does not induce withdrawal symptoms, nor do users develop a tolerance such that increasingly larger doses must be taken to produce the same effect. This is also true of LSD (although researchers report that some users do develop a tolerance).

The use of such hallucinogens has increased enormously within the last few years and experience with marihuana, once limited to fringe groups (beatniks, jazz musicians) and segregated ethnic minorities, is increasingly common among otherwise conventional, middle-class young people in quest of "kicks" and scorning as old-fashioned their elders' reliance on alcohol. More U.S. servicemen in Vietnam were arrested for smoking marihuana than for any other single major offense. The use of LSD is far less common if only because its sheer potency frightens off many would-be users, and those who venture on an LSD "trip" are less likely to be in quest of euphoria than are marihuana users. The power of LSD is, indeed, quite frightening: one authority reports that a two-suiter luggage piece could contain enough LSD to incapacitate the entire population of the United States.[1]

It is important to emphasize that, unlike most drug users, the so-called psychedelic who has recourse to the stronger psychochemicals (LSD and the weaker peyote or mescaline) is as a rule not hedonistically motivated. To overlook this is to miss the distinctive feature of the "movement," with its missionary quality and cult-like overtones. Most psychedelics claim not to be in search of pleasure, but of "understanding" through self-exploration, new experience, a sense of "oneness" with the universe, etc. The movement's onetime high-priest was Dr. Timothy Leary (not to mention a poet laureate, Allen Ginsberg) for whom the psychedelic drug meant "ecstasy, sensual unfolding, religious experience, revelation, illumination, contact with nature." Leary, now in prison, was quite undaunted by the vagueness and magnitude of the goal or the hazards of encouraging (albeit with an experienced guide) use of an

---

[1] Sidney Cohen, *The Beyond Within: The LSD Story* (New York: Atheneum, 1964), p. 231.

easily manufactured chemical so powerful that the slightest over-dose could produce disastrous consequences. Neither was he worried about the loss of motivation and lapse of interest in their normal social ties and usual occupations which characterize the "psychedelic dropouts." ("It's nothing to worry about; it's something to cheer.") His slogan was "Turn on, tune in, drop out," the import of which is to "detach yourself from the tribal game" and escape our "air-conditioned anthill." Leary rejected as unreliable a survey cited by *Time* finding 200 victims of bad trips in Los Angeles hospitals, as he does the conclusion of Dr. Jonathan Cole of the National Institute of Mental Health that psychedelic drugs "can be dangerous . . . People get into panic states in which they are ready to jump out of their skins . . . The benefits are obscure."

As everyone knows, the popularity of marihuana has increased enormously in recent years. Unfortunately, it is difficult to find in the voluminous literature on marihuana an intellectually respectable criticism that comes to grips with the really basic and overriding issue. Suppose, as may well be the case, that marihuana were as free of disadvantages and as superior to alcohol as its apologists claim it to be: no hazard to health from overuse, no hangover, no drain on a poor man's purse. Or, to avoid the legacy of controversy about marihuana, suppose that chemists were able to develop a cheap, completely harmless euphoriant. This is surely a theoretical possibility; the science of psychopharmacology is, after all, only in its infancy. In his *Brave New World* Aldous Huxley described such a drug, used by the dictatorship to keep the man in the street happy, which he called *soma.* Two questions at once suggest themselves, one psychological, the other moral: (1) Would most people avail themselves of such a drug? (2) How should we evaluate the consequences if they did? It could well be that the very virtues of a perfect euphoriant—and therefore, to a lesser degree, of marihuana—are paradoxically its real danger.

Satisfaction is usually purchased with effort, not merely in the obvious sense that most of us have to work in order to have the satisfaction of eating or living with a roof over our heads, but because in most circumstances (from which not even the rich are exempt) satisfaction is a concomitant of the successful pursuit of ends. We have enjoyment, satisfaction, gratification, whatever we choose to call it, when we have objectives and are able to encompass them, when, as Aristotle would have said, we realize ourselves. Such self-realization normally requires effort. And all such effort in its totality accounts for what we call civilization.

Suppose now that our cheap euphoriant were at hand with all its virtues. Since we have not claimed that it would also be an analgesic we would at least have to bestir ourselves to avoid the pain of hunger and exposure. Would we seek more than simple fare and shelter or, thanks to our euphoriant, live contentedly at a subsistence level? And, if we failed to seek more, what would the moral difference be? "It is better," J. S. Mill said, "to be a human being dissatisfied than a pig satisfied; better to be Socrates dissatisfied than a fool satisfied." Clearly Mill had no doubt about the moral difference. But a new breed of sybarites might respond, as exiles from the "straight" world in effect answer, that they would rather live like pigs than be caught in the "rat-race." That this attitude, if universal, would mean the decay of all culture, does not deter the committed "user." By dwelling exclusively on the defects of our culture he can find his rationalization in the charge that we have nothing worth saving.

Some light may be thrown on the question by Dr. C. J. Miras of the University of Athens who has observed chronic marihuana smokers in Greece for 20 years—much longer, according to UCLA drug experts, than American researchers. He reports that many of his subjects who were teachers and artists left their work for other jobs, but preferred most of all "to sleep and talk philosophy." One wonders if they "talked philosophy" or engaged in verbal reverie; the two are sometimes confused. As a state of vague and dreamy meditation the latter is not far from sleep. Pigs, we may suppose, do not engage in reverie, and yet one may well wonder if the state of torpor of which it is a variant is much different from the condition of porcine contentment eschewed by Mill.

As noted earlier, the effects of marihuana, LSD, and the hard drugs in general are widely disparate, and the motives of marihuana and LSD users are often quite different. It is therefore difficult to deal with them under the same rubric. The discussions below are limited to excerpts from an official report on the assumption that in the present climate of opinion the reader will be best served by a statement that both friends and foes of the punitive laws now in effect are bound to respect—although some advocates of the laws we have seem determined to respect nothing except demands for stiffer penalties. Meanwhile the reader may marvel at our inability to decide whether marihuana is a vicious scourge, an innocuous folk euphoriant, cheaper and less harmful than alcohol and tobacco, or possibly neither. At present our law is on the side of those who believe the first.

SOCIAL POLICY AND DRUG ABUSE[1]

National Commission on Marihuana and Drug Abuse

Established by Congress in 1970, the National Commission on Marihuana and Drug Abuse[2] has issued two lengthy reports entitled Marihuana: A Signal of Misunderstanding (*1972*) *and* Drug Use in America: Problem in Perspective (*1973*).[3] *The focus of the latter is on hard drugs. Mere excerpts from the reports are bound to do them an injustice; the interested reader should by all means consult the full text. Whatever one may think of the final recommendations of the commission, it must be said that the commissioners are fair and deliberate in their approach, and the reports do indeed achieve the "tone of cautious restraint" to which the commissioners say they aspired. The reports are heavily documented, different points of view have been solicited, and they are happily free of the emotionalism characteristic of earlier studies. Thus, even though the report of the commission reflects a point of view, it provides ample basis for a balanced discussion in the absence of the spectrum of viewpoints that would be included were space to permit.*

A constant tension exists in our society between individual liberties and the need for reasonable societal restraints. It is easy to go too far in either direction, and this tendency is particularly evident where drugs are concerned.

We have guided our decision-making by the belief that the state is obliged to justify restraints on individual behavior. Too often individual freedoms are submerged in the passions of the moment, and when that happens, the public policy may be determined more by rhetoric than by reason. Our effort has been to minimize the emotional and emphasize the rational in this Report.

---

[1] Excerpts from *Marihuana: A Signal of Misunderstanding* (1972). Superintendent of Documents, U.S. Government Printing Office, Washington, D.C.

[2] Commission members: Chairman Raymond Philip Shafer (Governor of Pennsylvania); Vice-chairman Dana L. Farnsworth, M.D.; T. L. Carter (Congressman, Kentucky); Joan Ganz Cooney; C. J. Galvin, S.J.D.; J. A. Howard, Ph.D.; Harold E. Hughes (Senator, Iowa); Jacob Javits (Senator, New York); Paul G. Rogers (Congressman, Florida); M. H. Seevers, M.D., Ph.D.; J. T. Ungerleider, M.D.; Mitchell Ware, J.D.

[3] Superintendent of Documents, U.S. Government Printing Office, Washington, D.C.

A free society seeks to provide conditions in which each of its members may develop his or her potentialities to the fullest extent. A premium is placed on individual choice in seeking self-fulfillment. This priority depends upon the capacity of free citizens not to abuse their freedom, and upon their willingness to act responsibly toward others and toward the society as a whole. Responsible behavior, through individual choice, is both the guarantor and the objective of a free society.

The use of drugs is not in itself an irresponsible act. Medical and scientific uses serve important individual and social needs and are often essential to our physical and mental well-being. Further, the use of drugs for pleasure or other non-medical purposes is not inherently irresponsible; alcohol is widely used as an acceptable part of social activities.

We do think the use of drugs is clearly irresponsible when it impedes the individual's integration into the economic and social system. A preference for individual productivity and contribution to social progress in a general sense still undergirds the American value structure, and we emphasize the policy-maker's duty to support this preference in a public policy judgment.

At the same time, in light of the emerging leisure ethic and the search for individual meaning and fulfillment . . . we cannot divorce social policy from the questions raised by the recreational use of drugs. Productivity and recreation both have a place in the American ethical system. They are not inconsistent unless the individual's use of leisure time inhibits his productive role in society.

Drugs should be servants, not masters. They become masters when they dominate an individual's existence or impair his faculties. To the extent that any drug, including alcohol, carries with it risks to the well-being of the user and seriously undermines his effectiveness in the society, that drug becomes a matter of concern for public policy.

An essential step in the process of policy-formation is a determination of the circumstances under which use of any given drug poses such risks. For some drugs, the risks may be so great that all permissible measures should be taken to eliminate use. For other drugs, such risks may be present only under certain specific circumstances, in which case society may defer to responsible individual choice on the matter of recreational use but take appropriate steps to minimize the incidence and consequences of dysfunctional use. . . .

In formulating a marihuana policy, our strongest concern is with irresponsible use, whether it be too often, too much, indiscriminate, or under improper circumstances. The excessive or indiscriminate use of any drug is a serious social concern; and this is particularly true of marihuana since we still know very little about the effects of long-term, heavy use. We have little doubt that the substantial majority of users, under any social control policy, including the existing system, do not and would not engage in irresponsible behavior.

In identifying the appropriate social control policy for marihuana, we have found it helpful to consider the following policy options:

    I   Approval of Use.
    II   Elimination of Use.
    III Discouragement of Use.
    IV Neutrality Toward Use.

Approval of Use

Society should not approve or encourage the recreational use of *any* drug, in public or private. Any semblance of encouragement enhances the possibility of abuse and removes, from a psychological standpoint, an effective support of individual restraint.

For example, so long as this society (not only the government, but other institutions and mass advertising as well) in effect approved of the use of tobacco, the growing medical consensus about the dangers of excessive use did not make a significant impression on individual judgment. With the Surgeon General's Report on Tobacco in 1964, *Smoking and Health,* a very real change has occurred in the way society now thinks about cigarettes.

The institutions of society definitely add their influences to the variety of social pressures which persuade individuals to use any kind of drugs. Rational social policy should seek to minimize such social pressures, whether they come from peers, from the media, from social custom, or from the user's sense of inadequacy. Official approval would inevitably encourage some people to use the drug who would not otherwise do so, and would also increase the incidence of heavy or otherwise irresponsible use and its complications. On this basis we reject policy option number one, approval of use.

Elimination of Use

For a half-century, official social policy has been not only to discourage use but to eliminate it (option number two). With the principal responsibility for this policy assigned to law enforcement, its implementation reached its zenith in the late 1950's and early 1960's when marihuana-related offenses were punishable by long periods of incarceration. This policy grew out of a distorted and greatly exaggerated concept of the drug's ordinary effects upon the individual and the society. On the basis of information then available, marihuana was not adequately distinguished from other problem drugs and was assumed to be as harmful as the others.

The increased incidence of use, intensive scientific reevaluation, and the spread of use to the middle and upper socioeconomic groups have brought about the informal adoption of a modified social policy. On the basis of our opinion surveys and our empirical studies of law enforcement behavior, we are convinced that officialdom and the public are no longer as punitive toward marihuana use as they once were.

Now there exists a more realistic estimate of the actual social impact of marihuana use. School and university administrators are seldom able to prevent the use of marihuana by their students and personnel and are increasingly reluctant to take disciplinary action against users. Within the criminal justice system, there has been a marked decline in the severity of the response to offenders charged with possession of marihuana.

In our survey of state enforcement activities, only 11% of all marihuana arrests resulted from active investigative activity, and most of those were in sale situations. For the most part, marihuana enforcement is a haphazard process; arrests occur on the street, in a park, in a car, or as a result of a phone call. Among those arrested, approximately 50% of the adults and 70% of the juveniles are not processed through the system; their cases are dismissed by the police, by the prosecutors or by the courts. Ultimately less than 6% of all those apprehended are incarcerated, and very few of these sentences are for possession of small amounts for personal use.

In the law enforcement community, the major concern is no longer marihuana but the tendency of some users to engage in other irresponsible activity, particularly the use of more dangerous drugs. Official sentiment now seems to be a desire to contain use of the drug as well as the drug subculture, and to minimize its spread to the rest of the youth population. Law enforcement policy, both at the Federal and State levels, implicitly recognizes that elimination is impossible at this time.

The active attempt to suppress all marihuana use has been replaced by an effort to keep it within reasonable bounds. Yet because this policy still reflects a view that marihuana smoking is itself destructive enough to justify punitive action against the user, we believe it is an inappropriate social response.

Marihuana's relative potential for harm to the vast majority of individual users and its actual impact on society does not justify a social policy designed to seek out and firmly punish those who use it. This judgment is based on prevalent use patterns, on behavior exhibited by the vast majority of users and on our interpretations of existing medical and scientific data. This position also is consistent with the estimate by law enforcement personnel that the elimination of use is unattainable.

In the case of experimental or intermittent use of marihuana, there is room for individual judgment. Some members of our society believe the decision to use marihuana is an immoral decision. However, even during Prohibition, when many people were concerned about the evils associated with excessive use of alcohol, possession of personal use was never outlawed federally and was made illegal in only five States.

Indeed, we suspect that the moral contempt in which some of our citizens hold the marihuana user is related to other behavior or other attitudes assumed to be associated with use of the drug. All of our data suggest that the moral views of the overwhelming majority of marihuana users are in general accord with those of the larger society.

Having previously rejected the approval policy (option number one), we now reject the eliminationist policy (option number two). This policy, if taken seriously, would require a great increase in manpower and resources in order to eliminate the use of a drug which simply does not warrant that kind of attention.

Discouragement or Neutrality

The unresolved question is whether society should try to dissuade its members from using marihuana or should defer entirely to individual judgment in the matter, remaining benignly neutral. We must choose between policies of discouragement (number three) and neutrality (number four). This choice is a difficult one and forces us to consider the limitations of our knowledge and the dynamics of social change. A number of considerations, none of which is conclusive by itself, point at the present time toward a discouragement policy. We will discuss each one of them separately.

Alcohol and tobacco have long been desired by large numbers within our society and their use is deeply ingrained in the American culture. Marihuana, on the other hand, has only recently achieved a significant foothold in the American experience, and it is still essentially used more by young people. Again, the unknown factor here is whether the sudden attraction to marihuana derives from its psychoactive virtues or from its symbolic status.

Throughout this Commission's deliberations there was a recurring awareness of the possibility that marihuana use may be a fad which, if not institutionalized, will recede substantially in time. Present data suggest that this is the case, and we do not hesitate to say that we would prefer that outcome. To the extent that conditions permit, society is well advised to minimize the number of drugs which may cause significant problems. By focusing our attention on fewer rather than more drugs, we may be better able to foster responsible use and diminish the consequences of irresponsible use.

The more prudent course seems to be to retain a social policy opposed to use, attempting to discourage use while at the same time seeking to deemphasize the issue. Such a policy leaves us with more options available when more definitive knowledge of the consequences of heavy and prolonged marihuana use becomes available.

In 1933 when Prohibition was repealed, society was cognizant of the effects of alcohol as a drug and the adverse consequences of abuse. But, because so many people wished to use the drug, policy-makers chose to run the risk of individual indiscretion and decided to abandon the abstentionist policy. There are many today who feel that if the social impact of alcohol use had then been more fully understood, a policy of discouragement rather than neutrality would have been adopted to minimize the negative aspects of alcohol use.

Misunderstanding also played an important part when the national government adopted an eliminationist marihuana policy in 1937. The policymakers knew very little about the effects or social impact of the drug; many of their hypotheses were speculative and, in large measure, incorrect.

Nevertheless, the argument that misinformation in 1937 automatically compels complete reversal of the action taken at that time is neither reasonable nor logical. While continuing concern about the effects of heavy, chronic use is not sufficient reason to maintain an overly harsh public policy, it is still a significant argument for choosing official discouragement in preference to official neutrality.

. . . two central influences in contemporary American life are the individual search for meaning within the context of an increasingly depersonalized society, and the collective search for enduring American values. . . . Society's present ambivalent response to marihuana use reflects these uncertainties.

. . . A sudden abandonment of an official policy of elimination in favor of one of neutrality toward marihuana would have a profound reverberating impact on social attitudes far beyond the one issue of marihuana use. We believe that society must have time to consider its image of the future. We believe that adoption of a discouragement policy toward marihuana at this time would facilitate such a reappraisal while official neutrality, under present circumstances, would impede it.

For whatever reasons, a substantial majority of the American public opposes the use of marihuana, and would prefer that their fellow citizens abstain from using it. In the National Survey, 64% of the adult public agreed with the statement that "using marihuana is morally offensive" (40% felt the same way about alcohol).

Although this majority opinion is not by any means conclusive, it cannot be ignored. We are well aware of the skepticism with which marihuana users, and those sympathetic to their wishes, view the policymaking process; and we are particularly concerned about the indifference to or disrespect for law manifested by many citizens and particularly the youth.

However, we are also apprehensive about the impact of a major change in social policy on that larger segment of our population which supports the implications of the existing social policy. They, too, might lose respect for a policy-making establishment which appeared to bend so easily to the wishes of a "lawless" and highly vocal minority.

This concern for minimizing cultural dislocation must, of course, be weighed against the relative importance of contrary arguments. For example, in the case of desegregation in the South, and now in the North, culture shock had to be accepted in the light of the fundamental precept at issue. In the case of marihuana, there is no fundamental principle supporting the use of the drug, and society is not compelled to approve or be neutral toward it. The opinion of the majority is entitled to greater weight.

Looking again to the experience with Prohibition, when an abstentionist policy for alcohol was adopted on the national level in 1918, its proponents were not blind to the vociferous opposition of a substantial minority of the people. By the late 1920's and early 1930's, the ambivalence of public opinion toward alcohol use and the unwillingness of large numbers of people to comply with the new social policy compelled reversal of that policy. Even many of its former supporters acknowledged its futility.

With marihuana, however, the prevailing policy of eliminating use had never been opposed to any significant degree until the mid-1960's. Unlike the prohibition of alcohol, which had been the subject of public debate off and on for 60 years before it was adopted, present marihuana policy has not until now engaged the public opinion process, some 50 years after it first began to be used. Majority sentiment does not appear to be as flexible as it was with alcohol.

Much of what was stated above bespeaks an acute awareness by the Commission of the subtleties of the collective consciousness of the American people, as shown in the National Survey. There is a legitimate concern about what the majority of the non-using population thinks about marihuana use and what the drug represents in the public mind. The question is appropriately asked if we are suggesting that the majority in a free society may impose its will on an unwilling minority even though, as it is claimed, uncertainty, speculation, and a large degree of misinformation form the basis of the predominant opinion. If we have nothing more substantial than this, the argument goes, society should remain neutral.

To deal with this contention, one must distinguish between ends and means. Policy-makers must choose their objectives with a sensitivity toward the entire social fabric and a vision of the good society. In such a decision, the general public attitude is a significant consideration. The preferred outcome in a democratic society cannot be that of the policy-makers alone; it must be that of an informed public. Accordingly, the policy-maker must consider the dynamic relationship between perception and reality in the public mind. Is the public consensus based on a real awareness of the facts? Does the public really understand what is at stake? Given the best evidence available, would the public consensus remain the same?

Assuming that dominant opinion opposes marihuana use, the philosophical issue is raised not by the goal but by how it is implemented. At this point, the interests of the unwilling become important. For example, the family unit and the institution of marriage are preferred means of group-living and child-rearing in our society. As a society, we are not neutral. We officially encourage matrimony by giving married couples favorable tax treatment; but we do not compel people to get married. If it should become public policy to try to reduce the birth rate, it is unlikely that there will be laws to punish those who exceed the preferred family size, although we may again utilize disincentives through the tax system. Similarly, this Commission believes society should continue actively to discourage people from using marihuana, and any philosophical limitation is relevant to the means employed, not to the goal itself.

FOR THESE REASONS, WE RECOMMEND TO THE PUBLIC AND ITS POLICY-MAKERS A SOCIAL CONTROL POLICY SEEKING TO DISCOURAGE MARIHUANA USE, WHILE CONCENTRATING PRIMARILY ON THE PREVENTION OF HEAVY AND VERY HEAVY USE.

We emphasize that this is a policy for today and the immediate future; we do not presume to suggest that this policy embodies eternal truth. Accordingly, we strongly recommend that our successor policy planners, at an appropriate time in the future, review the following factors to determine whether an altered social policy is in order: the state of public opinion, the extent to which members of the society continue to use the drug, the developing scientific knowledge about the effects and social impact of use of the drug, and the evolving social attitude toward the place of recreation and leisure in a work-oriented society. . . .

Choice of this social control policy does not automatically dictate any particular legal implementation. As we noted in Chapter I, there is a disturbing tendency among participants in the marihuana debate to assume that a given statement of the drug's effects, its number of users or its social impact compels a particular statutory scheme.

Law does not operate in a social vacuum, and it is only *one* of the institutional mechanisms which society can utilize to implement its policies. Consequently, the evaluation of alternative legal approaches demands not only logic but also a delicate assessment of the mutual relationship between the law and other institutions of social control, such as the church, the family and the school.

The Role of Law in Effective Social Control

Social control is most effectively guaranteed by the exercise of individual self-discipline. Elementary social psychology teaches us that restraint generated within is infinitely more effective and tenacious than restraint imposed from without. . . .

To this functional consideration of external restraint, we must also add the philosophical faith in the responsible exercise of individual judgment which is the essence of a free society. To illustrate, a preference for individual productivity underlies this society's opposition to indiscriminate drug use; the fact that so few of the 24 million Americans who have tried marihuana use it, or have used it, irresponsibly, testifies to the extent to which they have internalized that value.

The hypothesis that widespread irresponsibility would attend freer availability of marihuana suggests not that a restrictive policy is in order but rather that a basic premise of our free society is in doubt. We note that the escalation thesis, used as an argument *against* marihuana rather than as a tool for understanding individual behavior, is really a manifestation of skepticism about individual vulnerabilities. For example, one-half of the public agreed with the statement that "if marihuana were made legal, it would make drug addicts out of ordinary people."

At the same time, we do feel that the threat of excessive use is most potent with the young. In fact, we think *all* drug use should continue to be discouraged among the young, because of possible adverse effects on psychological development and because of the lesser ability of this part of the population to discriminate between limited and excessive use.

Social policy implementation in this regard is extraordinarily difficult. . . . The inclination of so many young people to experiment with drugs is a reflection of a so-called successful socialization process on one hand, and of society's ambivalence to the use of drugs on the other. . . .

This nation tries very hard to instill in its children independence, curiosity and a healthy self-assurance. These qualities guarantee a dynamic, progressive society. Where drugs are concerned, however, we have relied generally on authoritarianism and on obedience. Drug education has generally been characterized by overemphasis of scare tactics. Some segments of the population have been reluctant to inform for fear of arousing curiosity in young minds. Where drugs are concerned, young people are simply supposed to nod and obey.

This society has always been and continues to be ambivalent about the non-medical (in the strict sense) use of drugs. And this ambivalence does not escape our children. If we can come to grips with this issue, we might convince our youth that the curiosity that is encouraged in other aspects of our culture is undesirable where drugs are concerned.

The law is at best a highly imperfect reflection of drug policy. The laws proscribing sale of tobacco to minors are largely ignored. Prohibitions of sale of alcohol to minors are enforced sporadically. As to marihuana, there are areas throughout this nation where possession laws are not enforced at all. In other sections, such proscriptions are strictly enforced, with no apparent decrease in marihuana use.

As a guiding doctrine for parents and children, the law is certainly confusing when it imposes widely varying punishments in different states, and even in different courts of the same state, all for use of the same substance, marihuana. That marihuana use can be treated as a petty offense in one state and a felony in another is illogical and confusing to even the most sincere of parents.

The law is simply too blunt an instrument to manifest the subtle distinctions we draw between the motivations and the circumstances of use. At the same time, legal status carries a certain weight of its own, and other institutions must take account of the law in performing their functions.

In legally implementing our recommended social policy, we seek to maximize the ability of our schools, churches and families to be open and honest in discussing all drugs, including marihuana. The law must assist, not impede. In this respect, we note with concern the counterproductive tendency in our society to seek simple solutions to complex problems. Since the statutory law is a simple tool, the tendency in our society to look to the law for social control is particularly strong.

We have discussed the four basic social policy objectives of elimination, discouragement, neutrality and approval of marihuana use and have selected discouragement of use, with emphasis on prevention of heavy and very heavy use, as our generalized aim. We have considered three legal responses, each with a wide range of alternatives:

1. Total Prohibition.
2. Partial Prohibition.
3. Regulation.

Total Prohibition

The distinctive feature of a total prohibition scheme is that all marihuana-related behavior is prohibited by law. Under the total prohibition response now in force in every state and at the federal level, cultivation, importation, sale, gift or other transfer, and possession are all prohibited acts. In 11 states and the District of Columbia, simply being present knowingly in a place where marihuana is present is also prohibited; and many states prohibit the possession of pipes or other smoking paraphernalia. For our purposes, the key feature of the total prohibition approach is that even possession of a small amount in the home for personal use is prohibited by criminal law.

From the very inception of marihuana control legislation, this nation has utilized a policy of a total prohibition, far more comprehensive than the restrictions established during the prohibition of alcohol.

Until recent years, society was operating under an eliminationist policy. The exaggerated beliefs about the drug's effects, social impact, and user population virtually dictated this legal approach. During this entire period, total prohibition was sought through the use of heavier and heavier penalties until even first-time possession was a felony in every jurisdiction, and second possession offenses generally received a mandatory minimum sentence without parole or probation. Yet the last few years have seen society little by little abandoning the eliminationist policy in favor of a containment policy.

Under the total prohibition umbrella, this containment policy has been implemented by a unique patchwork of legislation, informal prosecutorial policy and judicial practice. Possession is now almost everywhere a misdemeanor. Although some term of incarceration remains as a penalty for possessors, it is generally not meted out to young first offenders or to possessors of small amounts. Instead, most such offenders are dismissed or informally diverted to agencies outside the criminal system by those within the system who are trying to help them avoid the stigma of a criminal record.

Offenders who are processed within the criminal justice system generally receive fines and/or probation. In many jurisdictions, enforcement officials make little or no effort to enforce possession proscriptions, concentrating instead on major trafficking. Possessors are generally arrested only when they are indiscreet or when marihuana is found incident to questioning or apprehension resulting from some other violation. From our surveys, state and federal, we have found that only minimal effort is made to investigate marihuana possession cases.

Such a tendency is a reflection of the adoption of a containment policy. By acting only when marihuana appears above ground, enforcement officials are helping to keep its use underground. The shift away from the elimination policy has been matched by a similar shift in legal implementation, but the distinctive feature of the total prohibition scheme still remains: all marihuana-related behavior, including possession for personal use within the home, is prohibited by criminal law.

Is such a response an appropriate technique for achieving the social control policy we outlined above? The key question for our purposes is whether total criminal prohibition is the most suitable or effective way to discourage use and whether it facilitates or inhibits a concentration on the reduction and treatment of irresponsible use. We are convinced that total prohibition frustrates both of these objectives for the following reasons.

With possession and use of marihuana, we are dealing with a form of behavior which occurs generally in private where a person possesses the drug for his own use. The social impact of this conduct is indirect, arising primarily in cases of heavy or otherwise irresponsible use and from the drug's symbolic aspects. We do not take the absolutist position that society is philosophically forbidden from criminalizing any kind of "private" behavior. The phrase "victimless crimes," like "public health hazard," has become a rhetorical excuse for avoiding basic social policy issues. We have chosen a discouragement policy on the basis of our evaluation of the actual and potential individual and social impact of marihuana use. Only now that we have done so can we accord appropriate weight to the nation's philosophical preference for individual privacy.

On the basis of this evaluation we believe that the criminal law is too harsh a tool to apply to personal possession even in the effort to discourage use. It implies an overwhelming indictment of the behavior which we believe is not appropriate. The actual and potential harm of use of the drug is not great enough to justify intrusion by the criminal law into private behavior, a step which our society takes only with the greatest reluctance.

The preference for individual privacy reflected in the debate over the philosophical limitations on the criminal law is also manifested in our constitutional jurisprudence. Although no court, to our knowledge, has held that government may not prohibit private possession of marihuana, two overlapping constitutional traditions do have important public policy implications in this area.

The first revolves around the concept that in a free society, the legislature may act only for public purposes. The "police powers" of the states extend only to the "public health, safety and morals." In the period of our history when the people most feared interference with their rights by the government, it was generally accepted that this broad power had an inherent limitation. For example, early prohibitions of alcohol possession were declared unconstitutional on the basis of reasoning such as that employed by the Supreme Court of Kentucky in 1915 in the case of *Commonwealth v. Campbell:*

> It is not within the competency of government to invade the privacy of the citizen's life and to regulate his conduct in matters in which he alone is concerned, or to prohibit him any liberty the exercise of which will not directly injure society.

Noting that the defendant was "not charged with having the liquor in his possession for the purpose of selling it, or even giving it to another," and that "ownership and possession cannot be denied when that ownership and possession is not in itself injurious to the public," the Kentucky court concluded that:

> The right to use liquor for one's own comfort, if they use it without
> direct injury to the public, is one of the citizen's natural and in-
> alienable rights. . . . We hold that the police power—vague and
> wide and undefined as it is—has limits. . . .

As a matter of constitutional history, a second tradition, the application of specific provisions in the Bill of Rights, has generally replaced the
notion of "inherent" limitations. The ultimate effect is virtually the same,
however. The Fourth Amendment's proscription of "unreasonable searches
and seizures" reflects a constitutional commitment to the value of individual
privacy. The importance of the Fourth Amendment to the entire constitutional scheme was eloquently described by Justice Brandeis in 1928 in the
case of *Olmstead v. U.S.:*

> The makers of our Constitution undertook to secure conditions fa-
> vorable to the pursuit of happiness. They recognized the signifi-
> cance of man's spiritual nature, of his feelings and his intellect.
> They knew that only a part of the pain, pleasure and satisfaction of
> life are to be found in material things. They sought to protect
> Americans in their beliefs, their thoughts, their emotions and their
> sensations. They conferred, as against the Government, the right to
> be let alone—the most comprehensive of rights and the right most
> valued by civilized men.

Although the Fourth Amendment is itself a procedural protection,
the value of privacy which it crystallizes is often read in conjunction with
other important values to set substantive limits on legislative power. The
Supreme Court, in the case of *Griswold v. Connecticut,* held in 1965 that
Connecticut could not constitutionally prohibit the use of birth control devices by married persons. Although the Justices did not agree completely on
the reasons for their decision, Justice Douglas stated in the opinion of the
Court:

> The present case, then, concerns a relationship lying within the
> zone of privacy created by several fundamental constitutional guar-
> antees. And it concerns a law which, in forbidding the use of con-
> traceptives rather than regulating their manufacture or sale, seeks
> to achieve its goals by means of having a maximum destructive im-
> pact upon that relationship. Such a law cannot stand in light of the
> familiar principle, so often applied by this Court, that a "govern-
> mental purpose to control or prevent activities constitutionally sub-
> ject to state regulation may not be achieved by means which sweep
> unnecessarily broadly and thereby invade the area of protected
> freedom." (citation omitted) Would we allow the police to search
> the sacred precincts of marital bedrooms for telltale signs of the
> use of contraceptives? The very idea is repulsive to the notions of
> privacy surrounding the marriage relationship.

Four years later, the Supreme Court, in *Stanley v. Georgia,* held that even though obscenity is not "speech" protected by the First Amendment, a state cannot constitutionally make private possession of obscene material a crime. . . .

Accordingly, we believe that government must show a compelling reason to justify invasion of the home in order to prevent personal use of marihuana. We find little in marihuana's effects or in its social impact to support such a determination. Legislators enacting Prohibition did not find such a compelling reason 40 years ago; and we do not find the situation any more compelling for marihuana today.

Apart from the philosophical and constitutional constraints outlined above, a total prohibition scheme carries with it significant institutional costs. Yet it contributes very little to the achievement of our social policy. In some ways it actually inhibits the success of that policy.

The primary goals of a prudent marihuana social control policy include preventing irresponsible use of the drug, attending to the consequences of such use, and deemphasizing use in general. Yet an absolute prohibition of possession and use inhibits the ability of other institutions to contribute actively to these objectives. For example, the possibility of criminal prosecution deters users who are experiencing medical problems from seeking assistance for fear of bringing attention to themselves. In addition, the illegality of possession and use creates difficulties in achieving an open, honest educational program, both in the schools and in the home.

In terms of the social policy objective of discouraging use of the drug, the legal system can assist that objective in three ways: first, by deterring people from use; second, by symbolizing social opposition to use; and finally, by cutting off supply of the drug.

The present illegal status of possession has not discouraged an estimated 24 million people from trying marihuana or an estimated eight million from continuing to use it. Our survey of the country's state prosecuting attorneys shows that 53% of them do not believe that the law has more than a minimal deterrent effect in this regard. Moreover, if the present trend toward passive enforcement of the marihuana law continues, the law ultimately will deter only indiscreet use, a result achieved as well by a partial prohibition scheme and with a great deal more honesty and fairness.

A major attraction of the law has been its symbolic value. Yet, society can symbolize its desire to discourage marihuana use in many other, less restrictive ways. The warning labels on cigarette packages serve this purpose, illustrating that even a regulatory scheme could serve a discouragement policy. During Prohibition, the chosen statutory implementation symbolized society's opposition to the use of intoxicating beverages; yet, most jurisdictions did not think it necessary to superimpose a proscription of possession for personal use in the home.

Finally, prohibiting possession for personal use has no substantive relation to interdicting supply. A possession penalty may make enforcement of proscriptions against sale a little easier, but we believe this benefit is of minimal importance in light of its costs.

The law enforcement goal repeatedly stated at both the federal and state levels has been the elimination of supply and the interdiction of trafficking. These avowed aims of law enforcement make sense, since they are the most profitable means of employing its manpower and resources in this area.

Indeed, the time consumed in arresting possessors is inefficiently used when contrasted with an equal amount of time invested in apprehending major dealers. Although a credible effort to eliminate supply requires prohibitions of importation, sale and possession-with-intent-to-sell, the enforcement of a proscription of possession for personal use is minimally productive. . . .

In addition to the misallocation of enforcement resources, another consequence of prohibition against possession for personal use is the social cost of criminalizing large numbers of users. Our empirical study of enforcement of state and federal marihuana laws indicates that almost all of those arrested are between the ages of 18 and 25, most have jobs or are in school, and most have had no prior contact with the criminal justice system. The high social cost of stigmatizing such persons as criminals is now generally acknowledged by the public at large as well as by those in the criminal justice system.

According to the National Survey, 53% of the public was unwilling to give young users a criminal record and 87% objected to putting them in jail. The nation's judges expressed an overwhelming disinclination to sentence and convict users for marihuana possession. Of these judges only 13% thought it was appropriate to incarcerate an adult for possession and only 4% would jail a juvenile for marihuana possession. This disinclination is reflected in the low percentage of arrested users who are convicted, and the even lower percentage who are jailed.

Even among the nation's prosecutors, a substantial majority favor the present trend toward avoiding incarceration for first offenders. Most jurisdictions have devised informal procedures for disposing of cases in lieu of prosecution. Our empirical study shows that 48% of the adult cases, and 70% of the juvenile cases, were dropped from the system at some point between arrest and conviction. The picture displayed is one of a large expenditure of police manpower to enforce a law most participants further along the line are not anxious to apply.

Other disturbing consequences of laws proscribing possession for personal use are the techniques required to enforce them. Possession of marihuana is generally a private behavior; in order to find it, the police many times must operate on the edge of constitutional limitations. Arrests without probable cause, illegal searches and selective enforcement occur often enough to arouse concern about the integrity of the criminal process.

Yet another consequence of marihuana possession laws is the clogging of judicial calendars. President Nixon has noted that one of the major impediments to our nation's efforts to combat serious crimes is the fact that the judicial machinery moves so slowly. Swift arrests, prosecution, trial and sentence would significantly improve the deterrent effect of law. Yet the judicial system is overloaded with petty cases, with public drunkenness accounting for about 50% of all non-traffic offenses. . . .

A final cost of the possession laws is the disrespect which the laws and their enforcement engender in the young. Our youth cannot understand why society chooses to criminalize a behavior with so little visible ill-effect or adverse social impact, particularly when so many members of the law enforcement community also question the same laws. These young people have jumped the fence and found no cliff. And the disrespect for the possession laws fosters a disrespect for all law and the system in general.

On top of all this is the distinct impression among the youth that some police may use the marihuana laws to arrest people they don't like for other reasons, whether it be their politics, their hair style or their ethnic background. Whether or not such selectivity actually exists, it is perceived to exist. . . . For all these reasons, we reject the total prohibition approach and its variations.

Regulation

Another general technique for implementing the recommended social policy is regulation. The distinguishing feature of this technique is that it institutionalizes the availability of the drug. By establishing a legitimate channel of supply and distribution, society can theoretically control the quality and potency of the product. The major alternatives within this approach lie in the variety of restraints which can be imposed on consumption of the drug and on the informational requirements to which its distribution can be subject.

We have given serious consideration to this set of alternatives; however, we are unanimously of the opinion that such a scheme, no matter how tightly it might restrict consumption, is presently unacceptable.

In rejecting the total prohibition approach, we emphasized the symbolic aspects. In essence, we do not believe prohibition of possession for personal use is necessary to symbolize a social policy disapproving the use. Theoretically, a tightly controlled regulatory scheme, with limited distribution outlets, significant restraints on consumption, prohibition of advertising and compulsory labeling, could possibly symbolize such disapproval. Our regulatory policy toward tobacco is beginning slowly to reflect a disapproval policy toward cigarette smoking. Nonetheless, given the social and historical context of such a major shift in legal policy toward marihuana, we are certain that such a change would instead symbolize approval of use, or at least a position of neutrality.

The Commission is concerned that even neutrality toward use as a matter of policy could invest an otherwise transient phenomenon with the status of an accepted behavior. If marihuana smoking were an already ingrained part of our culture, this objection would be dispelled. However, we do not believe that this is the case. We are inclined to believe, instead, that the present interest in marihuana is transient and will diminish in time of its own accord once the major symbolic aspects of use are deemphasized, leaving among our population only a relatively small coterie of users. With this possibility in mind, we are hesitant to adopt either a policy of neutrality or a regulatory implementation of our discouragement policy. The law would inevitably lose its discouragement character and would become even more ambiguous in its rationale and its enforcement.

The effect of changing a social policy direction may be seen with tobacco policy. In recent years, society has ostensibly adopted a policy of discouraging cigarette smoking. This new policy has been implemented primarily in the information area through prohibition of some forms of advertising and through compulsory labeling. Yet, the volume of cigarettes used increased last year. We believe that the failure of the new policy results from the fact that it supplants one that formerly approved use. This set of circumstances argues against any policy which would be regarded as approval of use, including a regulatory scheme. It is always extremely difficult to transform a previously acceptable behavior into a disapproved behavior.

We noted above that institutionalizing availability of the drug would inevitably increase the incidence of use, even though that incidence might otherwise decrease. Of greater concern is the prospect that a larger incidence of use would result in a larger incidence of long-term heavy and very heavy use of potent preparations. . . .

A significant segment of the public on both sides of the issue views marihuana and its "legalization" in a highly symbolic way. Any attempt to adopt a regulatory approach now would be counterproductive in this respect. The collision of values resulting from such a dramatic shift of policy would maintain the debate at a highly emotional level and would perpetuate the tendency to perceive marihuana use as a symbol of the struggle between two conflicting philosophies.

Advocates of legalization of marihuana are often inclined to propose a licensing scheme or an "alcohol model" without offering a specific program of regulation taking all the variables into account. Responsible policy planning cannot be so cursory. Consequently, we have given serious study to the many issues presented by such a scheme and to the nation's experience with other drug licensing schemes. On the basis of our inquiry, we are convinced that such a step should not be taken unless a realistic assessment of the efficacy of existing schemes and their potential application to marihuana indicates it would be successful. Such an assessment raises a number of disturbing questions.

The regulatory approaches which this nation has used in the cases of alcohol and tobacco have failed to accomplish two of their most important objectives: the minimization of excessive use and the limitation of accessibility to the young. . . .

Another important purpose of a regulatory scheme is to channel the product through a controlled system of supply and distribution. In that way the quality and quantity of the substance can be regulated. The efficacy of such a scheme as applied to marihuana is questionable.

Cannabis can be grown easily almost anywhere in the United States with little or no human assistance. Even if a legitimate source of supply were established, it is likely that many persons would choose to ignore the legitimate source and grow their own, the purity of which would not be in question. If such a practice were illegal, the necessity for a concerted governmental eradication program is raised, which would involve a monumental law enforcement effort. According to the U.S. Department of Agriculture, there are presently an estimated five million acres of wild marihuana growing in this country and an undetermined number of acres under cultivation. . . .

These are a few of the problems confronting the policy-maker if he seeks to devise an effective regulatory system of distribution for what is, in fact, a universally common plant. Our doubts about the efficacy of existing regulatory schemes, together with an uncertainty about the permanence of social interest in marihuana and the approval inevitably implied by adoption of such a scheme, all impel us to reject the regulatory approach as an appropriate implementation of a discouragement policy at the present time.

Future policy planners might well come to a different conclusion if further study of existing schemes suggests a feasible model; if responsible use of the drug does indeed take root in our society; if continuing scientific and medical research uncovers no long-term ill-effects; if potency control appears feasible; and if the passage of time and the adoption of a rational social policy sufficiently desymbolizes marihuana so that availability is not equated in the public mind with approval.

Partial Prohibition

The total prohibition scheme was rejected primarily because no sufficiently compelling social reason, predicated on existing knowledge, justifies intrusion by the criminal justice system into the private lives of individuals who use marihuana. The Commission is of the unanimous opinion that marihuana use is not such a grave problem that individuals who smoke marihuana, and possess it for that purpose, should be subject to criminal procedures. On the other hand, we have also rejected the regulatory or legalization scheme because it would institutionalize availability of a drug which has uncertain long-term effects and which may be of transient social interest.

Instead we recommend a partial prohibition scheme which we feel has the following benefits:

- Symbolizing a continuing societal discouragement of use;
- Facilitating the deemphasis of marihuana essential to answering dispassionately so many of the unanswered questions;
- Permitting a simultaneous medical, educational, religious, and parental effort to concentrate on reducing irresponsible use and remedying its consequences;
- Removing the criminal stigma and the threat of incarceration from a widespread behavior (possession for personal use) which does not warrant such treatment;
- Relieving the law enforcement community of the responsibility for enforcing a law of questionable utility, and one which they cannot fully enforce, thereby allowing concentration on drug trafficking and crimes against persons and property;
- Relieving the judicial calendar of a large volume of marihuana possession cases which delay the processing of more serious cases; and
- Maximizing the flexibility of future public responses as new information comes to light.

No major change is required in existing law to achieve all of these benefits. In general, we recommend only a decriminalization of possession of marihuana for personal use on both the state and federal levels. The major features of the recommended scheme are that: production and distribution of the drug would remain criminal activities as would possession with intent to distribute commercially; marihuana would be contraband subject to confiscation in public places; and criminal sanctions would be withdrawn from private use and possession incident to such use, but, at the state level, fines would be imposed for use in public.[1]

---

[1] Editor's note: In its 1973 report, the commission reaffirmed its position that, whatever the symbolic value of proscribing the use of marihuana for personal use, such legal measures are self-defeating; and "in the long run a measure of the success of this nation's drug policy will be how much we are able to disengage the criminal law from concern with consumption" (p. 256). However, with respect to other prohibited psychoactive substances (opiates, cocaine, amphetamines, and hallucinogens such as LSD) on which the second report focuses, the commission recommends:

that the unauthorized possession of any controlled substance except marihuana for personal use remain a prohibited act. The Commission further recommends that as a matter of statutory or enforcement policy, assertion of control over the consumer should not be tied to concepts of criminal accountability but rather to concepts of assistance appropriate in the individual case. The primary purpose of enforcement of the possession laws should be the detection and selection of those persons who would benefit by treatment or prevention services.

that all states attempt to rationalize the operation of the criminal justice system as a process for identifying drug-dependent persons and for securing their entry into a treatment system. The states should establish, as part of the comprehensive prevention and treatment program, a separate treatment process which runs parallel to the criminal process, and which may be formally or informally substituted for the criminal process.

In the long run, however, the Commission believes that coercive intervention should not rest simply on the need for therapy alone. Primarily, entry into treatment should become voluntary, and society should aim to maximize the number of drug-dependent persons who seek assistance on their own. The legal status of dependence on opiates, barbiturates or any other drug restricted to medical channels should compare to that of alcohol dependence: coercive intervention should be limited to those persons posing an immediate and substantial danger to their own safety or the safety of others [pp. 273, 267].

17

Escape from Alienation

Are we succumbing to a progressive malaise, or is it possible to revive a sense of belonging and, beyond this, a sense of commitment and a new spirit among those who need more than economic security and more than an endless succession of technological miracles to make them feel at home in their world? Does the latter require a redefinition of purpose in modern society and, if so, can this be accomplished within the framework of our existing values? Do the deep differences expressed throughout this volume suggest that such a redefinition of purpose is chimerical, or can we find a kind of value consensus within which difference thrives without degenerating into discord and distemper? The concluding essay in this volume is addressed to such basic questions.

TOWARD A MORE HUMAN SOCIETY

Kenneth Keniston

Dr. Keniston, a former Rhodes scholar, is professor of psychology and psychiatry at Yale. Much of his attention has been concentrated on chronicling and describing new tendencies in student life. In addition to the volume from which the following selection is taken, he has written Young Radicals: Notes on Committed Youth *(1968) and* Youth and Dissent: The Rise of a New Opposition *(1971).*

Our age inspires scant enthusiasm. In the industrial West, and increasingly now in the uncommitted nations, ardor is lacking; instead men talk of their growing distance from each other, from their social order, from their work and play, and from the values and heroes which in a perhaps romanticized past seem to have given order, meaning, and coherence to their lives. Horatio Alger is replaced by Timon, Napoleon by Ishmael, and even Lincoln now seems pallid before the defiant images of hoods and beats. Increasingly, the vocabulary of social commentary is dominated by terms that characterize the sense of growing distance between men and their former objects of affection. Alienation, estrangement, disaffection, anomie, withdrawal, disengagement, separation, noninvolvement, apathy, indifference, and neutralism—all of these terms point to a sense of loss, a growing gap between men and their social world. The drift of our time is away from connection, relation, communion, and dialogue, and our intellectual concerns reflect this conviction. Alienation, once seen as imposed *on* men by an unjust economic system, is increasingly chosen *by* men as their basic stance toward society.

These tendencies can of course be exaggerated in individual cases. As many or more men and women now lead individually decent and humane lives as ever did. There are pockets of enthusiasm in every nation. Old values are clung to the more tenaciously by some as they are disregarded by others. And the growing sense of alienation brings reactions in the form of new efforts to reconstruct commitment. But other facts are equally incontrovertible, at least in America: that there has seldom been so great a confusion about what is valid and good; that more and more men and women question what their society offers them and asks in return; that hopeful visions of the future are increasingly rare. The prevailing images of our culture are images of disintegration, decay, and despair; our highest art involves the fragmentation and distortion of traditional realities; our best drama depicts suffering, misunderstanding, and breakdown; our worthiest novels are narratives of loneliness, searching, and unfulfillment; even our best music is, by earlier standards, dissonant, discordant, and inhuman. Judged by the values of past generations, our culture seems obsessed with breakdown, splintering, disintegration, and destruction. Ours is an age not of synthesis but of analysis, not of constructive hopes but of awful destructive potentials, not of commitment but of alienation.

Thus it happens that terms like alienation gain ever wider currency, for despite all their vagueness they seem to point to something characteristic of our time. We feel this "something" in the growing belief in the inherent alienation of man from man and from the universe, in our preoccupation with the rifts, traumas, and discontinuities of psychological development, in the increasingly problematical relationship between men and their society, in our concern over national purposes and the breakdown of established values, even in our wavering faith in the progressive drift of history. And we see alienation especially clearly in American youth, poised hesitantly on the threshold of an adult world which elicits little deep commitment. Despite the achievement of many of the traditional aspirations of our society, we commonly feel a vague disappointment that goals that promised so much have somehow meant so little real improvement in the quality of human life. Whatever the gains of our technological age, whatever the decrease in objective suffering and want, whatever the increase in our "opportunities" and "freedoms," many Americans are left with an inarticulate sense of loss, of unrelatedness and lack of connection.

Thus, paradoxically, at the very moment when affluence is within our reach, we have grown discontented, confused, and aimless. The "new alienation" is a symptom and an expression of our current crisis. The individual and social roots of our modern alienation . . . are complex and interrelated; yet if there is any one crucial factor at the center of this alienation, it is the growing bankruptcy of technological values and visions. If we are to move toward a society that is less alienating, that releases rather than imprisons the energies of the dissident, that is truly worthy of dedication, devotion, idealism, and commitment, we must transcend our outworn visions of technological abundance, seeking new values beyond technology.

In the next decades of this century, Americans will be called upon to choose between three fundamentally different options concerning the future course of our society: whether to attempt to turn the clock back so as to "re-create" a bygone society in which our modern alienations did not yet exist, whether to "continue" the present triumphant march of a technological process which has created these same alienations, or whether to begin to define a new vision of a society whose values transcend technology. The first two choices would lead, I believe, to regression or stagnation; only by beginning now to articulate a vision of a society in which technology is used for truly human purposes can we create a nation of individuals, a society, that *merits* the commitment of its citizens. Yet such a redefinition of purpose has not been forthcoming, and social and political thought in America continues to be dominated by those who would have us regress to the past or those who would merely have us continue our present drift. What is it that prevents our imagining a society radically better than and different from our own?

. . . I have emphasized the inherent hostility of technology to Utopian and visionary thinking. The fundamental assumptions of technology and science are metrical, comparative, analytic, and reductive. Technology concerns itself with instrumental questions and dismisses Utopian visions as impractical or irrelevant. Moreover, the growing pressure for ego dictatorship increasingly subordinates and suppresses the passions and idealisms from which cogent criticisms of our society and radical propositions for its reform might spring. Convinced that all

Utopian thinking is impractical and self-defeating, we therefore cling to a technological empiricism that merely perpetuates the status quo. No doubt all established orders and all great ideologies resist fundamental change; but the technological society we live in is unusually well armored against attack, especially well equipped to subvert its critics, peculiarly able to discourage thinking that does not start from technological assumptions.

But beyond this, the very speed with which technology has accomplished its original goals has caught us off guard. The triumph of technology has occurred in an extraordinarily brief span of time: only one century separates our own era from the Civil War, technology triumphant from the beginning of the industrial era. Like a victorious and powerful army whose enemy unexpectedly surrenders, we now find ourselves without clear goals, mobilized for action that is no longer needed, and scarcely aware of the extent of our victory. We have been overtaken by success, surprised by triumph, caught off guard by victory. We have only begun to realize how far we have come, let alone to think of what might lie beyond.

Paradoxically, then, we live in a society in which unprecedented rates of technological change are accompanied by a fundamental unwillingness to look beyond the technological process which spurs this change. Even those who are most concerned over the future course of our society continue to conceive that course in primarily technological terms, emphasizing quantity, comparisons, economic output, and dollars and cents. And the imagination and commitment needed to define a future qualitatively different from the technological present are deflected—even for those most concerned with our social future—by a series of specific fallacies about the social process.

The fallacy of the psychosocial vise—A characteristic conviction of many modern men and women is the sense of being trapped in a social, cultural, and historical process they have no power to control. This sense of being inescapably locked in a psychosocial vise is often most paralyzing to precisely those men and women who have the greatest understanding of the complexity of their society, and who therefore might be best able to plan intelligently for its future. And although the sense of being trapped in history is widespread, it often appears to receive particularly cogent justification by social scientists. Recent years have seen a growing understanding of the connections between individual character, social process, cultural configuration, and historical change. Just as psychoanalysis has shown that even the most aberrant behavior "makes psychological sense" and serves definable psychic ends, so sociologists argue that social patterns that seem senseless also make a kind of sociological sense, serving "latent functions" corresponding to the unstated needs of individuals. We now know that the link between how men are raised as children and how they lead their lives as adults is a close one; that small changes in one sector of society can have enormous repercussions in other areas; and that apparently small historical transformations may spread and generalize to transform an entire community.

This awareness that individual, social, cultural, and historical processes are intimately connected is often taken as the basis for social pessimism. Because social institutions have a function, it is assumed this function can never be changed; because individual behavior, even the most irrational, has adaptive value, it is thought that no other behavior could be more adaptive. The fit between individual character and social structure is seen as a perfect fit, and the "gears" which convert historical pressures to psychological responses are seen as having a fixed and invariant ratio. The result is a deterministic sense of being caught in a psychosocial vise, locked so tightly it cannot be loosened without destroying it altogether. As a consequence, we dare change nothing at all.

In practice, the fallacy of the psychosocial vise can lead either to despair or complacency. Those who despair are usually all too aware of the enormous problems of our age: they despair because they can see no way of changing anything short of changing everything. Those who are complacent take comfort from the fact that (in retrospect) everything that happens in American society in some way "makes sense," can be explained and understood in terms of individual motives and social processes. The most dangerous trends in American society can be explained away as mere "reactions to social strain" which an omniscient sociologist could well have anticipated.

The facts, however, justify neither despair nor complacency. The "fit" between individuals and society, culture and history is never a perfect fit and is not always even a good fit. . . . the closeness of fit between, for example, family structure and social structure does not entail a comparable closeness of fit between family demands and the psychological needs of family members. There is, then, a kind of "slippage in the gears" of psychosocial transmission. Social institutions that now serve one function can later serve another or be replaced altogether; two men with essentially the same potential can end very differently; cultural needs and values that are salient today may become subordinate tomorrow. A "functional view" of social institutions does not require the assumption that comparable functions cannot be assumed by still other and better institutions.

To be sure, all social planning must be undertaken with the greatest possible understanding of its likely consequences. And we are probably in a better position than any previous generation to assess and gauge what these consequences will be. But the obvious fact that changes in one area of society have repercussions in others need not prevent social action. On the contrary, an understanding of the complexity of society can be an aid to social planning, helping us identify those points and moments of maximum leverage where small actions can have large consequences. There is often a kind of social "multiplier effect"; there are virtuous as well as vicious circles. Far from discouraging social planning and action, an understanding of psychosocial process can help us guide and direct it more intelligently.

The fallacy of romantic regression——One of the most common reactions against technological society is to deplore it by invoking images of a romanticized past as a guidepost for regressive social change. In future years, as at present, Americans will be increasingly called upon to accept or reject the ideology of romantic regression. This ideology starts from the valid observation that our post-industrial society has lost intact community, socially given identity, stable and accepted morality, certainty and a clear collective sense of direction. From this valid observation, the regressive position attempts to re-establish a simple "organic" community, longs for Jeffersonian agrarianism, seeks a "new conservatism" which will "preserve" the values of the nineteenth century, turns to Fascism with its appeal to blood feeling and the "corporate state," or is tempted by the syndicalist vision of re-attaining "genuine" self-governing communities of workers. All of these outlooks see the solution to the problems of post-industrial society as some form of restoration, re-creation, or reconstruction of the simpler, more intact world that technology has destroyed.

Given a romantic idealization of the past, programs for social action invariably have regressive aims: to *reduce* the complexity of the world, be it material or moral; to *limit* the choices and opportunities which now bewilder men; to *inhibit* freedoms to which men owe their modern anxieties; to *narrow* the alternatives which give rise to current indecision; to *constrain* those who complicate moral, social, political, and international life; to *simplify* moral dilemmas into clear-cut decisions between good and evil. In short, the romantic seeks to solve the problems of the modern world by regressing to his image of an earlier world where these problems did not exist—be it the New England village, the grit-and-gumption ethic of the nineteenth-century entrepreneur, or even the Polynesian island.

Among social scientists, this ideology often takes the form of an idealization of primitive communities or peasant life. In such static communities, the problems of social change cannot arise; in an undifferentiated society, the problems of a divided life, "not belonging," and being forced to choose do not exist; the family cannot be specialized because it has too much work to do to survive; and ideological crises rarely occur because men and women unthinkingly accept the ideology they were born to.

The image of such a primitive community is, I believe, useful in highlighting the contrasting qualities of our social order. But it is a grave mistake to take primitive society, peasant life, the New England village, medieval life, or the entrepreneurial ethos of the nineteenth century as an adequate model for the future of our own society. On the contrary, few of us would freely choose to inhabit such a world. However romantically appealing the technicolor image of the Polynesian village, the idealized portrait of the "intact" peasant community, or the zest and simplicity of the frontier, harsher realities lie behind these romanticized images: endemic disease, grinding poverty, high infant mortality, lawlessness, and often the absence of the most elementary requirements for subsistence. Nor is the low standard of living in such communities accidental: it results from attitudes to change, to social organization, and to child-rearing that make a prosperous society impossible. And even if we could put up with such material deprivations, few of us could tolerate the oppressive social demands of such communities. Americans today may "conform," but we usually do so from choice; in most primitive societies the issue of conformity cannot arise as such because there *is* no choice. Our society may demand the arduous achievement of individual identity, but peasant communities "solve" this problem simply by allowing the young no options. We may suffer from the pressures of chronic social change, but we would suffer more in a society that persisted in its traditional ways despite evidence that they were destructive. And we may lament the loss of mythic vitality in the twentieth century, but we would lament even more an age where those who challenged the collective myth were outlawed or destroyed.

Moreover, in appealing to the image of the primitive or "intact" community as a guide for social action, we forget the eagerness with which those who dwell in such communities seek to abandon them. The destruction of tribalism, of feudalism, and of "intact community" continues to correspond with the wishes of the vast majority of those who have a choice: in the emerging nations of the world men lust after affluence and technology, not after tribal embeddedness. And even in our own history, the development of political liberalism and representative government, like the growth of technological society, was a response to the felt wishes of those who sought to escape the rigors of previous societies. Those who hark back to the values of their grandparents forget the eagerness with which these same men and women sought to create a "better world" for their grandchildren. We would find even the rigidity, complacency, and intolerance of the recent Victorian era hard to live with; the total absorption of the individual in most "primitive" societies would be even more intolerable.

However instructive the comparison of our own society with "intact" communities may be, today's problems cannot be solved by regressing to that kind of society. The new problems, the new alienations of technological society, require not regression to a romanticized past but new definitions of purpose, new forms of social organization, new goals for personal development. We must not return to the past, but transcend the present.

The fallacy of unfinished business—Perhaps the most potent deterrent of all to any fresh thinking about the purposes of our lives and our society is the fallacy of unfinished business—exclusive concentration on the remaining problems of productivity, poverty, education, and inequality as defined by technological values. This fallacy is most dangerous because it affects most those who are genuinely concerned with the problems of our society, critical of its achievements, impatient with the slowness of its "progress." Politically and socially, the only articulate alternative to those who would have us regress to the past is found among those who emphasize the unfinished business of technology, the "incomplete revolutions" which must be completed. From Lyndon Baines Johnson to Paul Goodman, the main thread of "progressive" thinking about American society assumes that our task is to complete our unfinished technological business.

I do not mean to deprecate this position. It is not wrong but inadequate; the evils pointed to are real and urgent. Gross prejudice and inequality are daily realities in much of America; poverty is a grinding and destructive fact to a fifth of the nation; millions do not and cannot get the minimal education necessary for an honored place in American life; it is genuinely alarming that we have not solved the problems of chronic unemployment. Nor will it be politically easy to solve these problems; the programs so far proposed only scratch the surface.

But the adequacy of this view to the problems of our society can be questioned. The "unfinished business" of technological society is, on a historical scale, increasingly vestigial, a "mopping-up operation." Revolutionary causes lose their impact when they have been largely accomplished; men are seldom stirred to arms in a cause already victorious. What is historically most salient is that *only* a fifth of the nation remains, by today's high American standards, poor. What should astound us is that *only* 30 per cent fail today to complete twelve years of education. And even in very recent American history, an unemployment rate of *only* four to six per cent would have been an unprecedented breakthrough to prosperity. Our efforts to relieve these problems should not abate; on the contrary, these efforts are still inadequate. But our technological accomplishments mean that if real "new frontiers" are to be found, they must lie beyond technology; and that if we do not now live in a "Great Society," then expanded Medicare, poverty programs, job-retraining, and anti-dropout campaigns will not suffice to create it.

Moreover, the values and instruments of technology will no longer suffice even to finish a technological society's own unfinished business. Our pursuit of quantity leads us to focus on such numerical indices of national and social success as the gross national product, the growth rate, the percentages of Americans employed, the proportion in high school, the divorce rate, the number of cars, telephones, and washing machines. We rejoice when these indices of success show us "ahead" of the Russians, and worry when our growth rate falls below theirs. But in each area of "unfinished business" in American life, our traditional techniques are inadequate. That traditional panacea, an increase in national output, no longer affects the poor, insulated from the main streams of the economy. More money poured into existing schools does not solve the problem of drop-outs, whose prior problems are human and psychological, not merely educational. New technological innovations in industry are producing more, not less, chronic unemployment among the unskilled. And no matter how much we speed up the slow movement toward greater equality for Negro Americans, full citizenship cannot be achieved by traditional legal means alone. It also requires a deeper (and non-technological) effort to overcome the bitter legacies of slavery and oppression; and it may even require that we learn to recognize, accept, and enjoy the differences between white and Negro Americans that this legacy has created. In almost every area where our "technological revolutions" are incomplete, the instruments and values of technology will not alone suffice to carry us farther. Our urban sprawl, the chaos, disorganization, blight, and congestion of our society, our new alienations—all were *created* by our exploding, unplanned technological society; the technological process alone will not solve their problems.

But most important, the fallacy of unfinished business overlooks the crucial questions for most Americans today: What lies beyond the triumph of technology? After racial equality has been achieved, what then? Abundance for all for what? Full employment for today's empty jobs? More education that instills an ever more cognitive outlook?

It is all too easy to imagine a society in which the triumph of technology is complete. It would be an overwhelmingly rich society, dominated by a rampant technology and all of its corollaries—science, research and development, advertising, "conformity," secret invidiousness, overwhelming nostalgia for childhood, the dictatorship of the ego, a continuing deflection of the Utopian spirit. It would be a prosperous, ugly, sprawling society which men had learned not to see. It would have many entertainers but few artists, many superhighways but few open spaces to go to on them. It would be a science-fiction dream of automation, pre-processing, and home-care conveniences. Skyscrapers would rise ever taller and more sheer, and "developments" would burgeon outside the blighted urban cores.

Yet the central problems of today would merely be magnified. The pace of social change would increase and, without an over-all sense of direction, Americans would huddle ever more defensively in the present. For some, the romanticized stability of the past would grow more and more attractive, and this attraction would express itself more and more forcibly in political and social reaction. Life, already divided today, would be further divided tomorrow; and the vast majority of Americans, who could create no community within their own hearts, would be altogether without a home. As the pressures toward cognition grew, private escapes into ir-rationality, cults, and fads would flourish. The atmosphere would become ever more hostile to speculation, to idealism, and to Utopianism; the cult of efficiency, spread into human relations and industrial management, would relegate idealism and the noble dreams of youth to the hours after work or to "entertainment." In such a society the most talented would be alienated, yet they would be unable to find a positive voice; and their alienations would be, as now, self-destructive, carping, and self-defeating. To complete our incomplete revolutions, to finish our unfinished business, is therefore not enough, nor can it be accomplished by technological means alone. For their solution, the vestigial tasks of technology require values beyond technology.

If we are to seek values beyond technology, purposes beyond affluence, visions of the good life beyond material prosperity, where are these values, purposes, and visions to be found? Must we, as many secretly fear, await the coming of some new prophet who will create, out of nothing, a new Utopian vision for Americans? Are we condemned to a continuation of technological society until some Messiah arrives to save us?

I believe the answer is closer to home. When, a century ago, Americans began to take seriously the goals of prosperity and freedom from want, these values were not created out of nothing: they had long been part of the Western tradition. What changed was that a dream of the good life previously considered beyond the reach of the ordinary man passed into his hands and was accepted as a concrete goal that could be achieved by ordinary men and women. The turning point at which we stand today requires a similar translation of already existing dreams of human fulfillment and social diversity into the concrete goals of individuals and of our society. The values we need are deeply rooted in our own tradition: we must merely begin to take them seriously.

The ideal of full human wholeness is as old as Periclean Athens. But in the course of Western history, this goal could be taken seriously by few men and women: as in Athens, only a small number of the leisured and wealthy, supported by the vast majority of their fellow citizens, attained the freedom from want which is a prerequisite for the implementation of this ancient goal. Even in the Renaissance, when the Greek ideal of full humanity was rediscovered, the vast majority of men and women were far too preoccupied by their incessant struggle against poverty, oppression, and sickness to have time for such lofty ideals. And even today, for most citizens of most nations of the world, the vision of a more harmonious integration of self, a more complete development of talent and ability, must await the attainment of more urgent goals of attaining freedom from want and oppression. Only those who have been able to conquer poverty and tyranny have energy to cultivate their full humanity.

But for those who do not want materially and are not oppressed politically, the quest for fulfillment beyond material goods becomes possible and urgent. There is in human life a hierarchy of needs, such that the higher needs are fully felt when, and only when, the lower needs have been satisfied. Just as thirsty men do not seek food, and the starved have no strength for sex, so freedom from political oppression and material want are prerequisites for any attempt to achieve a more harmonious integration of self, a fuller development of human potentials. Today, in America, and increasingly in other technological nations, these preconditions are rapidly being met: we can now begin to imagine realistically that a whole society might commit itself to the attainment of the greatest possible fulfillment for its members.

To be sure, by the quantitative and reductionistic standards of our technological era, goals like "human wholeness," "personal integration," "the full development of human potentials" are inevitably vague and imprecise. They point to the quality of individual life, rather than to quantitatively measurable entities. Partly for this reason, our knowledge of the sources of human wholeness and fulfillment is woefully inadequate, despite a half-century's systematic study of man. But we do know more than previous generations about the causes of human malformation, distortion, and blighting. Our systematic and scientific knowledge is, no doubt, no more than a confirmation of what a few wise men have intuitively known in the past. But what was heretofore the special wisdom of the sagacious few (which they often carried to their graves) is on the way to becoming communicable public knowledge. Gradually, we are learning to pinpoint the obstacles to full human growth, specifying those especially "lethal" psychological combinations of parentage and social circumstance for children, defining more adequately the antecedents of human pathology, and even at times learning how to intervene positively to foster full human development.

Yet even today, it is far simpler to list the obstacles to full human development, to personal integration, to self-actualization, than to prescribe the precise path to these ancient goals. For just as there are from birth many distinct individuals, each with his own unique genetic and environmental potential, there must remain many paths to fulfillment. Our modern search for a single definition for "maturity" and "positive mental health" that will apply to everyone is probably doomed to failure from the start. Responsiveness, activity, excitability, and even the capacity to learn are not only shaped by the environment, but partly determined by birth. "Fulfillment" depends on individual potential and on social opportunity; human "wholeness" depends on what there is to be made whole.

But though no single definition of human fulfillment is possible, some of its results can be defined. A whole man or woman has the capacity for zest, exuberance, and passion, though this capacity may often be in abeyance. An integrated man does not cease to experience tension, anxiety, and psychic pain, but he is rarely overwhelmed by it. Though all men must at times "close" themselves to that which would be subversive of their commitments, a whole man nonetheless retains the *capacity* for openness, sensitivity, and responsiveness to the world around him: he can always be surprised because he remains open to that which is alien to himself.

Above all, human wholeness means a capacity for commitment, dedication, passionate concern, and care—a capacity for wholeheartedness and single-mindedness, for abandon without fear of self-annihilation and loss of identity. In psychological terms, this means that a whole man retains contact with his deepest passions at the same time that he remains responsive to his ethical sense. No one psychic potential destroys or subverts the others: his cognitive abilities remain in the service of his commitment, not vice versa; his ethical sense guides rather than tyrannizing over his basic passions; his deepest drives are the sources of his strength but not the dictators of his action. We recognize whole men and women because their wholeness is manifest in their lives: what they do is "of a piece."

If no unitary definition of fulfillment and integration is possible, then a society that is to support these goals must necessarily be a diverse, heterogeneous, pluralistic, and open society. And like the ideal of individual fulfillment, the goal of social diversity is one we have never seriously considered implementing. Although the ideal of political pluralism is entrenched in our liberal tradition, this ideal has most often meant the toleration of political factions, not the encouragement of the full diversity of human talents. Politically, we may tolerate lobbies and believe in political parties; but socially our goals are given by slogans like "Americanization," "the melting pot," and increasingly today "the search for excellence" defined in cognitive terms. Though we think of ourselves as a "tolerant" society, in ordinary speech we most often couple the term "tolerate" with the modifier "barely." All too often, the "tolerance" of Americans is a thin veneer over the discomfort created by all that is different, strange, and alien to them. Once, to be sure, the image of this nation as a vast melting pot suggested the noble vision that the millions of diverse immigrants who came to this shore could be welded into a single coherent nation. But today there is no menace of an America excessively fractured along ethnic, regional or class lines. The current danger is excessive homogeneity, sameness, uniformity. Already, ethnic distinctions, regional differences, even class lines have been blurred beyond recognition in a land where almost everyone lives in the same city apartments and suburban dwellings, eats the same frozen foods and watches the same television programs at the same time on the same networks. Even the current effort of some Americans who are fearful of conformity to be "different," to develop distinctive styles of consumption and life, paralleled by the attempts of advertisers and industry to promote "personalized" and "individualized" products, tends to become only another sign of the homogenization of American society.

Romantic regionalism or the idealization of ethnicity are of course not virtuous in themselves: and even if we chose, distinctions of region and ethnic background could not be naturally preserved. But there *is* an inherent virtue in the appreciation of genuine human differences and the encouragement of a new social diversity based not on region, ancestral origin, class, or race, but on the special accomplishments, potentials, talents, and vital commitments of each individual. Pluralism must be extended from politics to the individual, implemented as a concrete social goal. Human diversity and variety must not only be tolerated, but rejoiced in, applauded, and encouraged.

A society of whole men and women must, then, be a society which encourages diversity, enjoying the differences between men as well as the similarities among them. Social diversity has a double connection to individual fulfillment: not only is a diverse society a precondition for human wholeness, it is its consequence—the kind of society whole men and women choose to live in. Those who are inwardly torn, unsure of their psychic coherence and fearful of inner fragmentation, are naturally distrustful of all that is alien and strange. Those whose sense of inner unity is tenuous are easily threatened by others who remind them of that part of themselves they seek to suppress. Our "one-hundred-per-cent Americans" are those whose own Americanism is felt to be most tenuous; the bigoted and the prejudiced cannot live with the full gamut of their own feelings. And conversely, those who can still sense their shared humanity with others of different or opposite talents and commitments are those who are sure of their own intactness. The goals of human fulfillment and social diversity require each other.

Both of these ideals, I have argued, are ancient ones. They are rooted deep in our Western tradition, and they arise almost spontaneously in those whose material and physical wants have been satisfied. But it remains for us to implement these visions. These are values beyond technology, credal ideals of our civilization which we can now begin to take seriously. Probably for the first time in human history, we can move toward a fullness of life beyond a full larder, human fulfillment beyond material satiation, social diversity beyond consensus.

History is always made by men, even in an era like ours when men feel they are but the pawns of history. The inability to envision a future different from the present is not a historical imposition but a failure of imagination. It is individuals, not historical trends, that are possessed by a self-confirming sense of social powerlessness. The decision to continue along our present course rather than to take a new turning is still a decision made by men. One way men sometimes have of shaping the future is to be passive and acquiescent before it. Our collective and individual future, then, will inevitably be shaped by us, whether we choose inaction and passivity, regression and romanticism, or action, imagination, and resolve. Men cannot escape their historical role by merely denying its existence. The question is therefore not *whether* Americans will shape their future, but *how* they will shape it.

What is lacking today in America is certainly not the know-how, the imagination, or the intelligence to shape a future better than our present. Nor do we lack the values that might guide the transformation of our society to a more fully human and diverse one. Rather, we lack the conviction that these values might be implemented by ordinary men and women acting in concert for their common good. The Utopian impulse, I have argued, runs deep in all human life, and especially deep in American life. What is needed is to free that impulse once again, to redirect it toward the creation of a better society. We too often attempt to patch up our threadbare values and outworn purposes; we too rarely dare imagine a society radically different from our own.

Proposals for specific reforms are bound to be inadequate by themselves. However desirable, any specific reform will remain an empty intellectual exercise in the absence of a new collective myth, ideology, or Utopian vision. Politically, no potent or lasting change will be possible except as men can be roused from their current alienations by the vision of an attainable society more inviting than that in which they now listlessly live. Behind the need for any specific reform lies the greater need to create an intellectual, ideological, and cultural atmosphere in which it is possible for men to attempt affirmation without undue fear that their Utopian visions will collapse through neglect, ridicule or their own inherent errors. Such an ethos can only be built slowly and piecemeal, yet is it clear what some of its prerequisites must be.

For one, we need a more generous tolerance for synthetic and constructive ideas. Instead of concentrating on the possible bad motives from which they might arise (the genetic fallacy) or on the possible bad consequences which might follow from their misinterpretation (the progenitive fallacy), we must learn to assess them in terms of their present relevance and appropriateness. To accomplish this task will be a double work. Destructively, it will require subverting the methodologies of reduction that now dominate our intellectual life. Constructively, it will require replacing these with more just measures of relevance, subtlety and wisdom, learning to cherish and value the enriching complexity of motives, passions, ethical interests, and facts which will necessarily underlie and support any future vision of the good life.

Secondly, we must reappraise our current concepts and interpretations of man and society. It is characteristic of the intellectual stagnation of our era, an era so obviously different from former times, that we continue to operate with language more appropriate to past generations than to our own. Many of our critiques and interpretations of technological society, including most discussions of alienation, apply more accurately to the America of the 1880's than to the America of the 1960's. We require a radical reanalysis of the human and social present—a re-evaluation which, starting from uncritical openness to the experience, joys, and dissatisfactions of men today, can gradually develop concepts and theories that can more completely comprehend today's world. American society does not lack men and women with the fine discrimination, keen intelligence, and imagination to understand the modern world; but we have yet to focus these talents on our contemporary problems.

But above and beyond a more generous atmosphere and a more adequate understanding of our time, ordinary human courage is needed. To criticize one's society openly requires a strong heart, especially when criticism is interpreted as pathology; only a man of high mettle will propose a new interpretation of the facts now arranged in entrenched categories. And no matter how eagerly the audience awaits or how well prepared the set, only courage can take a performer to the stage. There are many kinds of courage: needed here is the courage to risk being wrong, to risk doing unintentional harm, and, above all, the courage to overcome one's own humility and sense of finite inadequacy. This is not merely a diffuse "courage to be," without protest, in a world of uncertainty, alienation, and anxiety, but the courage to be *for* something despite the perishability and transience of all human endeavors.

Commitment, I have said, is worthy only as its object is worthy. To try to "reconstruct" commitment to American society as it exists today is less than worthy, for our society is shot through with failings, failures, and flaws. It is, as the alienated truly perceive, "trashy, cheap, and commercial"; it is also, as the alienated seldom see, unjust, distorting of human growth and dignity, destructive of diversity. It has allowed itself to be dominated by the instruments of its own triumph over poverty and want, worshiping the values, virtues, and institutions of technology even when these now dominate those they should serve. Only if we can transform the technological process from a master to a servant, harnessing our scientific inventiveness and industrial productivity to the promotion of human fulfillment, will our society be worthy of commitment. And only the vision of a world beyond technology can now inspire the commitment of whole men and women.

America today possesses a vast reservoir of thwarted and displaced idealism; there are millions of men and women who sense vaguely that something is amiss in their lives, who search for something more, and yet who cannot find it. Their idealism will not be easily redirected to the creation of better lives in a better society; it will require imagination, vigor, conviction, and strong voices willing to call for many years, before we dare raise our aspirations beyond vistas of total technology to visions of fuller humanity. But for the first time in American history, and probably in the history of the world, it is conceivable that a whole nation might come to take seriously these ancient and honored visions.

In defining this new vision of life and society, we must remember the quests of the alienated. Though their goals are often confused and inarticulate, they converge on a passionate yearning for openness and immediacy of experience, on an intense desire to create, on a longing to express their perception of the world, and, above all, on a quest for values and commitments that will give their lives coherence. The [alienated] of modern American life are often self-defeating; they cannot be taken as exemplars of human integration or fulfillment. But the implicit goals they unsuccessfully seek to attain *are* those of integrated and whole men—openness, creativity, and dedication. Today we need men and women with the wisdom, passion, and courage to transform their private alienations into such public aspirations. We might then begin to move toward a society where such aspirations were more fully realized than in any the world has known.

We can hope for such new commitments in the future only if men now begin to resolve their alienations by committing themselves—through the analysis, synthesis, and reform of their own lives and worlds—to the preparation of such a new society, a society in which whole men and women can play with zest and spontaneity, can work with skill and dedication, can love with passion and care—a society that enjoys diversity and supports human fulfillment.